Illustrated Guide To The South Indian Railway: Including The Mayavaram-Mutupet, And Peralam-Karaikkal Railways ...

Ltd South Indian Railway Co.

BOARD OF DIRECTORS.

Chairman.

HENRY KIMBER, Esq., M.P.

Government Director.

COLONEL SIR W. S. S. BISSET, R.E., K.C.I.E.

SIR DOUGLAS FOX, M.I.C.E.

MAJOR-GENERAL J. H. M. SHAW-STEWART, R.E.

SIR JULAND DANVERS, K.C.S.I.

Managing Director.

HENRY W. NOTMAN, Esq.

Consulting Engineer.

SIR GEORGE B. BRUCE,

Past President, INST. C.E.

Officers in India.

MAJOR A. D. G. SHELLEY, R.E., *Agent, Trichinopoly.*

HENRY DAVIES, Esq., *Traffic Manager, Trichinopoly.*

T. J. McCLOUGHIN, Esq., *Dy. Traffic Manager, Trichinopoly.*

A. E. BICE, Esq., *District Traffic Supdt., Madras (Egmore).*

S. BRYANT, Esq., *District Traffic Superintendent, Pakala.*

J. O. SHOOBRIDGE, Esq., *District Traffic Supdt., Tanjore.*

R. SANGAR, Esq., *District Traffic Superintendent, Madura.*

All correspondence in connection with routes, fares, timing of trains, etc., should be addressed to the Traffic Officers named above by designation and not by name.

PREFACE.

THIS work being equally intended for the use of
those visiting India for the first time as for the
assistance of the more permanent residents in the
country, it has been considered advisable to supplement the information usually given in railway guide
books, by a brief account of the history, manners,
and religions of the various peoples who have inhabited the country traversed by the South Indian
Railway. To extract the information from standard
works of reference is a task which the ordinary pleasure seeker would hesitate to undertake, but it is
obvious that, without some knowledge of these
subjects, a tour in Southern India would for most
persons be largely deprived of its interest. To avoid
inflicting these details on the unwilling minority,
they have, as far as possible, been dealt with in the
Introduction, so that they can be readily skipped.
The historical section has been compiled in the
Agent's Office, but has had the advantage of revi-
sion by the Revd. Thomas Foulkes, the eminent
antiquarian. The sections dealing with races, religions, and architecture have obligingly been contributed by the same gentleman, while the articles on
sport are due to the kindness of Sir Frederick Price,
K.C.S.I. (whose name is a guarantee that the
subject is authoritatively treated), and Mr. R. H.
Morris. The remainder of the work has been compiled by the Company's officers of the Agent's and
Traffic Departments.

CONTENTS.

———•———

———◆◆◆———

LIST OF ILLUSTRATIONS.

B

MAHAMAKHAM FESTIVAL OF 1897 KUMBAKONAM

eastern from Beder through Adoni to Tirupati. *Telingana*, the original province in which Telugu is spoken, is situated between Dravida, Carnata, the Bay of Bengal, and a line from Ganjam to Beder. *Maharashtra*, or the Mahratta country, lies between the hills south of the Nerbudda and a line thence to Chanda, the remaining boundaries being the Arabian Sea and the territories of Carnata and Talinga. *Orissa*, the home of the Urya language, lies north of Talinga, and is bounded on the west by a line from Sohnpore to Midnapore and on the east by the Bay of Bengal. The *Konkana* consists of the belt between the Arabian Sea and the Western Ghâts, including the districts of Bombay, Kanara, Colaba, Ratnagherry, and Thana. The *Carnatic* was formerly the tableland in the south between the Eastern and Western Ghâts, but is now understood to be the country below the Eastern Ghâts. *Kalingana* may be defined as the land below the Eastern Ghâts between Dravida and Orissa.

Consideration of Southern Indian history is simplified by dividing it into three epochs, the first

Division of Subject.

embracing the period from earliest known times to the invasion of the Mussulmans under Malik Kafur in A. D. 1310, the second from this date to the fall of the Golkonda kingdom in 1687, and the third from 1687 to the establishment of the English supremacy. In dealing with this subject a brief account of the first two periods will be given, supplemented by fuller details in regard to such dynasties as more particularly affect the country served or likely to be served by the South Indian Railway.

The earliest recorded kingdoms in Southern India were the Pandiya, Chola, and Chera or Kerala,

General History to A. D. 1310.

which seem to have been existent in the 3rd century B. C. The Pandiyans then held the extreme south of the peninsula, occupying the present revenue districts of Madura and Tinnevelly, and South Travancore: the Cholas had possession of the belt of country between the Eastern Ghâts and the coast extending from the Madura district to the Ponniar river; and the Cheras were located in North Travancore, Cochin, Malabar and South Canara. In these remote times the ruling race in the north of the Madras Presidency were the Andhras—a nation which became extremely powerful about the beginning of the Christian era. The Andhras then held the whole of the inland country to the north of the Kistna. The country intervening between the dominions of the Andhras and those of the Pallavas seems to have been a wild and almost uninhabited region of rock and forest. The Pallava kingdom extended along the coast from the Ponniar river to the southern limit of the Kalingas, and stretched inland over the whole area of the basin of the Palar river up to the Palmaner and Kolar districts with the northern half of the present district of Salem. From about the 9th century onwards the Cholas began to forge their way westwards and northwards, conquering and annexing the old Konga kingdom from the neighbourhood of Karur westwards to the eastern limits of the present Mysore country, and overthrowing the fast-decaying Pallava kingdom to their north as far as the Eastern Chaluleyan kingdom in the delta of the Godaveri. In the course of centuries the Kurumbas—a branch of a once powerful old nomad race, according to one of the modern popular traditions—developed into the nation known as the Pallavas. This nation became at a very early period the dominant race in Southern India, and when in the zenith of its power embraced the whole of the Pallava region described above. The dynasty and nation of Kalingana are alluded to by early Grecian and Roman writers and it would seem that the kingdom was powerful and independent in very early times. The people were adventurous maritime traders undertaking lengthy voyages to distant countries. In later years their southern districts were ruled by Pallava kings until the country was ultimately absorbed by more powerful neighbours about A. D. 1000. The Pandiyan kingdom was the earliest to be civilized and it retained a leading position in the extreme South until the time of the upheaval of the Cholas, who in the 11th century attained a supremacy hitherto unknown in Southern India. During this period the balance of power was repeatedly disturbed by wars, invasions, and the formation of new nationalities, with the result that at the beginning of the 11th century the state of affairs had assumed the following aspect. The Pandiyan, Chola and Chera nations had maintained their independence, though the latter were much harassed upon their northern boundary by the attacks of the Hoysala Bellalas, a small but rising Yadava state founded in Mysore by a branch of the Western Chalukyas. The Chalukyas, a Rajput nation, settled near Kalyan, in the Nizam's Dominions, had intruded by expansion towards the Eastern Coast and had conquered and annexed the northern districts of the Pallava territories. The Chalukyas then became divided into two branches—the western remaining within their original limits in the Western Dakhan, the eastern settling in the provinces between the Kistna and Godaveri which it had taken from the Pallavas. In A. D. 1064 the Chola and Eastern Chalukyan dynasties were united under Rajandra Chola, his father having married a Chalukyan princess, and this increase in power was subsequently followed by the conquest of Ceylon, the Pallavas, and the Pandyan kingdom, where a short dynasty of Chola-Pandiyan kings was established. A little later the Hoysala Ballalas obtained a further extension of territory and would probably in time have defeated the ancient nations of the plains, had not their victorious career been checked by the first Mussulman invasion of the Dakhan in A. D. 1310, which resulted in a serious undermining of the ancient dynasties of the South.

The following additional information regarding the more

important kingdoms referred to in the foregoing paragraphs may be of interest.

Pandiyans. The Pandiyan nation is said to have been founded by an agriculturist named Pandiya in the 5th century B.C. The dynasty was also known as the Minavar, from the Tamil word *min*, a fish, this being the royal emblem. The original capital was Korkai, near the mouth of the Tinnevelly river, but it was moved to Kalyana, near Cape Comorin, and finally to Madura. The kingdom of Pandiya is referred to by Megasthenes (B.C. 302) under the name of Pandaia, and in the Periplus Maris Erythroei the capital Madura and the then king under the name of O Παυδιωυ being mentioned. In the sectarial legends of the Madura temple a list, more or less untrustworthy, of 73 Pandiyan kings who are supposed to have ruled the country prior to its conquest in 1064 by the Chola sovereign, Rajendra Koluttunga, is given in various works, but it will suffice to mention the 46th Vamsasekhara Pandiyan, who fortified and enlarged Madura, and established there the once celebrated Tamil College of Poets. On the death of the first Chola-Pandiyan monarch a short period of anarchy obtained till about 1100, when a line of kings about 41 in number commenced to reign. The most noteworthy events of this period were repeated wars and alliances with the Cholas, the conquest of the country in 1171 by King Parakrama Bahu I. of Ceylon, and the final subversion of the dynasty by the Mussulmans in 1310.

Cholas. The Chola kingdom was also of greater antiquity than the Pandiyan dynasty, but its history prior to 1023 is almost a blank. Under the name of Choda it is referred to in the edicts of Asoka, a celebrated king of Magadha in Northern India, who reigned from about the middle of the 3rd century B.C. The capital of the kingdom was at Warriore, near Trichinopoly, in the second century; at Kumbakonam in the seventh; and at

Tanjore in the tenth. Incessant struggles with the Pandiyans seem to have been the most prominent events in the early career of the Cholas, but later on they transferred their attention to their neighbours the Kongus, whom they defeated about A.D. 900. According to Singhalese narratives the Cholas invaded and conquered Ceylon before the Christian era, and ruled the island for a period of 44 years. Another and unsuccessful invasion is supposed to have occurred in the middle of the 10th century. King Rajaraja by marriage obtained for his son the dominions of the Eastern Chalukyas comprising the territories known as Kalinga and Vengi. In 1059 this monarch invaded Ceylon, took King Mihindu and his queen prisoners, seized the crown jewels and appointed a Chola viceroy to the government of the island. The succeeding king, Kulottunga I. or Rajendra Chola, was the most powerful sovereign of the dynasty. He consolidated his kingdom to the borders of Orissa, crushed the Pallavas of Conjeeveram, annexed for a time the Pandiyan kingdom, and seems to have devastated the country of the Western Chalukyas. After prolonged fighting Ceylon was lost, but a retaliatory invasion by the Singhalese in the following reign was easily repulsed. On the defeat of the Pandiyans, Gangaikondan, a son of Rajendra Chola, was placed on the throne of that kingdom, and took the name of Sundara Pandiyan. From the time of Kulottunga the power of the Cholas steadily diminished until the dynasty sank into obscurity after the invasion of the Mussulmans in 1310. The word "Coromandel" is derived from Cholamandalam.

According to the inscriptions of Asoka the Cheras were **Cheras and Kongus.** contemporaneous with the Pandiyans and Cholas. Little, however, is known about them and until recently it was a matter of opinion whether they were separate from, or identical with, the race dwelling in the Kongu country. Under these circumstances it is necessary to deal separately with the kingdoms of Kongu and Chera or Kerala. The first known reigning dynasty in the Kongu country consisted of seven kings of the Ratti tribe under whom the kingdom was extended by annexation of Carnata, and its prestige increased by victories over the Cholas, Cheras, and Pandiyans. The first six kings were Jains, but the seventh adopted the Shiva religion. It would appear that this last sovereign lost his life in battle against a Mysore chieftain, who then seized the vacant throne, and established a Ganga dynasty which lasted from A.D. 189 to about 878. Under these monarchs the kingdom was further enlarged, and their authority extended to the neighbourhood of Harihar. The country was finally annexed by the Cholas who held it till about the middle of the 11th century, when it revolted and broke up into numerous petty principalities. These were absorbed by the Hoysala Ballalas about A.D. 1080, who retained possession of them for some 250 years. Of the Cheras but little is known. In earliest times they appear to have occupied North Travancore, Cochin, Malabar and portions of Canara, but shortly after the commencement of the Christian era, Canara separated under an independent dynasty which lasted until the 12th century. According to tradition the Chera empire was divided into 24 divisions under Brahmin control. This arrangement did not prove satisfactory and after a system of government under four chiefs had been unsuccessfully tried, a Kshatriya king was appointed. The last of these sovereigns, Cheraman Perumal, embraced the Muhammadan religion and in A.D. 825 proceeded on a pilgrimage to Mecca from which he never returned. Before his departure he partitioned the kingdom among his principal nobles, thus originating the states of Travancore and Cochin, and the independency of the territories pertaining to the Zamorin of Calicut. The Jews are said to have settled on the Chera coast in the 6th century B. C., and their colonies exist there to this day.

The Pallavas are of more than ordinary interest by reason of their architectural remains. They claimed descent from Tadu, the common ancestor of the shepherd races of India, and, as before mentioned, belonged to the Kurumba tribe. The legends say that on their first settlement in Dravida they had no government, but dissensions arising they elected a king named Komandu Kurumba Prabhu and thus originated the Pallava dynasty. Under this king the country was divided into 24 divisions, each containing a fort, the principal stronghold being at Puralur, near Madras. The remains of other forts are still to be found at Mahendravadi, Amburpet, Narayanavanam, Vallimalai and Padaved, the ruins at the last-named place showing that the city had a circumference of about sixteen miles. The authentic history of the Pallavas is to be gathered from their copper-plate inscriptions and those of the rulers of the neighbour-ing kingdoms, which shew that when at the height of their prosperity at the end of the sixth century, they ruled over an empire extending from the Nerbudda and Orissa on the north, to the Southern Pennar river in the south, and from the sea on the east to a line through Salem and Bangalore to Berar on the west. The capital of the kingdom was Kanchipuram, the modern Conjeeveram, then one of the most civilized cities of India, and the religious capital of the South. The state religion at one period was Jainism, but apparently liberal views prevailed, as it is reported that both Buddhists and Brahmans were settled in Conjeeveram in the fourth century A. D. Commercial enterprise was vigorously pursued and through the numerous ports between Cuddalore and Ganjam, maritime trade was maintained with the Romans and other western nations. The celebrated monolithic temples and raths at Maha-mallapuram known as the Seven Pagodas are attributed to

Pallavas.

the Pallavas, inscriptions both on the Ganesha and southern-most temples disclosing the name of a king of this dynasty. The decline of the Pallava empire commenced in the seventh century, when Kubja Vishnuvardhana, the first of the Eastern Chalukyan kings, annexed the northern provinces of Vengi, Andhra, and Kalinga, and Pulakesi II of West Chalukya inflicted serious defeats in the south. The final conquest of the Pallavas occurred in the eleventh century when Adondai, the son of the Chola king Rajendra Kulottunga I, defeated them at Puralur and annexed the province of Dravida which was thereafter called by the name of Tondamandalam.

The Chalukyas, a Rajput race, first rose into prominence in the early part of the sixth century,

Chalukyas.

the founder of the dynasty, Jayasimha I, claiming descent from the kings of Ayodhya, the modern Oudh. The early capital of the kingdom was at Kalyan, in the Nizam's Dominions, whence the Chalukyas extended their territories eastward to the coast between the God-averi and Kistna, and northward as far as Daulatabad, a large portion of Mysore being included in their possessions. Raja Sinha, a posthumous son of Jayasimha, made extensive conquests, and cemented his power by an alliance with the Pallava king of Conjeeveram. About A. D. 610 the reigning family divided, Satyasraya I remaining in the Western Dakhan, and Kubja Vishnuvardhana founding the kingdom of Eastern Chalukya on territories wrested from the Pallavas. Satyasraya was one of the greatest kings of the Western Chalukyan branch, but after his death the dynasty was interrupted until about 670 when Vikramaditya I regained the throne. Some hundred years later another collapse of the dynasty occurred and the kingdom remained in obscurity for a period of about two hundred years, when it again became powerful and remained so until the year 1126. A rapid decline then set in and nothing is known of the Western

Chalukyan dynasty after the year 1189. The Eastern Chalukyans after their separation gradually extended their dominions to the borders of Orissa, the capital of the kingdom being fixed at Rajahmundry. In 1064 the dynasties of Eastern Chalukya and Chola were united under Rajendra Chola by the marriage of his father Rajaraja with the daughter of a Chalukyan king, when the kingdom became a northern province of the Cholas, to subsequently fall under the sway of the Ganapatis of Warangal. The Chalukyas were essentially a race of builders and have left many noble architectural remains in the territories they occupied. The defeat of the Pallavas was of importance from the fact that it was a victory of the Brahmanical religion over Buddhism and Jainism.

Returning to the general history of Southern India, we find that in 1306 Ala-ud-din, the Muhammadan Emperor of Delhi, despatched an army of 100,000 horse under an ennobled slave named Malek Kafur into the Dakhan for the purpose of compelling the Yadava Rajah of Devagiri to pay tribute which had been withheld for three years. In 1309 the same general was again sent into the Dakhan to reduce another principality to submission. In the following year Malek Kafur headed a third expedition against the Hoysala Ballalas of Dvarasamudra, the modern Halebidu. The Muhammadans were completely victorious, Halebidu being captured, its famous temple sacked, and the power of the Hoysala Ballala dynasty effectually shattered. The king Ballala was taken prisoner, but was subsequently released and allowed to exercise a nominal sovereignty, a privilege which seems to have been continued to his successors. The conquest of the Ballalas was followed by the reduction of both the Pandiyans and the Cholas, and on the withdrawal of the Muhammadan force complete anarchy prevailed over the southern portion of the peninsula for

General History, A. D. 1310 to A. D. 1687.

some years. In the struggle for supremacy the Mussulmans received a check by the defeat of a large Muhammadan army at the hands of a combination of Hindu rajahs, and a serious blow in 1347, when Ala-ud-din Hassan, the Mussulman viceroy of Daulatabad, revolted against the Emperor of Delhi and established in the Dakhan the independent Bahmani kingdom. Simultaneously with the consolidation of this State a powerful Hindu Empire was in course of formation at Vijayanagar on the ruins of the Hoysala Ballalas and other sovereignties. The growth of the new state was rapid, and it soon attained a degree of power far superior to that possessed by any prior southern kingdom. The Mussulmans seem to have held possession of the Chola country until 1347, when they were expelled and a short native dynasty established. In 1396 the Vijayanagar monarchs secured possession of the Chola kingdom, and probably in 1372 had expelled the Muhammadans from the Pandiyan territories. At the close of the 15th century the supremacy of Vijayanagar was acknowledged throughout the peninsula, although mall independent States as Mysore and Travancore continued to exist. About this time the Bahmani kingdom split up into five distinct principalities, their rivalry further increasing the power of the Hindu Empire. In 1564, however, the Muhammadan king combined against Vijayanagar, and after inflicting a crushing defeat at Talikota, sacked the city, slew the king and seized the Hindu possessions north of the Kistna. Owing to jealousy among the victors, and the loyalty of the Hindu provinces of the south, further partition of the Vijayanagar territories did not immediately follow the Mussulman success, but early in the next century serious dismemberment of the empire commenced. In 1657 a war broke out between the Rayar of Vijayanagar and the Nayakka of Madura, which led to interference by the kings of Golkonda and Bijapur. The most important results of these foreign invasions were the establishment of a Mahratta dynasty in Tanjore by Ekoji or Venkaji in 1674-5 and the invasion of the Carnatic by Sivaji in 1676.

The Bahmani kingdom established by Ala-ud-din Hassan in 1347 lasted 250 years, and had its

Bahmani Kingdoms of the Dakhan.

capital first at Kulbarga and subsequently at Bidar. Frequent wars with Vijayanagar were the principal events of the first ten reigns. The twelfth king, Nizan Shah, had to meet invasions from Orissa, Telingana, and Malwar which were successfully resisted. The succeeding monarch, Muhammad Shah II, came to the throne in 1463 at the youthful age of nine years, and in 1468 appointed the celebrated minister Mahmud Gawan to be his chief adviser. In 1469 the Konkana was captured from Vijayanagar and in 1471, Telingana was invaded, Kondapalle and Rajahmundry being taken. Six years later another expedition was made into Orissa, during which a flying visit was paid to Conjeeveram, when the town was sacked and an immense amount of loot secured. In 1481 Mahmud Gawan was believed by the king to be guilty of treason and was, in consequence, put to death. Though the dismemberment of the empire commenced in the following reign, the decline of the kingdom dated from the time of Mahmud's execution. Muhammad Shah II was succeeded in 1482 by his son Mahmud II, whose minister was Nizamu'l-mulk Bhavu. Within a few years of this king's accession the minister was murdered, an event which led to his son, Ahmad Nizam Shah, declaring his independence at Ahmadnagar in 1490. The Governor of Berar had previously revolted, establishing the 'Imad Shahi dynasty at Ellichpur, and a third kingdom was founded at Bijapur in 1489 by Yusuf 'Adil Shah. In 1504, on the death of his father, Amir Barid became minister to Mahmud and acquired extraordinary influence over the king. A fourth dynasty dates from 1512, when the Governor of Telingana, Qutbu'l-mulk, formed a new kingdom at Golkonda. On the death of Mahmud II, Amir Barid placed four successive kings on the throne, two of whom were murdered, and the fourth fled, presumably to avoid a like fate. On this Amir Barid threw off all pretence of allegiance to the Bahmani dynasty and established the Barid Shahi monarchy at Bidar. Space does not admit of the career of all these separate dynasties being traced, and it will suffice to mention that the Bijapur kingdom absorbed Bidar, and Ahmadnagar incorporated Ellichpur.

The Bijapur and Golkonda dynasties, however, call for more particular notice on account of the influence they subsequently exercised in the Carnatic. After the defeat at Talikota of the Rajah of Vijayanagar by the confederation of the Mussalman kings of Bijapur, Golkonda, Bidar and Ahmednagar, the doab between the Kistna and Godaveri was divided amongst the victors, while the Hindu Rajah was allowed to exercise a more or less nominal sovereignty over his southern possessions of Gingee, Tanjore and Madura. Some seventy years later the Nayakka or Viceroy of Madura rebelled against his suzerain and on the latter eventually proceeding to warlike measures solicited and obtained aid from the king of Golkonda. The Mussalmans after ravaging the country were ejected, but returning in greater force compelled the Rajah of Vijayanagar to take refuge in Mysore. On the Golkonda troops advancing further south the Viceroy of Tanjore submitted, but the Nayakka of Madura invoked the assistance of Bijapur, and in response a large force of cavalry was sent to his aid. At this time the Golkonda Army was besieging Gingee, but the two Mussalman forces having come to an understanding, the Golkonda troops drew off to hold the surrounding country, leaving the fort to be captured by the Bijapur contingent under Shahji, the father of the celebrated Sivaji. In 1646, after a further invasion, the forts of

Kingdoms of Bijapur and Golkonda.

Gingee and Vellore with the country south-east of Chandragiri were taken by Bijapur, while Chingleput and the
territories more to the north and around Madras were
annexed by Golkonda. An attempt in 1659 by the Nayakka
of Madura to throw off the Mussalman yoke produced
another invasion from Bijapur, when Gingee and Tanjore
were held for three years. No further attacks by Bijapur
and Golkonda are recorded, and these dynasties were
annihilated in 1686 and 1687 by the Mogul emperor
Aurangzeb.

The early history of the kingdom of Vijayanagar is
shrouded in obscurity. The first dynasty of which we have knowledge
claimed descent from the Yadava rajahs
of Magadha, the modern Behar, and the first king mentioned
in authentic history was Nanda, 1034 A.D., the founder of
Nandapur and Warangal. The city of Vijayanagar, now
known as Humpi, is situated on the right bank of the
Tungabadhra in the Bellary district. The town was
founded about 1338 in the reign of Mohammed Tughlak of
Delhi, according to one account by two fugitives who fled
from Telingana after the overthrow of Warangal by the
Mussalmans in 1323, and, according to another by Belal
Deo of Karnata. In 1380 a king named Harihara II expelled the Muhammadans from Goa and placed the captured
country under one of his ministers. About 1490 this
dynasty was succeeded by the powerful line of kings called
after Narasimha, the founder of the family, a monarch who
seems to have extended his power into the Dravida country.
One of his successors, Krishnadeva Raya, 1509-1530, was
the greatest monarch of the dynasty, and largely increased
the possessions of the empire. He commenced by settling
the district round Conjeeveram, and then captured the fort
of Sivasamudram and the city of Seringapatam from the
Mysore Rajah, Ganga Raja of Ummatur. In 1513 he captured the fortress and dependencies of Udayagiri in Cuttack,

Kingdom of Vijayanagar.

and two years later the hill fort of Kondavidu from a Gajapati chief. These victories were followed by numerous conquests between Nellore and the Kistna, including the subversion of Bezwada and Kondapalle. The southern forts of Chandragiri and Vellore are attributed to this monarch who, by his conquests, became ultimately the virtual ruler of a kingdom whose limits nearly coincided with those of the Madras Presidency of to-day. The chief officials under the Vijayanagar kings were always styled Nayakkas and as two persons, named Lakkana Nayakka and Mattanan Nayakka, ruled jointly in Madura from A. D. 1404 to 1451, it would appear that the power of Vijayanagar was felt in the extreme south prior to the accession of Narasimha. These Nayakkas were succeeded by four descendants of the old Pandiyan Kings, but in 1499 a second line of Nayakkas ruled in Madura till 1558 and a third till 1736. The second dynasty of Nayakkas are described in inscriptions as servants of the Rayar of Vijayanagar. In 1530 a line of four Nayakkas reigned till 1665 in Tanjore, so it is probable that Krishnadeva Raya had then established other Viceroys as rulers of his southern dependencies. Achyutya, the successor of the last mentioned king, finally reduced Tinnevelly in 1532-33 and was succeeded in 1542 by an infant son, Sadasiva, who was kept in subjection by his ministers, and can hardly be said to have ever reigned. In 1565, during the time when the minister Rama Raja was usurping the power of his sovereign, the Mussulman kings of the Dakhan combined and inflicted the disastrous defeat of Talikota on Vijayanagar. Rama Raja was killed in cold blood after the battle, and his head, smeared over with red paint and oil, was preserved as a trophy at Bijapur for a century afterwards. The victorious allies, after sacking the city of Vijayanagar and committing every conceivable atrocity, annexed all the Hindu possessions north of the Kistna. With Sadasiva terminated the Narasimha dynasty and henceforward the sovereignty passed to the line of the usurping minister, Rama Raja. The successor of this minister established himself in Pennakonda, 85 miles south-west of Bellary, and a successor, Timmah Raja, removed from there to Chandragiri in 1570, at which place he ruled with some degree of magnificence over his Nayakkas of Gingee, Tanjore, Madura, Madras, Seringapatam and Pennakonda. In 1577 a Muhammadan attack on Pennakonda was repelled by the Viceroy Jagadeva Raya, who received, as a reward for this service, large grants of land in Mysore and Salem. In 1597 the seat of Government was removed to Vellore and two years later war broke out with the Governor of Madura. In the reign of this king, Venkatapati, European Missionaries were well received and the trade of the East India Company encouraged ; but the Dutch, who were established at Pulicat, persuaded him to refuse the English a settlement. On the death of Venkatapati in 1614 wild disorder prevailed. The various Viceroys proclaimed their independence and the capture of Seringapatam by Raja Udaiyar of Mysore virtually destroyed the power of Vijayanagar above the ghats. In 1644 the Carnatic was invaded by armies from Bijapur and Golkonda and the then Rajah, Sri Ranga Rayel, escaped to Mysore, where he was afforded shelter, and from this time the dominion of Vijayanagar may be considered as finally terminated. It is to be remarked that in 1639 Damarla Venkatadri Nayudu, Zemindar of Kalahasti, gave to the English the village of Chennakuppum, and they obtained a *sanad* (warrant) for it from the then Rajah of Chandragiri. The Zemindar stipulated that the settlement was to be called Chenna-pattanam after his father Chennappa Nayudu, and on the site so granted Fort St. George was built, and the city founded, now known as Madras to Europeans and Chenna-pattanam by the natives.

The course of events in Southern India after 1687 can

A. D. 1687 to English Supremacy. best be followed by a perusal of separate narratives of the most important nationalities which influenced the history of the period. This method will, therefore, be adopted; but, to make matters clearer, a short general account of Carnatic history will also be given.

On the fall of Golkonda and Bijapur, the armies of the Moghul Emperors of Delhi, under **Carnatic History.** Zulfikar Khan, were set in motion against the Mahratta possessions in the Carnatic. Rajaram, a king who had usurped the Mahratta throne, established himself at Gingee, and for eight years resisted the attempts of the Muhammadans to capture the fortress. Gingee was, however, eventually taken, when Rajaram escaped to Vellore, and from thence proceeded to Satara, where he collected a large army. The Mussulmans at first intended to make Gingee their head-quarters, but increasing troubles with the Mahrattas in the north compelled Aurungzeb to abandon these designs. After the death of this Emperor in 1707, Zulfikar Khan was appointed subadar or viceroy of the Dakhan, but for political reasons he deputed one Daud Khan to act for him, when, in consequence of the unhealthiness of Gingee, the seat of government was removed to Arcot. Zulfikar Khan was murdered in 1713, and his deputy in the Carnatic was then replaced by a minister named Chin Kilick Khan, better known by the title of Nizam-ul-Mulk, still borne by his descendants in Hyderabad. The Nizam was removed from office within one year of his arrival at Arcot, and was succeeded by a subadar named Hussain Ali, who, before long, incurred the displeasure of his sovereign. In consequence of this Hussain Ali had soon to meet an attack by Muhammadan troops, followed by troubles with the Mahrattas who were persuaded to annoy him. Ultimately Hussain Ali bought off the Mahrattas by yielding to them the right to collect the "chout" or the fourth and the tenth of the revenues of the six provinces of the Dakhan, and of the tributary States of Tanjore, Mysore and Trichinopoly. Hussain

Ali then marched to Delhi and captured the Emperor, whose assassination he procured. Hussain Ali was shortly afterwards murdered, when the Nizam was appointed Vizier or Prime Minister at Delhi, which post he soon vacated. He retired to Hyderabad in 1724 and from that time became practically independent. The Carnatic was subordinate to him and was governed by a deputy or Nabob named Sadat-ulla with head-quarters at Arcot. On Sadatulla's death in 1732, his nephew Dost Ali, became Nabob, but without securing the Nizam's sanction. In 1736 Dost Ali attacked Trichinopoly capturing the fort there, but in 1740 the Mahrattas, at the instigation of the Nizam, sent a large army against him on the pretext of collecting the "chout," which had long remained unpaid. Dost Ali advanced to meet the invaders with what force he could collect and determined to make a stand at Damalcheru in North Arcot district until such time as re-inforcements could be despatched to his succour. Owing to treachery the Mahratta army was enabled to gain, during hours of darkness, a position in rear of the Nabob's line, and after a stubborn fight obtained a complete victory, both Dost Ali and his son Hussain Ali being killed. Safdar Ali, another son, eventually bought off the Mahrattas and assumed the governorship of the Carnatic. He was murdered by a Pathan, at the instigation of his nephew, Mortiz Ali, who succeeded to the vacancy. Owing to troubles with his army the latter had to retire in favour of Mahommed Ali, the infant son of Safdar Ali, who ruled under the guardianship of his uncle, Tuckia Sahib, at Wandiwash. About this time the Nizam with a large army visited Wandiwash, and confirmed Mahommed Ali as Nabob, but appointed one Anwar-ud-din as guardian. This change was followed by the retransfer of the court to Arcot.

In 1744 Mahommed Ali was murdered presumably at the initiation of Mortiz Ali, whereupon the Nizam elevated Anwar-ud-din to the vacant throne, and he became the ancestor of those Nabobs of the Carnatic from whom the country was obtained by the English. Subsequent events in the Carnatic will be referred to when dealing with the development of the British Empire in India.

There are some grounds for supposing that the territories of the Pandiyans were invaded by the **Kingdom of Madura.** Mussulmans prior to the subversion of the dynasty in 1310, but these earlier visits, if real, were of minor importance compared with the devastation wrought by the notorious Malik Kafur and his immediate successors. During the period when the Madura country was administered by Muhammadan chiefs, atrocities of every kind were perpetrated. Among other acts of vandalism, the outer wall of the town with its fourteen towers was levelled, and the magnificent temple, excepting only the shrines of the gods, Sundareshwara and Minakshi, was utterly destroyed. About 1372, a Mysorean General, named Kampana Udeiyar, presumably the agent of Buk'ha, the Rayar of Vijayanagar, marched on Madura and succeeded in expelling the Muhammadan rulers. After administering the country for some time and providing for its future government by Udeiyars, Kampana Udeiyar left the country. About 1404 the last Udeiyar, Porkasa, was succeeded by a Viceroy named Lakkana Nayakkan, who was either followed by or ruled jointly with another Nayakkan called Mathanan. In 1451 four persons supposed to be of Pandiyan origin were placed on the throne of Madura by one Lakkana Nayakkan and reigned for a period of 48 years. To these Pandiyans are attributed the four lofty gopuras (towers) connected with the enclosure walls of the great temple. About 1515 the government of the country again reverted to Vijayanagar agents and remained so until 1557 when, during a brief period of anarchy, another Pandiyan secured the throne for a short time until deposed by a Chola king, named Virashekhara. The fugitive Pandya fled to the court of Vijayanagar and besought the aid of the Rayar in regaining his kingdom. Help was given and a General, named Kotiya Naganna Nayakkan, was ordered to chastise the Tanjore Rajah and reinstate the Pandiyan at Madura. For this undertaking Naganna was successful, but soon assumed the reins of government on his own account. This disobedience was promptly dealt with, and Naganna's son Visvanatha, was despatched against his father whom he defeated and imprisoned until the rebel was ultimately pardoned. Visvanatha placed Chandrashekhara on the throne, but as he proved unequal to the position, Visvanatha, with the consent of the Rayar, became the viceroy of Vijayanagar. With Visvanatha commenced the well-known dynasty of the Nayakkas of Madura, the date of his accession being generally accepted as 1559. A very remarkable man, named Arya Nayaga Muthali, came to Madura with Visvanatha. He was the son of poor parents of the Vellala caste, but being possessed of energy and talent, rose rapidly to a position of trust in the service of the Rayar. The history of Arya Nayaga or Nat'ha, as he is frequently called, is much shrouded in legend, but there is no doubt that he was a man of great power and authority who was General and Prime Minister to Visvanatha and during the three succeeding reigns. The Madura Poligars pray to him as the founder of their order and his equestrian statue in Tirumala Nayakka's choultry is garlanded to this day. To him is due the hall of a thousand pillars within the enclosure of the great temple at Madura. Under Visvanatha the country was wisely governed, fortifications constructed, temples rebuilt, and irrigation works undertaken. Trichinopoly was obtained from the Tanjore king in exchange for Vallam, and its rock suitably fortified. The Tinnevelly District was put in order after some trouble from five chiefs who called themselves the "five Pandavas," and who allowed the dispute to be settled by personal combat between one of their number and a Madura champion. To provide for the stability of the kingdom, each of the 72 bastions of the Madura Fort was placed in charge of a particular chief, who was bound for himself and his heirs to keep his post at all times and under all circumstances, to maintain a body of troops for Imperial service, and to pay a fixed annual tribute. Thus originated the famous Madura Paliyakarans or Poligars, some of whose descendants still possess the family estates. Visvanatha died in December 1563 and was succeeded by his son, Kumara Krishnappa, who reigned until 1573. Arya Natha seems to have been the real ruler of the kingdom, so the beneficent policy of the previous Nayakka was continued. Kumara was succeeded by his two sons, Krishnappa and Visvanatha II, who ruled jointly until Visvanatha's death. During this reign a rebellion was quelled and Trichinopoly and Chidambaram were strengthened. Krishnappa died in 1595 and was succeeded by his two sons, Lingayya and Visvanatha III. The great Arya Nat'ha died in 1600, and Lingayya, the survivor of the two brothers in 1602. Kasturi Rangayya, the uncle of the previous kings, then usurped the kingdom ; but, being murdered a week later, Muttu Krishnappa, Lingayya's son, succeeded to the throne. The most important event of this reign was the re-establishment, in 1604, of the Setupati dynasty of Ramnad. The Setupatis claim to be of the ancient Marava race, and were probably vassals of the Pandiyan kings prior to the supremacy of Vijayanagar. At various times their capitals have been Devapura, or Rameshwara, Tondi, Raghunat'hapura, Verava Nallur and Ramnad. The Setupatis seem to have sunk into obscurity for a considerable time, and, at the accession of Muttu Krishnappa, the Ramnad country was under the management of two Commissioners appointed by the Viceroy of Madura. These officers having failed to maintain order within their charge, Sadeika Tevan Udeiyan Sethupati was appointed Governor of the territory between Madura and the sea coast and chief of the 72 Poligars.

This act of policy was productive of the happiest results, Ramnad and Pokalur were fortified and improved, the important villages of Vadakku Vattakei, Kaliyar-Kovil, and Pattamangalam were taken from refractory chiefs, and a considerable tribute was annually remitted to Madura. In 1606 Robert de Nobilibus visited Madura and finding that the spread of Christianity was prevented by the abhorrence in which the Portuguese were held by the Hindus on account of their eating beef, drinking spirits, and associating with pariahs, he determined to devote his life to missionary enterprise. With the consent of the Archbishop of Cranganore, he represented to the Brahmans that he was not a Portuguese, but a Roman prince and a religious devotee. He then commenced to live a life of strict Hindu asceticism and withdrew from all intercourse with Father Fernandez, the Portuguese Missionary. His efforts were soon crowned with some success, but this naturally resulted in provoking the hostility of the Brahman Gurus or priests, who lost a considerable portion of their customary fees. More serious, however, than this persecution was the peremptory suspension of de Nobilibus' administration by his superiors in Europe, an action undoubtedly due to hostile reports by Father Fernandez, and which was the severest blow ever inflicted on Christianity in India. Muttu Krishnappa died in 1609 leaving three sons, Muttu Verappa, Tirumala, and Kumara Muttu, the first of whom succeeded to the throne. This king resided at Trichinopoly and was hostile to Christianity. The only features of note during this reign of fourteen years were a small war with Tanjore and unimportant incursions of predatory bands from Mysore directed against Dindigul. Muttu Verappa's successor was Tirumala Nayakka, the greatest of all the modern rulers of Madura. He was at the time of his accession suffering from a severe attack of catarrh of long standing, which his physicians were unable to cure. During a halt at Dindigul, the god, Sundareshwara and the goddess,

Minakshi are said to have appeared to him in a vision and promised him a speedy recovery if he would make Madura his capital and permanently reside there. Tirumala therefore removed to Madura when his health was restored. In gratitude for his recovery he undertook the construction of the magnificent religious edifices unseparably connected with his name, and then built himself an enormous palace which he furnished with the greatest splendour. The first war in which Tirumala was engaged appears to have been against Cham Raj Udeiyar, the Rajah of Mysore. The Madura Dalavay (Commander-in-Chief) Ramappayya encountered the Mysore army near Dindigul and defeated it with great loss. This victory was followed by an active pursuit of the enemy into Mysore and the capture of one of the principal fortresses of that kingdom. A few years after the war with Mysore, troubles arose with the Setupati of Ramnad, and in the ensuing conflicts Tirumala was not particularly successful. Tirumala had from the first been desirous of freeing himself from subordination to Vijayanagar, and, in 1657, his want of loyalty led to war with the Rayar. Tanjore and Gingee combined with Madura, while the Mussulmans, at Tirumala's suggestion invaded the territories of Vijayanagar, and greatly extended their possessions. The Muhammadans then turned their attention to the south and captured Madura without bloodshed, when Tirumala entered into an alliance with the State of Golkonda which then ravaged Mysore and the remaining territories of Vijayanagar. In consequence of this, war broke out between Mysore and Madura and ultimately ended in favour of the latter kingdom in 1659, the year in which Tirumala died. In this war the Setupati particularly distinguished himself and was liberally rewarded with additions to his territories and exemption from payment of tribute. Tirumala is supposed to have had a strong leaning towards Christianity and Robert de Nobilibus resumed his ministrations in June 1625. There are some

grounds for concluding that Tirumala was murdered by the
Brahmans, one tradition being that he was enticed into a
supposed treasure vault and there confined until he died of
starvation. Tirumala was succeeded in 1659 by his
illegitimate son, Muttu Arakadri, the rightful heir, Kumara
Muttu, having been induced to waive his claims. This
reign only lasted a year; but during this period, the
Mussulmans invaded the country, and, after capturing
Tanjore and other places, unsuccessfully besieged Trichinopoly. This king was followed in 1660 by his son
Chokkanatha, a youth of sixteen, who, after outwitting
a plot to dethrone him, successfully besieged Tanjore,
whither the traitors had fled. In 1663-64 another Mussulman invasion occurred, during which Trichinopoly was
unsuccessfully besieged and fearful massacres of innocent
villagers took place. The Nayakka of Tanjore, Vijaya
Raghava, having assisted the Muhammadans, Chokkanatha
attacked and defeated him. Shortly after this the Setupati
rebelled and was unsuccessfully attacked. In 1674 Tanjore
was again invaded, reduced, the king Vijaya Raghava
slain with almost all his family, and Chokkanatha's foster
brother, Alagiri Nayakka, appointed Viceroy. In 1675
Chokkanatha married Mangammal, who afterwards became
Regent, and gave himself up to private enjoyments, living
at Trichinopoly and neglecting the government which was
carried on by his brother, Muttu Arakadri. The ministers
soon began to intrigue with Arakadri at Madura, and
finally induced him to declare his independence. At the
same time the Muhammadans in alliance with Ekoji, the
half-brother of Sivaji and a refugee Tanjore prince, seized
first Tanjore, and then almost all the Madura territory
without opposition. At length Chokkanatha assembled
an army for the attack of the Muhammadans in Tanjore,
and at the same time the Rajah of Mysore prepared to
attack Madura. A raid by Sivaji, as far south as the
Coleroon, was taken advantage of by the Muhammadans

4

to attack Gingee, but the effort was unsuccessful, and
Sivaji's armies returned in safety to garrison the fortress.
Chokkanatha had meanwhile advanced on Tanjore, but
remained inactive, and in 1677 the Rajah of Mysore invaded
Madura, when Chokkanatha was dethroned by his ministers
and his brother, Muttu Lingappa, placed on the throne.
This prince, however, only reigned a few months, when
Chokkanatha was restored. In 1680 the armies of Mysore
invested Trichinopoly, and the Nayakka was further
threatened by the Setupati, the Mahrattas and the Tanjore
Muhammadans. Eventually the Mahrattas, who nominally
were supposed to be in alliance with Chokkanatha, having
defeated the Mysoreans with great slaughter and retaken
their conquest in the Madura territories, proceeded to
besiege Trichinopoly on their own account. This last
misfortune proved too much for the Nayakka, who fell into
a profound melancholy and died of a broken heart in 1682.
The whole country was now in a state of anarchy and
the territories of Madura were divided between the new
Nayakka, Ranga Krishna Muttu Virappa, the Rajah of
Mysore, the Setupati, Sambuji of Gingee, and Ekoji of
Tanjore. Ranga Krishna gradually shook off the Mysore
control, recovered the lands annexed by the Setupati, and
regained possession of his capital. This Nayakka, who
governed well and energetically, died of small-pox in 1689.
The kingdom then fell under the regency of Mangammal,
a charitable but unscrupulous woman, who permitted
religious toleration. The Setupati of Ramnad, however,
was violently opposed to Christianity and in 1693 beheaded
the missionary John De Britto at the instigation of the
Brahmans. In 1698 troubles arose with Travancore, the
outcome of which is not definitely known, although the
Madura troops claim to have been victorious. In 1700 the
Dutch of Tuticorin acquired the monopoly of the pearl
fisheries, and a desultory war with Tanjore broke out,
during which the Madura forces ravaged Tanjore and had

to be bought off. In 1701 Madura and Tanjore combined against Mysore, but war was averted, and in the following year the Setupati defeated and killed the Delavay Narasappayya. The regency terminated in 1704, when the young prince Vijaya Ranga Chokkanatha came of age and Mangammal was starved to death. This reign was remarkable for a terrible flood in 1709 and a famine which lasted from 1709 to 1720. The Tondaman or Rajah of Pudukottai revolted against his liege lord the Setupati of Ramnad, who died whilst marching to chastise his rebellious vassal. On this a struggle ensued for the throne of Ramnad, which terminated in a division of territory, Tanjore securing a share. Vijaya Ranga died in 1731 without issue, when his widow, Minakshi, adopted the son of a person, named Vangaru Tirumala, who considered himself the legal heir. This led to further troubles and, in 1734, the Muhammadans under Safdar Ali Khan ravaged the country as well as Tanjore, Travancore, and the Western Coast. Vangaru Tirumala induced Safdar Ali Khan to declare him king, and Chanda Sahib, a son-in-law of Dost Ali was left to enforce the decision. Minakshi, however, bribed Chanda Sahib, who, in 1736, sent troops against Vangaru Tirumala at Dindigul and Madura. They were victorious and Chanda Sahib seized the sovereignty. Minakshi then committed suicide and the Hindu government of Madura was thus put an end to for ever. Vangaru Tirumala sought aid from the Mahrattas, when Raghuji Bhonsle with an immense army marched on Madura. The Muhammadans were defeated with great slaughter, Chanda Sahib taken prisoner, and Trichinopoly captured. Morari Rao, a Mahratta chief, was left in charge of Trichinopoly, while another Mahratta, Appaji Rao, administered Madura; this arrangement ceased in 1743, when the whole was yielded up to the Nizam on his invasion. Vangaru Tirumala gained the protection of the Nizam, but was shortly afterwards poisoned. From the time of the Mahratta expulsion the Madura country was governed by officers nominated by Anwar-ud-din. In 1750 the then ruler Allum Khan threw in his lot with Chanda Sahib who, after regaining his liberty in 1748, had, with the aid of the French and Muzaffir Jung, defeated and killed Anwar-ud-din at Ambur in 1749, when Muhammed Ali fled to Trichinopoly and proclaimed himself Nabob. In 1751 Muhammed Ali, in alliance with a small English force, made an unsuccessful attack on Madura. The next Governor, Mayana, is supposed to have sold the city to Mysore, but the English under Captain Cope returned and took possession. They were expelled by the Setupati who, in 1753, placed the adopted son of Minakshi upon the throne of Madura. Complete confusion for two years followed, when Muhammed Ali sent another expedition against Madura. The city was surrendered without a struggle, and a European garrison under a Muhammadan Governor was installed. In 1758 the English obtained permanent possession of Madura, but troubles in the surrounding district did not cease until 1783, when Colonel Fullarton quieted the whole country, which was thereafter administered solely by the English. The first "Collector of Madura," Mr. McLeod, was appointed in 1790.

Reverting to the history of Tanjore, which has been **Kingdom of Tanjore.** carried up to the time of the Mussalman invasion when dealing with the Cholas, it is to be noted that, as there is no record of the country having been ruled by the Muhammadans in the fourteenth century, it is probable it was only ravaged by a wing of Malek Kafur's army. During this century the old Chola kingdom seems to have become tributary to Vijayanagar under the Udeiyars. Little, however, is known of Tanjore history during this period until the expedition of the Vijayanagar General, Kotriya Naganna Nayakka, against Madura, after which a Nayakkan dynasty appears to have been established in Tanjore. In all four

Nayakkas—Sevappa, Acutappa, Raghunatha, and Vijaya
Raghava, governed the country.   These rulers soon became
virtually independent of Vijayanagar, but were never so
powerful as the Madura Viceroys.   Although they did not
undertake any very great utilitarian works, several forts,
tanks and temples were constructed by the first and last
two Nayakkas.   During the existence of this dynasty,
which terminated about 1665, the Portuguese, in 1612,
formed a settlement at Negapatam, and the Danes at
Tranquebar in 1620.   Negapatam was taken by the Dutch
in 1660 and possession confirmed by a grant from the
last Nayakka.   Vijaya Raghava and his son, Mannaru,
were killed in a final and desperate *sortie* from Tanjore
during the attack of the Madura army under Alagiri.   To
prevent any member of his family, or of his numerous
zenana falling into the hands of his enemies, Vijaya
Raghava caused the female apartments to be blown-up just
before he sallied forth, but the crown Rani managed to
save her male baby.   The nurse, who had charge of the
child, fled to Negapatam, where she was received into the
house of a Chetty and allowed to bring up the infant as
her own.   Twelve years later, a Brahman named Venkanna,
who had been Vijaya Raghava's secretary, collected a
number of the old Nayakka's dependents and took the boy
to Bijapur, where he laid his unfortunate case before the
king.   After some delay an army was sent under the
command of Ekoji, a Mahratta General, then in charge
of the recent Bijapur conquests in the Carnatic.   Ekoji
defeated Alagiri, who, in the meantime, had usurped the
throne, and conducted the young prince in triumph to the
palace, where he was crowned with due solemnity.
Troubles soon arose in connection with the appointment
of a Minister, which resulted on the death of the Bijapur
sovereign, in Ekoji ejecting the young king, Sengamal-
adas, and securing the throne for himself.   It is generally
agreed that Ekoji seized Tanjore in 1674.   He came of a

respectable Mahratta family surnamed Bhonsle and was half-brother of the great Sivaji. In 1677 Sivaji raided the Carnatic, capturing all the Bijapur conquests, and claiming a moiety of the Tanjore possessions. Eventually, Ekoji was allowed to retain Tanjore and the family estate in Mysore, but had to pay a large sum of money and divide his father's jewels and the revenues of the territories left to him. The Mysore property was captured by a Moghul General and Chikka Deva Rajah of Mysore about 1683. Ekoji died either in 1686 or 1687, leaving three sons, Shahji, Sharabhoji, and Tukkoji. Shahji reigned for 25 years and in 1691 was compelled by Zulfikar Khan, the Moghul Deputy, to pay an annual tribute of 4 lakhs of rupees. In 1696 Zulfikar Khan compelled the Rajah to restore several places he had wrested from the Nayakka of Trichinopoly. The reign of Sharabhoji, 1712—1727, was uneventful, but that of the following king, Tukkoji, was noteworthy for the extension of the Tanjore territory southwards into the Marava country. In 1725 the succession to the throne of Ramnad was violently disputed by two rival claimants, Tanda Tevan and Bhavani Shankara. The cause of the latter, an illegitimate son of the preceding Setupati, was espoused by Tukkoji, while the Nayakka of Ramnad and the Tondaman of Pudukottai supported the former. The Tanjore General, Ananda Rao Peshva, was victorious, and, having slain Tanda Tevan, placed Bhavani Shankara on the throne. Soon after this event two other claimants appeared named Katta Tevan and Sheshavarna Tevan, who succeeded in enlisting the active sympathy of the Tanjore Rajah. This resulted in the Ramnad territory being divided into three portions : the country north of the Pamban river fell to Tanjore ; that around Ramnad to Katta, and the present Zemindari of Sivaganga to Sheshavarna. Shortly afterwards Katta Tevan captured from Tanjore all the Ramnad territory, except Arantanji and its dependent districts. Tukkoji was succeeded in 1736 by his son Baba Sahib, who reigned only a year, when his wife Sujana Bai was appointed regent. Some two years later a pretender named Savai Shahji or Kattu Raja succeeded, with the aid of the Muhammadan Commander of the fort, in ousting Sujana Bai. He was, however, soon deposed and Saiyaji, the second son of Tukkoji, placed on the throne. For some unknown reason, Saiyaji also was removed from power, and his illegitimate brother, Pratapsing, appointed Rajah in 1740. Pratapsing's reign of 24 years embraced an eventful period in South Indian history, for, during his time, the Carnatic was the scene of fierce contests for supremacy between two rival Muhammadan families aspiring to the rank of Moghul Deputy, and of the first intervention of the English and French in the political affairs of India. Early in 1749 Saiyaji, the deposed Rajah, solicited the aid of the English in deposing Pratapsing, promising to pay the expenses of the expedition if successful, and to give them the fort of Divikkottei, near the mouth of the Coleroon. The offer was accepted ; but the expedition was unsuccessful. To retrieve the lost prestige, a second and more powerful force, under Major Stringer Lawrence, was sent against Divikkottei in May 1749. The fort was taken in the following month, the assault being led by Lieutenant, afterwards Lord, Clive, the founder of the British Empire in India. After a temple at Achavaram had been captured, Pratapsing agreed to cede for ever the fort of Divikkottei with its adjoining territory worth 31,500 rupees per annum, pay a war indemnity of a lakh of rupees, and allow a yearly pension of Rs. 4,000 to Saiyaji. In December 1749, Pratapsing was pressed by Chanda Sahib, and Muzaffar Jung, a claimant to the Subadarship of the Dakhan for payment of 4 crores of rupees on account of arrears of tribute and as a contribution towards the expenses of the war against Anwar-ud-din. The confeder-ates, who were then on their way to attack Muhammed

Ali in Trichinopoly, forced the Rajah by bombarding Tanjore to make heavy payments in money and to give extensive grants of land. The attack on Trichinopoly was postponed in consequence of the approach of a large army under Nazir Jung, the second son of the Nizam. A battle was fought at Valdavur, in which the allies were utterly defeated, and after which Muzaffar Jung was thrown into prison. The victorious army retired to Arcot, where Nazir Jung gave himself up to a life of ease and luxury, after having sent large numbers of his troops back to the north. Advantage was taken of this inaction by Chanda Sahib, who proceeded to besiege Muhammed Ali in Trichinopoly, and by the French, who secured Gingee. Trichinopoly was eventually relieved by Clive with the assistance of some Mysore troops, the Mahratta Horse under Murari Rao, and a Mahratta contingent under Mankoji. Chanda Sahib surrendered himself to Mankoji, who caused him to be beheaded. As a reward for his assistance, Mahommed Ali granted to Pratapsing a release of ten years' arrears of tribute and the districts of Koiladi and Yalangudu. Subsequently Mysore and the Mahratta Horse went over to the French, and the intrigues of Dupleix nearly resulted in Pratapsing taking their side in the struggle against the Nabob and the English. However, the Tanjore prince remained staunch, and, in revenge, the Mahratta contingent plundered the country until driven out by Mankoji. In May 1754 the French ravaged the country, inflicting a most wanton injury on the cultivators by cutting through the large irrigation bank, which prevented the waters of the Cauvery escaping into the Coleroon. The bank was, however, repaired when the French withdrew, the labourers working under the protection of the Tanjore army. In 1758 the French Governor, Lally, looted Nagore and Kivalur, and finally encamped in front of Tanjore, but soon raised the siege on hearing that an English fleet had anchored off Karaikkal. Pratapsing

died in 1763 and was succeeded by his son Tulzaji.
Hyder Ali from Mysore invaded the Carnatic in 1769, but
spared Tanjore in consideration of a heavy payment exacted
from Tulzaji. At the persuasion of Muhammed Ali, the
English undertook an expedition against Tanjore in 1771
for the purpose of enforcing tribute due by Tulzaji. The
fort of Vallam, near Tanjore, was taken in September of
that year, and in October the siege of the capital was raised
on the Rajah coming to terms. The Nabob, however, was
not satisfied, and, in 1773, induced the English to undertake
the reduction of the country. This resulted in Tulzaji being
deposed and Muhammed Ali being put in possession of the
district together with the port of Nagore. The Court
of Directors of the East India Company, however, dis-
approved of these unjust wars, and, after removing from
office the President of the Madras Council, directed the
re-installation of Tulzaji, who, on 11th April 1776, was
formally put in possession of all his territories, including
Vallam, Yalangudu and Koiladi. During the two years
Muhammed Ali held Tanjore, the country was subjected
to the most cruel oppressions and exactions. In 1781
Hyder Ali for a second time invaded Tanjore, ravaged the
country, and, with the exception of the capital, made
himself master of the whole district. He was, however,
signally defeated by Sir Eyre Coote at Porto Novo on
1st July 1781, and by November of that year, except for
occasional raids, the troops of Hyder had left the country.
A lamentable disaster occurred to a force under Colonel
Brathwaite, in February 1782, which was overpowered on
the banks of the Coleroon by an overwhelming army under
Tippu, Hyder's son. Tulzaji died in 1787, and was succeeded by his half-brother Amarsing, his adopted son Sharabhoji
being set aside on the grounds of illegal adoption and the
imbecile state of Tulzaji's mind when the selection was
made. Sharabhoji was educated at Tanjore under the care
of the celebrated German Missionary Mr. Schwartz. In

5

1792 loud complaints were made of the ill-treatment of Sharabhoji by Amarsing, and the Madras Government interfering, Sharabhoji was removed to Madras and placed under the care of the Revd. W. Fr. Gericke, of the Lutheran Mission. On arrival at Madras, and by the advice of Mr. Schwartz, Government was memorialized to reinvestigate Sharabhoji's claim to the throne of Tanjore. The appeal was ultimately successful and, in June 1798, Amarsing was deposed and Sharabhoji installed. Soon after Sharabhoji consented to resign the Government of Tanjore wholly into the hands of the Company, and under a treaty, dated 25th October 1799, Tanjore became a British province. Sharabhoji lived till 1832 and made an extensive collection of English and Sanskrit works, his library being probably the largest and most valuable in Southern India. He was succeeded by his son Sivaji, who died in 1855 without male heirs, when the title and dignity of the Tanjore raj became extinct. The whole of the late Rajah's property, real and personal, excepting only the insignia of royalty, are now in possession of his family, subject to the ordinary laws of Hindu succession. The palace is State property, and the estate is managed under the control of the Collector by a receiver appointed by Government.

The cradle of the Maharatta race is known as Maharashtra, being all the southern portion of the Bombay Presidency, and large areas in the Central Provinces, Central India Agency, and Nizam's Dominions. Nothing authentic is known of the early history of the Mahrattas; but they were conquered by the Mussulmans before the fall of the Pathan dynasty of Delhi, and, between the times of the Moghul emperors, Akbar and Aurangzeb, were partly subject to the Moghuls and partly to Ahmadnagar and Bijapur. The Mahratta dynasty sprang from a family named Bhonsle, residing at Ellora, and which traced its descent from the royal house

The Mahrattas.

of Oudipur. Babaji Bhonsle, the head man of three villages, had a son named Maloji, who rose in 1577 to be a cavalry commander under Nizam Shah II of Ahmadnagar. Maloji's eldest son, Shahji, became prominent first under Nizam Shah and then under the Moghuls and Ibrahim Adil Shah of Bijapur, governing the southern conquests of the last king. Shahji had three legitimate sons, the first of whom was killed in action; the second was the great Sivaji, the founder of the Mahratta power; and the third was Ekoji, who seized Tanjore from its Nayakkan Governor, and established the last dynasty, which ruled the ancient Chola kingdom. In 1638 Shahji came into the Carnatic as second-in-command of the Bijapur force, which eventually conquered a considerable portion of modern Mysore, the fortresses of Vellore, Gingee and Arni, and other places of minor importance. On his own account, Shahji acquired extensive landed property near Bangalore, and estates at Arni and Porto Novo. Sivaji's connection with the Carnatic was comparatively of small consequence. In 1677 he invaded the country, seizing the Bijapur conquests and the family possessions in Mysore and Arni, and in 1680, the year of his death, obtained from the Bijapur Government a grant of all the territories he had conquered in the Carnatic, together with the principality of Tanjore. The further history of the Mahratta race, except as regards the Tanjore branch already narrated, is connected with districts beyond the limits of the Madras Presidency, and is, therefore, outside the scope of this work.

The family of the Rajahs of Mysore is supposed to be

Mysore. descended from Vijaya, the elder of two Yadava brothers, who left the Court of Vijayanagar, and, after rescuing the daughter of the ruler of Hadanad or Udaiyar from an enforced marriage with the chieftain of Karugakalli in Mysore, married her himself and finally became lord of Hadanad. Very little is known of the early history of the dynasty. The first ruler of note was Hire Chama Raja (1571—76), who became independent on the fall of the Vijayanagar empire. Rajah Udaiyar (1578—1617) largely increased the extent of his dominions, and in 1609 ejected the Viceroy of Vijayanagar from Seringapatam, which town he then occupied. The next Rajah Kanthirava Narasa (1638—1659), and his successor, Kempa Deva (1659—1672), further enlarged their kingdom, the latter takingErode from the Nayakka of Madura. The following Rajah, Chikka Deva (1672—1704), was the most powerful sovereign of the dynasty. He governed well, reformed the land-tenure system, defeated the Mahrattas, and added several new tracts, including Bangalore, to the State. With Chama Raja (1731—1733) the dynasty was interrupted for a period of 66 years by anarchy, the elevation to the throne of puppet sovereigns of distant branches, and by the usurpation of Hyder Ali Khan and his son Tippu Sultan. Hyder Ali, who made himself master of the kingdom in 1760, was the grandson of a religious mendicant from the Panjab, and the son of a dashing cavalry officer. He was born at Kolar in 1702, and, at the age of thirty, entered the Mysore service, in which he was soon promoted to the leadership of 50 horse and 200 infantry and the command of the Dindigul district. In June 1761, after fighting and negotiation, Hyder Ali obtained from the weak Rajah a formal renunciation of the kingdom of Mysore. Two years later he attacked and took the large city of Bednor or Nagar, where he obtained immense treasure. In 1765 he was signally defeated by the Mahrattas and compelled to relinquish his new conquest. The following year Hyder invaded Malabar and took Calicut, the Zamorin burning himself in his palace to avoid captivity. A confederacy against Hyder was now formed by the Mahrattas, into which the English were unfortunately drawn by their treaty with the Nizam, but Hyder managed to detach the Mahrattas and Mussulmans, leaving the English to meet him unsupported. The Europeans, however, proved equal to the occasion, and were victorious at Changamma and Tiruvannamalai in the South Arcot district. The subsequent history of Hyder Ali and his son, Tippu, will be found in the account of the rise of the English power in India. After the death of Tippu, the British Government placed the son of Chama Raja on the throne, since which time the succession has been continued in the same line.

Portugal was the first European nation to form settlements in India. On 28th May 1498

The Portuguese.

. Vasco da Gama having rounded the Cape of Good Hope, anchored off Calicut. He soon got into trouble with the Zamorin, and the hostility thus excited was extended to the Rajah of Cochin and the succeeding Portuguese captains, Alvarez Cabral, Alphonso and Francisco Albuquerque, Duarte Pacheco, and Lope Soarez. The Portuguese had further to face hostility from Egypt, Gujarat and the Arabian Moors. The first two Viceroys, Francisco Almeyda (1505—1508) and Alphonso Albuquerque (1508—1515), did much to extend the empire, but their religious intolerance, subjection to Spain, and the hostility of the Dutch, soon led to a decline, and the Portuguese now possess only Goa, Damaun, and Diu.

The Portuguese were followed in 1594 by the Dutch, who, after a struggle of fifty years' dura-

The Dutch.

tion, gained decided but brief supremacy among European settlers. The chief Dutch possessions were, Negapatam, taken from the Portuguese in 1660, Sadras, Pulicat, Tuticorin and Bimlipatam, all of which have now fallen into the hands of the English.

The Danes arrived in India in 1616, but only held two settlements, Tranquebar, bought

The Danes.

from the Rajah of Tanjore in 1616, and Serampore on the Hoogly. Both these places were bought by the English in 1845, and were principally noted for the learned ecclesiastics attached to their missions. Ziegenbalg (1706—1719), Fabricius (1739—1791) and

Schwartz (1750—1798) are names still justly respected in connection with the religious establishments at Tranquebar.

The French appeared on the scene in 1668, when Francis **The French.** Caron formed the first settlement at Surat in connection with the East India Company formed by Colbert. In 1669 a site was obtained at Masulipatam, and three years later Trincomalee and Mylapore (St. Thomé) were captured from the Dutch, to be lost after two years' possession. In April 1674 the site of Pondicherry was bought from the Bijapur Government and the city founded by Francois Martin. In 1693 the Dutch captured the settlement, but restored it on the peace of Ryswick being signed in 1697. In 1688 Chandernagore was obtained from Aurungzeb and in 1725 Mâhe was added to the French possessions. In 1731 Joseph Francois Dupleix, the ablest Indian statesman ever produced by France, was appointed Director of Chandernagore. The French history from this time is so involved with that of the English, that it can be profitably dealt with when discussing the English struggle for supremacy in India.

The British East India Company was incorporated in **The English.** 1600, during the reign of Queen Elizabeth, and a second charter was obtained in 1661. The Moghul Emperor, Jehangir, in 1611, gave permission for the establishment of four factories in his dominions, and from time to time other settlements were made in various parts of India. A second company was formed in 1698, but the two rival concerns were united by King William III in 1702. The first trading settlement in the Madras Presidency was formed at Masulipatam in 1620 and shortly afterwards a second was established at Armogum, about forty miles north of Pulicat. In 1639 Fort St. George was constructed at Madras, and in 1691 Fort St. David at Tegnapatam, near Cuddalore. Until the end of the first-half of the 17th century, trading operations were carried on in comparative peace amid the perpetual wars between the Mahrattas and Mussalmans, the only event really affecting the future of the settlements being the acquisition of Pondicherry by the French in 1672. In 1744 war broke out between the English and the French, when Fort St. George was taken to be restored five years later at the peace of Aix-la-Chapelle. Nearly the whole of Southern India was at this time subject to the Nizam of Hyderabad, the country in the neighbourhood of Madras being immediately under the Nabob of the Carnatic, while the Mahrattas held Tanjore and the adjoining districts. The assistance of the English given to Saiyaji in 1749 and their espousal of the cause of Muhammed Ali have already been referred to. The French went to the aid of Chanda Sahib, who, in alliance with Muzaffir Jung, opposed Muhammed Ali. Muzaffir Jung succeeded in securing the throne of the Nizam, and the triumph of the French under Dupleix was complete, until Clive appeared on the scene. He changed the whole course of the war by seizing Arcot on 30th August 1751, at the time when Chanda Sahib and the French were besieging Muhammed Ali in Trichinopoly. Clive in turn was besieged, and, after brilliantly repulsing all attacks, followed up his success by a victory at Arni, which virtually placed the Carnatic once more under the rule of the Nabob. The siege of Trichinopoly, however, was not raised until the French detachment surrendered in June 1752 to Clive and Major Lawrence at Srirangam. A quarrel next broke out between the Nabob and Nunjeraj, the minister of the Rajah of Mysore. The English at first hesitated to assist Muhammed Ali, but Nunjeraj's conduct was such as forced them to treat him as an enemy. The French supported Nunjeraj, and a succession of combats took place, chiefly in the immediate vicinity of Trichinopoly, in which the English were almost uniformly successful. The recall of Dupleix, on 14th October 1754, led to a cessation of hostilities, but the English continued to aid the Nabob in his internal administration, while the French, under M. Bussy, performed a similar office for the then Nizam, Salabut Jung. Hostilities in Southern India were resumed in 1757, when it became known that war had broken out in Europe between England and France. The French taking advantage of the English forces being dispersed in various expeditions, unsuccessfully attacked Trichinopoly, and captured Vizagapatam. In 1758 a French fleet appeared off Fort St. David and the fort fell on 2nd June; Devikkottei was next reduced, but an expedition against Tanjore completely failed. In December Madras was besieged and was not relieved until February 1758, when an English fleet appeared in the roads. In the North Clive captured Masulipatam on 7th April, securing to the English a tract of territory around the town extending eighty miles along the coast and twenty miles inland, and destroying French influence with the Nizam. In the South, Colonel Coote, on 22nd January 1760, completely defeated the French under Lally, at Wandewash, and followed up the victory by taking both Gingee and Arcot. Minor forts then fell in rapid succession and by May the English were in a position to lay siege to Pondicherry. Lally then invoked the aid of Hyder Ali, who totally defeated an English detachment, but was then obliged to return home on account of internal troubles. The withdrawal of the Mysoreans rendered the French cause hopeless, and, on 16th January 1761, Pondicherry surrendered. With this event the power of the French in the Carnatic may be considered to have ended. In 1765 the Northern Circars, consisting of the districts of Ganjam, Vizagapatam, Godaveri, and Kistna, were transferred to the Company by the Emperor of Delhi, whose paramount authority was recognized by the Nizam. The Madras Council, however, hesitated to take over these territories until the consent of the Nizam had been given to the acquisition; and in 1776 a treaty was entered into with Nizam Ali agreeing to pay tribute for the Circars and to defend the Nizam against his enemies. The English were soon required, under this latter stipulation, to assist the Nizam and the Mahrattas in checking the aggression of Hyder Ali. No sooner had operations commenced than Hyder bought off the Mahrattas, and induced the Nizam to desert the British and join him in a descent upon the Carnatic. Colonel Smith, who commanded the English forces, finding himself opposed to an infinitely superior force, commenced a retreat, but was overtaken in South Arcot. The first attack, made at Changamma, was repulsed, the second, at Tiruvannamalai, resulted in a decisive English victory, and the disorderly flight of the troops of Hyder and the Nizam. Colonel Smith was too weak to follow up his victory and withdrew into cantonments for the rainy season. Hyder availed himself of this inaction to reduce a few unimportant fortresses, but was checked by Captain Calvert's defence of Ambur. On its relief by Colonel Smith in December 1767, Hyder drew off to commence operations on the West Coast, where a Bombay expedition had captured his fleet. The Madras Government continued their offensive operations, one corps under Colonel Wood proceeding to the reduction of the fortresses under the south-eastern slopes of the Ghâts, while another force, under Colonel Smith, entered Mysore. Hyder could not be induced to risk a general engagement, and, after he had retaken a few forts, concluded a treaty with the English on 4th April 1769. From this time until 1780, the only military operations, beyond assisting the Nabob in his quarrels with the Rajah of Tanjore, were the capture of Pondicherry and Mâhe in 1779. In 1880 war broke out with Hyder owing to the Nabob failing to provide the English with means to fulfil the treaty of 1769. In alliance with the Nizam and Mahrattas, Hyder invaded the Carnatic, burning crops and devastating villages, until Madras was enclosed by a blackened area of desolation.

The English Commander-in-Chief, Sir Hector Munro, proceeded to Conjeeveram, directing Colonel Baillie to join him there with troops from the North. Hyder managed to overwhelm Baillie's force on 9th September 1780, when Munro retreated to Madras, leaving the field open to Hyder. On receipt of the intelligence of this disaster, Warren Hastings, the Governor-General in Calcutta, despatched Sir Eyre Coote to Madras with reinforcements. The latter took the field on 17th January 1781, relieved Chingleput on the 19th, retook Carangooly on the 21st, and caused the siege of Wandewash, which had been brilliantly resisted by Lieutenant Flint, to be raised. Coote, after proceeding to Pondicherry, turned his attention to the protection of Cuddalore. Hyder, who had followed him down the coast, shirked a general engagement, until he heard of an unsuccessful attack on Cellumbrum, when he advanced and took up a position close to Sir Eyre Coote's camp at Porto Novo, some fourteen miles south of Cuddalore. The battle commenced early on 1st July 1781, and was long and severe; but by 4 P.M. the enemy were in precipitate retreat. The want of proper equipment prevented Coote from following up his success, but he again relieved Wandewash, and eluding Hyder's troops, captured Tripassore on 22nd August. Five days later an indecisive general engagement was fought, but on 27th September the Mysoreans were surprised near Sholinghur and a decisive victory was gained, which enabled provisions to be thrown into Vellore. In November the English army retired into Madras for the monsoon, where it remained till January 1782, when it proceeded once more to the relief of Vellore. Hyder then turned his attention to Cuddalore, and with the assistance of a French contingent captured it and also Permacoil, but Sir Eyre Coote arrived in time to save Wandewash. In the meantime, war had broken out with the Dutch as well as with the French, and the Dutch settlements of Sadras, Pulicat, and Negapatam had been taken. A portion of the force employed for the reduction of Negapatam, while proceeding under Colonel Brathwaite to operate in Tanjore, was surprised by Hyder's son, Tippu Sultan, and annihilated almost to a man. At this juncture a rebellion against Hyder broke out in Malabar, and with the assistance of the English a considerable victory was gained at Tellicherry. This necessitated the immediate despatch of Tippu to the West Coast, when Hyder feeling himself overmatched determined to quit the Coromandel Coast. The death of Hyder at Chittoor, on 7th December 1782, left the field open to the English, and after being reinforced from Bombay they took several places on the West Coast, penetrating as far as Bednor above the Ghâts. Tippu succeeded in stopping further progress, retook Bednor on 3rd May, and laid siege to Mangalore, which, after a gallant resistance, capitulated on 30th January 1784. After much evasion and delay, peace was concluded on 10th March on the basis of mutual restoration of conquests. On account of Tippu's fanatical zeal, many rebellions of the Nairs of Malabar arose from time to time. Eventually Tippu resolved to invade Travancore, where many Nairs had taken refuge, although cautioned that such a proceeding would involve him in another war with the English. His first attempt to enter Travancore was a failure; a second was successful, and the country was overrun in his usual cruel manner. However, on Tippu's return to Coimbatore, he found an English army in the field under General Medows, the Governor of Madras. Tippu first withdrew to Seringapatam, and the English experienced little opposition in the reduction of the various forts on the south-eastern slopes of the Ghâts until 7th September 1790, when an army, commanded by Tippu in person, descended by the Guzalhatti Pass. General Medows repulsed the attack, but Tippu declined to commit himself to anything more serious than skirmishes.

On 29th January 1791 the Governor-General, Lord Cornwallis, took command in person, and proceeded to concentrate his army at Vellore preparatory to a march on Bangalore. Tippu hastened to oppose the advance which he expected would be made by the passes near Ambur. In this Tippu was deceived, as the tableland was reached by the more northerly Moogly Pass. The town of Bangalore fell early in March, and, on the night of the 20th, the fort was taken by assault. While these operations were in progress in Mysore, Colonel Hartly had defeated Tippu's troops near Calicut, and General Abercrombie, the Governor of Bombay, had reduced Cannanore, so that in a very short time the whole of Malabar was in possession of the English. On 4th May 1791 the English marched against Seringapatam, but, notwithstanding a victory at Arikera, only nine miles distant from that place, were compelled to retire on Bangalore, in consequence of the devastated nature of the country. The Nizam and Mahrattas, who were in alliance with Lord Cornwallis, worked their way up from the North and reinforced his army, both with men and supplies, so that Lord Cornwallis again was able to appear before Seringapatam. On 6th February 1792 the outlying encampment and redoubts were carried and the city closely invested on two sides. On 24th February a peace was agreed to, under which Tippu had to pay three crores and thirty lakhs of rupees, and to surrender half his kingdom. By this treaty the English came into possession of the Baramahal, Dindigul, Malabar and Coorg, the latter being restored to the Rajah, who had rendered material aid to the British. In 1798 it became known that Tippu was intriguing with the French, and it was decided to act against him before he had matured his plans. The Madras army was placed on a war footing and an alliance was entered into by him with the French. General Harris was placed in command of the army of the Carnatic, while another force from Malabar, under General Stuart, entered Coorg in 1799. Tippu directed his first efforts against the latter army, but was beaten at Sedasseer, near Periapatam, and, in the meantime, General Harris and the Nizam's troops crossed the Mysore frontier. Tippu turned to meet them and was defeated with severe loss at Malvelly, on 27th March. He then retired to Seringapatam, and the allies there besieged him for a month before a practical breach was made. The assault commenced at one o'clock on the 4th May, and before evening Tippu was dead, and the whole town in the possession of the English. With Tippu terminated the dynasty of Hyder, and the settlement of the country was effected by the restoration of Mysore to the ancient royal family. The greater portion of the remainder of Tippu's empire was then divided between the English and the Nizam, the districts of Canara, Coimbatore, and Wynad falling to the share of the former. On the fall of Seringapatam, it was discovered that Muhammed Ali had been carrying on treasonable correspondence with Mysore, and the treaty of 1792 having thus been infringed, the British Government assumed the entire management of the Carnatic, thus securing the whole of the country from the Northern Circars to Cape Comorin, with the exception of the French settlements of Pondicherry and Karaikkal, and the Danish settlement of Tranquebar. The titular dignity of Nabob of the Carnatic was continued until 1855, when there was a failure of direct heirs. The present representative of the family bears the title of Prince of Arcot, and has the position of the first native nobleman of Madras. In 1838 internal misadministration led to the Nabob of Kurnool being deposed and his territory annexed, and since then no territory has been acquired by conquest.

(B).—POPULATION.

THE Districts of the Madras Presidency served by the South Indian Railway are the following twelve, namely :—
Madras, Chingleput, South Arcot, Tanjore, Trichinopoly, Coimbatore, Madura, Tinnevelly, North Arcot, Anantapur, Cuddapah, and Nellore.

The following Table shows the principal statistics of these districts respecting their population :—

Districts.	Area in sq. miles.	Population.	Density per sq. mile.	Towns and Villages.	Ratio of Population.		Percentage of Thatched Houses.
					Urban.	Rural.	
Madras	29	452,518	15,604	1	100·00	..	24·25
Chingleput	2,842	1,136,928	400	1,997	8·28	91·72	75·68
South Arcot	5,217	2,162,851	415	2,897	6·10	93·90	89·56
Tanjore	3,709	2,228,114	601	3,550	14·87	85·13	74·95
Trichinopoly	3,631	1,372,717	378	1,502	9·77	90·23	91·10
Coimbatore	7,860	2,004,839	255	1,478	5·50	94·50	76·40
Madura	8,808	2,608,404	296	4,103	9·23	90·77	89·79
Tinnevelly	5,387	1,916,095	356	1,538	17·20	82·80	89·62
North Arcot	7,616	2,180,487	286	4,465	7·26	92·74	81·38
Anantapur	5,275	708,549	134	941	9·77	90·23	27·69
Cuddapah	8,722	1,272,072	146	1,276	5·56	94·44	79·92
Nellore	8,765	1,463,736	167	1,793	5·57	94·43	91·09
Total	67,861	19,507,310	..	25,541	9·92	90·08	74·29

With regard to the languages spoken in them, the first nine have the Tamil language for their true vernacular, and the other three Telugu; but the Telugu language is largely spoken throughout the Tamil districts, as Hindustani also is in the whole twelve; and, in some portions of their western fringe, Canarese has a small place.

The census divides the population, in regard to their

occupation, into seven classes. These classes, with the
total number in each of them, are as follows :—

Class.	Name.	Number.
A	Government Service	522,055
B	Pasture and Agriculture	12,111,177
C	Personal Service	575,094
D	Trades, &c. ..	8,558,781
E	Commerce	479,925
F	Professions	423,855
G	Indefinite	1,824,457
	Others	11,966
	Total ..	19,507,310

By far the most numerous class of the population is that
which is connected directly or indirectly with the cultivation of the soil. They number 61 per cent. of the whole
people. Fifty-two per cent. of them are in immediate
connection with the land, either as landlords or tenants ;
and 7 per cent. more are dependent on these as agricultural labourers. The proportions of this class differ
much in town and country. In the urban population,
only 20 per cent. are connected with the land, while, in
the rural population, there are 66 per cent. The great
majority of the farmers, therefore, either reside on the land
which they cultivate, or close to it. Corresponding with
this distribution, there are only 34 per cent. of the rural
population belonging to the classes of tradesmen, merchants, domestic servants, general labourers, the learned
professions, the Government service, and all others,
whereas in the towns these classes absorb 80 per cent.
of their inhabitants.

The most numerous class of these non-agriculturists is
that which contains the traders and artizans, dealing in
all articles of general consumption and use—Class D.
They form 15 per cent. of the people. Closely allied to them
are the upper commercial classes, merchants, bankers,
brokers, and their agents, forming class E, and representing

3 per cent. of the population. These two classes, who carry on the trade and commerce of these districts, form together nearly a moiety of the non-agricultural classes.

Next to them, in point of numbers, is the class of General Labour, which includes the unskilled workers of all sorts. It represents 9 per cent. of the people : 4 per cent. are engaged in different kinds of personal service, (Class C), of whom about 3½ per cent. are domestic servants. Of the remaining number, Government officials (Class A), the members of the different learned-professions (Class F), and persons of independent means take about 2 per cent. each ; and the final balance consists of those persons whose occupations have not been recorded, and includes the fractions omitted in all the above round numbers.

It may be asked here, where the pauper-class falls in under this distribution. Strictly speaking, the only paupers in India are the destitute members of the European and Eurasian communities : for, though there may be the usual proportions of infirm and constitutionally idle members in this as in all other nations, the recognized right of the indigent to share the better fortune of their more prosperous relatives excludes the necessity for the poor-laws and workhouses of England from the shores of happier India.

There are, indeed, various classes of professional mendicants, so called, in this country ; but more properly these are to be regarded as members of the tail of the religious, and the low artistic classes than as vagrant paupers.

It would not be an easy task to frame an exact estimate of the material condition of these people ; for there are intricacies on both the income and the expenditure sides of the problem which would have to be explained.

But a fairly approximate estimate of it can be made from wellknown facts sufficient to afford a general idea of the kind and amount of comfort in which they live their ordinary lives. It is obvious from the very names of some of the census groups that their ordinary members are respectable, well-to-do people. It is evident enough also that the large section engaged in trade and commerce can only continue to belong to those classes so long as they earn that margin of profit which is necessary to maintain them in those positions. Even the domestic servants have all their necessary wants secured to them, while they continue to be employed. The existing standard of comfort, in every community, is a thing which has grown-up in the natural course of things, and it has taken its present shape upon lines which are inherent in the circumstances of that community. It is therefore in a state of constant development, continually rising, in the ordinary slow, but sure processes of nature, by the side of the growth of the prosperity of the community.

These general remarks apply especially to classes A, C, D, E, and F, in whole or in part; and these sections cover 6 millions of the 20 million inhabitants of the twelve districts which we are here considering. The great agricultural section (class B), and the class of indefinite occupations (class G) require to be considered separately.

There is a considerable difference in the percentage of class B in the different districts. While it forms only 53·78 per cent. of the general population in Nellore, it rises to 57·83 in Coimbatore, 59·62 in Tinnevelly, 60·42 in Chingleput, 61·02 in Tanjore, 61·55 in Anantapur, 64·19 in Cuddapah, 65·14 in Madura, 69·84 in North Arcot, 69·89 in Trichinopoly, and 70·64 in South Arcot.

The full title of this class in the census is "Pasture and Agriculture," and its separate sections must therefore be discriminated. Those who have to do with cattle, and those who have only an indirect connection with the land, together with the tea-and-coffee planters, market gardeners, &c., form 2·36 per cent. of the population, the landlord and the ryot sections cover 52·20 per cent., and the section of agricultural labourers 6·50 per cent.

7

These labourers again are sub-divided into those who are constantly employed on the land and thus form part of the farmer's families, and those who are only temporarily hired. These last, who are a little more numerous than the others, fall back into the class of unskilled labour when they are not needed on the farms, and become amongst the earliest to feel the first pinches of famine.

A great deal was said and written some little time back regarding the supposed poverty of this large class of the population. It is to be hoped that better information has now become available for an estimate of their true condition, while some erroneous impressions have been removed in the meantime. It is not at all improbable that some of them may be in comparatively low circumstances; but to those who have an intimate knowledge of their condition no signs of indigence are to be found in the class as a whole body: on the contrary it is not difficult to see that, except in years of bad agricultural seasons, most of them possess a fair amount of prosperity judged from the standpoint of their position in the community. They pay their land-assessment with fair punctuality: they spend considerable sums of money upon their marriages: they are able to afford a large expenditure of time and money upon their numerous law suits: and they maintain in all respects a remarkable amount of hereditary independence of character. These things are not tokens of a state of semi-starvation such as has been said to be their normal condition.

The census gives 12,111,117 as the number of this class in the twelve districts which we are now considering: and this number of individuals represents 2,422,288 families at the rate of five members to each family. It is required to know, as nearly as it can be made out, what annual income each of these families derives from the produce of his land and the other products of his industry. An answer to this question may be obtained in a general way by the following concise process. The area of these twelve districts, as shown by the table on page 46, is 67,861 square miles: and this, in agricultural terms, represents 43,431,040 acres. Of this area, according to the proportions given in the last Parliamentary Statistical Abstract, 10,857,760 acres are cultivated, namely, 2,714,440 acres with rice crops, 6,333,693 acres with several kinds of dry grain, and 1,809,627 acres with various other kinds of field and garden food-stuff. The yield per acre of these crops varies from year to year according to the character of the seasons: and hence the quantity of the yield of the grain crops in any year is the key to the valuation of the farmers' income for that year. As a medium yield, that of the rice crops may be taken to be 2,400 lbs. per acre, and that of the dry (unirrigated) grains 1,200 lbs. Calculated on this basis the total yield of the rice crops in an ordinary year is 6,514,656,000 lbs., and that of the dry grains 7,600,431,600 lbs. The quantity required by the ryots for their own use during the succeeding year is put aside and stored at home, and the rest is sold. The quantity stored is about 11 million pounds: and about 3,115,087,600 lbs. is available for sale.

Thus the whole of the food of this class of the population is grown by themselves upon their own farms, for they are all vegetarians, using flesh-meat only on special occasions: and even when any outside labour is needed to supplement their own, those labourers also are paid in grain. As the rule of their life, therefore, their food is secured to them in all years, except those when the yield falls below one-third of a full crop of both the wet and dry grains, a circumstance of very rare occurrence. Even then the pinch is not of vital importance until a second year of bad crops follows the first.

With regard to the section of petty ryots whose holdings are too small for them to live upon, most of them have some other employment, and the deficiency of their non-earnings is made up by those of their very industrious wives. In times of difficulty, or perhaps for some domestic ceremony, these men mortgage their holdings, arranging to pay off their debt from the proceeds of their future crops.

The lenders are usually some of the more thriving members of their own class, and not infrequently the grain merchants of the neighbouring towns.

When the necessity is only temporary they soon succeed in extricating themselves; but if they are unable to do so within a reasonable number of years they relinquish their holdings to the creditor, receiving some additional sum to cover the value of the land.

The case of the agricultural labourers stands apart from these, and is very simple. They form one-eighth part of the whole agricultural class, and are 1,365,511 in number in these twelve districts. They live in the families of their employers, receiving their wages in grain, together with certain recognized perquisites at certain times of the year. When a famine comes on they share the troubles of their masters : and when that stage arrives when the master has to curtail his daily doles from the grain-store, the labourer is obliged to seek a subsistence abroad or to seek help from the Famine Commissioner. For the greater part of his life he lives in stolid contentment, with all his necessary wants always ready to his hands, and then he is scarcely ever heard of; but when the fatal famine year arrives, the poor fellow falls into a practically helpless condition.

The value of the surplus rice thus available for sale, at its present market price, is Rs. 38,457,871, and that of the dry grains Rs. 39,183,492, making together Rs. 77,641,363. Besides these grains the ryots sell the unused surplus of their pulses, fruit-trees, oil-seeds, narcotics, condiments, and other similar products of their land : and these have been calculated to be of about the same value as the serial crops. And further they sell their dairy produce, surplus straw, hides and skins, wool, pigs, cow and buffalo calves, lambs and poultry, the estimated value of which is Rs. 19,410,325. All these sources together bring their income in a year of ordinarily good seasons up to Rs. 174,693,051. Out of this income the first great payment is the Government land-assessment, which in the year 1897-8, the last at present available, amounted to Rs. 30,426,807. When this has been paid they have a balance of Rs. 144,266,244 in hand for their clothing, the repairs of their houses and out-houses, to cover the wear and tear of their stock, and to meet the expenses of their domestic ceremonies, festivals, travelling, and sundry luxuries.

This balance when divided amongst the 2,422,288 families of which this class consists, gives to each of them Rs. 60 a year after abundant provision has been made for their food-supply, and after the full payment of their Government dues. They have no house-rent to pay ; for their houses are their own property. This result represents the outcome of the calculation for an ordinary year when the yield is three-quarters of a full crop,—a twelve-anna crop in agricultural terms,—which may be taken to be the average for a long series of years, subject to the fluctuations in the market price of all the produce.

In years when the yield reaches a higher rate than this the final balance is correspondingly greater. Such years are not of infrequent occurrence ; for it has been shown for one of the neighbouring districts that in a series of 49 consecutive years the rice crops were above this average in 14 years, and the dry crops in 13 years. In that series there were also 13 years of rice crops of the average yield and 11 similar years of the dry grains. Putting it in another form 27 years of the 49 had good rice crops ranging from three-fourths of a full crop upwards, 11 years had crops of medium yield, and there were 11 years of poor crops below the half of a full crop : and similarly for the dry-grain crops, 24 years had good crops, 12 years medium, and 13 years poor crops.

Some valuable data for an estimate of the general condition of the people are afforded by the taxes which they pay. Table II. shows the principal items of the taxation for the official year 1897-8. Besides these there are Municipal taxes which fall upon the inhabitants of the great towns, and Local-Fund cesses which fall upon the occupiers of the land, and tolls paid by those who use the roads.

TABLE II.

District.	Land Revenue.	Income Tax.	Stamps.	Abkari.	Opium.	Customs and Excise.	Salt.
	Rs.	Rs.	Rs.	Rs.	Rs.	Rs.	Rs.
Madras ..	80,609	4,87,134	8,14,151	16	15,400	29,37,749	11,03,415
Chingleput ..	17,23,555	55,273	2,12,999	3,47,470	1,722	25	43,96,350
South Arcot.	39,87,111	70,835	3,47,493	7,40,700	1,491	1,58,352	7,05,888
Tanjore ..	57,50,608	1,49,076	8,77,957	13,53,701	3,501	7,05,658	13,75,132
Trichinopoly.	20,47,996	60,908	2,96,194	3,83,131	2,389	..	3,816
Coimbatore ...	29,10,668	60,867	4,00,692	7,83,541	4,554	..	..
Madura ..	29,07,689	2,57,715	6,54,999	5,57,852	4,429	23,876	..
Tinnevelly ..	30,59,591	1,21,413	5,89,846	3,94,966	2,302	2,74,365	30,31,886
North Arcot.	27,37,685	1,18,842	3,29,249	15,75,433	7,288	..	595
Anantapur ..	7,43,083	34,317	91,374	4,36,227	1,839	..	..
Cuddapah ..	18,53,049	77,841	2,01,891	2,83,136	6,965	..	..
Nellore ..	26,25,263	84,937	2,49,288	2,83,974	6,578	17	24,94,336
Total ..	304,26,807	15,79,158	50,66,133	71,40,141	58,458	41,00,042	131,11,418

With regard to the Income-tax in the above table, the total collections, Rs. 15,79,158, represent an income of Rs. 606,39,667 from which it was collected, taking the assessment at the uniform rate of 5 pies per rupee. This tax is paid by those whose income is Rs. 500 a year and upwards, the Agricultural class alone being exempted, as they are taxed under separate legislation. To obtain the number of those who pay the tax, therefore, the 12,111,177 who constitute class B. must be eliminated from the total population, as well as all those members of the other classes whose income is less than Rs. 41-10-8 a month. The actual number of those who pay the tax in our twelve districts is computed to be only 39,014. The incidence of the tax has been calculated to be Rs. 25 a head on those who pay the tax, or 6 annas a head on the whole population. In the North Arcot District,—and presumably the other districts do not widely differ,—the percentages of the tax-payers, according to the amount of their income, is as follows:—71 per cent. have taxable incomes from Rs. 500 to Rs. 1,000 a year; 23·5 per cent. from Rs. 1,000 to Rs. 2,000; 4·5 per cent. from Rs. 2,000 to Rs. 5,000; 0·8 per cent. from Rs. 5,000 to Rs. 10,000, and 0·2 per cent. over Rs. 10,000.

Regarding the column headed "Stamps" it may be worth noticing that one-third of these stamps represent the value of those used for commercial purposes of all kinds, and the rest of them are judicial stamps. It thus appears that the large sum of Rs. 33,77,422 per annum is spent upon the stamps attached to the documents used in the people's lawsuits. This is considerably more than double the amount of the Income-tax: and yet it forms but a small portion of the whole amount of their litigation bill, which includes, in addition to that sum, advocates' fees, payments to witnesses and various Court expenses.

The column headed "Abkari" is made up of license fees for distilleries, and for the shops and taverns in which the liquors are sold, also the tax upon the trees from which the toddy is drawn, and the excise duty. These things amount to Rs. 71,40,141. To this sum must be added the value of the liquors as produced or purchased by the vendors, and the amount of the vendors' profit upon the retail sales; which last is apparently said to be about 25 per cent. upon the cost price. Nevertheless the "drink bill" of the North Arcot District, which may probably be taken as a general example, is said to be only 8½ annas per head per annum, notwithstanding that some of the lower castes of the community are notorious drinkers. The average consumption of the spirits (arrack) is about one-twentieth of a gallon per head per annum, but in the towns it is much higher, rising in some of them to over half a gallon per head.

(C.)—THE HINDU RELIGION.

The Hindu religion of the present day is regarded by its votaries as the representative of the ancient religion of the Veda, which, in obedience to the tendencies always inherent in it, has passed through a long series of developments on the lines of those natural laws of its growth. This theory furnishes a satisfactory basis for a sketch of this ancient and eminently interesting religion. Here the word 'Veda' should be understood to mean that collection of the hymns of the ancient Riṣhis known as the 'Rig-veda,' which is the root and source of all that great body of vedic literature,—the accumulated growth of all the intermediate ages,—to which the name 'Veda' is also sometimes applied. It stands alone at the head of the three other collections,—the Sáma-veda, the Yajur-veda, and the Atharva-veda, which have, in considerable proportion, borrowed their contents from it for the special purposes of their ritual or other objects.

The Rig-veda consists of a body of 1,017 hymns of various lengths, written in many varieties of metre. The Riṣhis, to whom these hymns are attributed, belonged, for the most part, to several ancient Brahminical families; and many of them are assigned to members of the old royal dynasties, and some few to persons of the inferior classes. There are female Riṣhis also among them, and even some of the older divinities themselves and their human offspring. The hymns are distributed into ten books (maṇḍalas) of various dimensions, in which they are arranged primarily with regard to the gods addressed in them, partly to the authors of the hymns, and partly to the number of the verses in them. No attempt appears to have been made by any vedic writer to fix the date of any of the Riṣhis, though some of them at least are evidently historical personages; but in the later literature an eternal existence is claimed for the hymns, their Ṛishis being merely privileged Seers, and not their actual authors, having "seen" them by means of their supernatural sight, and the special favour of the gods.

The form in which this hymn-book has come down to modern times is admittedly the last of a long series of "arrangements" which it has undergone from time to time; but the changes which were made in it at those times are said to have been confined to minor matters such as the distribution of the hymns or the order of their verses. Great care has been taken from a very early period to prevent any further alterations being made in them in any respect, by recording the number of the hymns, and their verses and words, together with the names of the god or gods to whom each of them is addressed, their Ṛishis, and the metres in which they are composed. It is clear, however, that no attempt was ever made to arrange them in any form of historical or chronological order.

The language in which they are written is an archaic form of Sanskrit, representing, it is supposed, a transition state of that language during the process of its evolution into classical Sanskrit. The meaning of many words is consequently not known in the present day, and some of its grammatical forms have become obsolete. It has been remarked by an oriental scholar, that there are apparently no varieties of this archaic language notwithstanding the long period covered by the hymns, such as we should naturally expect to find if this dialect was ever the vernacular of the people or even of the Ṛishis themselves.

The theory which seems best to combine the traditions regarding the current recension of these hymns is that it is a collection of the hymnals of several vedic families which were originally distinct, each of which had for its nucleus the hymns composed by the founder of that family, to which those of his sons and descendants were

8

added from time to time, which were hoarded up in the undivided priestly family as a religious treasure, and transmitted from generation to generation as a sacred family inheritance, and the source of its wealth and influence. Later on, these separate hymn-books were gathered together to form a general collection for the use of the whole sacerdotal community ; to which other new hymns were subsequently added until the compilation, after undergoing the several re-arrangements referred to above, attained its present dimensions and shape. In its present form there stand, side by side in it, the extensive collections of those mighty old rivals Vasishtha and Vishvámitra and their descendants, whose ritual warfare once shook the whole vedic world to its foundations : and it may be presumed that the bitterness of that strife had, in some great measure, passed away, when it became possible to bring their songs together into one book. Of the ten books in this recension, seven are family collections of the above description, bearing the names of Gritsamada, (the son of the Rishi Bhrigu), Vishvámitra, Vámadeva, (of the Gotama sub-division of the race of the Rishi Angiras), Atri, Bharadvája, Vasishtha, and Kaṇva, respectively, and containing hymns addressed to different gods. Books I and X, on the other hand, are miscellaneous collections by a great variety of authors, and similarly addressed to many different gods, while Book IX contains hymns to Soma alone by various Rishis.

The number of the vedic gods is usually said to be thirty-three ; but to these are sometimes added Agni, or Soma, or some other special divinity, and sometimes the two Ashvins or Dyaus, and Prithiví, making them thirty-four or thirty-five. They are divided into three classes, eleven upon earth, eleven in the lower firmament, and eleven in the upper sky. According to another classification, there are eight Vasus, eleven Rudras, twelve Ádityas, and the two Ashvins. These thirty-three are privileged to drink the soma-juice offerings which occupy an important place in the vedic worship; and there is another class of thirty-three who are not entitled to that privilege, or who abstain from drinking that beverage. They are not always limited to this number, however; and other more numerous groups are mentioned. In two of the hymns, 3,339 deities are said to have worshipped Agni. In the hymnal itself each hymn is addressed to its own appropriate divinity or combination of divinities, selected by the worshipper or the priest for the special occasion on which it was to be used, or as their favourite object of worship. It is but seldom that hymns are addressed to the whole pantheon together.

The actual number of gods and other divinities, to whom hymns are addressed individually in the Ṛig-veda, is sixty-two. Their relative importance in the ritual may be gathered from the number of hymns addressed to them. At the head of them, in his proper position as king of the gods, stands Indra with 226 hymns: next to him comes the god of fire, Agni, the convener of the gods and their official-general, with 187 hymns: and then Soma, the Moon, who is often not to be distinguished from the intoxicating beverage of that name which forms the chief offering at the sacrifices,—with 115 hymns. The 528 hymns addressed to these three gods thus make up considerably more than half of the whole hymnal: and the proportion is really much greater than this; for of the remaining 489 hymns, only 291 are addressed to individual gods. Following the above three principal gods come the Vishvadevas, or general assembly, with 59 hymns, the Ashvins, or heavenly twins, with 50, the Maruts, or Winds, with 34, and Ushas, the beautiful Dawn, with 20, and Savitṛi, the Ribhus, and the Ápris with 10 each. Thus the gods, who own ten hymns each and upwards, are only 10 in number. Of the lesser groups of hymns, Varuṇa has 8; Púshan 7; Súrya (the sun) and the A'dityas 6 each; Brihaspati 5; Váyu and the Waters 4 each; Rudra, Vishnu, and Parjanya 3 each; Kapinjala, Vishvakarman, Manyu, the Cows, and the Horse, 2 each; and Mitra, Sarasvatí, Prithiví, Yama, the Pitris, the Frogs, and 33 others have a single hymn each. Thus 819 of the hymns are addressed to individual gods; the remaining 198 are combination hymns addressed to groups of two or more gods, impersonal things, charms, and such like. Of these last hymns, 61 occur in the tenth book alone, which is, perhaps, to be regarded as a book of final gleanings and of later date. The relative importance of Indra becomes enhanced when we add the 77 hymns which he shares with various other gods to the above 226 addressed to him alone, which will bring up his whole number to 303. Similarly Agni's 26 combinations, added to his 187 personal hymns, bring up his total to 213. Then the hymns of Indra and Agni together become 516 against the 291 of the other single gods: and the predominance of the relative position of these two gods in the vedic system becomes very marked.

The comprehensive character of the religion of these hymns is shown by the great variety of the objects of worship to which they are addressed, covering, as they are evidently designed to do, the whole cycle of nature. Thus there are hymns to the two Ashvin brothers (Castor and Pollux), the martial outriders in the van of the daily procession of the Sun through the heavens to inspect his vast dominions, and to the exquisitely lovely Ushas, (Aurora), gambolling in front of his gorgeous chariot, as he comes forth, full of glory and power, attended by his mighty celestial body-guard clothed in an inexhaustible variety of shape and colour; hymns also to the route of his progress, the great ocean above the earth, weighted with its heavy waters ready to be poured forth "as nourishing milk from the udder of the cow," for the fructification of the Earth-goddess and the sustenance of all her worship-

ping children,—along which are built the cities of the gods
and of their many formidable enemies; hymns to the
Night-Sun also when he has descended below the horizon
to visit the realm of the timidly worshipped Yama, the
abode of the dead. There are many hymns to "King
Soma" also, for the vedic moon is of the male sex, the
secondary ruler of the heavens, during the nightly inter-
regnum of the greater lord of light,—the polygamous
husband of the twenty-seven lunar mansions, the separate
abodes of his wives, with each of whom, by stellar law, it
is his marital duty to spend each well-measured day of his
monthly tour of the sky; but, notwithstanding that law,
in his actual practice willingly lingering some while longer
in the abode of his favourite Rohini (Aldebaran), under the
pretence of filling up the unexhausted interval until the
exact moment for starting on his succeeding tour, and so
exposing himself to charges of unjust partiality towards
her, and causing inevitable irritations in the others, and
deceptions and assumed repentances on his part, and
general heart-burnings all round. There are hymns also
to the grave and wise Brihaspati, the philosophical teacher
and sage counsellor of the gods; hymns for the peaceful
periods of man's life addressed to the lord of the fields and
their cultivation, and for times of strife addressed to his
weapons of war; hymns for his ceremonial duties addressed
to the post to which the victims of their sacrifices were
bound, to the fire which consumed their oblations and carried
them upwards into the mouths of the gods, and to the sacri-
ficing priests, to the stones with which the Soma-juice was
expressed for their offerings, as well as to the Soma-juice
itself which they produced; hymns to Heaven and Earth,
to the Rivers and the Floods, to the seasons and times, to
their Cattle and Horses, to the nutritious and the medicinal
Herbs of the field; to things on earth, things in the sky,
and things in the upper heavens above the firmament.

Each of these gods has his own particular sphere,

especially the Sun and the Moon, the planets and the greater stars and the constellations. But they have also a common home, separated from all other localities, to which is given the special name of "the abode of the gods." The heaven above is distributed into seven well-defined regions, each of them increasing in sanctity and in the quality of its happiness in the proportion of its elevation above the earth :—1, the abode of the ancestors of mankind ; 2, the abode of Indra ; 3, the abode of the Maruts, or wind-gods ; 4, the abode of the celestial choristers ; 5, the abode of saintly men ; 6, the abode of the Ṛishis, and 7, the abode of the Supreme Being. The limits of some of these regions are marked out astronomically : thus the abode of the ancestors extends northwards from Canopus to the constellations Scorpio and Sagittarius ; the abode of the seven Ṛishis is in the constellation of the Great Bear and its adjacent belt ; between these two regions, and particularly between the constellations Aries and Taurus and the Great Bear, is the abode of the gods. It is from this region that their convener, the god Agni, calls them when he summons them to partake of the sacrifices prepared for them. For their locomotion on these journeys, as well as for their more ordinary requirements, decorated chariots of various degrees of splendour, built by the divine artificer, are at their disposal, drawn by highly bred horses, harnessed and yoked by the mere effort of their will ; and in a more modern period, these primitive vehicles were improved into aërial cars, whose wheels, thought-guided, moved noiselessly and with enormous rapidity along the friction-less paths of the sky, straight on to the place of sacrifice upon the earth.

The following hymn to Agni, in his capacity as convener of the gods, contains a vivid illustration of the vedic worship, and will also serve as a suitable specimen of the general style of the hymns. It is the 14th hymn of the first book.

"1. Come, Agni, to our adoration and to our praises, with all these gods to drink the Soma-juice: and do thou offer sacrifice.

"2. The Kaṇvas invoke thee, sapient Agni, and extol thy deeds: come, Agni, with the gods."

"3. Sacrifice, Agni, to Indra, Váyu, Bṛihaspati, Mitra, Agni, Púshan, and Bhaga, the Ádityas, and the troop of Maruts.

"4. For all of you are poured out these juices, satisfying, exhilarating, sweet, falling in drops, or gathered in ladles.

"5. The wise priests desirous of the protection of the gods, having spread the sacred grass, presenting oblations, and offering ornaments, praise thee.

"6. Let the coursers who convey thee, glossy-backed and harnessed at will, being the gods to drink the Soma-juice.

"7. Agni, make those objects of veneration, augmenters of pious acts, participiant of the offering, together with their wives: give them, bright-tongued, to drink the Soma-juice.

"8. Let those objects of veneration and of praise drink with thy tongue of the Soma-juice at the moment of libation.

"9. Let the wise invokers of the gods bring hither from the shining sphere of the sun all the divinities awaking with the dawn.

"10. With all the gods, with Indra, Váyu, and the glories of Mitra, drink Agni, the sweet Soma-juice.

"11. Thou, Agni, appointed by man as the invoker of the gods, art present at sacrifices: do thou present this our oblation.

"12. Yoke, divine Agni, thy fleet and powerful mares, Rohits, to thy chariot, and by them hither bring the gods."

The Soma-juice which occupies so prominent a place in the hymn, is the expressed juice of the moon-plant, and was frequently, perhaps always, mixed with milk. It was prepared with prescribed ceremony by the priest the day before it was used, to give it time to ferment, in sufficient quantity for two sacrifices : it was pressed between two boards, which were beaten with the sacred soma-stones, and allowed to trickle into troughs resting on the skin of a goat, and then strained through a cloth for its purification. After pouring out the libation to the gods, the remainder was drunk by the officiating priest. Its effects on Indra are described in the 175th hymn of the same book.

"1. Lord of Steeds, thou art exhilarated when the sacred Soma-juice has been imbibed by thee as by its appropriate vessel ; for to thee, showerer of benefits, it is exhilarating, inebriating, invigorating, the yielder of delight, satisfying as food, and the giver of a thousand pleasures.

"2. May our Soma-libation reach you, for it is exhilarating, invigorating, inebriating, most precious: it is companionable, Indra, enjoyable, the overthrower of hosts, immortal. . . . .

"5. Thy inebriety is most intense ; nevertheless thy acts for our good are most beneficent. Thou desirest, bountiful giver of horses, that both thy inebriety and thy beneficence should be the means of destroying enemies and distributing riches."

In the 119th hymn of the 10th book, he himself thus describes those effects :—

"1. Thus, indeed, thus my mind resolved,—I will give cows and horses to my worshippers ; for I have often drunk of the Soma.

"2. Like the winds, violently shaking the trees the draughts of Soma have lifted me up ; for I have often drunk of the Soma.

"3. The draughts of Soma have lifted me up like swift horses ; for I have often drunk of the Soma. . . . . . .

"6. The five castes have not eluded the glance of my eye ; for I have often drunk of the Soma. . . . .

"12. I am the Sun, the greatest of the great, raised to the firmament ; for I have often drunk of the Soma.

"13. Receiving the offering, I go, graced by the worshippers, bearing the oblation to the gods; for I have often drunk of the Soma."

A rapid view of the vedic conception of the character of the gods may be obtained from the epithets applied to them in the hymns. The matter available for this purpose is very abundant, and it may be sufficient here to collect some of those which occur in the first book and in the hymns to Indra alone :—"Indra of wonderful splendour," "apprehended by the understanding, and appreciated by the wise," "the mighty in battle," "the protector of wealth, the mighty, the accomplisher of good deeds, the friend of the offerer of the libation," "the discomfiter of many enemies, the lord of many blessings," "the lord of food," "the protector of the virtuous," "ever young, ever wise," "wielder of the thunderbolt," "the ruler of the world," "of boundless wealth," "who delights in the sacrificial food," "the lord of the vast god-frequented Svarga," "of whom the waters of heaven have not reached the limit," "the giver of horses, of cattle, of barley," "haughty," "ambitious of renown," "whose irresistible impetuosity is like the rush of water down a precipice," "the showerer of desires, who is the co-dweller with all energies, the supreme ruler over the vast heaven and earth," "the lord of all moving and breathing creatures," "whose great power pervades heaven and earth, in whose service Varuṇa and Súrya are steadfast, and whose command the rivers obey," "the seven rivers display his glory; heaven and earth and sky display his visible form; the Sun and Moon, Indra, perform their revolutions that we may see and have faith in what we see," "strong as a twice-twisted rope thou art the type of strength." "Protector of man, thou art more than able to sustain the three spheres, the three luminaries, and all this world of beings, Indra, who hast from thy birth been without a rival."

A similar general view of the hopes and desires with

9

which the worshippers approached Indra with their sacrifices may be gathered from the prayers and direct statements contained in their hymns to him :—" May he be to us for the acquirement of riches; may he be to us for the acquisition of knowledge; may he come to us with food :" " let not men do injury to our persons :" " shedder of rain . . . . set open this cloud :" " whatever men have recourse to Indra in battle, or for the acquirement of offspring, and the wise who are desirous of understanding, obtain their desires :" " grant to us, Indra, wealth beyond measure or calculation, inexhaustible, the source of cattle, of food, and of all life :" " set open the cowpastures :" " cast asleep the two female messengers of Yama; looking at each other let them sleep never waking :" " destroy this ass praising thee with such discordant speech :" " Let the adverse breeze with a crooked course alight far off in the forest :" " destroy everyone that reviles us; slay everyone that does us injury :" " bestow upon us abundance of cows with projecting jaws, . . . robust and rich in milk, with which we may be happy :" " may we prosper through thy divine favour, the source of prowess, of cattle, and of horses :" " bestow upon us, Indra, increasing reputation; bestow upon us great, augmenting, and foesubduing strength; preserve us in affluence; cherish those who are wise; and supply us with wealth from which proceed excellent progeny and food :" " do thou who art possessed of horses sit down with pleasure upon the sacred grass, attended by the Maruts, at this sacrifice :" " rejoice, Indra, with the steeds who are of thy nature, open thy jaws, set wide thy throat, and drink the Soma-juice; let thy horses bring thee who hast a handsome chin hither; and benignant towards us, be pleased by our oblations :" " excite in us, Indra, veneration for the Sun, for the Waters, and for those who are worthy of the praise of living beings : . . . harm us not, Indra, abandon us not; deprive us not of the enjoyments that are dear to

us ; injure not, affluent Shakra, our unborn offspring ;
harm not those who are capable only of crawling on their
knees ;" " come into our presence, they have called thee,
fond of the Soma-juice ; it is prepared, drink of it for
thine exhilaration ; vast of limb, distend thy stomach, and
when invoked hear us as a father listens to the words of
his sons :" " preserve us from this poverty that is so difficult to be destroyed, and from misfortune in war ; grant
us riches conspicuous for chariots, remarkable for horses,
for the sake of food, of fame and of truth :" "annihilate,
Maghavan, the might of malignant hosts ; hurl them into
the vile pit, the vast and vile pit :" " destroy, Indra, the
tawny-coloured, fearfully roaring Pisháchas [goblins],
annihilate all the Rákshasas [giants]:" " quickly grant us
that wealth that thou possessest, for we gratify the donor
with a most worthy present :" " this is the sacrifice ; these
are the prayers ; this, Indra, is the Soma-juice ; the sacred
grass is ready strewn ; come, therefore, Indra, quickly ;
sit down, drink the libation, here let loose thy steeds."

It remains to be said that the vedic gods were of human
birth and of anthropological nature and character in all
respects : their parentage and marriages and offspring,
their food and clothing and ornaments, their passions and
elevations and griefs, are mentioned in the most matter-of-
fact terms ; and their helpless infancy and mischievous
childhood, and the great deeds and moral defects of their
more mature years are illustrated by legends of the ordinary type. They earned their elevation to the Heavens,
with its accompanying immortality, by their austerities
and righteousness ; and their continuance in that exalt-
ation was subject to the usual contingencies. Their immortality too was intermittent, and passed away with all
the other things of time at the end of each divine period
of the world, to be renewed, however, with them, when
the seeds of the new heavens and the new earth begin to
germinate at the rising of the new Brahmá in the navel lotus
of Náráyaṇa at the dawn of each succeeding dispensation.

THE RISHIS.

The names of the Rishis to whom the hymns of the Rig-veda are ascribed have been handed down from early times in carefully prepared indices; and that ascription is upheld in many instances by the contents of the hymns. They are distributed into the three classes of Brahmarshis, Devarshis, and Rájarshis. The individual names of the authors of the Brahmarshi class are very numerous, namely, 938 including combinations: in the clans to which they belong these family groups are only seven in number. Arranging them alphabetically, Agastya and his family have 34 of the hymns; Angiras, in the two sub-divisions of his family, has the greatly preponderating number of 454, namely, 351 in the Bháradvája sub-division, and 103 in the Gotama sub-division; Yamadagni has 59; Kashyapa 46; Vasishtha 144; and Vishvámitra 105. These Rishis represent the seven primitive sages who constitute the constellation of the Great Bear, in which the star Alpha, is the Rishi Pulaha; Béta is Kratu; Gamma is Atri; Delta is Pulastya, Epsilon is Angiras; Zéta is Vasishtha and Éta is Maríchi. Here the Brahmarshis represent the five founders of the principal Brahmanical families, namely, Angiras, Atri, Bhrigu (who stands for his father Maríchi), Kashyapa, and Vasishtha: the Devarshis are represented by Kratu, Kardama the son of Pulaha, Kuvera the son of Pulastya, Nárada and Parvata the sons of Agastya, and some others: and the Rájarshis are Ikshváku and other similar princes. It is not that the hymns call this constellation "the Great Bear," although that name is at least as old as Homer; for the vedic map of the heavens is a religious map, scientifically divided into regions whose limits are defined by their astronomy while their names are derived from their mythology; the vedic name for it is simply "the seven Rishis," because the surrounding region is the heaven assigned to these sages as the reward of their piety on earth, and where they still continue to offer their prolonged sacrifices and prayers for the good of mankind. Meanwhile their wives are separated from them; for these are the Pleiades,—the seven nursing mothers of the fiery Mars (Kártikeya); and yet not all of the seven, for one of them, Arundhatí, the devoted wife of Vasishtha, has wandered far away from her companions in search of her husband, and is now pointed out to young Hindu brides as the model for their own fidelity, in the little star of the sixth magnitude below the middle star of the Bear's tail. One of the most remarkable of the vedic songsters, however, is not with them there, *viz.*, Agastya the son of Pulastya, the civilizer of Southern India, and the paternal uncle of Rávaṇa the demon-king of the Rámáyaṇa legend, whose stellar abode is far down in the opposite hemisphere in the great star Canopus.

The pedigree, which the hymns with their indices enable us to construct, shows that a more or less close relationship existed amongst these vedic Ṛishis, and that this natural connexion was extended from time to time by intermarriages. The following skeleton pedigree compiled from full genealogical tables for each of the great families, will show this inter-connexion more effectively than a description in words at length. The names of the seven primitive Ṛishis are in capital letters; and those of the daughters of the families, by whose marriages the completion of the unity was effected, are in italics. The figures in brackets after the names show the number of hymns ascribed to each of them. The " generations," A, B, &c., in the first column of this pedigree, correspond with those in the heading of the diagram on page 70. A few other names of hymn-makers have been omitted for want of space.

SKELETON PEDIGREE.

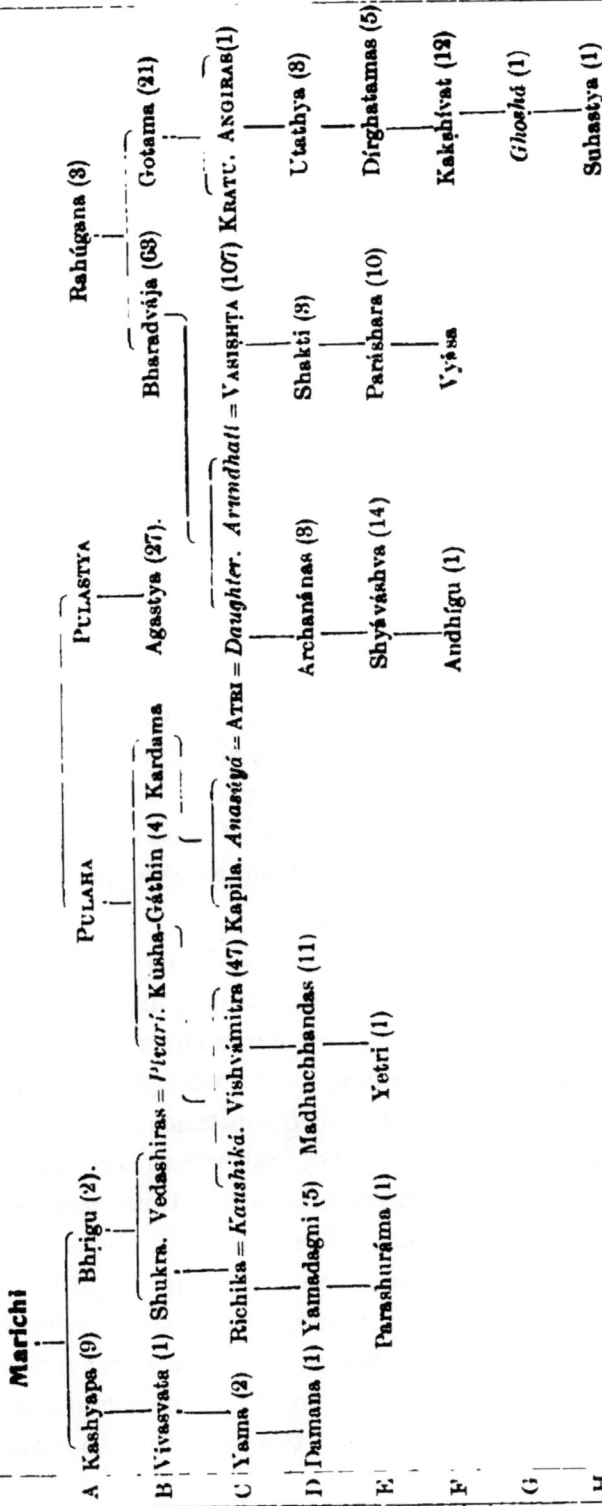

(Generations.)

Marichi

A Kashyapa (9)   Bhrigu (2).

B Vivasvata (1)   Shukra. Vedashiras = *Pitarí*. Kusha-Gáthin (4) Kardama   PULAHA   PULASTYA   Rahúgana (3)

C Yama (2)   Richika = *Kaushiká*. Vishvámitra (47) Kapila. *Anasúyá* = ATRI = *Daughter*. *Arundhatí* = VASISHTA (107) KRATU. ANGIRAS (1)   Agastya (27).   Bharadvája (63)   Gotama (21)

D Damana (1) Yamadagni (5)   Madhuchhandas (11)   Archanánas (8)   Shakti (8)   Utathya (8)

E Parashuráma (1)   Yetri (1)   Shyáváshva (14)   Paráshara (10)   Dírghatamas (5)

F   Andhígu (1)   Vyása   Kakshívat (12)

G   *Ghoshá* (1)

H   Suhastya (1)

This pedigree shows that an alliance between the houses of Maríchi and the brothers Pulaha and Pulastya was formed at an early period by the marriage of Vedashiras, the grandson of Maríchi, with Pívarí the daughter of Pulaha, that in the next generation, Atri joined that alliance by his marriage with Pulaha's grand-daughter, and then extended it to Vasishṭha by his second marriage with the daughter of Bharadvája, whose other daughter was Vasish-ṭha's wife, and who was himself first cousin of Kratu and Angiras, the remaining two of the seven sages of the Great Bear. Another great hymn-maker, though not of the primitive families, Vishvámitra, was brought into the connexion about the same time by the marriage of his sister with Richika, one of Bhṛigu's grandsons.

Moreover this pedigree shows the number of generations that the poetical afflatus continued in each of the families, culminating in the important result, that the whole period covered by the Ṛig-Veda hymns, from Bhṛigu, Kashyapa, and Rahúgaṇa down to Suhastya of the house of Angiras, the latest poet in Vyása's recension, was eight genera-tions, or 240 years at the rate of thirty years to a generation. The diagram on page 75 will show this latter circum-stance in a more definite form.

THE HOME OF THE ṚIṢHIS.

The legends scattered through the hymns regarding the Ṛiṣhis and the royal and other personages connected with them contain many geographical references which throw light upon the position of their hermitages and the localities which they frequented. Several rivers are mentioned, which are capable of precise identification, some of them in the basin of the Indus, the Sarasvatí, the Dṛishadvatí, the Sutlej and the Beas,—and others in the great eastern basin, the Ganges, the Jumna, the Sarayu, the Gumti, the Gogra, and the Gandak. The river Sarasvatí is men-tioned definitely only four times: in a few other places there is a double reference to the river and the goddess of the same name : but in the great majority of the passages where this name occurs, the goddess alone is meant quite apart from the river. The confluence of the Beas and the Sutlej is mentioned once, namely, in the hymn in which the Ṛiṣhi Vishvámitra prayed them to heap up their waters and grant him a passage over their dry bed. With these exceptions, it is by no means certain that the Panjáb and its rivers are referred to in any of the hymns. The expression, "the seven rivers" is of very frequent occurrence : but it is evident that it does not refer specially to the rivers of the Panjáb, but is a mere set phrase for any group of seven ; for it includes, when the rivers are named, several distinct groups which, in the words of one of the hymns, "flowed by sevens through the three worlds ;" and not one of these groups is confined to the Panjáb streams. The name "Sindhu," which might be supposed to mean the Indus, occurs in the hymns upwards of two hundred times ; but, with very few exceptions when it applies to other rivers of that name, as the context shows, it is a general term for any stream or other form of running water, and even the ocean.

As regards the hermitages of the Ṛiṣhis, if we supplement the information obtained from the hymns by the legends of the epic poems and puráṇas, they were all situated within an area extending from the Jumna on the west to the neighbourhood of Patna on the east, and from the mountains at the head-waters of the Ganges southwards through its confluence with the Jumna to the Chitra-kúṭa hills in Bundelkhand : southwestwards from this spot they spread themselves to the sources of the Godávari in the neighbourhood of Nasik and throughout the great Daṇḍakáraṇya wilderness.

More particularly, the usual spheres of action of the two great Ṛiṣhis, Vasiṣhṭha and Vishvámitra were confined to the two doabs on the right and left banks of the Ganges, above its junction with the Jumna, with a special visit to

Mithila, to the eastwards and to the confluence of the Sutlej and the Beas to the westwards in the case of Vishvámitra. The Ṛiṣhi region of the hymns is thus limited to the north-western districts of the basin of the Ganges and the adjoining wild country to the south, having the Upper Panjáb and less known farther west on its left hand, and on its right hand the sphere of the preaching tours of Buddha.

THE DATE OF THE ṚIṢHIS.

It is very much to be desired that some reliable clue should be found to fix the date of these Ṛiṣhis, in order to settle the time when these hymns were written, and to place this particular phase of religious development in its chronological position in the general history of religion. Various extreme dates have been put forward as not unreasonable; but they have been calculated from data which no one considers to be satisfactory; and this important question remains still open for solution.

It is possible that one of the Vasiṣhṭha-Vishvámitra legends may supply the required answer. One of Vishvá-mitra's hymns alludes in strong language to an enemy who entertained a deadly hatred against him, whom he calls upon Indra to destroy :—" Indra, hero, possessor of wealth, protect us this day against our foes with many and excellent defences : may the vile wretch who hates us fall before us; may the breath of life depart from him whom we hate." According to the commentator, following the general tradition, the enemy referred to is the Ṛiṣhi Vasiṣhṭha with reference to the remarkable legend which pervades the epic and puraṇik literature, and even more modern tradition. Vishvámitra, when on one of his conquering expeditions in his pre-Ṛiṣhi days, encamped with his army in the neighbourhood of Vasiṣhṭha's her-mitage, and admired the tokens of great affluence which he saw there. Vasiṣhṭha explained that these were the gifts of his cow-of-plenty. Vishvámitra made great efforts to

10

purchase the cow ; and when Vasishtha declined to sell her at any price, the king with his men proceeded to take her by force. The cow herself then took the matter into her own hands, and produced from her different limbs large bodies of foreign and unregenerate warriors—Shaka-Scythians, Bactrian-Greeks, Parthians, Persians, Kabúli-Kaffirs, together with the uncivilized mountaineers of Central India, and various races of the Dakhan,—by whose aid she defeated the army of Vishvámitra and drove him from his kingdom to seek refuge in exile amongst the hermitages of Southern India.

The mention of the foreign members of this alliance, assuming that this wide-spread legend has a historical significance, points to a time when it was possible for an alliance of this formidable and heterogeneous character to have been formed ; and it can only point to the time when the Greek Kings of Bactria (the Yavanas) had been defeated by the Parthians in confederacy with the Shaka-Scythians and driven over the Hindu-Kush, and had been followed in their flight into Afghanistan by their implacable foes, who there completed their final overthrow. At that time alone in history had these Scythians won for themselves the dominant position over all the nationalities mentioned here, which the legend implies that they possessed.

Without entering into the details of the invasion which this interpretation suggests, it will be sufficient to note here that Kanishka, the great king of the Khorán-Scythians had well established his power as far as the river Jumna in the 5th year of the Vikrama era, or 52 B.C., as is shown by an inscription of that date, bearing his name as paramount king, upon an image dug out of the ruins of the ancient city of Mathura. In accordance with the above theory, this date may probably not be far from the time of the overthrow of Vishvámitra's kingly power by the Scythian confederacy, and may mark the commencement of the second part of his career as an ascetic among the Rishis.

It would therefore correspond with generation C in the genealogical tree on page 70 : and from this date the other generations marked on that tree may be calculated backwards and forwards.

The following Diagram will now show the relative positions of these Ṛishis in their generations, together with the dates which the above method of calculation roughly assigns to them. It shows the number of generations during which the members of the different families continued to write hymns : and it also shows that the whole period which the Rig-Veda covers was somewhat over two centuries, namely, from the last quarter of the second century B.C. down to the close of the first century of the Christian era.

DIAGRAM OF THE GENERATIONS OF THE ṚISHIS.

First Rishi.	GENERATIONS.								Last Rishi.
	A. B.C. 112	B. B.C. 82	C. B.C. 52	D. B.C. 22	E. A.D. 8	F. A.D. 38	G. A.D. 68	H. A.D. 98	
Bhrigu	———	———				..	..	..	Parashuráma.
Kashyapa	———	———			..	..	..	..	Damana.
Agastya	..	———	———	———	..	..	..	..	Idhmavaha.
Bharadvája	..	———	———		..	..	..	..	Mudgala.
Gotama	..	———	———						Suhastya.
Atri	..	..	———	———	———	..	..		Andhigu.
Vasishtha	..	..	———	———		..	..	..	Paráshara.
Vishvámitra	..	..	———	———		..	..	..	Jetri.

It is, however, due to another group of oriental scholars, whose views are deserving of high consideration, to mention here, that the epoch which they assign to the Scythian invasion is not the Vikrama era of 57 B.C., upon which the above diagram is built, but the Shálivâhana era of A.D. 78. The effect of this preference, while not disturbing the construction of the above skeleton-pedigree, would be to bring each of its generations 135 years lower down in the chronology, by dating Kanishka's inscription of the year 5, in A.D. 83 instead of in 52 B.C.

We may now proceed to enquire what religions held possession of the countries to the east and west of this well-defined Rishi-region during the period when the vedic sages were singing their hymns there.

EASTERN INDIA.

We may begin with the region beyond its eastern boundary. Here we find that the Jaina and Buddhist religions had taken firm root, and had been progressing on strangely parallel lines of time, locality, and personal circumstances, from the seventh century B. C. downwards,—that is to say, from the second century after the building of Rome, or about the time when Nebuchadnezzar carried the Jews captive to Babylon (B. C. 598), and when Solon (B. C. 594) was legislating in Greece.

THE JAINA RELIGION.

The founder of the Jaina Religion was Vardhamána, the son of a respectable member of the Kshatriya caste living in the suburbs of the city of Vaishála, the capital of the old Kingdom of Videha on the northern banks of the Ganges opposite Patna. He was born about the year 639 B. C. On the death of his parents, when he was twenty-eight years old, he became an ascetic, and spent twelve years performing austerities in the wilderness. In the second of those years he cast off all clothing, and carried his self-mortification to the utmost conceivable lengths. Having thus acquired the necessary qualification he reappeared to the world in 599 B. C. in the character of an omniscient jina, and spent the remaining thirty years of his life as the prophet of his new religion under the title of ' Mahávíra,' or ' The Great Hero.' He went about preaching his doctrines throughout the kingdoms of Videha, Magadha, and Anga, that is to say, all the region to the east of Patna, on both sides of the Ganges, as far as the neighbourhood of Bhágalpur, and paying occasional visits to the wilder country at the foot of the Himalayas. He appointed eleven of his principal followers as the heads of his sect ; and with them he organised a regular order of ascetics. The five vows of his community are, (1) Not to destroy life ; (2) Not to tell an untruth; (3) Not to take anything which is not given ; (4) To observe complete celibacy ; (5) To renounce all interest in worldly things. Their views of the sacredness of life is carried to a greater length than by all other sects ; for they hold that not only all breathing animals, and the whole vegetable kingdom, but also every particle of matter included in the category of the prime elements, earth, fire, water, and air, have individual souls endowed with self-consciousness and the knowledge of surrounding things, and are subject to all the vicissitudes of soul-life.

Their ultimate hope is in a final emancipation from all imperfection through the attainment of perfect knowledge and absolute purity and goodness, which will then stamp the condition of the jina for eternity.

They have temples, in which one of their own sect is always the *reader*; but a Brahmin is usually the officiating *priest* at their services. The objects of worship in their temples are the images of the old saints of their sect, whose memorials are kept up by annual festivals in their honour.

The total Jaina population of India at the last census was 1,416,638. In Southern India there are only 68,588, of whom the greater part belong to the Nizam's territory and Mysore. Their chief seats are in the Bombay Presidency and the native states connected with it, and in Rajputana, Central India, the Central Provinces, Baroda and Ajmere, where they number 1,140,086, or about four-fifths of the whole Jaina population of India.

THE BUDDHIST RELIGION.

Buddhism until very lately might have seemed to have but a slight claim to a place in a brief sketch of this kind, seeing how few real Buddhists were to be found in the land of its birth. The name had indeed a place in the census classification; but the Jainas were at that time taken to be Buddhists. The inclusion of Burmah with its seven million Buddhists out of a total population of seven-and-a-half millions, has now altered that case; and India has once more to be reckoned amongst the Buddhist nations.

Siddhárta or Gautama Buddha, the founder of this religion, was the son of the king of Kapilavastu in the old kingdom of Kosala, a few days journey to the north of Benares, which was a dependency of the kings of Magadha. The young prince was born there about 623 B.C., a few years later than the birth of the founder of Jainism. While still a young man he was overcome by a pessimistic view of the present life; and after a series of mental struggles for 10 years, he secretly fled from the luxuries of his father's palace to become a homeless ascetic.

He settled for a time in the suburbs of the capital of Magadha, and gave himself up to profound philosophical study under the successive guidance of two Ṛishis resident there; but all the highest attainable knowledge failed to give him the mental repose which he was seeking. He then retired into the jungles of the Vindhya mountains to go through a course of self-torture and sin-annihilating austerities, with the same object, and with a similar disappointing result. At length, at the end of five years of that miserable life, the enlightenment came to him suddenly and in the last extremity of his emaciated body and his exhausted mind. His future course became clear to him: and he came forth from the mountains to preach his new doctrine of emancipation from the five passions.

He began his work in a grove in the outskirts of Benares; and there by degrees he became surrounded by a number of disciples. At the end of the rainy season he sent each of his leading converts separately into different parts of the country round about to propagate his teaching and to initiate disciples into his order. He himself returned to the neighbourhood of his old hermitage in the Vindhyas, where there was already an extensive settlement of older Ṛishis, the 'Rathees' of the Burmese legend, with their numerous disciples, all of whom became his converts.

This preaching itineration became the established custom of his order, all returning to some appointed centre to spend each rainy season together with their master, each of them bringing one or more of his new converts with him. Buddha's itinerating circuits extended to a distance of 150 miles around Benares, the kings of Magadha sometimes patronizing his work, and at others persecuting him and his followers. Thus he passed his life for forty-five years after his enlightenment. He died on one of these tours at Kusinagara, a few day's journey to the east of his birthplace, in 543 B. C. in the 80th year of his age.

The Buddhist holds, in common with some other sects, that his position in each of his successive transmigrations is the direct result of his character and conduct in some one or more of his previous existences, and consequently that all life is a connected chain of causes and effects. Birth itself is one of those effects, and is itself an evil of downward growth: and the present life is therefore a misery, made up of mental and bodily pains. The sole cause of all this misery is desire in its various forms: and the remedy for this evil is to stamp out that cause,—to uproot every form of desire, (1) by embracing the faith of Buddha, (2) by forming a right judgment in all things, (3) by bridling the tongue, (4) by setting up right aims for one's life, (5) by avoiding all wrong actions, (6) by cultivating a meek and reverential spirit, (7) by maintaining a memory of all that is good, and (8) by solemn meditation upon spiritual things. The final result of all this, the supreme object of his hope is the Nirvána, namely, the complete extinction of all desire in his nature, and a consequent state of spiritual tranquillity and unadulterated joy. It is not the extinction of the man's existence; for the cessation of spiritual life is an inconceivable thing, especially to such a philosopher as Buddha: it is not that the "lamp is blown out at the casement," nor is it that the sources of the hopes and fears and sorrows of man have been removed from his surroundings; but that the emancipated man himself has been raised above them, far beyond their reach, and that no attracting or repelling force exists which can thenceforward put him in contact with them any more throughout the ages to come.

WESTERN INDIA.

Beyond the western boundary of our Rishi-region lies the Panjáb, and the countries bordering on the Indus westwards and northwards, together with those to the north of the Hindu-Kush which have always largely shared the destinies of Afghanistan.

Our true chronological starting-point for this region is the reign of Cyrus the Great; for it was through his conquests that it was brought within the circle of Persian civilization and to share the influences of the great religious movement which was so largely fostered by him.

Cyrus won the decisive battles of Pasargadæ in 558 B.C., and so became the founder of the empire of the Medes and Persians. The early years of his reign were occupied by his conquest of Asia Minor. Sardis fell in 554 B.C., and then he turned his face towards the mysterious East. He spent fourteen years in his eastern wars; and at their close he had added to his dominions the vast tract from the Caspian Sea to the plains of Kashgar and the right bank of the Indus, and from the Jaxartes to the Indian Ocean.

It is expressly stated that he never crossed the Indus. From 539 B. C. onwards he conquered Susiana, Babylonia, Syria and Palestine, and there dealt a mortal blow to the Semitic civilization of those nations with its debasing idolatry, from which it never recovered.

It was after his return to Babylon at the close of those western conquests that he permitted the Jews of the captivity to return to their native land; and he gave them his help to rebuild their temple at Jerusalem. He thus became the restorer of pure monotheism to its old home, and so relaid the foundation of that spiritual life for mankind which, in the natural course of its evolution, has grown into the Christian civilization of the persent day.

Egypt still remained unconquered: but he was now 65 years of age; and his great empire also required rest and much prudent care. He was apparently seventy years old when something unrecorded occurred to set him once more upon the war-path This time it was against the Massagetæ beyond the Jaxartes : and there, in the ends of the earth, this mighty warrior met his death. He survived his mortal wound long enough to know that his army had inflicted a crushing defeat upon the enemy.

At the time of his conquest of the country north of the Hindu-Kush he found the religion of Zoroaster well established on both banks of the river Oxus; for Bactria was the cradle of that religion. To the north of that region, beyond the Jaxartes, it had not spread : the Massagetæ who inhabited it had some form of solar worship; for they sacrificed horses to the Sun, and their queen, when she gave her oath to Cyrus, swore " by the Sun, the Lord of the Massagetæ."

Cyrus died in 529 B. C. We have therefore a solid basis for the religious history of the Bactrian provinces with their southern continuation in Afghanistan and Baluchistan from the 6th century downwards. The state religion was necessarily the religion of the king: and as regards the

11

masses of his subjects, while they paid due respect to the religion of the state, they continued free, under the king's well-understood toleration, to worship the old gods of their fathers. Cyrus' own early life and education fell in a time when a great religious movement, under various phases, was stirring up the whole oriental world: he lived the first fifteen years of his life during the last days of Zoroaster, and he survived Mahávíra by forty years, and Buddha by fourteen years; Confucius also was transforming the religion of China during the last twenty-one years of his reign. His great genius was susceptible of all purely spiritual influences: and the religious character which they contributed to mould in him, and which fascinated his own contemporaries, became the type of the religion of his empire for many generations to come.

We may here pass by the short reigns of Cambyses and the Pseudo-Smerdis, as they contain nothing which permanently affects our subject. Darius I. the son of Hystaspes, began to reign in 521 B.C. The absence of Cambyses from his kingdom for so long a time led to a general relaxation of authority throughout the empire, and that state of semi-anarchy burst out into a succession of rebellions in several provinces during the first five years of the new king's reign. There was more or less of a religious element in these revolts, connected with the old idolatries of Babylon and the adjacent provinces; but the eastern provinces, Bactria and its neighbours, which were the chief seats of Zoroastrianism, remained faithful to Darius throughout the struggle. When these disturbances had been quelled the empire had rest for ten years. Darius then entered upon a series of conquests which occupied the remaining twenty-one years of his reign; but it is only necessary here to follow his Indian campaign.

Cyrus' conquests stopped short at the Indus: and Darius now desired to extend that eastern boundary. He sent forward an exploring party from some point upon the

Cabul river, with the Carian navigator Scylax at its head, to descend that river, and to trace its connexion with his western dominions, not from mere curiosity, but with the practical object of establishing a continuous commercial route from the Indus to the Nile by way of the Erythræan sea. The spirit of Milesian maritime enterprise was incarnate in Scylax : and the successful completion of his task marked a new epoch in the commerce of the East. When Scylax returned from this voyage, Darius crossed the Indus and conquered the Panjáb and Sind. This large acquisition of territory added upwards of a million pounds sterling per annum to the tribute-revenue of his empire, and extended its boundary eastwards to the line of the river Sutlej. At the same time, it put forward the sphere of Persian civilization, both political and religious, over the same additional extent of area.

Darius I, died in 486 B.C. after a reign of 35 years, at the age of 63, leaving behind him a character as one of the wisest and most successful of the rulers of men, and from our present point of view, as one of the chief promoters of the religious education of the oriental world. His religious character corresponds in its main features with that of Cyrus. All through his life he was a consistent disciple of Zoroaster; and he observed the same large toleration as Cyrus towards the different religions of his subjects. This is well illustrated in his inscriptions. In his great rock inscription at Behistun, in which he recorded the events of the early years of his reign, he attributes all his successes, one after the other, to the grace of Auramazda. "This is what I accomplished, what I accomplished with the grace of Auramazda; I have fought nineteen battles and taken captive nine kings :" At the foot of the principal inscription there is another explanatory one which has a remarkable addition illustrative of his toleration,—" What I have done, I have done by the grace of Auramazda; Auramazda came to my aid. *and the other gods*, who did so because I was *not hostile*" (to them). And similarly in an inscription at Persepolis belonging to the later years of his reign,—" By the grace of Auramazda I have founded this fortress, strong, beautiful and complete. May Auramazda and all the gods protect me and this fortress and all that is in it." The kindliness of Darius' nature together with his personal piety are well seen in his sympathy with the Jewish prophet Daniel when in tribulation, and in his joy at his deliverance; for this is that same Darius who published his proclamation throughout his empire,— " Peace be multiplied to you. I make a decree, that in every dominion of my kingdom men tremble before the god of Daniel: for he is the living God, and stedfast for ever, and his kingdom that which shall not be destroyed, and his dominion shall be even unto the end. He delivereth and rescueth, and he worketh signs and wonders in heaven and in earth, who hath delivered Daniel from the power of the lions."

No material change is mentioned regarding the eastern limits of the Persian empire during the reigns of its subsequent kings: the Sutlej continued to mark its boundary in that direction down to its collapse in the reign of Darius III. The satraps of the Panjáb may have conducted their affairs with various degrees of independence in the meantime; nevertheless they sent in their tribute. For, if they had not done so, the loss of a million sterling a year, or one-third of the whole land-revenue of the empire, could hardly have occurred without some reference being made to it and to its cause. Even in the time of Darius Nothus (B.C. 424 to 405), whose reign was a constant scene of revolts and insurrections, India does not appear among the revolting provinces: and the presence of elephants with Indian troops in the place of honour around the king's person in the battle of Gaugamela is sufficient to show that the Panjáb was still faithful down to Darius' last struggle in defence of his throne.

Nor on the other hand, had there been any material change in the state religion of Persia during this period. Laxness regarding the "other gods" no doubt waxed and waned in the proportion of the firmness or weakness of the personal character of the kings, and of the influence of their queens; but the empire was supported by other strong conservative forces all the while, sufficient to maintain a steady equilibrium in its religious and all its other leading principles. Mithra, the ancient Sun-god, retained his influence over both throne and people down to the end: his ten sacred sacrificial horses and his splendid chariot were prominent features of the magnificent procession of Xerxes when he went forth to the invasion of Greece: and when he was about to cross the straits, he waited for the moment of sunrise to worship Mithra with a libation, and with a prayer that he would enable him to conquer Europe. It was also not without some reference to the worship of Mithra that he transported the whole body of the priests of the Milesian Phœbus-Apollo into the interior of his empire, and built them a city, and endowed them with lands, where Alexander found them in their sixth generation still maintaining the traditions of Didyma, and propagating the worship of their Sun-god among the surrounding Scythian hordes. It was in the reign of Xerxes also that the worship of Anaitis, the Babylonian Venus, the Isis of the Egyptians, the Aphrodite, Artemis, or Héra of the Greeks, the great goddess Diana of the Ephesians,—was introduced into Persia. But his great-grandson Alexander Mnemon (B. C. 405 to 359) went much further, and did his utmost to raise her previous casual worship into a full national idolatry; for he set up images of this goddess for the worship of the people at Susa, Persepolis, and Ecbatana, at Babylon and Damascus, at Sardis in the far west, and at Balkh in the far east. Magnificent temples were also built for her worship with pillars plated with gold, and bricks of solid silver and gold. This king set up a statue of

Mithra also, to whom the form of an idol had never before been given in Zoroastrian lands, and invoked him as his special protector: and his example in this respect was followed by his son Ochus (B. C. 359 to 338). And yet Zoroaster's Auramazda, the nearest approach to Jehovah which man had thus far discovered, was never deposed from his supremacy in the midst of all these decadencies; and the religion of Cyrus, " the anointed shepherd of the Lord," continued to be the paramount religion of his empire down to its fall.

We are now approaching the time of the conquest of the Persian empire by Alexander the Great. He started from Macedon on this great enterprise in 334 B. C.: and it may well be doubted whether he then quite realized the full extent of the work which was before him; for at that moment Darius' dominions extended from the Nile to the Sutlej, and from the northern extremity of the Caspian Sea to the shore of the Erythræan, covering along the crow-line a distance of 2,820 miles of longitude by 1,380 of latitude. He did, however, realize the necessity of divine help for the work; for he offered sacrifices to Jupiter, Pallas-Athene and Hercules for the success of the expedition when he started upon it, and committed both himself and his army to the patronage of these divinities for protection and victory. There is a running record throughout his campaigns of similar public sacrifices being offered on every special occasion. Arrian says of him that he was "strictly observant of his duty to the deity," and that it was his custom to offer sacrifices daily. There are also repeated instances of his desire to conciliate the religious feelings of his army and the people through whose territory he was marching, and to impress a religious character upon his movements. For instance, he built a temple to Olympian Zeus at Sardis; he celebrated the festival of Hercules at Tyre; he sacrificed to the Egyptian god Apis at Memphis; he rebuilt the ancient temple of Bel at Babylon, which Xerxes had destroyed, and sacrificed there in the way prescribed by the Chaldean priests ; he sacrificed to Apollo when he was about to take his army across the Hindu-Kush to Bactria ; he made libations to the divinities of the Panjáb rivers when he was about to sail on them, and to Neptune and the other water-gods when he dismissed his fleet from the mouths of the Indus on their ocean-voyage to Persia ; `he offered thanksgiving sacrifices at the end of his distressing march through Beluchistan ; and by some strange arrangement he induced the Greek soothsayers and the Persian Magi to hold a mixed religious service at the feast of reconciliation at Susa, when 9,000 men made their libations together and raised a united hymn of praise for their happy deliverance from the great perils and dangers which they had passed through.

Alexander's Persian campaigns occupied altogether eleven years ; he crossed over into Asia in 334 B. C., and he returned to Babylon to die in 323 B.C.   Of this period, five years, namely, from 330 to 325 B.C. were spent in the reduction of the Bactrian and Indian provinces, two of which he spent in the Panjáb : he turned his back on the Sutlej in 326 B.C., and finally left the mouths of the Indus in 325 B.C.

He found the Panjáb in a flourishing condition.   The first of its doabs (mesopotamias) lying between the Indus and the Jhelum, was said to be as large as Egypt.   Its capital then and for a long time afterwards was Taxila, which gave its name to Taxiles who occupies a prominent place in the histories as the regal satrap who welcomed the new master of the empire into his satrapy with right loyal services.   In the second doab, between the Jhelum and the Chenab (Acesines) lay the dominions of Porus, another of the regal satraps of the empire, whose greater distance from its heart had led to the assumption of a large degree of independence.   Alexander conquered him, but treated him with great generosity, restoring him to his government, and making large additions to his territory, which Arrian says comprised seven nations and contained more than two thousand cities.

When he had advanced into the last of the doabs he stood face to face with the river Sutlej, the furthest limit of the empire of Darius, and he had therefore substantially fulfilled the real object of his march into India, namely, to recover and settle the whole of the satrapies which he had won at Gaugamela. On the other side of the Sutlej runs the main waterparting which separates the basins of the Indus and the Ganges: and in the latter basin lay the great empire of Magadha, whose enormous military power had become known, probably in an exaggerated degree, to Alexander's soldiers during the year they had now been in the Panjáb. The veterans of the army formed an adverse opinion of the prudence of the proposed advance into altogether new territory: and they respectfully but firmly declined to be led beyond their present position. The gods were consulted; but the auspices were unfavourable; and preparations were made for the return march. Alexander built here twelve colossal altars to mark the site of his last camp; and after celebrating a farewell festival there, he took the army back to the Jhelum where he completed the erection of the two cities, one on each side of the river, which he had previously founded there, and established colonies of Europeans in them. The garrisons of these two cities commanded the doabs which formed the two satrapies of Taxiles and Porus respectively: and the latter was at this time raised to the dignity of Mahá-Kshatrapa, or Governor-General, of the whole of the Panjáb.

The twelve gods to whom the above tower-altars were dedicated, and who were thus elevated into an official pantheon for the Greek dominions in India, can be identified by the help of a passage in Arrian which names those who were worshipped on a corresponding occasion when Alexander started on his homeward voyage down the

Hydaspes. They are there distributed into two groups; (1) "the gods of his fathers," namely, the triad worshipped when he started on this expedition,—Jupiter, Pallas-Athene, and Hercules; (2) "those who were named by the soothsayers," of whom Ammon and Apollo have been named already, to "Poseidon, Amphitrite, and the Nereids, to Oceanus himself, to the river Hydaspes from which he was starting, to the Acesines into which the Hydaspes falls, and to the Indus into which they both fall." A very large number of animals were sacrificed on these altars; for, at the accompanying feast, he "distributed the flesh of the slaughtered animals throughout the divisions of the whole army."

With regard to the religions of "the Indians" of the Panjáb at this time, one circumstance is particularly interesting and important, and is related by all the leading classical authorities. During his stay at Taxila, Alexander made the acquaintance of some Indian sages whose hermitages were in the neighbourhood of that city. One of these groups were "Gymnosophists," or "Naked Sages:" and as the Digambara-Jainas were the only *naked* ascetics in those days, it follows that Calanus and his campanions belonged to that sect. Their great reverence for every thing that has life, which is particularly mentioned, is also an indication to the same effect. Another group is also mentioned whose doctrines and customs, where they differed from those of Calanus, show that they were Buddhist monks. There is also a third group mentioned as distinct from those two, namely the Brahmins, who were the counsellers and ministers of the kings, and the directors of their religious duties, who also occupied themselves with the sciences of physiology and astronomy. These Brahmins also had their own class of ascetics, both male and female, who lived in the forests, and there perpetually supplicated the gods on behalf of the kings. Their gods were "Jupiter-Ombrius, the river Ganges, and the indigenous deities of the country." Lower down the Indus also, as well as on the banks of the Rávi, there was a fringe of Brahmin settlements. One of these was a walled city with a citadel and fortifications, which had a population whose fighting men numbered over 5,000.

Alexander founded a large number of cities during this expedition, in which he settled numerous colonies of Europeans both to garrison them and also to carry out his favourite intention of amalgamating the people of Europe and Asia and their civilizations. There were several of these colonies in both the Bactrian and Indian provinces: and from these centres there went forth a continuous influence of Greek ideas connected with their manners, recreations, sciences, literature, language and religion upon the surrounding population, with far-reaching results for many succeeding generations.

When the fragments of Alexander's empire came to be permanently divided amongst his generals after the battle of Ipsus in 301 B. C., the provinces of old Percia from the borders of Phœnicia eastwards fell to the share of Seleucus. He had been in more or less precarious possession of Baby-lon and all that naturally went with it from B. C. 321. Now he transferred the capital of the East from Babylon to Antioch in Syria, thus rendering his control over the Bactrian and Indian satrapies little better than nominal. Difficulties had already arisen in the Indian satrapies. Porus, whom Alexander left there as governor-general, was slain in B. C. 317 by Eudemus: and Chandragupta, king of Magadha, then overran the Panjáb. Seleucus, after an unsuccessful effort to defend the province, ceded it to Chandragupta about B. C. 302: and thenceforward it ceased to form part of the Persian empire, whose boundary was thus thrown back to the line of the Indus which had formerly been Cyrus' eastern limit.

The religion followed the king, according to the general rule: and for a short time the state religion of the Panjáb

became the old Brahminical religion of the Nandas and
Mauryas, for the kings of Magadha had not yet become
Buddhists.

It remained in this position during the rest of Chandragupta's reign, and also throughout the reign of his son and
successor Bindusára (B. C. 291 to 263). This king appointed his son, the famous Ashoka, viceroy of the Punjáb,
with old Taxila as his capital, which was at that time a
rich and flourishing city and very populous. Chandragupta
extended his dominions in another direction also, along the
southern boundary of the Punjáb, through Rajputana and
the Vindhya territories as far as Gujarat. Over these
conquests with Ujain as their capital he made Ashoka his
viceroy, while he was still a young man.

Ashoka succeeded his father on the throne of Magadha
in B. C. 263 and reigned down to 222. Other dates are
also given; but the reader of a sketch like this will not
care to be troubled with them.

He began his career as a pronounced enemy of Buddhism,
and then became its ardent supporter, devoting to it the
immense resources of his great empire. Under his zealous
patronage, and by means of an organized propaganda, this
religion was disseminated throughout the whole of his
dominions, and in all the adjoining countries. Monuments
containing relics of Buddha, or to serve as memorials of
the localities connected with his career, were erected by
this king in many places, and he also established a large
number of monasteries, with their appendages, to accommodate many thousand monks. Several rock inscriptions
ascribed to him have survived to the present day, in which
he commands full toleration to be observed towards all
religions, and general encouragement to be given to ascetics
of all denominations. According to the legends of later
times, Ashoka extended his dominions much beyond the
limits of his grandfather's conquests. As regards Southern
India, there are traces of his presence in Conjeveram, in the

neigbourhood of Madras : and one of his edict-inscriptions has been discovered quite recently in the Mysore territory. Upon his death, the provinces of his empire were divided amongst his four sons : Magadha and Central India fell to Sujasus, and Kunála established himself in the Punjáb and Rajputana.

We have seen above when Seleucus Nicator made over the Punjab to Chandragupta, Bactria, together with the country to the south of the Hindu Kush and along the right bank of the Indus, still remained part of the Persian empire. This territory continued in the hands of Seleucus and his two successors, Antiochus I. (B. C. 281—261), and Antiochus II. (B. C. 261 to 246), down to the revolt of Bactria and its formation into a separate kingdom about 250 B. C. The religion of the Seleucid kings was substantially the same as Alexander's, as is shown by their coins ; and the Greek colonists maintained the popular cults of their nation in their new homes during that period, with such modifications, as time went on, as came in the natural course of things from the influence of their Bactrian wives and other local and personal influences. One circumstance, however, there was which drew forth a special preference for the worship of Apollo. The ancestors of Seleucus claimed to be the children of this god, and his worship, already well established in eastern Persia, since the days of Xerxes, was consistently encouraged now through the Seleucid empire. And concerning Bactriana in particular, a new Antioch was founded amongst the Scythians beyond the Jaxartes by Antiochus II., and altars were dedicated there to his patron divinity, the Apollo of Didyma, as if to replace the city of the Branchidæ priests in Sogdiana, whose temple and sacred groves had been destroyed by Alexander.

The revolt of Bactria in 250 B. C. cut off from the Seleucid dominions not only the province properly so called, but also all to the east of it beyond the " Roof of the World' in the Kashgarvan plains, in the Sogdianian territory also, and the oasis of Merv, together with the whole region to the south of the Hindu Kush as far as the Indus. And when Parthia soon afterwards followed the example of Bactria, the eastern boundary of Khorasan thenceforward marked the frontier of the empire. During the period at which we have now arrived, Bactria, practically and historically, consisted of two divisions: (1) Old Bactria and its appendages on the northern side of the Hindu Kush, with Balkh, "the mother of cities," for its capital, and (2) the region to the south of that great range with Alexander's great colony, Alexandria ad Caucasum, for its chief city, the Alasadda of the Buddhist literature, whose colossal ruins still lie in the plain of Beghran, 25 miles north of Kabul.

The northern division remained under the rule of the revolting dynasty for two successions of its kings down to 209 B. C., when it was extinguished by the Satrap of the adjoining province, Enthydemus of Magnesia. Shortly after this event, Antiochus III. (B. C. 222 to 187), marched at the head of a great army to recover his lost Satrapies. He defeated Enthydemus in the neighbourhood of Herat, and shut him up in Balkh. After a prolonged siege the Bactrian king threatened to call in the neighbouring Scythian hordes to his aid, and thus succeeded in inducing Antiochus to enter into a friendly treaty with him leaving him in possession of his kingdom, Antiochus then crossed the Hindu Kush (208 B. C.), and marched down the Kabul river towards India, where he spent three years in an ineffectual attempt to restore the Punjáb to his empire. Nearly a century had now elapsed since Seleucus left this province in the hands of Chandragupta; and the rule of the Magadha kings there has been traced above, from the Indian side of its history, down to Chandragupta's great grandson Kunála. In the early part of that century, Seleucus' son, Antiochus I., renewed friendly relations with Chandragupta's son, Amítragháta; and nothing had disturbed the good feeling on either side down to the time of their grandsons, Antiochus II. and the Great Ashoka. At the end of that century, Antiochus III. now found Subhaga-send, who appears to have been either Ashoka's son or his grandson, representing the old Magadha power here; and these two princes once more renewed the old treaties of their ancestors. At that time Ashoka had been dead about twenty years; and as Kunála remained in the religion of his father, Buddhism still continued to be the predominant religion of the Punjáb.

While the negotiations for peace between Antiochus and Enthydemus were in progress, Demetrius, the youthful son of the latter, visited the camp of the Syrian emperor, who formed a high opinion of him, and promised him his daughter in marriage. This marriage could not fail to have an important influence upon the young prince's future circumstances.

Not long afterwards we find Demetrius in full career of conquest in the Punjáb. He reduced the whole of the Indus provinces down to the delta, and also the further country eastwards and southwards through Rajputana and Guzerat, to the basins of the Nerbudda and the Tapti. He made old Sákala (Sangala), on the Rávi, his capital, and changed its name to Enthydemia in honour of his father. Some years had now gone by; and, in the mean-time, Enthydemus had been driven from his throne by Eucratides about the time when Mithradates I. began to reign in Parthia (*Justian* Book XLI), *i.e.*, B. C. 171.

Demetrius, backed by the full power of his Indian triumphs marched his army into Bactria to recover his father's throne, and laid siege to Balkh for several months. Eucratides having received seasonable succours, at length defeated the invading army, and followed up his victory until he had conquered some large portion of Demetrius' possessions in India. The strain of this and his numerous other wars at length proved too much for him; and Mithridates took advantage of this exhaustion, and, finally, in the reign of Heliodes the son of Eucratides, annexed Bactria to the rapidly extending Parthian empire about 135 B. C.

The extinction of the parent kingdom on the northern side of the mountains led to a variety of changes in the dependent Satrapies on their southern side. But presently a prince of enduring fame restored the eclipsed Greek power and, with his two successors, carried forward the hellenizing traditions of Alexander down to the time of their absorption in the new order of things in the middle of the century before the Christian era. This prince is Menander of the classical historians, the Milinda of the southern Buddhist literature.

Menander was born in the neighbourhood of Alexander's great colony of Alexandria ad Caucasum (Alasadda), under the hills to the north of Cabul. He began to reign while he was a young man, as his earlier coins show : the portraits on his later coins make him a man of mature years ; but none of them have the marks of old age. This accords with the tradition which assigns to him a reign of thirty years, and with another tradition that he died in camp. His coins have been found in great abundance and in great variety—indicating a long and prosperous reign—and over a very large extent of country, from Beghran and Cabul eastwards to Mathura on the Jumna, and southwards to the mouth of the Indus. This shows the credibility of the statement that he consolidated the whole of the Greek conquests in India under his rule ; while it also illustrated the statement of Greek authors that he was one of the two kings who advanced the Greek power farthest to the East. His coins were current in the sea-port town of Baroach, at the mouth of the Nerbudda river, during the first century of the Christian era. He was a wise and just king, and an eminently learned philosopher ; eloquent also, and very skilful and successful in controversy. He made the ancient city of Sákala in the heart of the Punjáb his capital; and he converted it into a kind of Indian Athens by the encouragement which he gave to learned men who resorted thither in great numbers, and with whom he spent much time in public discussions and religious investigations. The controversies of this Greek prince, well versed in the philosophy of his own nation, with the most learned of the Buddhist and other Indian philosophers of his time during the long period of thirty years, form an interesting episode in the religious history of India, and are suggestive of an interchange of oriental and western ideas, which could hardly be without some permanent result.

The legends of the Singhalese say that he became a convert to Buddhism; but his coins do not support this statement. They show him to have been a consistent worshipper of Minerva during the whole of his reign. Amongst his subjects, however, Buddhism was in a more flourishing condition than ever before; and upon his death his subjects are said to have given him the imperial funeral rights of a Chakravarti in imitation of the obsequies of Buddha.

During the reign of Menander, Pushpamitra, a Parthian ruling a portion of the country upon the Nerbudda, and the General of the forces of the last prince of Ashoka's line, slew his master and usurped his throne. By the advice of his Brahmin minister he persecuted the Buddhists throughout India from the Ganges to the Indus. In particular he massacred the Buddhist monks of Sákala and Pátaliputra and destroyed their monasteries. Menander delivered them from this oppressor, and raised them again to a state of high prosperity.

During the three centuries when these Greek kings reigned in Bactria and Bactrian India, a great movement was in progress amongst their Scythian neighbours making for their ultimate overthrow and supersession. It would be out of place here to relate the details of this movement. It will be enough to mark the progress of the two races whose influence was most directly felt in India.

The Saca tribes became troublesome from the earliest days of the Bactrian and Parthian revolts (B. C. 250). They were ultimately impelled southwards by the pressure of their northern neighbours the Tochari; and, passing along the south-eastern borders of Parthia and around Herat, they settled in the province to which they have permanently attached their name, Sistan (Seistan, Sakastene), "the abode of the Sakas." From this new home they sent forward detachments later on towards India; and, passing through southern Afghanistan (Arachosia) by the double route of the Ghazni Mountains and the Bolan pass, they struck the lower Indus and formed there the Indo-Scythian kingdom of the early historians.

The Tochari tribes then occupied Sogdiana, between the Jaxartes and the Oxus, and subsequently Bactria proper, between the Oxus and the Hindu Kush; and by about 126 B. C. they had driven the last of the Greek rulers of that province across the mountains into Afghanistan. Then, finally, following up these conquests, they themselves passed the great mountain barrier in the course of the succeeding half-century; and under Kadphises, their king, they extended their empire to the seashore of the Indian ocean southwards, and to Kashmir and the Punjáb eastwards, and ultimately to the river Jumna.

Upon his coins Kadphises calls himself "King of Kings, the great Saviour Kadphises," thus asserting a suzerainty over all the surviving remnants of Alexander's successors and all the separate tribes of the Tochari hordes. His name is added to that of Hermæus, the last of the Greek kings, upon the latest coins of that prince, thus indicating that he was left in possession of his kingdom as a regal satrap of the new empire after its conquest by Kadphises. Moreover, he issued gold coins, thus showing his independence of all external control; for this was one of the exclusive prerogatives of a paramount sovereign.

King Kadphises is an important personage from our present point of view. He represents a great revolution in the religious history of India, and a new starting point of religious thought and worship in a direction which has retained its predominance down to the present day. His people had been in possession of the country on both banks of the Oxus at this time for about a century, making this the meeting place of the commerce of India and China with Parthia and China, and all the world beyond, at the time when these nations represented the sources of the wealth of the eastern and of the luxuries of the western world, and where the intellectual wealth of mankind also found a common resting place and a new centre for its dissemination in the grand old "mother of cities." The religious surroundings in which he was brought up were also of a cosmopolitan character representing the intermingling of the Zoroastrianism of the older Persian period of his country's history with the Greek faiths of its more recent rulers, and with the polytheistic nature worship of his Scythian ancestors, and the all-embracing Buddhism of his Indian neighbours.

The principal subject upon the reverse side of the coins of Kadphises is the figure of the god **Shiva.** It appears there for the first time in the records of the religious history of Indra; but it is continuously repeated upon the coins of his Scythian successors. A good specimen of these reverses occurs on a large gold coin of this king. It has a bi-form androgynous standing figure of Shiva (Ardha-Naríshvara), with his hair coiled into a pointed top-knot (jaḍa), in the special fashion of this god, with a rayed nimbus around his head to indicate that he is the solar divinity, and wearing a garland of skulls suspended from his right shoulder, holding, moreover, a trident, Shiva's special weapon, in his right hand, with his left hand resting on the bull, Nandi, Shiva's constant companion, dressed with housings like the sapient bulls taken about down to the present time by the professional mendicants of the Shaivas.

Kadphises was succeeded by Kanishka (Kanerki), in whose reign the worship of the sun underwent some modification. The legend on some of his reverses is " Helios," the sun of the Greeks, written, like all the other legends of these kings in the Greek language and character : on others it is " Mithro," " Mioro," or " Miiro," the sun of the Persians, wearing a royal fillet on his head surrounded by a rayed nimbus, and clothed in Persian costume. Some of his coins have the legend " Mao," the moon of the old Persian language, accompanied by a figure with the horns of the moon rising from his head and sometimes from his shoulders. The legend on some of his coins is " Nanaia," " Nana," or " Nana Rao," accompanied by a female figure, the goddess Anaitis or Anahid of the Persians representing that Artemis, the twin sister of Phœbus Apollo, whose worship Artaxerxes Mnemon made great efforts to spread throughout his dominions, and in whose temple in Elymais, in the second book of Maccabees, king Antiochus was slain. Her figure has sometimes four arms; and this is the earliest appearance on these pictures of a many-membered figure to signify superhuman power : in one of her hands she holds a royal fillet, in another she has Shiva's trident, and in a third Shiva's small drum. Sometimes she has a fawn standing on its hind legs by her side, which is another of Shiva's emblems.

Huvishka, the successor of Kanishka, returned in the main to the simpler form of worship of Kadphises' Shiva ; although both he and his successors have the legends " Mithra," " Mao," and " Nana " in some of their reverses.

These Indo-Scythian kings have sometimes been described as zealous Buddhists. Their coins, which are the official and contemporaneous records of their religion, do not support this view. Buddhist emblems are not entirely absent; but they are found on only a few small copper coins of

Kanishka amongst the many thousands of these Scythian coins which have been discovered. These few are, nevertheless, sufficient to point to the religious tolerance of these kings while they themselves continued to be staunch worshippers of Shiva throughout their career.

The coins of Kadphises were minted in immense quantities sufficient to supply the necessities of the people for many generations. To this day they are met with in the bazaars of Northern India, and they are found buried in the earth throughout that part of the country. They served, therefore, from the beginning as a popular medium for the propagation of the new religion amongst the masses of the people who used them in their daily bazaar transactions and familiarized them with Shiva's form and symbols.

Shiva is usually represented as the destructive power of the Hindu triad; but he is in reality much more than that: like the sun in nature he has also nourishing, recuperating, and regenerating attributes: in the Shaiva literature he is a creator and a preserver, as well as a destroyer. Brahmá, the author of the first creation, completed his work when he had produced the first generation of created things: and he then retired to rest until the beginning of a new dispensation. During the intervening time for the reproduction of each succeeding generation, the secondary creative attribute of procreation in all the spheres of nature belongs to Shiva. He is moreover the rival of Vishnu in his attribute of preservation to all who regard that god as a separate and independent divinity; for Shiva, like Apollo, is the averter of evil, as well as the god of destruction, the healer of diseases also, and the protector of all medicinal herbs: and, again, like Apollo, he has the special care of all flocks and herds.

The worship of Phœbus Apollo had been cultivated in Sogdiana for several centuries before the time of Kadphises: the great treasures of the Milesian Apollo, whose oracle was second only to that of Delphi together with the whole race of the priests attached to his temple, had been carried into Persia by Xerxes on his return from his expedition against Greece: and a new strong walled city, a new Branchide, had been founded for them midway between Balkh and Samarkand, which was endowed with lands and surrounded with sacred groves. There they were found by Alexander, still keeping up their old worship and home customs, and speaking the Greek language modified by the vernacular tongue. As the reputed ancestor and cherished patron of the Seleucid kings, the worship of Apollo was naturally fostered by them in these distant satrapies of their empire, and especially so during the period when Antiochus I. ruled them as a subordinate kingdom in the lifetime of his father (B. C. 293 to 281). Later on another temple of this god was established farther to the north amongst the Scythians beyond the Jaxartes. It would be no difficult thing for the hellenized nomads of Kadphises race to recognize in the splendid Phœbus Apollo thus presented to them their own old solar divinity, that god of their ancestors by whom the Queen of the Massgetæ swore her oath to Cyrus: and in the course of those centuries the ancient traditions of that divinity would readily entwine themselves around this new form of the god of their fathers.

Here then we find the making of Shiva whose origin is nowhere distinctly made known to us in the early Indian record, but who appears later on in the bi-form androgynous Brahmá of Manu's code, and more clearly in the still later legends of the Puránas, which literally interpret the mysterious effigy on these Scythian coins. The glorious Apollo of the Milesians was transformed into the "great god" (Mahádeva) of India by successive stages: first, by the identification of the Mithra of the old Persians with the Apollo of the Greeks; secondly, by his elevation to the supreme place in the court religion of the Seleucid kings and their semi-orientalized Bactrian successors;

thirdly, by his acceptance as the representative of their own primitive sun-god by the Scythians; to be finally introduced into his new home in India, destined there to occupy the supreme place in its religious firmament for two successive millenniums. Nor was he brought there, by Kadphises as a totally unknown guest; for, in his simpler Greek form, Apollo had a place on the coins of Enthydemus, Demetrius, Eucratides, Agathocles, Apollodotus and Hermæus down to the last years of Greek rule in India.

It is quite in accordance with these facts, and is also a confirmation of their historical value, that legends of the solar worship of the early centuries of the Christian era, and ruins of ancient temples of the sun should be found in various places along the track of these mighty conquerors from Cabul through Jalalabad and Peshawur to Kashmir, and from Kashmir down the course of the Rávi to Multan, and from Taxila in the neighbourhood of the great ford of the upper Indus at Attock through Umballa and Thanesar to Muthra (Mathurá) on the Jumná, and still farther eastwards to Shahabad, Budda-Gáya and Behar, and far southwards also to Somnáth in Kathiawar and Saurishtra in the Dakhan.

On the other hand, the religious toleration of these kings is illustrated by the colossal Buddhist topes of Beghram, Peshawur, Taxila, and Manikyala; for their foundation contained caskets of Kadphises, Kanishka, Huvishka, and Vásudeva. In addition to these we have the invaluable Muthra (Mathurá) inscriptions recording gifts of temple-pillars and statuary to both Buddhist and Jaina buildings erected by disciples of those sects, containing the names of these same Scythian kings as the reigning kings there at the time when these donations were made, together with the dates of the donations.

Moreover the ruins are still in existence of the immense memorial mound of Kanishka at Peshawur with its accompanying Buddhist monastery, and also of the Buddhist monastery of Huvishka at Muthrá, and to crown this evidence, the last general council of the Buddhists, at which the canon of the Buddhist sacred books was finally settled, was held in Kashmir under the protection of Kanishka.

The date of these Indo-Scythian kings, and the great revolution effected by their invasion in the political and religious history of India, is ascertained by means of two kinds of evidence, namely, (1) from Roman coins, whose dates are well known ; and (2) from dated contemporaneous inscriptions engraved upon ancient monuments.

As a good example of the first class of this evidence, seven silver Roman coins have been found deposited in a memorial mound (tope, stúpa), erected by one of these kings at Manikyála in the Punjáb, together with a few coins of Kadphises and many others of Kanishka. The date of these Roman coins thus deposited, after the fashion which has survived to the present time in laying the foundation stones of our public buildings, tells us the date of the erection of these buildings, and also the date of the kings whose current coins are found deposited with them. Three of these Roman coins are denarii of Julius Cæsar, Augustus, and Mark Antony. They belong therefore to the last half of the century before the Christian era ; and the end of the period covered by these coins may therefore be taken as the date of Kanishka's reign.

The second kind of evidence referred to above is obtained from the dated inscriptions of these kings. An inscription found in the southern great tope of Manikyála states that it was built in the Samvat year 18, during the reign of Kanishka. Similarly, numerous dated inscriptions have been obtained from the ruins of Mathurá referred to above, giving full particulars of the serial day and month, the season of the year, and the era-year or Samvat of the gift recorded in them, together with the name of the reigning king. The Samvat, to which these dates are to be referred, is most probably, perhaps certainly, the Vikrama-Samvat commencing in the year 57 B. C., the initial year of Kanishka's reign. Upon this basis the reign of the four earliest of these kings, as gathered from their inscriptions, may be arranged as follows:—

(1) Kadphises reigned down to B. C. 57.

(2) Kanishka reigned down to B. C. 57 to B. C. 27.

(3) Huvishka reigned down to B. C. 27 to A. D. 13.

(4) Vámadeva reigned down to A. D. 13 to A. D. 41.

The excavations at Mathurá have yielded Jaina and Buddhist statues in equally large numbers, some of them of colossal size, together with many richly carved railings which usually encircle the larger memorial mounds of the Buddhists; and similarly the gifts recorded in the inscriptions were made by people of both these sects. A "splendid" Buddhist monastery of king Huvishka has also been discovered amongst the ruins. Thus these monuments, together with the coins found with them, afford ample proof that the Jaina and Buddhist religions flourished in great vigour side by side under the patronage of these Scythian kings upon the western bank of the Jumna at the commencement of the Christian era. We have previously found the ascetics of both these sects dwelling at Taxila in the north-western extremity of the Punjab three centuries before this period at the time of Alexander's invasion; and there appears to be no reason to doubt that these two classes had continued to enjoy equal freedom in the profession of their religions throughout the intermediate period in these parts of India.

Moreover, we may here remind ourselves that we have now come back to the western limits of the region where we left the sages of the Rig-veda performing their hymned sacrifices to a pantheon of nature-gods not entirely dissimilar to the system of divinities prevailing amongst the mixed Bactrian and Scythian, Persian and Greek people of the land of the Oxus during the centuries when Kadphises' ancestors

were moulding the Milesian Apollo into the form of that
Shiva which he ultimately brought with him to India; and,
before proceeding to the next stage of development, we may
also recall the fact that Shiva was quite unknown to the
Vedic sages.   He does not enter into the Hindu mythology
until a comparatively late period of the Scythian conquest.

It is said that the Tochari can be traced by inscriptions
down to A.D. 213 and 239; and the Chinese records
have statements to the same effect.   The prevalence of
Buddhism is also mentioned in those records; and several
classical authors, such as Clemens of Alexandria, (A.D.
180 to 230), and the Neo-Platonist Porphyry, (A.D. 270 to
305), bring down this record to the beginning of the fourth
century.   But the Scythian ascendancy was in a condition
of decay at that time; and by A.D. 319 the paramount
power had passed from them into the hands of the Gupta
kings to remain with them for the succeeding three
centuries.

The territory of the Guptas, at the time of its full extension, was conterminous with the whole basin of the
Ganges and its affluents.   In the middle of the fifth
century they ruled over the whole of Northern India from
Gujerat to the Gangetic delta; and for at least some
portion of their period the petty kings of the Nerbudda
region were tributary to them.   The capital of this great
empire was still the old Patna (Pátaliputra) of Gautama
Buddha's days.

Buddhism maintained its ground to a considerable extent
during the whole of the Gupta period, but not without
various vicissitudes.   At least three of the Guptas supported the orthodox Vedic religion of the Brahmins, and
offered great sacrifices to the old gods Indra, Varuna, and
Yama; and two of them were worshippers of the more recent
divinities, Krishṇa and Vishṇu.   Under one of them Buddhism suffered grievous persecution; and another of them
was a successful student of the secret and incommunicable

14

" wisdom of the Tantras." It was during this period that Buddhism was introduced into Nepal and Tibet; but it was laden with the Tantrika ritual and the gross sensual form of the worship of Shiva and his consort which have remained engrafted on it to the present day.

The Shiva brought to India by Kadphises was an androgynous divinity formed by the unification of the Phœbus Apollo introduced into Bactria by Xerxes with his twin-sister Artemis (Nanaia) introduced by Artaxerxes. On the reverses of Kanishka's coins the bi-form figure has disappeared; a bisection of its two halves has taken place, and each of them appears there as a separate divinity, sometimes standing, sometimes sitting, but each of them, in some instances, with four arms, bearing the usual emblems of Shiva, to indicate their superhuman power, and both with a nimbus around their heads to indicate that they are forms of the solar divinity; or, rather, forms of the sun and his female complement, or Shakti, who bears a cornucopia in his hand to indicate that she is the earth-goddess, the nourisher of all living beings, the many-breast-ed Diana of the Ephesians; and having the title of "Ardokro" (Arddhárka), "the half-sun" to show that she has sprung from her husband's side. The same legend is repeated in the Puránas with several variations of its details, in one of which, the Vishṇu Puráṇa, this bi-fold god is distinctly named "Rudra, radiant as the noon-tide sun, fierce and of vast bulk."

Hitherto no female divinity has been particularly promi-nent upon these coins; but in the Gupta period a great change came over the religious ideas of Northern India; for the principal feature of the Gupta coins is the absence of male divinities from their reverses. The male side of the bi-form Shiva of Kadphises has disappeared, and its female side now stands alone. There are several symbols on these reverses which show plainly who this female divinity is. On some of them her head is encircled with the nimbus of the solar divinity, on others, she bears Shiva's trident in her hand: on some of them she feeds a peacock, the vehicle of Skanda, the son of Shiva; and in others, she is mounted on the peacock; in many of them, she carries the cornucopia of the earth-goddess in her left hand, and holds out a royal fillet in her right hand. There is also another very distinct mark, for some of these coins represent her riding on a lion, which is the special vehicle of Durgá, the fierce consort of the still fiercer Shiva, and, to complete her identification, she sometimes sits on the high-backed chair of Nanaia as in the Kanishka coins, which does not appear in any other connection in these Indian mintages.

Much valuable information regarding the state of religion in Northern India at this period is obtained from the record of the travels of a Chinese pilgrim, Fa Hian, who came on purpose to visit the sacred places connected with the life of Buddha, and to collect Buddhist books to take back with him to China. He left China in A.D. 399, and returned there in A.D. 415. He visited old Patna (Pátaliputra) in the early part of the reign of Chandra-gupta-Vikramáditya, who was a munificent patron of the Buddhists, and, at the same time, a believer in the spiritual power of the Jaina divinities. All religious sects appear to have been treated with full toleration along the route by which he travelled; but the Buddhists greatly exceeded the other sects in point of numbers at that time. The annual festival of Buddha was celebrated at Patna with great pomp, while he (Fa Hian) was in that city. He specially mentions that the " Brahmans came to visit Buddha (Foe) on these occasions," and that the whole population of the city, and of the surrounding country, and " from all the provinces " joined in the festivities. From Patna he continued his journey down to the mouth of the Ganges, where he took ship and passed on to Ceylon.

About two centuries later another Chinese, Hwen-Thsang, paid India a similar visit, and extended his tour to Southern India. He left China in A.D. 629 and returned in 645. He came to India by the Tashkand, Samarkand, Balkh and Bamian route, and returned thither by way of Ghazni and the Helmand crossing the Hindu-Kush,* by the Khawak Pass above Kunduz,† and through Badakshan across the Pamirs to Kashgar.

His route in Northern India extended from the neighbourhood of Kabul down to Atrek on the Indus and across the Punjab through Jalandhara to Muttra (Mathurá) on the Jumna, where he found Buddhism to be the preponderating religion. There were also a few temples of various Hindu gods flourishing in its midst. At Thanesar, a hundred miles to the north of Muttra, the religious condition of the people was reversed; there were only three Buddhist establishments there, while there were " some hundred" temples of the Hindu gods, and sectaries of various kinds in great number. Farther east, across the Ganges, he found the temples of the gods in considerable numbers; but the Buddhist establishments outnumbered them. At Kanouj (Kanya Kubja) he found a Rajput King reigning, who had obtained a throne by election. This was Shiláditya-Shri Harshavardhana, the conqueror of the five Indies.‡ He was a great patron of Sanskrit literature, and promoted religion in all its forms. For the Buddhists, he erected very many memorial-mounds (stupas) and settled numerous Buddhist establishments along the course of the Ganges ; and (in the interest of the Jainas) he forbade the slaughter of animals for food throughout his empire. He also fed large numbers of people of all religions daily at his palace. Moreover, there was a great temple of the Sun§ at Kanouj at this time, and not far from

---

* Beal's *Buddhist Records, Introd.*, p. xix.
† Ward's *Oxus*, p. 274.
‡ *A. D. 610 to 650*, by Max Müller, but *A. D 606 or 607*, by Bendall.
§ Dual 1, p. 229.

it there was a temple of Shiva, both of them elegantly built and adorned with rich sculptures. There was also a large Buddhist monastery, two hundred feet high, in the close neighbourhood of these temples, in which there was a colossal bronze statue of Buddha, thirty feet high, decorated with costly gems, and its four walls were sculptured with pictures of the various incidents of Buddha's life.

At Oudh (Ayodhyá), the old home of Ráma, the hero of the Rámáyana epic and of the solar race of kings, he found one hundred Buddhist establishments and ten temples of the gods of the Brahmins. At Allahabad (Pray'ga), however, the ancient capital of Vikrama, the hero of Kalidása's drama "Vikramorvashí," and the lunar race of kings, on the other hand, there were only two small Buddhist establishments with several Brahminical temples, one of which was beautifully ornamented and has become famous for its many miracles and as a popular place for the self-immolation of its worshippers practised there from very ancient times. "The undecaying banyan tree" of this temple is still an object of worship at Allahabad.[*] At Kausambí, another ancient place on the Jumna (the scene of Bána's drama, the Ratnávalí), Hwen-Thsang found the ten old Buddhist establishments deserted and in ruins, while there were fifty Brahminical temples there, the number of whose votaries was "enormous." In an old palace in this place there was a large Buddhist chapel which had a sandal-wood statue of Buddha under a stone canopy.

SALEM,   THOS. FOULKES.
24th January 1900.

---

[*] Beal 1, p. 282.

(D.)—ARCHITECTURE.

The Dravidian or Carnatic style comprises nine-tenths of the architectural objects in the whole of peninsular India, though it is actually confined for the most part to a small angle of it in the south. The style shows the ancient inhabitants of the south to have been one of the chief building races of the world. The Dravidians are constructive as the Aryans are literary. The typical Dravidian style consists of a square base ornamented with pilasters externally and containing the cell in which the image or emblem of the deity is placed. Above this rises a pyramid the general outline of which is straight-lined, but always divided into storeys; ·in small temples [còil, pagoda] generally three, but frequently, as in the great pagoda at Tanjore, into as many as fourteen storeys. Upwards the building terminates in a small dome of polygonal or circular shape. The second feature belonging to Dravidian temples consists in the great gateways, or gopoorams which are frequently more important in size than the vimaunams or pyramids themselves. They form the entrance through the large circumvallating wall [praucauram]. Their outline and general design is the same as that of the temples, except that in plan they are generally twice as wide as they are deep, and are always crowned by an oblong roof instead of a circular dome [goombaz]. In the Dravidian style again the temple almost invariably includes, beside the vimaunam or towered shrine and the gopooram or gateway, the mantapam or porch leading to the shrine; the choultry or pillared hall; numerous other buildings; elegant stamb-hams or pillars bearing the images or flags [dhwajam] of the gods, or numberless lamps all connected with the temple worship and service [poojah]; tanks and gardens and avenues [shaulay] of palms [taur] and sacred trees [poonyoshadhy]; all within the temple enclosure. The Dravidian form of design has apparently arisen from a form of building in receding terraces which prevailed in earlier times, though existing only in wood. In such early forms it is to be concluded that the basement was probably a pillared hall like those of Buddhist [booddha] monasteries [vihauram] found in Burmah at the present day. Above this was apparently a smaller hall, with detached cells in the edge of the platform on which it stood ; though whether these were chapels, or sleeping apartments, or cooking rooms, cannot now be determined. In the oldest buildings belonging to the style, the cells are still observable detached from the vimaunam and used as chapels. Later the cells are only semi-detached, and afterwards they become mere ornaments of the pyramid. Another feature by which this style is to be recognized is the double curve of the cornices. In all other Indian styles the cornice is straight-lined and sloping downwards to throw off the wet. In the Dravidian style they are universally formed with a double curvature. In connection with this style, it is necessary to point out that no Dravidian architect uses the arch as part of his art. According to a Tamil proverb, an arch never sleeps. An arch in fact contains in its principle an active force, always tending to thrust outwards. A pillar supporting a beam is on the contrary in stable equilibrium ; and the Tamulians prefer it, though its use frequently limits their interiors to an undesirable extent. When they find it necessary to cover larger spaces than can be done by single stones, they bracket out one stone beyond another, as was done in ancient Etruria and Greece, till the stones approach near enough to be covered by one stone. The special exhibition of Dravidian architecture known as the south-east style arose under the Chola or Tanjore king in the eleventh century A.D., when nearly all the great temples to Shiva in Southern India were built, and it continued in use in the twelfth and thirteenth centuries, during which time the great temples to Vishnoo were erected. Up to the beginning of the sixteenth century these temples remained almost unchanged; but at that time all Southern India became subject to the kings of Vijayanagar, and Krishnaroya, A.D. 1509—30, rebuilt or added to most of the great buildings of the south. The chief feature of the architecture of this later period is the construction of the enormous gopooram which are so conspicuous at Conjeeveram, Chidambaram, and Shree-rungam. All these were built by Krishnaroya, they do not form part of the original south-east style, but were intended as fortifications to protect the shrines from foreign invaders. The following may be taken as a descriptive catalogue of the chief present South Indian specimens of Dravidian architecture.—(i) First, the Dravidian rock-cut temples at Mahavallipore [seven pagodas]; (ii) Secondly, Dravidian temples of the ordinary description. Those at Chidambaram, Kumbakonam, Conjeeveram, Madura, Peroor, Rameshwaram, Srirungam, Tanjore, Tinnevelly, Trivellore, and Vijayanagar may be taken as typical. The temple at Chidambaram is one of the most venerated, and has also the reputation of being one of the most ancient temples in Southern India. This temple has been aggregated at different ages. At Kumbakonam there is a fine gopooram. The two towns, Great and Small Conjeeveram, possess groups of temples as picturesque and nearly as vast as any to be found elsewhere. The great temple at the first-named place possesses some remarkable gopooram. At Madura the most important of Tirumala Nayakka's original buildings is the celebrated choultry which he built for the reception of the presiding deity of the place. The great temple at Madura is, however, a larger and far more important building than the choultry, and it also owes all its magnificence to Tirumala Nayakka. Although the temple at Peroor, near Coimbatore, can only rank among the second class as regards size, it possesses a portico of extreme interest to architectural history. Of Rameshwaram it may be said that in no other temple has the same amount of patient industry been exhibited. It was begun and finished on a previously settled plan, as regularly and as undeviatingly carried out as that at Tanjore, but on a principle diametrically opposed to it. It is double the dimensions of Tanjore and has ten times its elaboration. The chief ornament of this temple resides in its corridors. Srirungam is certainly the largest, and, of its principle of design could be reverse would be one of the finest temples in the south of India. Here the central enclosure is quite as insignificant as that at Trivellore. Tanjore has a very celebrated temple. In nine cases out of ten, Dravidian temples are a fortuitous aggregation of parts, arranged without plan, as accident dictated at the time of their erection. The principal exception to this rule is to be found at Tanjore. The great pagoda there was commenced on a well-defined plan, which was persevered in till its completion. One of the peculiarities of the Tanjore temple is that all the sculptures of the gopoorams belong to the religion of Vishnu, while everything in the courtyard is dedicated to the worship of Shiva. Tinnevelly temple also has the advantage of having been built on one plan, and at one time without subsequent alteration or change. The great thousand-pillared portico in the temple is well known. Trivellore is about 30 miles west of Madras. The nucleus was a small village temple drawn to the same scale as the plan of Tanjore. It, however, at some subsequent period, became enriched and a second or outer court was added. Additions were again made at some subsequent date. The buildings mentioned in the above catalogue are in number rather more than one-third of the great Dravidian temples known

15

to exist in the Presidency. Of the remainder, none have vimaunams like that of Tanjore, nor corridors [praucauram] like those of Rameshwaram; but several have gopoorams quite equal to or exceeding those mentioned above and many have mantapams of great beauty and extent. Several, such as Avadaiyarkovil, Tauramungalam, Virinjipooram, and others, possess features unsurpassed by any in the south, especially the first-named, which may, perhaps, be considered as one of the most elegant of its class as well as one of the oldest. (iii) Thirdly, Forts. Among the most remarkable of these are those of Dindigul, Ginjee, Oodayagherry, Palamcottah, Penucondah, Seringapatam, Trichinopoly, and Vellore; with the droogs or hill forts in the Baramahaul, Mysore, Canara, &c. Many of these are very ancient. The works of Ginjee are specially interesting [aursham, chauvady, coil, dewal, droog, goody, gopooram, mantapam, pagoda, rath, stambham, vimaunam].—" b " Chalukyan architecture is easily distinguished from either the Dravidian or the North Indian. In plan the temples are generally star-shaped and of sixteen sides. The typical characteristic is that four of these sides are flat and form the principal faces, and between each of these are three facets arranged angularly. The same principle pervades the design of the spire, which is always rectilinear in outline, and generally made up of miniature repetitions of itself heaped one over the other. The peculiarity, however, which is more characteristic of the style than the outline of its form, is the great richness and beauty of the details with which the buildings are elaborated. The most celebrated temples are those at Halabidu in Mysore.

CHAPTER I.

(A)—DESCRIPTION OF THE SOUTH INDIAN RAILWAY.

The South Indian Railway is a metre (3′-3⅜″) gauge,

Extent of the S. I. Ry. System. single-track system comprising with worked lines a total length of 1,121 miles. The main line runs from the Beach at Madras to Tuticorin, a distance of 446 miles, serving the important towns of Chingleput, Cuddalore, Mayavaram, Kumbakonam, Tanjore, Trichinopoly, Dindigul and Madura. From Chingleput, 34½ miles from Madras, Egmore, a branch line, 39 miles in length, and which passes through the historic city of Conjeeveram, connects the main line with the Madras Railway at Arkonam. From Villupuram, 98¼ miles from Egmore, connection is made with the French Town of Pondicherry, 24 miles distant. Another line, 223½ miles in length, leaves at this Junction, and crossing the Madras Railway at Katpadi and Renigunta Junctions, meets the East Coast Railway at Gudur. At Pakala Junction on this branch, a line 142 miles long, forms a connection with the Southern Mahratta Railway at Dharmavaram. At Mayavaram, 174 miles from Egmore, a branch railway, 54 miles in length, takes off for Mutupet. From Peralam on the Mayavaram-Mutupet Railway, a short line of 15 miles gives railway facilities to the French port of Karaikkal. Tanjore, 217½ miles from Egmore, is the junction with a 48-mile branch to the large port of Negapatam ; and from Trichinopoly 248½ miles from Egmore, a line 88 miles in length, gives another connection with the Madras Railway at Erode. At

Maniyachi Junction, a branch, 19 miles in length, serves Tinnevelly and Palamcottah, through which latter town passes the road to Trevandram, the capital of Travancore State. A railway, some 100 miles in length, which will form a portion of the express route between India and Ceylon, is about to be made from Madura to the mainland coast at Palks Straits; and another extension, slightly longer, is to be made from Tinnevelly to Quilon on the West Coast. It is also probable that the Mayavaram-Mutupet Railway will be continued to Avadayarkovil.

The South Indian Railway system has developed from the amalgamation and extension of two **History of the** prior lines, the "Great Southern of **S. I. Ry.** India" connecting Negapatam and Erode, and the "Indian Tramway" extending from Conjeevaram to Arkonam. The former of these railways was commenced in May 1859 and was completed on the 5'-6" gauge in December 1867, the latter a 3'-6" gauge line was begun in March 1864 and was completed in May 1865, its name being subsequently changed to the "Carnatic Railway." Later on, the Great Southern of India Railway Company was entrusted with the construction on the metre gauge, of a line from the Coleroon river to Tanjore and from Trichinopoly to Tuticorin and Tinnevelly, while the Carnatic Railway Company undertook the making of a line on this gauge from the Coleroon to Madras. On July 1st, 1874, the two Companies were amalgamated under the name of the South Indian Railway Company and this was followed by the conversion of their respective lines to the metre gauge. The extensions from Trichinopoly to Tuticorin and Tinnevelly, and from Tanjore to Madras were opened in January 1876 and July 1879 respectively. In December 1879 a branch line from Villupuram to the French frontier on the Gingee river was opened in connection with a line constructed by

the French Government between the frontier and Pondicherry, and in January 1881 the old Tramway Company's
line was connected at Chingleput with the rest of the
system. The remaining lengths of the South Indian
Railway were opened on the following dates :—

Tirupati to Nellore ... September 1887.

Villupuram to Tirupati ... March 1891.

Pakala to Dharmavaram ... March 1892.

In April 1894 the Mayavaram-Mutupet Railway, which
is the property of the Tanjore District Board, was opened
for traffic and handed over for working to the South
Indian Railway Company.

The extensions from Villupuram to Nellore and Dharmavaram were made for the protection against famine
of certain districts which suffered severely in 1876-78.
The construction of the Mayavaram-Mutupet Railway,
which traverses the Cauvery delta, is due to the enterprise
of the Tanjore District Board. This corporation for years
past has levied a special land cess for the provision of
such railways as are required for the development of the
district, and funds are now sufficient to enable further
extensions to be undertaken. On the 1st January 1891 the
South Indian Railway was purchased by the Secretary of
State, and together with the Villupuram-Dharmavaram
and Pakala Nellore branches was handed over to the present
South Indian Railway Company for working, which Company, in addition to these lines, and the Mayavaram-
Mutupet Railway, also works the French lines from
the Gingee river to Pondicherry and from Peralam to
Karaikkal. On 1st November 1898, the section between
Nellore and Gudur was transferred to the East Coast
Railway after conversion to the standard 5'-6" gauge.

With the exception of the length between Vellore and
Dharmavaram, the whole of the South
Indian Railway system lies between
the Bay of Bengal and the Eastern

General descrip-
tion of country tra-
versed.

Ghâts, a mountain range averaging 1,500 feet in elevation and forming in the South the Eastern scarp of the Mysore plateau. The general scenery in the neighbour-hood of the coast is flat and somewhat monotonous; but inland, particularly in the proximity of the ghâts, the country becomes undulating and in places even moun-tainous. Between Madras and Trichinopoly, the line traverses alternating stretches of paddy (rice) fields, dry cultivation, and scrub jungle, the country, on the whole, being decidedly fertile. The landscape is occasionally diversified by low hills, sometimes in the form of solitary peaks of crystalline rock, and sometimes as continuous ranges, the former class of eminence being often crowned by a Hindu Temple, or by the remains of an ancient fort. Numerous tanks are also met with, which, before they have dried up under the demands of irrigation, form, with their fringes of palmyra and cocoa-nut palms, a prominent feature in the South Indian land-scape. When the tanks are exhausted, or in places where none exist, the ryots (agriculturists) may often be seen raising water from wells and channels with the assistance of bullocks, or by means of the picottah. This appliance consists of a balanced lever, suspended several feet from the ground on stout posts, and which is actuated by one or more men who, by moving along the beam, cause it to swing and thus raise or lower a bucket suspended from one end. From Porto Novo to Tanjore, Tanjore to Negapatam, and Mayavaram to Mutupet, it will be noticed that the country for miles is one enormous flat of paddy, the level being only broken by clumps of cocoanut or other fruit trees interspersed among the rice-fields. This area is known as the Cauvery delta, and is a large and extremely fertile alluvial plain falling gently towards the sea, and irrigated from artificial channels fed by the con-trolled waters of the river. So successfully is the water distributed that the Cauvery which, at Trichinopoly, is about half a mile wide is crossed at Mayavaram by the railway on a bridge of three spans of twenty feet.

At Ayyalur, 291 miles from Madras, the main line reaches its highest elevation (1,090 feet above sea level) in passing over the Sem Mullai hills. For several miles, on either side of the summit, the scenery is charming, particularly in the morning and evening, when the varying lights on the wooded hills are very beautiful. From here southwards the curious umbrella tree, so called from the mushroom-like growth of its foliage, is of frequent occurrence. After passing Madura the railway enters a district where large plains of black cotton soil or regar are met with. This is a fine, dark, highly argillaceous and adhesive soil which was probably at one time covered with luxuriant forest. The fertility of black cotton soil is generally very remarkable, and it is said that, in some districts, it has produced crops for 2000 years without manure, irrigation, or periods of fallow.

The branch line, which runs from Trichinopoly to Erode, passes for some 50 miles through extremely fertile country irrigated by the Cauvery; but, after traversing this tract, continues in a barren region for the remaining 37 miles of its length. The section of the railway, which ascends the Mysore plateau towards Dharmavaram, passes through picturesque but, on the whole, unfertile country. The scenery is, in many places grand, weird-shaped rocks and weathered boulders being piled up on every side in wild confusion, sometimes simulating fantastic forms, and sometimes threatening in their apparent instability, to crash down the hill-sides on the least disturbance of their tottering equilibrium.

As is naturally to be expected in the case of a railway, a long mileage of which crosses the drainage of the country near its outflow into the sea, many and large bridges are necessary to protect the line against flood damage. The

Bridging and floods.

extent of waterway originally provided was very insufficient; but, as this defect became apparent, the deficiency was remedied until it is now hoped that the line is safe from any but phenomenal floods. As an example of the severity of the inundations which have occurred, it may be mentioned that in November and December 1884 the railway was breached for an aggregate length of five miles and several large bridges were wrecked. The force of the floods was so great that six of the girders of a bridge of seven spans of 150 feet were broken up, and that a forty feet girder was found in the bed of a river about half a mile below the site of the bridge to which it belonged.

The mileage of the railway is measured from Egmore and is shown on the telegraph poles **System of shew-ing the mileage.** alongside the line. To identify mileages of the same value the number-plates on the branches bear a distinguishing letter. Thus $\frac{G}{V}\frac{}{14}$ denotes the Villupuram-Dharmavaram branch, and the fourteenth telegraph post in mile 210 from Egmore. On the main line no distinguishing letter is shown on the mileage-plate.

(B.)—INFORMATION FOR TRAVELLERS.

Southern India should be visited, if possible, during November, December, January and February, which are the coolest and pleasantest months in the year. During this period, the mean temperature below the Ghâts varies from 69° to 79°, with a daily range of about 20°. May is the hottest month, the thermometer occasionally registering as much as 110° in the shade and 170° in the sun. The greatest rainfall on the Eastern Coast of the Madras Presidency occurs during October and November. The total annual fall varies greatly in different places ; but an average of 35 inches is probably near the mark. The higher temperatures of the land over the sea surfaces during the day and the converse during the night produce the daily sea and land breezes, which, except during the full force of the monsoon, are gratefully felt on the Coromandel Coast.

Climatic temperature and rainfall.

The monsoons are properly the periodic winds which blow from the South-West from April to October, and from the North-East from about the middle of October to the end of February. The monsoons especially the North-East, are frequently ushered in by heavy gales, occasionally cyclonic, and produce the seasonable rain fall popularly known as the South-West and North-East monsoons. The elevation of the Western Ghâts is sufficient to deprive the South-West monsoon of most of its vapour, so that it produces but little rain on the Eastern side of these mountains. This monsoon produces the periodical rains with such unfailing certainty that agricultural distress, as the result of a bad season, is unknown. A similar condition, unfortunately, does not obtain with the North-East monsoon on which the greater portion of the Presidency is dependent for its rainfall

Monsoons.

The irregularity of its rainfall has forced cultivators to guard
against deficiency by the construction of tanks, and has induced
Government to undertake its large schemes of canal and river
irrigation.

Though the Carnatic may be said to enjoy an equable
climate, the temperature must be considered
as varying between hot and hotter. The
clothing required by travellers is therefore light; but, at the
same time, it is not advisable to adopt the extreme course of
wearing such thin clothes that the body is insufficiently protected against the sun, or the difference between day and night
temperatures. Light English summer clothes can generally be
worn with comfort during the cold weather on the plains in
Southern India, and there is no necessity to incur the expense
of a special Indian outfit. Warm clothes are necessary on the
hills, and, during the cold weather, in Northern India, where
it should be remembered that a sudden fall in temperature
occurs soon after sun down. Warm clothes should be easily
accessible, so that they can be worn directly a feeling of cold
is felt. When within the tropics, it is well to treat the sun with
respect, and, in addition to the proper protection of the head,
care should be taken that the spine is not exposed to the
prolonged action of the sun through an insufficient thickness of
clothes. A pad, four inches wide buttoning to the inside of
the coat from the collar to the small of the back, will afford the
necessary protection without inconvenience to the wearer. A
kummarband, or woollen waist belt, should be worn at night,
especially when travelling. Sun-hats are, of course, a necessity
for all Europeans, and can be purchased either in England or
India. The most convenient pattern for men is that known as
the Shikar hat, its one fault being its weight. Clothes of all
descriptions can be procured in the largest towns as Madras,
Bangalore and Secunderabad; and in most towns of any size
there are native tailors who can make-up shooting, riding, and
travelling clothes sufficiently well for wear in the country.

Travellers will find it very essential to take bedding with
them everywhere in India. A waterproof
valise containing a couple of blankets, a

Clothing.

Bedding.

razai or padded quilt, a pair of sheets and having a pocket to hold two pillows and sleeping clothes will be found the most convenient arrangement for railway travelling. It is also advisable to take a small tiffin or luncheon basket in the train, although it is not absolutely necessary when travelling on the main line of the South Indian Railway, where refreshment rooms are numerous, and ice and aerated waters are procurable on the day mail trains.

Tourist coupons. Messrs. Thomas Cook & Son and Messrs. Henry Gaze & Sons, under agreement with the South Indian Railway Company, issue first and second-class single journey coupons available for two months and return journey coupons available for six months to tourists visiting India, and third-class coupons for servants accompanying them to and from stations on this railway. These coupons are treated, in every respect, as ordinary paper tickets. Each coupon must bear the perforated stamp of Messrs. Thomas Cook & Son, or Messrs. Henry Gaze & Sons, as the case may be.

The holders of these coupons are allowed to break journey at any station within the distance for which the coupons are available, provided the line is not travelled over more than once in the same direction, and the period allowed free for the journey is not exceeded.

The ordinary rules as to luggage apply in all respects to the holders of these coupons. Any luggage in excess of the free allowance should be paid for by the holders of the coupons on the spot, before the journey commences, at the ordinary rates for excess luggage.

Booking of passengers. Passengers can be booked at intermediate stations only on condition that there shall be room in the train and class of carriages for which their tickets shall have been issued. To insure being booked, passengers should be at the station at least thirty minutes before the time mentioned in the tables. The door of the Booking office will be closed five minutes before the train is expected at the station. Passengers cannot be re-booked at roadside stations to proceed by the train in which they have arrived.

The scale of fares for passengers is as follows :—

	Rate per mile.	Minimum charge.
	Rs. a. p.	Rs. a. p.
For a first-class passenger	0 1 0	0 3 0
For a second-class do.	0 0 6	0 1 6
For a third-class do.	0 0 2	0 0 6

Children under three years of age travel free; above that and under twelve years of age are charged half-fare.

Fractions of miles and of annas are calculated as whole numbers.

Servants' Tickets. First and second-class passengers are advised not to keep their servants' tickets with them. The tickets should be given to their servants, so that they may produce them when called upon to do so.

The following charges will be made for servants travelling in the servants' compartments in addition to the ordinary third-class fare :—

For distances from 15 to 25 miles inclusive ... 1 anna.

,, ,, 25 to 50 ,, ,, ... 2 annas.

,, above 50 ,, ... 4 ,,

These tickets will not be issued for distances under 15 miles. Children are not allowed in these compartments.

Tickets. The tickets given to passengers on payment of their fares, will be required to be produced to the Company's servants or given up to them whenever demanded. Passengers unable or refusing to produce their tickets are liable to be charged the fare from the *most* distant station whence the train started. The tickets are not transferable, are only available for the station named thereon, and can only be used on the day or for the journey issued.

Tickets which have been torn or mutilated, particularly when the date or progressive number is off, will not be recognised and the holder will be charged the full fare.

A person to whom a ticket has been issued, and for whom there is not room available in the train for which the ticket was issued, shall, on returning the ticket within three hours after the departure of the train, be entitled to have his fare at once refunded.

Passengers who have purchased tickets and are unable to travel in consequence of their own private business or fault, should report the matter at once to the Station Master, get the tickets endorsed to the effect that they did not travel and apply to the Traffic Manager who will, if the circumstances of the case are of an exceptional nature, allow a refund of the amount paid for the *unused ticket*, less a commission of 10 per cent.

No return of any portion of the fare will be allowed on tickets used for part of a journey, except in cases where passengers cannot complete their journey, owing to accidents to trains or to any other default of the Company.

Examining tickets and change. Passengers are requested to examine their tickets before leaving the Booking Office counter, as mistakes in tickets or money will not be afterwards recognised.

Correction of charges. It must be distinctly understood that the Railway Company reserves the right to correct any charges that may have been incorrectly entered in railway receipts or tickets.

Claims. Notice of intention to prefer a claim for loss of, or damage to, luggage or parcels must be given in writing to the Station Master previous to removal from the railway premises, and a written statement of the nature of the damage received or of the articles missing should be sent to the Traffic Manager, Trichinopoly, without delay.

Break of Journey. Holders of single tickets for distances over 100 miles will be allowed one day extra for every additional 100 miles or part of 100 miles in the through distance, to enable them to break their journey if they wish to do so at any place along the route at which the train stops. Holders of single tickets between stations less than 100 miles apart will be allowed to halt at one or more stations on the route, provided they reach the place of destination within 24 hours from the time the ticket was issued. This break of journey can be made at one or more places along the route for one or more days at each provided the time of arrival at destination, reckoned at one day for every one hundred miles, from the place of starting to the place of destination, is not exceeded; but *it will be incumbent upon passengers breaking their journey immediately they alight, to have their tickets endorsed on the back at the halting station* to the effect that they broke their journey at that station. Each ticket so endorsed must bear the Station Master's signature and date, failing which passengers will be liable to be charged excess fare at destination for travelling on an out-of-date ticket.

Passengers will not be allowed to travel in superior class of carriage when the accommodation for which they hold tickets is fully occupied, unless the difference in fare is paid.

Passengers may either travel by the train following or the value of the ticket will be refunded if application be made.

Passengers wishing to exchange their tickets at a *starting station* for a superior class of carriage should return the ticket they originally purchased to the Booking clerk, who is authorized to issue a ticket for the higher class collecting only the difference of fare.

Passengers wishing to change to a superior class of carriage at an intermediate station, either for a part or the remainder of the journey, can do so with the permission of the Station Master, who will advise the Guard of the train to give the required information at the end of the journey. When passengers so travel, *the difference of fare only* should be collected and no excess penalty charged.

Travelling beyond destination. Any passenger who unintentionally travels beyond the distance for which he has paid fare, will be allowed to return to the station to which he was booked, on payment of a single fare for the distance over-ridden provided he returns by the next passenger train.

Waking passengers at night. As a matter of convenience, guards in charge of night passenger and mixed trains have been instructed to awake first and second class passengers at any station, on request of passengers to do so. It must be understood, however, that the Company accepts no responsibility in the matter.

In all cases of excess being paid, an exce s ticket should be

Excess fare tickets. obtained from the Station Master, and passengers are requested to satisfy themselves that the excess ticket specifies the amount paid.

Passengers who allege they have *lost or mislaid their tickets* and apply for a return of their fares, are requested to take notice that the Company do not hold themselves liable to make any return to passengers who, from neglect or any cause, fail to produce their tickets.

Each dog must be provided with a muzzle and collar, or

Dogs for despatch by rail without the owners accompanying them. chain, or the dog must be properly secured in a strong basket or crate. A full and legible address must be tendered with each consignment. Dogs are conveyed in special compartments provided for the purpose.

The charge for dogs in dog boxes or brake-vans   RS. A. P.

Rate for dogs. is for each dog for every 50 miles or any part of 50 miles ..   0 4 0

The charge for dogs in passenger carriages is for each dog for every 50 miles or any part of 50 miles 0 8 0

Food for dogs whilst on rail should be provided by the owner.

Food and water. Water will be obtained for them from the Company's water carriers at station where there is sufficient time.

No passenger is allowed to take any dog into a passenger

Dogs in passengers' carriages. carriage (unless the owner of the dog has reserved a carriage or compartment) except with the consent of the Station Master at the starting station, and also with the concurrence of fellow-passengers. Dogs so carried will be charged at double the dog rate for each animal. The acceptance of a dog at the double rate for conveyance with the owner at the starting station is subject to the condition that the dog shall be *removed if subsequently* objected to, no refund being given.

128

Cats, monkeys, &c., also **birds,** accompanying passengers are not to be considered as luggage, but must be separately charged for.

Live Animals.

The following are charged at the dog rates :—

(*a*) Puppies, cats, kittens, mongooses, ferrets, rabbits, monkeys, guinea-pigs, and other small animals not in cages separately for each animal.

(*b*) Live turkeys, geese, ducks, and other poultry, if not in baskets, hampers or coops, separately for each bird.

Conveyance of pet animals in passenger carriages with the owner.

Puppies, cats, kittens, mongooses, ferrets, rabbits, monkeys, guinea-pigs, and other small animals, will be allowed to be carried in passenger carriages *in cages only*, with the permission of the Station Master at the starting station, and also with the consent of the fellow-passengers, and then only on payment of double the dog rate for each animal, subject to the condition that they will be removed if subsequently objected to, no refund being given.

This prohibition does not apply to pet animals conveyed in reserved compartments or carriages or in private special trains ; but the number to be taken by the owner into a reserved compartment must not exceed three cages.

Bicycles, Tricycles, Perambulators, etc.

On the South Indian Railway packed bicycles and tricycles are charged at full parcels rates.

The charge for an unpacked bicycle shall be as for one maund and that for an unpacked perambulator or tricycle shall be as for two maunds if accompanying the owner as luggage at these weights, subject to the ordinary free allowance.

Bicycles and tricycles are carried at Company's risk if packed in cases or protected by wood work, and at owner's risk if not so packed. Bicycles and tricycles merely packed in straw or gunny are to be considered as unpacked.

Bicycles and tricycles are not allowed to be taken in carriages with owners, but must always be loaded in the guard's van. When conveyed by passenger trains with owners, they may be taken out of the guard's van at any station short of destination at which the owner may wish and is entitled to break his journey free of extra cost.

Luggage should be delivered twenty minutes before train time to be booked.

Free allowance of Passengers' Luggage. Luggage accompanying passengers will be weighed, and after a deduction has been made of the weight allowed free by the Company, the balance will be charged for. In the case of first- and second-class passengers, the bundle of rugs, tiffin baskets, and small hand-bags, walking sticks, or umbrellas, and in the case of third-class passengers the razai or blanket, which passengers usually take into the carriage with them for their requirements on the journey, shall not be weighed. Furniture, live animals, treasure, opium, indigo, dangerous goods, wet skins, and other offensive articles, are not considered as luggage. The company reserves the right to refuse to receive for conveyance as passengers' luggage bulky articles which it would be inconvenient to carry as luggage by passenger train.

The free allowance of luggage for first-class passengers is $1\frac{1}{2}$ maunds; for second-class passengers 30 seers, and for third-class 15 seers.

Passengers' Luggage. Calculation of charges in through booking where the free allowance differs :—In cases where the class of ticket, or the free allowance differs in through booking, charges on passengers' excess luggage will be calculated at the through rate on the through distance, granting the lowest free allowance.

No free allowance on unbooked Luggage. All passengers neglecting or failing to obtain a ticket for luggage at the station where he purchases a ticket for himself will be required to pay at destination for the gross weight of the luggage, and no allowance whatever will be made.

No luggage is allowed in the carriages, which cannot be placed under the seat occupied by the owner. Station Masters and guards are required to remove all packages which cannot be deposited under the seat.

Luggage will not be accepted and booked at the Beach, Fort, Park, Chetpat, and Kodambakam stations; but passengers using

17

those stations are allowed to take with them small **packages** under 30 lbs. in weight that can go under the seat of a **carriage**.

The charge for excess luggage must be prepaid at the booking station, and to insure its being sent away it mûst be delivered at that station twenty minutes before the time announced for the departure of the train. Passengers not conforming to the rule run the risk of travelling without their luggage being sent in the same train.

It is particularly requested that each package of luggage be well secured and plainly addressed in **Luggage to be** English with the name of the owner and **addressed.** destination; in the absence of which the Company will not be responsible for damage or loss.

Passengers intending to break their journey at one or more places *en route* may either book their lug- **Booking Luggage** gage to accompany them throughout, or **in advance.** book the heavy portion, or the whole direct to the station for which they have taken tickets. Luggage booked through to destination will be allowed to remain at the station free of charge up to the day on which (after allowing for break of journey) the passenger would be due to arrive, after which it will be charged at the rate for left luggage.

Passengers requiring their luggage at stations where they intend to break journey should give to the **Luggage required** Station Master or clerk, at the commence- **en route.** ment of the journey, the names of the stations at which halts will be made, and the places will be entered on the back of the luggage ticket. When starting from such halting places, any luggage in excess of the quantity booked at the commencement of the journey, will be booked and charged at the luggage rates. Passengers cannot be permitted to take with them any portion of their luggage in the Company's charge, unless they consent to relinquish the luggage ticket unconditionally, as the Company is liable for the safe custody of such luggage until the luggage ticket is given up.

Passengers desiring to leave their luggage until called for, at the station to which it is booked, may **Left Luggage.** do so at the following rates :—

2 annas per package for the first twenty-four hours or part
of twenty-four hours.

1 anna per package for each subsequent day or part
of a day.

*The Company is not responsible for the loss, destruction or
deterioration of any luggage belonging to,*

Responsibility for Luggage. *or in charge of, a passenger, unless a railway servant has booked and given a receipt therefor.*

Unclaimed Articles found in railway carriages, or at stations, will be kept at the station where found forty-eight hours, and if not then claimed will be sent to the Lost Property Office at Trichinopoly Junction. Applications concerning *lost property* so lost should be made to the nearest Station Master, or to the Traffic Manager, Trichinopoly.

A fee of 2 annas will be charged for each article of luggage when claimed from the Lost Luggage Office ; and, if articles be not claimed within one month, an additional storage charge of As. 4 per month, or portion of a month afterwards, will be made. All lost luggage, if not claimed within six months, will be sold by the Company to pay expenses.

The cost of transmitting telegrams giving directions regarding luggage or property that has been left at any of the Company's stations or in trains must be borne by the owner.

No part of a consignment booked as passenger's luggage left in charge of the Company, can be delivered unless the owner or holder of the luggage tickets delivers up the ticket granted at the forwarding station.

Penalty for Offensive or Dangerous goods :—

(*a*) No person shall take with him upon the railway any offensive or dangerous goods, such as gunpowder, lucifer or congreve matches, vitriol, ardent spirits, turpentine, naphtha, sulphuric acid, gun cotton or other articles of an explosive or highly combustible nature without giving notice of their nature to the Station Master or other railway servant in charge of the place where he brings the goods on the railway.

(*b*) And no person shall tender or deliver any such goods

for carriage upon the railway without distinctly mark-
ing their nature on the outside of the package containing them, or otherwise giving notice in writing of
their nature to the railway servant to whom he tenders
or delivers them. Any one guilty of these offences
will be liable to a fine which may extend to Rs. 500,
and shall also be responsible for any loss, injury or
damage which may be caused by reason of such goods
having been brought upon the railway. (See Secs. 59
and 67 of the Indian Railway Act of 1890.)

Smoking. Any traveller who smokes without the consent of his fellow-passengers, if any, in the same compartment (except in a compartment specially
provided for the purpose), is liable to be punished with a fine
which may extend to Rs. 20.

Fees to Railway servants. The Company's servants are prohibited
from receiving any gratuity under pain of
dismissal.

Refreshment Rooms. Guards are authorized on requisition by first- and second-class
passengers to order meals at the refresh-
ment rooms, but to prevent disappointment telegraphic notice ought to be given
at least six hours before a meal is required. For tariff rates, see
page 141.

Sleeping Accommodation for Europeans is provided at Villupuram, Negapatam, Trichinopoly Junction and Madura stations
at the following charges :—

	RS.	A.	P.
Not exceeding three hours for each adult	0	8	0
And for each child of twelve years and under	0	4	0
Exceeding three hours and not exceeding twenty-four hours or *one night only* for each adult	1	0	0
And for each child of twelve years and under	0	8	0

Dogs are not allowed inside these rooms.—Punkah-
pullers and hot and cold water baths are charged as extras.
Application should be made to the Station Masters at the stations
mentioned.

European, Eurasian and Native Women Servants are
allowed to accompany their mistress in a first-class carriage, on

payment of second-class fare, and in a second-class carriage on payment of third-class fare. The same arrangement applies when they accompany young children, with or without the parents of such children. This concession will not be allowed to servants in charge of children under three years of age travelling free.

The wives of officers travelling under Government warrant are allowed the same privilege in respect to women servants.

Invalids, producing a certificate from a medical man, approved by the Company showing that personal attendance during the journey is necessary, will be allowed to take an attendant in a first-class carriage on payment of second-class fare and in a second-class carriage on payment of third-class fare.

One servant only is allowed to travel in each of the foregoing cases at the reduced fare.

Except on occasions of festivals, reserved accommodation will be provided, *when available*, at the **Reserved Accommodation.** following rates on application to **Station Masters**; but to prevent disappointment twelve hours' notice must be given at the undermentioned stations and twenty-four hours' notice at all other stations :—

Madras.	Madura.	Pondicherry.
Chingleput.	Tuticorin.	Tiruvallur J.
Villupuram.	Tinnevelly.	Peralam.
Cuddalore O. T.	Pakala.	Negapatam.
Mayavaram.	Tirupati West.	Karaikkal.
Tanjore.	Dharmavaram.	Erode.
Trichinopoly J.	Arkonam.	

The payment to be made for a reserved compartment or carriage will be :—

(a) **First-class Accommodation.**—One double saloon carriage, on payment for eight first-class tickets.

Half of a double saloon, on payment for four first-class tickets.

(b) **Second-class Accommodation.**—The whole of a second-class carriage on payment for twelve second-class tickets.

A second-class compartment on payment for six second-class tickets.

(c) **Third-class Accommodation.**—The whole of an ordinary third-class carriage on payment for thirty-two third-class tickets.

A compartment on payment for eight third-class tickets.

(d) **Clemenson's Third-class Carriage.**—The whole of a third-class Clemenson's carriage on payment for sixty-four third-class tickets.

A compartment on payment for eight third-class tickets.

(c) There are 4 kinds of Composite carriages as stated below, and the charges will be made as follows :—

D. *Composite carriages.*—Four first-class seats and six second-class seats.

E. *Composite carriages.*—Six first-class seats and six third-class seats.

F. *Composite carriages.*—Two first-class seats and eight second-class seats.

T. *Composite carriages* (*Bogie*).—Four first-class seats and eight second-class seats.

Charge will be made for actual number only of servants.

Whenever the number of tickets taken for reserved accommodation or special train accommodation is exceeded by the number of persons actually travelling, each passenger in excess of the number specified will be charged ordinary fare.

The fares, on payment of which, first-, second-, and third-class reserved accommodation as shewn above, will be provided, are the ordinary fares.

A Ladies' Compartment will be provided in a first- or second-class carriage without extra charge if twenty-four hours' notice be given. None but women and young children can travel in compartments so reserved.

A reserved second-class compartment is set aside on the through main line mail train running between Madras and Tuticorin for the accommodation of ladies travelling second-class.

A reserved third-class carriage or compartment is set aside in every passenger-train for the accommodation of women travelling third-class.

Passengers reserving carriages or compartments from stations on the branch lines to main line stations will be required to change carriages at the main line junctions if they wish to travel by the fast Bogie mail trains.

When a carriage is ordered but is not used, a demurrage charge of 4 annas for an ordinary carriage and 8 annas for a Bogie carriage will be made per hour, or part of an hour, with a minimum charge of Rs. 3 in the former and Rs. 5 in the latter case. The charge will be reckoned from the time the vehicle is available until intimation is received that it is not required, subject to a maximum charge of Rs. 6 for an ordinary carriage and Rs. 12 for a Bogie carriage.

Demurrage and haulage charges on carriages not used.

When first-, second- and third-class carriages are fully reserved, they can be run through to stations on the Southern Mahratta Railway on twenty-four hours' previous notice being given.

Reserved through carriages.

The charges for Passengers by Special Train are—

		Tickets.
Double saloon with compartment for servants, carrying capacity sixteen first- and six second-class passengers	Rs. 1-6-0 per mile.	
First-class carriage	..	8
Double saloon carriage	..	8
D. Composite carriage { First class	..	4
{ Second class	..	6
E. Composite carriage { First class	..	6
{ Third class	..	6
F. Composite carriage { First class	..	2
{ Second class	..	8
T. Composite carriage (Bogie) { First class	..	4
{ Second class	..	8
Second-class carriage	..	12
Third-class carriage (ordinary)	..	32
Do. Clemenson's	..	64

Charges will be made for actual number only of servants.

Each passenger by special train is entitled to the ordinary allowance of luggage, and any excess will be charged for.

Application for *Special Trains* must be made to the Traffic Manager, Trichinopoly, or to the District Traffic Superintendents, at Madras, Pakala, Tanjore, and Madura, and should reach them at least thirty-six hours before the special trains are required.

The charge for engine-power is, for any distance less than 100 miles, Rs. 4 per mile, subject to a minimum charge of Rs. 100 and a maximum of Rs. 300.

For 100 miles and upwards Rs. 3 per mile.

For through special trains over the Madras Railway and South Indian Railway, when the charge over either or both Companies' lines at the above rates is under Rs. 100, a minimum charge of Rs. 100 for either or both Companies will be made.

Outside porters are engaged at some of the principal stations

Outside Porters. to carry passengers' luggage from outside the stations to carriages of trains and *vice versá*. These men wear a brass badge marked " S. I. R. outside porters " on their right arm. The charges are 6 pies for each head-load with a maximum of 2 annas for clearing the whole of a passenger's belongings to or from the carriage.

TELEGRAPH RULES AND RATES.

The South Indian Railway Company forward telegraph messages for the public on the following conditions, *viz.* :—

That the wires are not occupied by messages relating to the Company's service.

The accuracy of telegrams is not guaranteed ; and the sender and receiver must accept all risks arising from non-delivery, errors, or delays.

The address includes the addressee's name and address and the name of the office to which the telegram is to go. Care should be taken that the latter is written as given in the List of Telegraph Offices published in the *Telegraph Guide*. The address must contain all the information necessary to ensure delivery without search or enquiry. The sender in all cases has to bear the consequence of insufficiency in the address, which, after the telegram has been despatched, can neither be completed nor altered, except by a paid service advice.

No private telegram or series of telegrams containing more than *five hundred* words can be sent at any one time by any individual or firm, and no subsequent telegram by the same individual or firm till after the lapse of three hours, unless the telegraph lines be free of all other traffic.

The following are the rates of charges for messages between any two stations in India :—

No charge is made for the transmission of the address.	First eight words or groups of five figures.	Each additional word or group of five figures.
	RS. A. P.	RS. A. P.
Urgent messages	2 0 0	0 4 0
Ordinary do.	1 0 0	0 2 0
Deferred do.	0 8 0	0 1 0

Between any station in India and any station in Ceylon.

For each word including those in the address, 3 annas.

A message for Ceylon can be sent from any station on the South Indian Railway.

(a) Urgent telegrams receive instant transmission, and have precedence over ordinary telegrams and the right of special delivery at destination. In cases of life and death, or of extraordinary emergency, an urgent telegram can be sent from any office at any time.

(b) Ordinary telegrams are transmitted in their turn after urgent telegrams, and are delivered by messengers between day-break and 9 P. M. (local time).

(c) Deferred telegrams are transmitted when the lines are clear of urgent and ordinary telegrams, and are delivered by messengers between day-break and 9 P. M. (local time).

The words comprising the address of a telegram are not charged for; the address includes names of stations from and to which the telegram is to be despatched, the *bonâ-fide* names or designation of the sender and addressee, and the latter's address.

18

Every word of fifteen letters or less is counted as one word. Words containing more than fifteen letters are charged for as two words up to thirty letters, and so on by multiples of fifteen *plus* one word for any excess.

When numbers are expressed in figures, all the characters, figures, letters, or signs in each group are added together, the total divided by five, and the quotient, *plus* one for remainder, if there be any, gives the number of words the group represents. Signs used to separate groups, and letters added to figures to form ordinal numbers, are counted each as a figure or letter. Groups of letters not forming words (letter cipher) cannot be transmitted in private telegrams.

Delivery. Telegrams are delivered free of charge within five miles of a Telegraph Office.

(*a*) Beyond the free delivery circle, telegrams will be sent by post without charge, or by such other means as the sender may arrange and pay for.

(*b*) Should the addressee of a telegram have left the place to which it is addressed, it will, if returned unopened with definite instructions as to the new address, be re-transmitted without extra charge. Similarly it will be re-transmitted immediately to any new destination, without being sent out for delivery at the first address, if the addressee has left written instructions at the Telegraph Office, or if his new address is known.

(*c*) The messenger who delivers a telegram may be entrusted with the reply, provided he be not detained for this purpose more than five minutes. The fact of the reply having been given to the messenger, and the amount paid to him, should be mentioned on the receipt given for the original telegram.

If the sender desires his message to be delivered open, he is to write the instructions (R. O.) in the space marked " official instructions" on the form.

Open delivery.

The sender of a message can pre-pay a reply, depositing for this purpose a sum not less than 8 annas and not more than 2 rupees and not including any fraction of an anna ; but the message to which a

Reply pre-paid.

reply is pre-paid must not be addressed to more than one
person.   On depositing the corresponding sum, the sender can
add (free) to the words " Reply paid" or " Answer paid" the
amount to which he wishes the reply to be limited.   The
terminal station sends to the receiver a pass for the amount
pre-paid, leaving it to him to send his answer within thirty days
to what address he pleases.   Should the cost of the reply exceed
the sum deposited as specified above, the difference must be paid
by the sender of the reply.   Should the cost of the reply be less
than the amount of the pass, no refund will be given for the
amount not availed of; but, if the pass be not used, the amount,
which has been pre-paid for it, will be refunded upon application
to the Check Office, Calcutta.   Application must, however, be
made within two months and be supported by this pass, without
which no refund will be granted.   It should be distinctly understood that the pass is only available for thirty days.   Should it
be impossible to effect delivery of a reply pre-paid message, the
terminal station sends a service telegram to that effect to the
sender.

If an ordinary or urgent private telegram be not delivered,
or be subjected to serious delay, through the fault of any
telegraph administration in India, the whole charge made for
it will be returned to the sender.

(a) If an ordinary or urgent private telegram be delivered wholly
or partially in an unintelligible state, a refund will be
made only when the extra -charge for repetition has
been paid by the sender.

(b) No refund will, under any circumstances, be made for a
deferred private telegram.

Full and detailed information respecting the transmission of
messages may be had on application to any of the Station Masters,
Traffic Manager, Trichinopoly, District Traffic Superintendents,
Madras, Pakala, Tanjore and Madura.

The stations on the South Indian Railway, where there is no
Government Telegraph office, are authorized to accept messages
for despatch to stations other than those in India.   (For rules
and charges, *vide* Government Telegraph Tariff Book.)

Urgent paid telegrams are accepted at roadside stations

where a night station staff is employed for transmission only to stations where a night signalling staff is employed.

The Office hours for receipt of paid messages are from 6 A.M., to 6 P.M., daily on this railway. Exception will be made in cases of *bond-fide* travellers by railway from whom messages may be received for despatch, at any time an office is open ; but they must be given to understand that the Company do not guarantee immediate despatch as delay may occur in consequence of the station, to which they are addressed, being closed.

The following Railway stations are opened for receipt and despatch of paid messages from 6 A.M. to 9. P.M. :—

St. Thomas' Mount.	Ayyampet.
Pallavaram.	Dindigul.
Chingleput Junction.	Ammayanayakanur.
Panruti.	Chittoor.
Porto Novo.	Chandragiri.
Chidambaram.	Tirupati West.
Mayavaram.	Tiruvallur Junction.

REFRESHMENT ROOMS.

The Refreshment Rooms on the South Indian Railway are under the management of Messrs. Spencer & Co., Ld., Madras.

Refreshment Rooms are provided at the undermentioned stations and meals will be served at the times shewn, if previous notice has been given and tickets purchased :—

Stations.	Breakfast.	Tiffin.	Dinner.
Madras-Egmore (Refreshment Buffet)..	..	..	..
Chingleput J.	9 0, / 9 22	15 17	19 43
Villupuram J.	11 50	13 0	21 30 / 22 16
Katpadi J.	10 20	14 28	20 45
Pakala J.	12 25 / 12 38	..	..
Dharmavaram J.	..	..	22 10
Renigunta J.	10 25	..	22 5
Cuddalore (Old Town)	9 51	14 45	18 45
Tanjore J.	8 40	14 25 / 14 52	19 56 / 21 16
Negapatam	..	13 45	18 55 / 20 50
Trichinopoly J.	10 40 / 11 0 / 12 35	..	19 38
Madura	10 51	14 40	20 10
Tuticorin	9 0	..	..

A Refreshment Buffet has been opened at the Egmore station.

A compartment of a third-class carriage is set apart for the sale of *ice* and *aerated waters* to passengers in certain trains.

NOTE.—*Passengers intending to travel by the evening Mail from Madras are requested to purchase tickets early in the day.*

REFRESHMENT CHARGES.

When ticket is previously purchased, or a telegram giving six hours' notice is sent.				When ticket is not previously purchased, or telegram giving six hours' notice is not sent.			
	RS.	A.	P.		RS.	A.	P.
Breakfast	1	0	0	Breakfast	1	8	0
Tiffin	1	0	0	Tiffin	1	8	0
Dinner	1	8	0	Dinner	2	0	0

Children will be charged half these rates.

Meals do not include Drinks and Ice.

Light refreshments, such as tea, coffee, biscuits, aerated waters and a variety of English tinned provisions can also be obtained at Tiruvannamalai, Chinna Tippa Samudram, Mayavaram, Kumbakonam, Dindigul, Virudupati and Koilpati stations. At Tiruvannamalai, Chinna Tippa Samudram and Kumbakonam, if not less than twelve hours' notice is given, breakfast, tiffin and dinner can be got ready for two or three passengers only.

Tea or coffee will be served free of charge at breakfast.

Coffee after dinner must be paid for at 2 annas per cup.

At least six hours' notice should be given for refreshments required to avoid disappointment. Passengers joining the railway at roadside stations should notify to the guard of the train if there is sufficient interval, and, in such cases, a message will be sent by the guard to the refreshment room to provide meals; but if six hours' notice is not given passengers must pay the higher rates.

Passengers are requested to purchase the tickets themselves at the booking offices.

Butlers will reserve seats at the refreshment room tables for the number of meals ordered on tickets. Passengers will be required to give up their breakfast, tiffin, or dinner tickets before taking their seats, and the proprietors of the refreshment rooms will be responsible for seeing that those passengers who have obtained tickets for meals are fully supplied, before other passengers are attended to, unless there happens to be sufficient for all.

Refreshments are not served in carriages.

Breakfast, Tiffin and Dinner Tickets will be sold at the Booking Offices of the following stations :—

S.I.R. Booking Office, Mount Road to Chingleput J. .. Breakfast and dinner tickets.

Do.	Mount Road	to Cuddalore O. T. ..	Tiffin tickets.
Do.	Do.	to Tanjore J. ..	Dinner do.
Do.	Do.	to Madura ..	Breakfast tickets.
Do.	Madras (Egmore)	to Chingleput J. ..	Breakfast and dinner tickets.
Do.	Do.	to Villupuram J. ...	Tiffin tickets.
Do.	Do.	to Cuddalore O. T. ..	Do.
Do.	Do.	to Tanjore J. ..	Dinner tickets.
Do.	Do.	to Madura ..	Breakfast do.
Do.	Chingleput J.	to Cuddalore O. T. ..	Tiffin do.
Do.	Do.	to Tanjore J. ..	Dinner do.
Do.	Do.	to Madura ..	Breakfast tickets.
Do.	Do.	to Tuticorin ..	Do.
Do.	Arkonam J.	to Chingleput J. ...	Do.
Do.	Do.	to Cuddalore O. T. ..	Tiffin tickets.
Do.	Do.	to Tanjore J. ..	Dinner tickets.
Do.	Villupuram J.	to Do. ..	Do.
Do.	Do.	to Pakala J. ..	Breakfast tickets.
Do.	Do.	to Cuddalore O. T. ..	Tiffin do.
Do.	Do.	to Tuticorin ..	Breakfast do.
Do.	Cuddalore N. T.	to Negapatam ..	Dinner do.
Do.	Cuddalore O. T.	to Tanjore J. ..	Tiffin and dinner tickets.
Do.	Do.	to Villupuram J. ...	Breakfast and dinner tickets.
Do.	Do.	to Kumbakonam ..	Breakfast tickets.
Do.	Do.	to Negapatam ..	Dinner do.
Do.	Do.	to Trichinopoly J. ..	Breakfast tickets.
Do.	Do.	to Tuticorin ..	Do.
Do.	Do.	to Chingleput J. ...	Tiffin tickets.
Do.	Coleroon	to Kumbakonam ..	Breakfast tickets.
Do.	Tanjore J.	to Madura ..	Do.
Do.	Do.	to Trichinopoly J. ..	Do.
Do.	Do.	to Tuticorin :.	Do.
Do.	Do.	to Kumbakonam ..	Do.

S.I.R. Booking Office, Cuddalore	to Villupuram J.	.. Breakfast and dinner tickets.
Do.	Cuddalore	to Negapatam	.. Do.
Do.	Negapatam	to Tanjore J.	.. Dinner tickets.
Do.	Do.	to Trichinopoly J.	.. Breakfast do.
Do.	Do.	to Madura	.. Breakfast and dinner tickets.
Do.	Trichinopoly J.	to Negapatam	.. Breakfast, tiffin and dinner tickets.
Do.	Do.	to Cuddalore O.T.	.. Breakfast tickets.
Do.	Do.	to Kumbakonam	.. Do.
Do.	Do.	to Madura	.. Do.
Do.	Do.	to Tuticorin	.. Do.
Do.	Karur	to Trichinopoly J.	.. Breakfast and dinner tickets.
Do.	Erode J.	to Negapatam	.. Tiffin and dinner tickets.
Do.	Do.	to Trichinopoly J.	.. Breakfast tickets.
Do.	Do.	to Madura	.. Dinner do.
Do.	Manaparai	to Do.	.. Breakfast do.
Do.	Dindigul	to Do.	.. Breakfast and dinner tickets.
Do.	Do.	to Trichinopoly J.	.. Dinner tickets.
Do.	Do.	to Negapatam	.. Breakfast and dinner tickets.
Do.	Ammayanayaka-nur	to Trichinopoly J.	.. Do.
Do.	Do.	to Madura	.. Do.
Do.	Do.	to Cuddalore O.T.	.. Breakfast tickets.
Do.	Madura	to Trichinopoly J.	.. Breakfast and dinner tickets.
Do.	Do.	to Tanjore J.	.. Tiffin tickets.
Do.	Do.	to Negapatam	.. Breakfast and dinner tickets.
Do.	Do.	to Cuddalore O.T.	.. Breakfast tickets.
Do.	Do.	to Tuticorin	.. Do.
Do.	Virudupati	to Negapatam	.. Breakfast and dinner tickets.
Do.	Tuticorin	to Madura	.. Tiffin and dinner tickets.
Do.	Do.	to Trichinopoly J.	.. Dinner tickets.
Do.	Do.	to Negapatam	.. Breakfast and dinner tickets.
Do.	Tinnevelly	to Katpadi J.	.. Breakfast tickets.
Do.	Do.	to Madura	.. Tiffin and dinner tickets.
Do.	Do.	to Negapatam	.. Breakfast and dinner tickets.

S.I.R. Booking Office, Pondicherry to Cuddalore O.T. .. Tiffin tickets.

Do.	Do.	to Renigunta J. ..	Do.
Do.	Do.	to Katpadi J. & Vil- lupuram J.	.. Breakfast tickets.
Do.	Tiruvannamalai	to Villupuram J. ...	Do.
Do.	Do.	to Pakala J.	.. Breakfast and tiffin tickets.
Do.	Polur	to Katpadi J.	.. Breakfast tickets.
Do.	Do.	to Villupuram J. ...	Do.
Do.	Vellore	to Renigunta J. ..	Tiffin tickets.
Do.	Do.	to Pakala J.	.. Breakfast and tiffin tickets.
Do.	Do.	to Tiruvannamalai.	Dinner tickets.
Do.	Do.	to Villupuram J. ...	Breakfast tickets.
Do.	Katpadi J.	to Do. ..	Do.
Do.	Do.	to Pakala J. ..	Do.
Do.	Pakala J.	to Tiruvannamalai.	Dinner tickets.
Do.	Renigunta J.	to Pakala J.	.. Breakfast and dinner tickets.
Do.	Venkatagiri	to Renigunta J. ..	Breakfast tickets.
Do.	Do.	to Pakala J. ..	Do.
Do.	Gudur	to Renigunta J. ..	Breakfast and dinner tickets.
Do.	Dharmavaram J.	to Katpadi J.	.. Breakfast tickets.
Do.	Do.	to Pakala J. ..	Do.

Breakfast, tiffin and dinner tickets can also be had at Chingleput J., Villupuram J., Tiruvannamalai, Pakala J., Cuddalore O. T., Tanjore J., Negapatam, Trichinopoly J., Madura and Tuticorin for meals required at these stations, but the prescribed notice must be given to the butler.

Refreshment Tickets may also be obtained at the Hotel of Messrs. Spencer & Co., Ld., Mount Road.

SCALE OF CHARGES.

	RS.	A.
Chota Hazaree consisting of 2 cups tea or coffee, toast and 2 eggs, or bread, butter and jam	0	8
Plate of Bread, butter and cheese	0	8
Do Cold meat, or sandwiches	0	8
Do. Bread, butter and 2 eggs	0	6
Do. Curry and rice	0	6
Do. Soup	0	4
Cup of tea or coffee, and toast with butter (if with jam 2 annas extra)	0	4
Cup of tea or coffee with 6 biscuits	0	3
Do. or coffee	0	2
Pint of milk	0	2
Eggs cooked	0	1
Glass of iced water each	0	1

WINES, SPIRITS, ETC.

	Qt.	Pt.	Meas.
	RS. A.	RS. A.	RS. A.
Champagne, Spencer's, Carte Blanche Extra Sec. ..	5 0	2 12	..
Sherry do. Red Seal ..	2 2	..	0 3
Port do. Yellow Seal...	2 0	1 2	..
Claret do. Medoc ..	1 2	0 11	..
Do. Vin Ordinaire ..	0 14	0 8	..
St. Raphael Wine in half-litres ..	2 10	..	..
Ginger Wine, Crabbie's ..	1 14	..	0 3
Vermouth, Italian, Silver Label ..	2 2	..	0 3
Bull, or Swan Brandy, Spencer's ..	3 0	..	0 4
Brandy, Spencer's, 2 Stars ..	3 8	2 0	0 5
Whiskey, Spencer's, Club No. 1 ..	3 12	..	0 6
Do. do. Imperial Highland ..	3 0	..	0 4
Do. do. Glenlivet ..	2 12	..	0 4
Gin, Plymouth ..	3 0	..	0 4
Do. Old Tom, Boord & Sons ..	2 4	..	0 4
Do. Hollands, Eagle Brand flasks ..	2 12	1 14	0 3
Beer, Bass' "Dog's Head" brand ..	0 13	0 9	..
Stout, Guinness' do. ..	0 13	0 9	..
Beer, Pilsener, Beck & Co.'s ..	0 9	0 6	..
Do. do. Tennent's ..	0 9	0 6	..

STORES, ETC.

		RS. A.
Arrowroot, Speed's ..		1 0
Asparagus, C. & B.'s ..		1 5
Bacon, Wiltshire in Tins, C. & B.'s 1½ to 3 lbs. each	per lb..	1 8
Do. Finest Wiltshire on cut ..	,,	1 4
Barley, Finest Pearl, C. & B.'s ..		0 14
Biscuits, Huntley & Palmer's assorted	per tin..	1 0
Do. Mixed (20 different kinds)		1 5
Bloaters, Yarmouth 1 lb., C. & B.'s		0 14
Butter, Esbensen's Danish ..	½ lb...	1 1
Catsup, Walnut or Mushroom ..	pint..	0 15
Cheese, Gouda on cut ..	per lb..	1 0
Do. Dutch Ball ..	,,	1 0
Do. do. ..	(4-lb.) per ball..	3 4
Do. Cheddar or Berkeley in ..	..2 lb. tins..	2 8
Chutnies and Pickles, Indian assorted		0 14
Cocoa (Van Houten's)..	..½ lb. tin..	1 0
Coffee, Finest Ground	1 lb..	1 9
Do. Essence, Branson's	small..	0 9
Do. Medium ..		0 14
Corn Flour, Brown & Polson's ..		0 15
Herrings, Kippered, C. & B.'s ..		0 12
Jams, Moir's assorted ..		0 8
Do. Strawberry and Raspberry		0 9
Marmalade, Moir's ..		0 7
Mellin's food	large bottles..	2 4

STORES, ETO.—*continued.*

		RS. A.
Milk, Swiss, Milkmaid brand		0 9
Do. do. small		0 4½
Mustard, Coleman's	¼-lb. tins	0 13
Oatmeal, Round, Moir's	1 lb.	0 8
Olives, French	½ pint	0 9
Peas, Green, Petits Pois	2 lb.	0 12
Pickles, assorted	pint	0 15
Do. do.	½ „	0 9
Potted Meats, C. & B.'s and Moir's		0 8
Do. Maconochies, small		0 1
Salad oil, S. & Co.'s	pint	1 0
Salmon, Oregon, C. & B.'s		0 13
Salt, English, Table	2 lbs.	0 9
Sardines, Philippe & Canads	large tin	1 6
Do. do	small	1 0
Do. Victor Tertrais	large	0 9
Do. do.	small	0 7
Sauce, L. & P.'s Worcester	pints	1 14
Do. Sutton's do.	„	0 15
Do. Essence of Anchovies	„	1 9
Sausages, Oxford, small		1 5
Soups, assorted, Moir's	pint	0 14
Tapioca, C. & B.'s		0 10
Tea, K. T. E., Orange Pekoe	per lb.	1 6
Do. do. Pekoe	each	1 2
Do. do. Pekoe Souchong	„	0 15
Do. do. Souchong	„	0 12
Do. do. Congou	„	0 9
Vinegar Malt, Cas. & S.		0 7

AERATED WATERS.

	Without bottle.		With bottle.	
	RS.	A.	RS.	A.
Soda water, large	0	2	0	6
Do. per dozen	1	2	4	2
Do. Splits	0	1	0	5
Lemonade	0	3	0	7
Do. per dozen	1	10	4	10
Ginger Ale	0	3	0	7
Orange Ale	0	3	0	7
Kola Tonic	0	3	0	7
Quinine Tonic	0	3	0	7
Any of the above, per dozen	1	12	4	12

AUSTRALIAN STORES.

		RS.	A.
Beef, Roast	per lb..	0	10
Do. Spiced 2 lbs.	,,	1	2
Do. Luncheon	,,	0	10
Mutton, Roast	,,	0	10
Do. Corned	,,	0	10
Do. Spiced	,,	0	10
Minced Collops	,,	0	10
Ox Cheeks..	,,	0	9
Lunch Tongues	,,	1	4
Cambridge Sausages ..	,,	1	11
Oxford do.	,,	0	11

A suggestion book is kept in each refreshment room and passengers are invited to enter therein any remarks they have to offer.

It is requested that complaints of inattention may be addressed to the Traffic Manager.

Dinner Tickets for service on the *Madras Railway* are sold, at the following stations at the reduced rate of Rs. 1-8-0 each provided sufficient notice is given and tickets purchased, otherwise the fixed rate, Rs. 2, will be charged :—

Stations at which Tickets are sold.	*Stations at which Dinner is supplied.
Trichinopoly J. Trichinopoly Fort Karur	} Erode J., or Salem, as passenger may require.
Cuddalore (New Town) Villupuram J. Pondicherry Conjeeveram	} Arkonam J.

DHARMAVARAM JUNCTION JOINT STATION REFRESHMENT ROOM.

Refreshments are provided in the above room at the following rates :—

	RS.	A.
Chota Hazaree, tea or coffee, bread, butter and eggs	0	8
Breakfast, hot with meat, eggs, &c.	1	8
Tiffin, hot	1	8
Do. cold	1	0

* Salem is the proper dinner station for passengers travelling from stations on the South Indian Railway to Salem or beyond.

						RS.	A.
Dinner, hot..	..	..	..	..	..	2	0
Supper	..	..	..	..	..	1	0
Meat sandwiches, per plate	..	..	..	..	0	8
Ham do. do.	..	..	..	..	0	12
Cup of tea ..	..	..	..	..	..	0	2
Do. with bread and butter ..	..	..	..	0	6
Do. with bread and eggs	..	..	..	0	8
Cup of coffee	..	..	..	..	..	0	3
Milk, per seer	..	..	..	..	..	0	4
Plate of soup	..	..	..	..	..	0	8
Do. bread, butter and cheese ..	..	..	..	0	8
Do. bread and butter	..	..	..	..	0	4

Children under twelve years of age half-rates for Breakfast, Tiffin or Dinner.

Refreshment rooms are provided by the Madras Railway Company at Erode, Katpadi, Arkonam and Renigunta; and by the Southern Mahratta Railway Company at Dharmavaram.

For tariff charges at these rooms, see the time-tables of those Companies.

Refreshments are not served in the carriages.

REFRESHMENT ROOM FOR NATIVE PASSENGERS AT VILLUPURAM J.

Refreshments prepared *under Brahmin management* are supplied in the refreshment room for Native passengers at Villupuram J. station, at the rates shewn below :—

				RS.	A.	P.
Superior meals, per head	..	..	..	0	3	0
Sweet pongul, one full cake	..	..	..	0	2	6
Pongul do.	..	..	..	0	2	0
Pooliyorai do.	..	..	..	0	1	9
Thathyovannam do.	..	..	..	0	1	6
Coffee, per tumbler	..	..	..	0	1	3
Tea do.	..	..	..	0	1	0

(C).—TOURIST ROUTES.

It has hitherto been customary for persons visiting India to commence and finish their tour at Bombay, a practice which has resulted in Southern India being either excluded from their programme or only visited at the expense of needless travelling. A far better arrangement is to either disembark or embark at Colombo, and commence or conclude the Indian tour at Tuticorin. This will enable the beautiful and interesting Island of Ceylon to be seen without materially adding to the duration of the trip. The passage between Colombo and Tuticorin has been greatly improved during recent years; but, in rough weather, the crossing is not altogether a pleasant experience to in-different sailors. It is, however, intended to construct a line of railway from Madura to l'amban which, when opened, will enable the more comfortable sea route between Colombo and Pamban to be adopted. During the North-East monsoon months the Gulf of Manaar is generally smooth, and tourists are therefore advised to so arrange their programmes as to admit of the crossings being made during these months.

Assuming that the visitor to India has decided to commence his trip from Tuticorin, the following itinerary might advantageously be adopted.

There being but little to be seen in Tuticorin, the town should be left, if possible, by the express train running in connection with the Colombo boat. Madura will be reached after a journey of five hours, and in this town a day can profitably be spent in visiting the temples and palace. The tourist, limiting his stay to this period, should proceed by the express train of the following day to Trichinopoly, which is reached in about four and three quarter hours. During this journey, Ammayanayakanur and Dindigul are passed, the former being the station for Kodaikanal (altitude 7,209 feet), in the Pulney Hills, and the latter being noted for its old rock fort and large cigar industry. The journey to Kodaikanal occupies about twelve hours, and is usually made in a comfortable bullock-cart, as far as the foot of the hills, and thence in a chair carried by coolies, or on horseback. This expedition is, however, somewhat fatiguing, and tourists, desirous of visiting a southern hill station, should go from Trichinopoly to Coonoor (altitude 5,616 feet), a journey which can now be performed entirely by train. Ootacamund, the summer residence of the Madras Government, is eleven miles from Coonoor, and will repay a visit. If this trip to the Nilgiris is made, the tourist should return to Trichinopoly, where two days can be spent seeing the rock temples, and irrigation works. The next town to be visited is Tanjore, which is only 31 miles from Trichinopoly. The objects of interest in Tanjore can easily be seen in a day, when the visitor should proceed to Chidambaram, four hours' journey by rail. There is no refreshment room at this station, and the dâk bungalow is unfurnished; so travellers should bring food with them from Tanjore. On leaving Chidambaram, the train should be taken to Chingleput, the journey occupying nearly seven hours by the ordinary mail train. From Chingleput, Conjeeveram should be visited and an expedition of about eighteen miles by road should be made to the extremely interesting rock-cut and monolithic temples known as the Seven Pagodas. Near the temples is a Public Works Rest House, permission to occupy which can generally be obtained on application to the Executive Engineer, Buckingham Canal

GRAPHIC ART SOCIETY

THE PERIYAR DAM

NEGATIVE BY MESSʳˢ NICHOLAS & Cᵒ MADRAS

Division, Madras. The Pagodas can also be visited by
canal from Madras, unfurnished house-boats being obtainable on payment through this officer. This journey is,
however, dreary, as it takes about a day to travel 33 miles
of canal; but it has the convenience that the boats afford
shelter, and that meals can be cooked on board. From
Chingleput to Madras, the distance is only 34½ miles, and
several trains are run daily. Tourists, desirous of visiting
places of interest on the South Indian Railway other than
those specified above, should consult the " Itinerary "
section of this guide. On leaving Madras, the tourist is
recommended to travel by the Madras Railway to Katpadi,
taking an early train, and, after having inspected the
buildings in Vellore Fort, either to proceed to Renigunta
by the South Indian Railway, or to return to Arkonam,
and from there travel to Hospet (viâ Guntakal) on the
Southern Mahratta Railway. The metre-gauge line to
Renigunta passes by Chandragiri, where there are buildings worth seeing; but the journey viâ Arkonam, while
offering no such inducements, will be found the more
comfortable, as the mail train to Guntakal leaves at a
more convenient hour from Arkonam than from Renigunta.
From Hospet, the extremely interesting ruins of Vijayanagar, or Humpi, can be easily reached, if previous
arrangements for conveyance can be made with the
Station-master. From Hospet, the journey should be
continued to Bijapur, a ruined Masalman city, well worth
seeing, and where board, lodging and conveyance can be
obtained, without trouble, on more than a few hours' notice.
The country in the neighbourhood of Dharwar abounds
in beautiful architectural remains in the Chalukyan style;
but special arrangements, involving a lengthy stay in the
district, will probably be necessary to enable them to be
visited. Haiderabad, the capital of the Nizam's Dominions, might next be seen, and the journey continued
thence to Puri and Cuttack, where there is much of inter-

est to be viewed. From Cuttack, the tourist should go to Calcutta, by the Bengal-Nagpur Railway, when the route is open for traffic, or by launch and steamer. On leaving Calcutta, the tour should be arranged to include Darjeeling, Benares, Allahabad, Cawnpore, Lucknow, Agra, Delhi, Ulwar, Jeypore, Ajmere, Oodeypore, Ahmedabad, Baroda and Bombay. From Bombay, interesting expeditions should be made to the caves of Nasik, Ellora and Ajanta, and an excursion to the caves of Elephanta in the Harbour.

CHAPTER II.

MAIN LINE.

ITINERARY.

1. **Madras** (lat. 13°·4' 6" N.; long. 80°·17' 22" E.) is the principal town of the Presidency which bears its name, and in 1891 had a population of 452,518 souls. It is the third largest city in India, and with its suburbs, extends 9 miles along the Coromandel Coast and 3½ miles inland, covering an area of 27 square miles. It is bounded on the East by the sea, on the West by Shambian, Shirloor, Shembadanbaukam, Einavaram, Kodambakam, Saidapet and Guindy, on the North by Shattancaud, Kodangiyur and Yeroocancherry, and on the South by the river Adyar.

The site on which the city of Madras is built was obtained from one Darmala Venkadri in 1639 by Mr. Francis Day, the then Chief of the Settlement of Armegam of the East India Company on the Coromandel Coast. The transfer of the land to the Company was ratified in Chandragiri Palace by Shree Runga Royal Rajah of Vijayanagar. Darmala Venkadri stipulated that the new factory should be called Chennapatnam in memory of his father Chennappa, and the city is known to the natives under this name at the present time. There has been considerable speculation as to the origin of the word Madras, the most generally accepted theory being that it is derived from Madre Dios, the supposed name of the old Armenian Church of St. Mary in Black Town. Roughly

20

speaking, Madras may be considered as divided into the following districts :—

(1) The Northern suburb of Thandiyarpet, Viyasar-padi and Royapuram. The general offices of the Madras Railway Company and the original terminus of its system are situated in the last named sub-division.

(2) Black Town, a densely populated block about a mile square lying immediately South of the Northern suburbs and having a sea frontage of about a mile and a half. The name of Black Town was given to the district by the early English settlers, because of its occupation by natives, and in contradistinction to their own quarters then known by the now obsolete name of White Town. This is the business portion of the town and contains the Banks, Customs, Port and Harbour offices, the High Court and Law College, the Presidency Post office, and the offices of the principal European mercantile firms. The Madras Harbour lies opposite the Northern portion of Black Town, and is controlled by Trustees appointed under special legislative enactment. The works were originally designed by William Parkes, Esq., M. INST. C.E., and the construction was commenced under the superintendence of James Walker, Esq., M. INST. C.E., in June 1875. By the end of October 1881 the two break-waters were nearly finished, but on 12th November 1881, a cyclone wrecked the Eastern walls from the elbows to the entrance, half a mile of break-water being breached or otherwise damaged. The work of reconstruction on an amended design was commenced in July 1884, and the Harbour may now be considered as practically completed. An earthen embankment from the centre of the shore face of the Harbour gives access to a screw pile pier which extends 1,000 feet beyond high water mark and accommodates four lines of rails. The pier has a cross-head 160 feet long by 40 feet broad which, together with the main portion of the pier, is furnished with fixed and travelling cranes.

155

(3) A fairly open block with a sea frontage of about
two miles and a depth of three-quarters of a mile. In
this area are situated Fort St. George, Government
House, the Island, Government offices, the Presidency
College, Senate House, and the district of Chepauk.

(4) The suburbs of Vepery, Pursevaukam, Perambur
and Kilpauk lying to the West of Black Town.

(5) The densely populated native and Eurasian districts of Triplicane and Mylapore including Royapetta
and St. Thomé. The latter constitutes a Roman Catholic
Diocese and contains the Cathedral pertaining to the See.

(6) The residential suburbs of Egmore, Chetpat,
Nungambaukam and Teynampet, where the principal
Europeans live, and in which are situated the South Indian
Railway stations of Egmore and Chetpat, the Civil Orphan
Asylum, the Presidency Magistrate's Court, Police Commis-
sioner's office, the Scotch Kirk, School of Arts, Government
Central Museum, Lying-in Hospital, Eye Infirmary, the
Madras Club, St. George's Cathedral, the Horticultural
Gardens and the Observatory.

(7) The district of Adyar in the extreme South containing some of the finest European Mansions in Madras,
the Adyar Ladies' and Gentlemen's Club, and the Boat
House of the Madras Rowing Club.

Madras stretches along the Coromandel Coast for some
10 miles, and, owing to the large size of the compounds or
grounds attached to the European houses has been appro-
priately styled, "The city of magnificent distances." The
town is traversed from East to West by the river Cooum,
and from North to South by the Buckingham Canal.
Except after heavy rain the Cooum is a body of stagnant
water noted for its offensive smell, a condition of affairs
which Government has long proposed to remedy. To the
West of Madras lie two tanks, the Spur Tank principally
used by the washermen, and the Long Tank on which
boating may be obtained after the rains. Extending along

the sea face from the Fort to St. Thomé is a fine Marina having on its Western side a long length of tan ride. In the evening it is a place of much resort for the sake of the cool sea breeze which rarely fails throughout the year. Despite the unpleasant odours arising from the Cooum, Madras is not ordinarily an unhealthy place either for Europeans or natives, the death-rate averaging 40 per 1,000 per annum. The mean temperature in the shade ranges between 86°.7 and 75°.1 Fahrenheit, the extremes being 98°.3 in June and 67°.5 in January.

The distances from Egmore to the principal junctions on the South Indian Railway are :—

Chingleput Junction (for Conjeeveram)	..	.. 35 miles.
Villupuram Junction (for Pondicherry)	..	.. 98 ,.
Tanjore Junction (for Negapatam and Mutupet)		.. 218 .,
Trichinopoly Junction (for Erode)	..	.. 249 ,,
Maniyachi Junction (for Tinnevelly)	..	.. 425 ,,

2. **Local Accommodation.**—The following is a list of the principal hotels :—

The " Connemara "	..Commander-in-Chief's Road, Egmore.
The " Buckingham "	..Westcott Road.
" Capper House "	..South Beach, St. Thomé.
" Central "	..Rundall's Road, Vepery.
" Dents Garden "	..Mount Road.
" Elphinstone "	..Mount Road.
" Elphinstone " (Branch).	..Commander-in-Chief's Road, Egmore.
" Esplanade "	..Errabauloo Chetty Street, Black Town.
" Harbour "	..Beach.
" National "	..Armenian Street, Black Town.
" Royal "	..Mount Road.
" Union "	..Esplanade Row, Black Town.
" Victoria "	..Commander-in-Chief's Road, Egmore.

With the exception of the Bachelors' quarters of the Connemara Hotel, the Madras Hotels are not celebrated for comfort, cleanliness, or cuisine.

For natives there are a large number of hotels, the best being in Munnadi and Periamettoo. There are also a few choultries, the most important of which are the " Monegar," the " Venkatagiri Rajah's," and " Sir Ramasamy Mudaliar's," where many poor natives are fed daily.

3. Road Conveyance.—The following are the rates for hackney carriages, carts and coolies :—

From Egmore station—

To	HACKNEY CARRIAGES.			Per Cooly.
	First class.	Second class.	Jutkas or Bullock-carts.	
	RS. A. P.	RS. A. P.	RS. A. P.	RS. A. P.
Chintadripet, Vepery, New Town, Periamettoo, Central Station, Puthupet, Komaraswarampet.	0 8 0	0 6 0	0 2 0	0 1 0
Black Town, Mount Road, Pursewaulkam, Choolay, Fort St. George, Goojelly, China Bazaar, General Market, Patchiappah's Hall, Napier Park, Salt Cottaurs, High Court, Law College.	0 10 0	0 8 0	0 3 0	0 1 0
Triplicane, North Black Town, Royapuram, Mint, Kilpauk, Chetpat, Nungumbaukam, Thousand Lights, Beach, Presidency College, Chepauk.	0 12 0	0 10 0	0 4 0	0 2 0
Royapettah, Puthupakam, Teynampet, Botanical Gardens, Washermanpet, The Luz, Perambore, Kodambakam, Office of Inspector-General of Police.	1 0 0	0 12 0	0 5 0	0 3 0
Mylapore, St. Thomé, Thondiarpet.	1 4 0	0 14 0	0 6 0	0 3 0
The Adyar, Saidapet, Kalahipet, Trivettore, Toll Bar.	1 8 0	1 2 0	0 7 0	0 4 0

The better description of carriages and bullock-carts are allowed inside the station compound, but jutkas are not allowed inside and must be engaged at the Stand outside the station.

Conveyances plying from Egmore station can be hired by the day or half-day at the following rates :—

Periods of time for which hired.	FIRST CLASS CONVEYANCE.		SECOND CLASS CONVEYANCE.	
	15th Mar to 15th Oct.	15th Oct. to 15th Mar	15th Mar to 15th Oct.	15th Oct. to 15th Mar
	RS. A. P.	RS. A. P.	RS. A. P.	RS. A. P.
For the day 6 A.M. to 6 P.M.	3 8 0	3 8 0	2 8 0	2 8 0
For the half-day. { 6 A.M. to 12 noon. 12 noon to 6 P.M. 6 P.M. to midnight. }	1 8 0	1 8 0	1 4 0	1 4 0

	RS. A. P.
Or per mile at the following rates :—	
First-class conveyances, 1st mile	0 8 0
For every subsequent mile	0 4 0
Second-class conveyances, 1st mile	0 6 0
For every subsequent mile	0 3 0

Stoppages of over quarter hour to be paid for at the rate of 2 annas for each quarter hour.

4. Railway Facilities.—The South Indian Railway has six stations in Madras, *viz.* :—

Beach.	Park.	Chetpat.
Fort.	Egmore.	Kodambakam.

Egmore is the most important station and passengers for Madras generally alight here. There is a Refreshment Buffet and a waiting-room for ladies. The Beach station situated near the Harbour is the most convenient station for those employed in the offices at Black Town and for passengers arriving by or disembarking from steamers.

The Fort station is principally used by those attending the Government and Military Offices in Fort St. George. Passengers for Madras Railway trains, Vepery and for Sir Ramaswamy Mudaliar's choultry should book to the Park station. Chetpat is used by the residents of Kilpauk, Nungumbaukam and Chetpat.

Kodambakam is the nearest station to Teynampet. In addition to the above stations the Company maintains an office in the Mount Road for booking passengers and receiving parcels and small consignments.

5. Shipping arrangements.—The following steamship Companies have agencies in Madras as under :—

P. & O. S. N. Co. ..	..Messrs. Arbuthnot & Co.
B. I. S. N. Co. ..	..Messrs. Binny & Co.
Messageries Maritimes	..M. Œsinger.
Clan Line ..	..Messrs. Gordon, Woodroffe & Co.
Austro-Hungarian Lloyds.	..Messrs. Binny & Co.
Anchor Line ..	..Messrs. Best & Co.

Passengers and goods are landed or embarked in jolly and masula boats, the charges being :—

	RS. A. P.
For jolly boats	1 0 0
For masula boats	2 8 0

6. Local Manufactures and Products.—The trade of Madras does not depend upon any special local manufactures or products, such industries as once flourished—weaving for instance—have decayed and no others have taken their place.

7. Officials.—Madras is the seat of Government during the cold season of the year, and is the head-quarters of the Eastern Division of the Madras Army, of many Military and Civil Departments, and the seat of the High Court of Judicature of the Presidency. The garrison usually numbers 3,000 men, of whom about one-third are Europeans. The City Police consists of a Commissioner, a Deputy Commissioner, an Assistant Commissioner and 980 subordinate officers and constables. The Municipality is controlled by a President appointed by Government, and thirty-two Commissioners, of whom one-fourth are nominated by Government, and three-fourths are elected by the rate-payers.

8. Missions, Churches, etc.—Churches, chapels and other places of religious worship are numerous in Madras, presenting almost every phase of Christian belief. The principal churches are :—

St. George's Cathedral built in 1815, and situated in Teynampet on the Mount Road. Visitors are admitted daily from 6 A.M. to 6 P.M. The exterior is far from handsome, but the interior is well worth inspection. At the east end of the north aisle is a fine monument to the Right Rev. Daniel Corrie, L.L.D., first Bishop of Madras, and on the north wall of the north aisle, one to Bishop Heber, who died in 1826. There is also a monument to Major Broadfoot, C.B., who was one of the illustrious garrison of Jellalabad.

St. Mary's Church in the Fort was built in 1680 and is the oldest and most interesting church in the Presidency. It contains several monuments of interest and antiquity, notably those in memory of the celebrated German Missionary Schwartz, Sir Francis Wittingham, Sir Henry Ward, Sir Thomas Munro, and Lord Hobart.

St. Andrew's, the Scotch Church, is architecturally superior to any other European religious edifice in the Presidency. The building was designed by Major de Havilland, and is entirely constructed of solid masonry, no timber work of any description being used. The steeple, which is 165 feet in height, is visible far out at sea.

St. Matthias' Church (originally known as the New Mission Church) at Vepery was built at the expense of Admiral Boscawen, in replacement of one near the Beach, which was destroyed during the war between the French and the English.

St. Thomé Cathedral.—This spacious and elegant Roman Catholic edifice is supposed to be built over the remains of St. Thomas, whose reputed tomb lies beneath a large trap-door on the south side of the building.

Holy Emmanuel Church in South Black Town has a tastefully laid out compound with a handsome fountain at the east end.

The Armenian Church of St. Mary bears on its street portal the date A. D. 1712. The slabs in the court are covered with inscriptions indicating that the Armenian community at Madras was once a large and wealthy body, forming the leading merchants of the place.

The Roman Cathedral (St. Mary of Angels) situated in Armenian Street, was built in 1785 and is under the immediate charge of the Archbishop of Madras.

Among religious Societies the principal are :—

Church Missionary Society.
Society for Promoting Christian Knowledge.
Society for the Propagation of the Gospel.
London Missionary Society.
Wesleyan Missionary Society.
Danish Evangelical Lutheran Missionary Society.
American Baptist Telugu Mission.
Free Church of Scotland Mission.
Young Men's Christian Association.

9. Clubs. The Madras Club, for many years considered the best in India, is situated near the Mount Road. The main entrance is opposite to Neil's statue, about two miles from Fort St. George. All members of Her Majesty's services, of the Bar and clergy and gentlemen received in general society are eligible for membership. Gentlemen visiting Madras for a period not exceeding three months, and who are not residents within the limits of the Presidency, can be admitted as Honorary Members for an aggregate of 30 days, upon being proposed and seconded by members. The subscription payable by Honorary Members is Rs. 10 per mensem, after a residence of 48 hours.

The Madras Gymkhana Club has its head-quarters on the Island near the Fort. It has separate departments for Racing, Paper-chasing, Polo, Golf, Football, and Trap-shooting.

The Madras Cricket Club has a nicely laid out ground at Chepauk, where both cricket and lawn-tennis are played.

The Cosmopolitan Club is situated on the Mount Road, and was established in 1873 to promote familiar intercourse between Europeans and Natives.

In addition to the above, there are a large number of less important Clubs and Societies, among which may be mentioned the Amateur Photographic, the Philharmonic, and the Dramatic Societies.

10. Historical. As before mentioned, Mr. Francis Day, obtained in March 1639, from the representative of the waning power of Vijianagar, Shree Runga Royal, Rajah of Chandragiri, the confirmatory grant of the site on which Madras now stands. A factory with some slight fortifications was at once constructed; and induced by favourable terms, a gradually increasing number of natives settled round the buildings. In 1702, Dawood Khan, Aurungzebe's General, blockaded the town for a few weeks, and in 1741, the Mahrattas attacked the place unsuccess-

21

fully. The Fort was extended and strengthened in 1743, and by this time the city had already become the largest in South India.

In 1746, Labourdonnais bombarded and captured the Fort; but the settlement was restored to the English two years later by the treaty of Aix-la-Chapelle. In 1758, the French under Lally occupied Black Town and invested the Fort; but it was relieved after a siege of two months on the arrival of a British fleet, when the besiegers retired with precipitation.

With the exception of the threatened approach of Hyder Ali's horsemen in 1769, and again in 1787, Madras has, since the French siege, been free from external attack.

11. Objects of Interest. *The School of Arts* (near Egmore Station) was established by Dr. Alexander Hunter in 1850 and was taken over by Government some five years later. The subjects taught are drawing, painting, engraving in metal and wood, modelling, moulding, carpet-weaving and pottery-making, etc.

The Gun Carriage Factory was originally established in 1802 at Seringapatam; but, as the supply of timber from the teak forests of Mysore and Coorg failed, it was removed to Madras in 1830. The Factory is replete with all the requisite machinery.

The Peoples' Park, for which Madras is indebted to Sir Charles Trevelyan, is near the Central Station of the Madras Railway. It was established in 1859, and is controlled by a Superintendent under the orders of the Municipal Commissioners. The main entrance, open from 5 A.M. to 8-30 P.M., is in the Poonamallee Road adjacent to the Hospital Bridge. The Park contains 116 acres of land, eleven lakes, $5\frac{1}{2}$ miles of road, a band-stand, public bath, two lawn-tennis courts, and a small zoological and ornithological collection. A portion of the Park has been taken up for the Victoria Public Hall in the neighbourhood of the Poonamallee Road.

The Victoria Public Hall.—This building was erected in 1887 at a cost of Rs. 1,79,000, with funds partly raised by public subscription and partly borrowed from the late Rajah of Vizianagaram. The hall is intended for public or private meetings, exhibitions, lectures, concerts, dinners, balls, theatrical or musical performances, and for any other purpose conducing to the moral, social, and intellectual welfare, or rational recreation of the public of Madras. The upper hall will accommodate 600, the gallery 200, and the lower hall 600 persons. Applications for the use of the building should be made to the Honorary Secretary.

The following is the present scale of charges :—

UPPER HALL.

1. For professional theatrical parties. For one single night, Rs. 50.
   If engaged for more than one night—

From 1st to 6th both inclusive	.. ..	Rs. 40 per night.
„ 7th to 12th „ „	.. ..	„ 35 „
„ 13th to 18th „ „	.. ..	„ 30 „
„ 19th to 24th „ „	.. ..	„ 20 „

2. For Amateur Dramatic Societies—half the above rates.
3. For private entertainments .. .. Rs. 30 per night
4. For purely charitable purposes .. .. „ 20 „
5. For meetings and lectures when the public
   are admitted free .. .. Rs. 15-0-0 on each occasion.
   Lower Hall .. .. „ 10-0-0 „ „
   North and South rooms .. „ 3-8-0 „ „

Munro's Statue.—Midway between Government House and the Fort stands the noble equestrian statue of Sir Thomas Munro, by Chantrey, erected by public subscription at a cost of over £12,000.

The Napier Park is a memorial of Lord Napier and Ettrick, who was Governor of Madras in 1866—72. On the west side there is a native girls' school, the last gift of Lord Napier.

The Memorial Hall, near the General Hospital, was erected by public subscription in commemoration of " the goodness and forbearance of Almighty God in sparing this Presidency from the Sepoy Mutiny which devastated the sister Presidency of Bengal in the year 1857. It is available for public meetings of a religious, educational, charitable, or scientific character; its doors being closed against balls, concerts, theatrical exhibitions and such like entertainments as of the character of mere worldly amusements." It is managed by a committee of gentlemen representing the various religious bodies of Madras.

Pachaiyappa's Hall, on the Esplanade Road, Black Town, was built in 1850 from funds bequeathed by Pachaiyappa Mudaliyar for public charities. The building is in the Greek Ionic style; but the general effect is marred by its environment of insignificant native buildings.

The High Court and Law College form a handsome and extensive group of buildings recently constructed from the designs of Messrs. Brassington and Irvin, Consulting Architects to Government. The elevation of the buildings is imposing and the internal decorations of the High Court in carving, ornamental tiling, stained glass, and iron works is particularly good. The new light for the Madras roadstead is exhibited from the main dome of the High Court, the old light-house being consequently no longer used. This light has a full power service intensity of 18,000 candles showing all round the compass, and giving white double flashes of half-minute periods.

Fort St. George contains extensive barracks for the accommodation of the troops in garrison, St. Mary's church, the principal Government Secretariat offices and the Arsenal. Here in writers buildings, Clive twice attempted suicide by snapping a pistol at his head. From this Fort he marched to his first victories and from it went the army which on May 4th, 1799, defeated Tippoo and captured Seringapatam. For some years past the walls of the Fort have showed signs of failure and in places the masonry has been replaced by earthen parapets.

Lord Cornwallis' Statue.—This statue within the Fort was erected in 1800, and represents in a standing attitude the British General, who conquered Tippoo Sultan at

GRAPHIC ART SOCIETY

THE HIGH COURT MADRAS

NEGATIVE BY W. A. CROSS

Seringapatam. A panel illustrating the surrender of Tippoo's two sons in 1792 is sculptured in *alto relievo* on one side of the pedestal.

Chepauk Park and Palace.—The site of this park once belonged to the Nawabs of the Carnatic; but, on the death of the last occupant of the musnud, the property escheated to Government.

The palace is built in the Moorish style and with its stately tower presents a most imposing appearance. It is occupied by the offices of the Board of Revenue, and an addition to the south accommodates the College of Civil Engineering.

The Senate House.—North of the offices of the Board of Revenue is the Senate House of the Madras University. It was begun in 1874 and completed in 1879 at a cost of Rs. 289,000.

The Presidency College is situated on the Marina, south of the Public Works Secretariat. Within its walls stands a statue of Mr. E. B. Powell, C.S.I., once a leading educationalist of this city and a late Director of Public Instruction.

Government House is situated in an extensive deer park lying between the Cooum, the Marina, and the Mount and Wallajah Roads. There are many interesting pictures in it, including a portrait of Lady Munro (by Sir Thomas Lawrence) and one of Clive. The Banqueting Hall is a lofty detached building, 80 feet long by 60 feet broad, principally used for State functions and Balls. It was constructed during Lord Clive's government to commemorate the fall of Seringapatam. Among the portraits of past Governors of Madras are many pictures of interest including the following:—

George III. (taken at the beginning of his reign), Queen Charlotte, a full length portrait of Sir Thomas Munro, Lord Hobart, Lord Harris, Lord Mornington (afterwards Marquis Wellesley), and General Wellesley (Duke of Wellington).

The Government Museum in Pantheon Road dates from 1851 when the collections previously kept in Fort St. George were removed to the older portion of the present buildings. In this section is a small vivarium of indigenous snakes and collections illustrating the fauna, flora, mineralogy, archæology, and economic products (including timbers) of Southern India. The new building is devoted to the arts, industries, and ethnology of the Madras Presidency, and contains a very fine selection of arms, and armour obtained from the Tanjore armoury, and by transfer from the arsenal in Fort St. George. The museum possesses an excellent collection of Indian coins which can be seen by those interested in numismatics on application to the superintendent and an anthropometrical Laboratory for research purposes which is not open to the public. Under Dr. Edgar Thurston's control the museum has developed largely in recent years and is well worth visiting. Attached to the museum is the Connemara public library and theatre. The interior of the library is beautifully decorated and should certainly be seen. The museum and library are open gratuitously to the public daily, Fridays excepted, from 7 A.M. to 5 P.M., but on the first Saturday of every month male visitors are required to leave after 12-noon to enable native gosha women to view the collections.

General Neill's Statue occupies a prominent position on the Mount Road near to the Club Road.

The Government Observatory, established in 1792, is situated in Nungambaukam and has been under the control of very eminent men.

The Agri-Horticultural Society's Gardens are in Teynampet, opposite to the chief entrance of the cathedral, the nurseries being located in a separate plot of land on the east of the cathedral. The gardens are mainly due to the late Dr. Wight, formerly a Surgeon in the Madras Army and a distinguished botanist. They occupy an area of 22 acres and are well laid out and stocked with many rare plants, tropical palms and Australian trees. The gardens are open free to the public at all times, and seeds can be bought by non-members at the office. A botanical library is attached to the gardens which can be used by permission of the Honorary Secretary.

Madras Literary Society.—This Society possesses a library of over 40,000 volumes, especially complete in history, biography, fiction, travel, and literature, attached to which are reading and writing rooms. The library is situated in the Pantheon Road and is open to members from 7 A. M. to 6 P. M. on week days. Any one wishing to join the Society should communicate with the Honorary Secretary.

SAIDAPET.

Saidapet (pop. 5,702) is a union town situated in a taluq of the same name, 5¼ miles from Madras (Egmore), and is the head-quarters of the Collector of the District of Chingleput.

Local Accommodation.—There is no accommodation for Europeans, except the waiting room at the Railway station.

In the town are 4 hotels for Brahmins and 3 for native travellers of other castes, the charges varying from 2½ to 4 annas per meal, according to quality. At "Muniappa's Choultry," three-quarter of a mile from the station, free lodging for three days is allowed to all classes of natives.

Road Conveyance.—Jutkas and single bullock-carts are procurable at the station, the fares being—

Jutkas—

To the town	..	..	..	.. 1½ annas.
To St. Thomas' Mount	..	..	.. 2 „
To Madras	..	..	..	.. 8 „

Bullock-carts—

To the town	..	..	..	.. 1½ „
To St. Thomas' Mount	..	..	.. 1¼ „
To Madras	..	..	..	.. 6 „

Local Manufactures and Products.—Weaving is the principal industry, sufficient cloth being made to supply local wants.

Local Officials.—Besides the Collector, an Assistant Collector, Treasury Deputy Collector, and a District Surgeon are stationed at Saidapet. The offices of the Collector are located in a house known as Holmes Gardens. The central depôt for salt from the south is at this place. There is a local fund dispensary and a high school.

Objects of Interest.—Two small temples, one dedicated to Siva, the other to Vishnu.

The College of Agriculture, which has been in existence for about 25 years, gives instruction in agriculture and allied subjects, as veterinary knowledge, chemistry, botany, etc. The buildings include lecture rooms, offices, two laboratories, a museum and a library, the two latter being open to the public during working hours. Within the college compound are the Principal's quarters and several cottages for students. Attached to the institution are a botanical garden containing specimen crops and plants, a model farm of 168 acres, and a veterinary hospital. On the farm a herd of pure bred Nellore cattle is maintained and a collection of agricultural implements is open to inspection. The veterinary hospital can accommodate about 20 inpatients, and owners can send their animals for treatment at any time either as in- or out-patient at a moderate charge.

GUINDY.

Guindy is a small station, about a mile south of Saidapet, and between that station and St. Thomas' Mount, at which trains only stop, by arrangement, when H. E. the Governor is in residence at his country-house and during the Madras Races.

The Governor's residence at Guindy is in many respects superior to that at Madras, and owes its modern form to Lord Elphinstone. The house has a very handsome appearance, being faced with the beautiful shell lime plaster for which Madras is so famous and is surrounded by a large and beautiful Park.

The Madras Race Course, one of the best in Southern India, is close to the station.

Local Officials.—The following officials have offices in Guindy, the District Registrar, Divisional Deputy Collector, Tahsildar and Sub-Magistrate.

Local Manufactures and Products.—Messrs. Oakes & Co. have established a cigar factory and tobacco depôt so as to be outside the Municipal limits of Madras.

ST. THOMAS' MOUNT.

St. Thomas' Mount (pop. 13,290) is a cantonment town in the Saidapet taluq of the Chingleput District, 8 miles from Madras (Egmore).

The Mount, which is 220 feet above sea level, is composed of green stone and syenite and is ascended by masonry steps. On the plain at the Eastern side of the base, lies the military cantonment, which is the head-quarters of the Artillery in the Madras Presidency, and the station of a brigade of Field Artillery. The cantonment contains the usual neatly built barracks, offices, hospitals and stores, necessitated by military occupation.

The bungalows of the officers and other residents with their trimly-kept gardens, give the place a pleasant appearance, while the absence of bazaars and native huts, which are hidden away to the eastward, adds to the favourable impression made on the visitor who sees the cantonment for the first time.

Local Accommodation.—With the exception of the waiting room at the station, there is no accommodation for Europeans. There are two choultries about half a mile north of the station, where meals are served to natives of all classes at the rate of $2\frac{1}{2}$ to 3 annas per meal.

Road Conveyance.—Jutkas and bullock-carts are procurable at the station at train times ; and hackney carriages, if previously arranged for.   The charge to the town is :—

Hackney carriages	..	..	..	..12 annas.
Jutkas	..	..	..	.. 4 ,,
Bullock-carts	..	..	..	.. 2 ,,

Local Officials.—The officials having offices in the cantonment are the Cantonment Magistrate, Superintendent of Police, officers commanding the batteries of Artillery and the Madras Infantry.

Missions and Churches.—Below the hill are the well built Protestant Church of St. Thomas' a Wesleyan and two Roman Catholic Chapels.   The summit of the Mount is crowned by an old Roman Catholic Church called the "Expectation of the Blessed Virgin," which belongs to the Armenian Catholics.   Behind the altar is a curiously carved stone cross, bearing a very ancient inscription, which translated, reads :—

" Who believes in the Messiah and in God above
" And in the Holy Ghost, is in favour with him
" Who bore the cross."

Historical.—St. Thomas' Mount figured in British History long before it was made a cantonment.   The battle of the Mount, fought on February 7th, 1759, was one of the fiercest struggles of the Franco-British war in India.   It lasted from early morning till 5 P.M., when the French retreated, the British at that time having only sufficient ammunition left to last another two minutes.

In 1774 the Cantonment became the head-quarters of the Artillery in the Madras Presidency and six years later a well equipped expedition was despatched from it to assist Colonel Baillie, who was then operating against a triple confederation of native princes headed by Hyder Ali.   Baillie's detachment was cut up and the force had to return to cantonments, harassed by countless swarms of Mahratta horse.

Objects of Interest.—The Little Mount, the traditionary site of St. Thomas' martyrdom, lies to the south-east of the cantonment and contains a cave in which is a spring of water. St. Thomas is said to have taken refuge in the cave when pressed by his pursuers, and by the miraculous creation of the spring inside the cave he was protected against thirst. Two stones are pointed out as impress of his feet and knees, while a third stone is supposed to be stained with his blood. A church has been erected over the cave at which a large festival is annually held. At the foot of the steps leading to the church is a stone slab inscribed in Armenian characters.

PALLAVARAM.

Pallavaram (pop. 4,222) is a cantonment town in the Saidapet taluq of the Chingleput district, 12 miles south of Madras (Egmore). It was formerly known as the Presidency Cantonment, native troops being stationed in it for garrisoning Madras. The lines were originally constructed for four regiments, but at present are only occupied as a European pensioner's depôt.

A range of hills separates Pallavaram from the sea, so that the temperature is high. The place is, however, healthy, and the water good and abundant. There are two peaks from 400 to 500 feet in height rising from the range in question, each of which is crowned by a bungalow.

Local Accommodation.—There is a choultry close to the station, where free lodging is allowed for three days to all classes of natives. After three days, 2½ to 4 annas per meal is charged.

Road Conveyance.—Jutkas and bullock-carts can be had at the station, if previous notice is given, the fares being:—

To the town	..	..	..	.. 2 annas.
Elsewhere (per mile)		..	..	.. 1½ ,,

Railway Facilities.—There is a good local train service to and from Madras. Waiting accommodation is provided at the station for first and second class passengers.

Local Manufactures and Products.—The principal industries are the tanning of hides for the Madras market, and the quarrying of stone for the Madras Harbour works and for road metal.

Local Officials.—The Cantonment Magistrate of St. Thomas' Mount holds court here twice a week.

Missions, Churches, etc.—There is a Roman Catholic church.

Objects of Interest.—In the neighbourhood is the Pancha-pandava hill which contains ancient remains.

There is a small bungalow on the top of a hill near the station containing a relic of the prophet, kept by Nawab Feroz Hussein Sahib. An annual festival is held in May. There is also a Durga (cemetery) about a mile east of the station containing the tomb of one Buddoo Shaheed Sahib, a hero who fought with the Portuguese, about three centuries ago.

VANDALUR.

Vandalur (pop. 541) is situated in the Chingleput taluq of the Chingleput district, 18½ miles from Madras (Egmore). During the wars of the Carnatic troops were frequently quartered in an entrenched camp, near the village, and a substantial house of two storeys erected by General Joseph Smith in 1765 is still existent.

Pilgrims proceeding to Sriperumbudur, the reputed birth place of Ramanujachari, the great Vaishnavite teacher, and, of Udaiyavar, a Vaishnavite devotee, usually break their journey at Vandalur. The local temple also attracts a large number of pilgrims during the annual festival in May.

Local Accommodation.—A free P. W. D. rest-house having accommodation for one person is close to station; but has no furniture nor cook. Another bungalow near the station can be occupied on payment of one rupee per adult per day. It contains neither furniture nor crockery, and has no cook. Provisions are not procurable.

Road Conveyance.—Bullock-carts can be procured at a minimum charge of one rupee, but can be kept the whole day for a payment of two rupees.

Local Manufactures and Products.—Pumpkins are grown here in large numbers.

Objects of Interest.—The Vishnu temple having an inscription of Vijianugur dynasty is worth a visit.

Sport.—In the reserved forest close to this station hare and partridge are fairly plentiful, and excellent snipe shooting can also be had in the season. The wages of shikarries is one to two rupees daily according to sport, and coolies receive 4 to 6 annas per diem.

GUDUVANCHERI.

Guduvancheri (pop. 831) is situated in the Chingleput taluq of the Chingleput district, 22¼ miles from Madras (Egmore), and is one of the healthiest villages in the district.

Local Accommodation.—For Europeans there is a fully, furnished travellers' bungalow, which can accommodate two persons; but occupants must provide their own cook. The rent is one rupee per diem for each person. Provisions are procurable at the bazaar close by. For natives of all classes a choultry is provided, where free lodging is allowed for three days. It has no cook nor cooking utensils; so travellers must make their own arrangements for food.

Road Conveyance.—Bullock-carts are procurable on previous notice being given. The minimum charge for a cart is one rupee; but the vehicle can be used the whole day for two rupees.

Local Manufactures and Products.—Rice is grown in large quantities and is sent to Madras for sale.

Sport.—In the reserved forest near the station hare and partridge can be obtained, and the snipe ground is considered one of the best in the neighbourhood of Madras. Shikarries can be procured at a charge of from one to two rupees daily according to sport and coolies at from 4 to 6 annas per diem.

SINGAPERUMALKOIL.

Singaperumalkoil (pop. 430) is situated in the Chingleput taluq of the Chingleput district, 29¼ miles from Madras (Egmore). The village, which is about half a mile from the station, is the scene of a yearly festival held in May.

Road Conveyance.—Bullock-carts can be procured if previous notice be given to the local officials. The minimum charge is one rupee; but the cart can be used the whole day on payment of two rupees.

Object of Interest.—The village contains an old temple which bears inscriptions both in Telugu and Nagari.

Sport.—Hare and partridge can be obtained in the reserved forest near the station, and there is good snipe shooting during the cold weather. The charge for a shikarry is from one to two rupees *per diem* according to the sport shown and for a cooly 4 to 6 annas.

CHINGLEPUT JUNCTION.

Chingleput (lat. 12·42, long. 80·01, pop. 3,466) is the chief town of the Collectorate and Taluq of the same name. It is 34½ miles from Madras (Egmore), and is the Junction station for a branch line to Arkonam on the Madras Railway. It stands half a mile from the northern bank of the river Palar, the intermediate space being occupied by a ridge of low hills. The health of Chingleput is generally good and the climate wonderfully cool. It is nearly surrounded by a number of hills, none of them much exceeding 500 feet in height, and these, together with the large tank, and several lesser sheets of water, lend to the scenery, especially after the rains, an appearance of picturesque beauty, seldom met with on the plains. The large tank is two miles long by one mile broad, and is

formed by the damming of the surplus water of the country
for 10 miles to the north. Passengers for the " Seven
Pagodas " can alight at this station.

The distances to the principal junctions on the South
Indian Railway are :—

To Arkonam Junction (for Madras Railway, etc.)	..	39 miles.
Villupuram Junction (for Pondicherry) ..	..	64 ,,
Mayavaram Junction (for Negapatam and Mutupet)	..	139 ,,
Tanjore	..	198 ,,
Trichinopoly Junction (for Erode) ..	..	214 ,,
Ammayanayakanur (for Kodaikanal) ..	..	285 ,,
Madura	..	310 ,,
Maniyachi (for Tinnevelly)	..	391 ,,
Tuticorin	..	409 ,,

Local Accommodation.—There is a good travellers'
bungalow close to the Railway station, which is fully
furnished and has a butler in charge, who can supply
meals, if required. This bungalow can accommodate four
persons at one time. If previous notice is given, arrangements can be made to accommodate as many as twelve as
there are sufficient servants, crockery, etc., at the bungalow.
The rent is one rupee *per diem* for a single person, and
Re. 1 and As. 8 for a married couple. Near the station are
four Brahmin hotels where meals are served to all classes of
natives at from 2½ to 4 annas per head. There is also a
commodious choultry, where free lodging for three days
is allowed.

Road Conveyance.—Jutkas and bullock-carts are procurable at the station at 2 annas per mile.

Railway Facilities.—There is a first and second class
waiting-room at the station, also refreshment rooms for first
and second-class passengers, at which a small stock of
travellers' requisites is kept by Messrs. Spencer & Co.,
Limited.

Missions, Churches, etc.—Near the travellers' bungalow
are Protestant and Roman Cotholic churches, the former
of which maintains a Mission High School.

Local Officials.—The District Judge, Joint Magistrate,

Civil Surgeon, Superintendent of the Jail, District Munsif, Tahsildar, Sub-Magistrate and the Superintendent of the Reformatory.

Local Manufactures and Products.—Brick-making is the principal industry, the clay being the best in the district for bricks. Weaving is also carried on at the Reformatory.

Historical.—The Fort was erected at the end of the sixteenth century, when the Vijianagar Rajahs held their court alternately here and at Chandragiri. Its trace is nearly a parallelogram of 400 yards from north to south, and 320 yards from east to west, and it is built of roughly dressed stone. About 1644 it passed into the hands of the Golcondah Chiefs, who gave it up to the Nawabs of Arcot, and by the latter, it was surrendered in 1751 to Chunda Sahib. In 1752, Clive bombarded it, and compelled the French garrison to yield. After the reduction of Fort St. David in 1758, the English, apprehensive of an attack on Madras, called in all the garrisons and stores from outlying forts, and Chingleput was consequently abandoned. On the advance of the French from the south it was again garrisoned, but Lally, the French Governor, finding it impregnable, left it in his rear and passed on to Madras. In 1780, the British force operating against Hyder Ali found refuge here after the destruction of General Baillie's column. During the later wars with Mysore, this fortress was once taken by the enemy, re-occupied by the British, and twice unsuccessfully besieged, from which time it remained uninterruptedly in the hands of the East India Company.

Objects of Interest.—The remains of the old Fort, the Reformatory School, the Shrine of Tirukalikundram, Sadras, the Fort at Tiruvadisulam and the old Cemetery.

Sport.—Excellent snipe shooting can be had in the season. Shikarries are available at a charge of rupee one to rupees two daily, according to sport shown. Coolies are paid 4 annas per day.

BASTION, CHINGLEPUT FORT

GRAPHIC ART SOCIETY

TIRUKALIKUNDRAM

NEGATIVE BY A. D. G. SHELLEY

The "*Seven Pagodas*" or Mahavellipore, stand midway between Sadras and Covelong and are conveniently reached *via* Chingleput on the South Indian Railway. There is a good metalled road from Chingleput to Sadras bridge (18 miles), the fare by jutka for this portion of the journey being Rs. 2 and As. 8. At Sadras bridge it is necessary to take a boat, and application for one to be in readiness should be made previously to Varatha Rajalu Chetty, though generally boats can be picked up at the bridge without prior notice. The charge for a boat from Sadras to Mahavellipore (5 miles) is about Rs. 2. An alternative road branches off from the Sadras road at Tirukalikundram (sacred kite village) leading to the point on the Buckingham Canal opposite to Mahavellipore (Seven Pagodas). This is an unmetalled road and difficult in the rainy season, but it is nine miles shorter than *via* Sadras, and bullock-carts frequently prefer to take it. Assuming that Chingleput is left early in the morning, the following would be the approximate time-table for the journey by jutka and boat:—

Leave Chingleput	..	.. 7-15
Arrive Sadras Bridge	..	..10-15
Leave Sadras Bridge	..	..10-30
Arrive Seven Pagodas		{ 12-0 if wind is favourable.
		{ 1-30 with head wind.

If the journey were made entirely by road, it would take 4 hours by jutka and $7\frac{1}{2}$ to 8 hours by bullock-cart and the fares would be—

By jutka	..	..	..	..Rs. 4 0 0
By bullock-cart	..	..	..	.. „ 1 8 0

At Mahavellipore there is a rest-house which is in charge of the Executive Engineer, Buckingham Canal Division, and will shortly afford accommodation for six persons, at one time. Eggs, fowls, sea-fish and milk are procurable; also food for servants. The charge for the use of this building (which is furnished and contains cutlery, crockery and a cook) is 8 annas *per diem* or portion of a day of 24 hours per person. Should accommodation be required by a Government official on duty, private individuals must

23

vacate. As it is improbable, however, that more than one Government official would be there at one time and the bungalow will be furnished for six persons, this is a remote contingency. The best way for tourists to see the place is to go from the rest-house to the monolithic temples and figures called the raths, thence to the structural Shore Pagoda, then through the village to the low range of hills containinig several excavations, the sculpture of Arjuna's Penance and the light-house on top of a pagoda. The raths are situated close together about ⅛ mile from the sea. With regard to these Mr. Fergusson, in his History of Indian and Eastern Architecture, says :—" The oldest and most interesting group of monuments are the so-called five raths, or monolithic temples standing on the sea-shore. One of these, that with the apsidal termination, stands a little detached from the rest. The other four stand in a line north and south, and look as if they had been carved out of a single stone or rock, which originally, if that were so, must have been between 35 feet and 40 feet high at its southern end sinking to half that height at its northern extremity, and its width diminishing in a like proportion. The first on the north is a mere Pausala or cell, 11 feet square externally, and 16 feet high. It is the only one too that seems finished or nearly so, but it has no throne or image internally from which we might guess its destination. The next is a small copy of the last to the southward, and measures 11 feet by 16 feet in plan and 20 feet in height. The third is very remarkable : it is an oblong building with a curvilinear-shaped roof with a straight ridge. Its dimensions are 42 feet long, 25 feet wide and 25 feet high. Externally it seems to have been completely carved, but internally only partially excavated, the works being apparently stopped by an accident. It is cracked completely through, so that daylight can be seen through it, and several masses of the rock have fallen to the ground. This has been ascribed to an earthquake and

THE SHORE TEMPLE MAHAVALLIPORE

other causes. My impression is, the explanation is not far to seek, but arose from unskilfulness on the part of the workmen employed in a first attempt. Having completed the exterior, they set to work to excavate the interior, so as to make it resemble a structural building of the same class, leaving only such pillars and supports as were sufficient to support a wooden roof of the ordinary construction. In this instance it was a mass of solid granite which, had the excavation been completed, would certainly have crushed the lower storey to powder. As it was, the builders seem to have taken the hint of the crack, and stopped the further progress of the works. The last, however, is the most interesting of the series. Its dimentions are 27 feet by 25 feet in plan, 34 feet in height. Its upper part is entirely finished with its sculptures, the lower merely blocked out. It may be that, frightened by the crack in the last-named rath, or from some other cause, they desisted, and it still remains in an unfinished state." Mr. Fergusson adds : " I see no reason for doubting the inference drawn by Sir Walter Elliot from their inscriptions that the excavations could not well have been made later than the 6th century." Add to all this that the raths are certainly very much like Buddhist buildings as we learn to know them from the early caves, and it seems hardly to admit of doubt that we have here petrifactions of the last forms of Buddhist architecture, and the first forms of that of the Dravidian.

The Shore Temple (plate No. 6) has, owing partly to its romantic position within range of the spray from the surf, attracted more general attention than the whole of the rest of the remains put together. It is in the purest early Dravidian style, the vimanah or tower over the shrine forming the central and principal mass, while the gopuram, or original gateway alongside is comparatively insignificant. The superficial extent of this temple is small, about 1,600 feet, and the height of the vimanah is about 60 feet. Like the smaller one, it is surmounted by the umbrella-shaped summit called Kalasa, made of basaltic rock which, unlike the granite below, bears no signs of destruction by the sea-air. It is built of blocks of granite, but time and religious strife have done much to conceal and alter the original design. What was no doubt the gateway on the eastern side has afterwards been converted into a separate shrine, and the passage of communication between the two has been blocked up at each end.

Additional support is given to this view by the fact that a stone screen surrounds the larger vimanah, but stops opposite the smaller. Moreover, the only entrance at present to the larger is through a large bare doorway cut in the screen, the only access to which is by scrambling along the edge of precipitous rocks, while that to the smaller is from the south over bare ground; but these rocks bear marks of the cutting of the rude stone steps, and apparently of platforms to support some terrace or superstructure. A pillar supposed to be a Dhipastamba, or lamp-pillar, such as is found in all pagodas, stands in the surf, but there is no visible means of ascent, and, except a sort of peg at the top, no appliance for fixing a light. Near the temple lie various figures of small crouching bulls and a mahishesura, all much eaten away by the action of the sea-air. The garbhagriha or " womb of the temple " under the principal vimanah, is occupied by a large lingam, sixteen sided made of black marble which is much mutilated. In a sort of verandah behind is a recumbent figure of Vishnu with the ordinary Nagasesha above and below him. This unusual presence of the two deities under one roof is unexplained, unless it be that the temple like the raths was erected before the intolerance of sects had produced irreconcilable antagonism between the Sivite and Vishnuvite faiths. In confirmation of this theory, images of Brahma and Vishnu are found carved on the wall along with those of Parvati, Param------wara and the young Subramanyaswami.

NEGATIVE BY A. D. G. SHELLEY

Dr. Hunter, late of the Madras School of Arts, thus describes the great bass-relief which goes by the name of "Arjuna's Penance" (plate No. 7). On the left side of the rock, which is divided by a deep natural cleft, the chief figure in the upper part appears to be the giant rajah, Mahabali Chakravurthi, with his attendant dwarfs, five rajahs with their wives, four warriors, five ascetics, and a holy rishi in his cave temple. The lions, tigers, cheetahs and deer, in different parts of the sculpture, show that the people have travelled from a distance through the jungles. In the central part of the cleft at the bottom, on the left, is a figure seated, which I take to be Buddha, with his five disciples in front of the cave temple with the holy Rishi. The heads of three of the disciples have been broken off. In the deep recess formed by the natural cleft in the centre of the rock sculpture is the lower part of the body and tail of the snake deity Vasuki, the Naga Rajah, and below this is the entire figure of Ulipi, his daughter, with a canopy of three snakes rising over the head. The upper portion of the Naga deity had been broken off and was said to be buried in front of the sculptures. I made search for it, found it and got it dug up, set upright and photographed; it is the figure of a man with his hands raised in prayer, and a canopy of seven snakes rising over a pyramidal head-dress, and with the usual emblems of the Buddhist religion. To the right of these are several rajahs and men, each accompained by his wife, six dwarfs, and eight garudas, or figures of men and women with the legs of birds; several monkeys, a cat doing penance, while rats are running near it. Two large, and several small elephants, lions, tigers, geese, cocks and hens. I thought at first that all the figures were coming to do reverence, or to worship the snake deity, but when we first took photographs of this rock sculpture, the whole of the central cleft was overgrown with trees and brushwood and the five disciples of Buddha were buried. Lord Napier, then Governor of Madras, visited the spot about a week after the snake deity was dug up, and had excavations made to the depth of 7 or 8 feet, which exposed a great number of figures and animals, and showed that the old road must have passed in front of the rock at a depth of five or six feet below the present level, the ground having been filled up chiefly with broken bricks and earth, with here and there large fragments of sculptured rocks, dressed stone, and cornices from the adjoining temples. The broken tusk of the large elephant was also found. To the left and below the five disciples of Buddha is a deer, in a very natural attitude, scratching its nose with its hind foot. The male and female elephants with their young behind them, and some of the figures of crouching tigers and cheetahs, are in a very natural and spirited style, and there is a great look of natural animation, movement and bustle in the whole group of which Buddha and his five disciples appear to occupy the principal position and to attract the greatest attention, while the snake deity and his daughter are, as it were, in the background, and ascetics are scattered about in several parts . . . One point of great importance in these early rock sculptures is that they represent scenes of peace, with men and their wives, a single wife accompanying each, and the animals, garudas, and birds in pairs, while the Rajah Mahabali is accompanied by dwarfs, and other rajahs, whose rank is indicated by umbrella-bearers, have each his wife beside him. The ascetics, of whom there are five or six, have no wives. It appears to me that the story is one which represents the establishment of the Buddhist religion or one of peace, goodwill, toleration, and kindness to all men, and to animals and birds."

With regard to the return journey from Mahavellipore, the best time to leave is in the afternoon, the following being an approximate time-table with a fair wind. With a head-wind the boat journey to Sadras bridge will occupy about three hours, unless extra coolies be engaged for towing when the time may be shortened by one hour.

Leave Seven Pagodas	..	..	.. 2- 0 p.m.
Arrive Sadras Bridge	..	..	.. 3-15 ,,
Leave Sadras Bridge	..	..	.. 3-25 ,,
Arrive Chingleput	..	..	.. 6-30 ,,

The cost of the return journey is the same as that of the outward.

The Seven Pagodas can also be reached from Madras, the journey being made entirely by boat, and occupying about 8 hours in one direction and 17 in the other, according to the wind. Applications for house, boats and particulars as to charge should be made to the Wharf Superintendent, the Basin, Madras. For this journey, furniture must be hired, and servants and provisions taken. It is usual to go on board and leave the boats at the bridge near Searle's Gardens at the Adyar.

KOLATUR (NORTH).

Kolatur (North) (pop. 2,017) is situated in the Chingleput taluq of the Chingleput district, about 1½ miles, north of the river Palar, on the main line, 40¼ miles from Madras (Egmore). The native name of this place is "Porkalanthy" and it was the birthplace of the Tamil poet, Puhalandipulavar.

Road Conveyance.—Bullock-carts are available, if previous notice given, at a charge of 2 annas per mile.

Local Officials.—The Village Munsiff and kurnam.

Missions, Churches, etc.—There is a Mission School under the management of Rev. A. Andrews, of Chingleput, near the station.

Objects of Interest.—In the village of Manapakam, about ¾ of a mile south, is a temple dedicated to "Kanney-ammon" where a festival is held every Friday.

Sport.—Snipe shooting can be had during the season. Shikaries are not available; but coolies can be engaged at 4 annas per day.

PADALAM.

Padalam (pop. 900) is situated in the Madurantakam taluq of the Chingleput district, on the southern bank of the river Palar, on the main line, 42½ miles from Madras (Egmore). Men in this village are credited with the power of curing snake-bite.

Road Conveyance.—Bullock-carts can be obtained, on previous notice, at 2 annas per mile.

Local Officials.—The Village Munsiff and kurnam.

Objects of Interest.—The Railway Bridge near the station is one of the largest on the line, having 18 spans of 120 feet.

Sport.—Snipe shooting can be had here in the cold season. Shikaries are not available ; but coolies can be hired at 4 annas per diem.

MADURANTAKAM.

Madurantakam (pop. 5,143) is situated in the Madurantakam taluq of the Chingleput district, on the main line, 51 miles from Madras (Egmore). The village is about ¼ of a mile west of the station, which commands a view of cocoanut and plantain groves on all sides. The chief residents of this place are Brahmins of the Vishnava sect.

Local Accommodation.—There is a travellers' bungalow about 2½ miles west of the station which is fully furnished. No cook is kept, and fowls, milk and eggs are the only eatables for Europeans obtainable in the village.

For Hindus there are four hotels close to the railway station, where meals are served at from 2½ to 3 annas per head.

A choultry is also being constructed.

Road Conveyance.—Jutkas and bullock-carts are procurable at the station.

Charges—

Jutkas	.. ..	2 annas per mile.
Bullock-carts ..	..	1½ „ „

Local Manufactures and Products—Rice is largely grown and laced and other cloths are woven. Salt is brought into this station in great quantities from Seyyur and Soonampet.

Local Officials.—The Tahsildar, Sub-Magistrate, Sub-Registrar, and Inspector of Police.

Missions, Churches, etc.—About 1½ miles, east of the station, is a Roman Catholic Church.

Clubs.—Madurantakam possesses a Reading-room attached to the Hindu High School, a Tennis Court for the officials of the place, and a Literary Society called the Hindu Young Men's Association, which possesses a fairly good library.

Objects of Interest.—The large tank about half a mile, south-west of the station, formed by damming up the Kiliyaur, is 1½ miles long, and its circumference when full is seven miles. Its overflow or surplusing weir is a very fine work, the height from the crest to the bed of the river below being 30 feet. The southern portion is a curious and beautiful specimen of masonry. Instead of being built in steps, the face of this part of the weir is parabolic in section and consists of huge blocks of granite dressed to this shape and clamped together.

About two miles, north of the station, at Karunguli, are the remains of an old fort apparently Muhammedan, surrounded by a moat and containing the ruins of granaries.

Sport.—During the cold season, snipe shooting can be had in the neighbourhood of Madurantakam.

ACHARAPAKAM.

Acharapakam (pop. 1,272) is situated in the Maduranta-kam taluq of the Chingleput district, the village being about ½ mile, south-west of the station.

Local Accommodation.—About ½ mile, west of the station, is a travellers' bungalow, containing one cot, one chair and a table and which can be occupied free of charge. There is no cook, and, except eggs, fowls and milk, no provisions are to be had.

24

For natives, there is a choultry which can be occupied three days free of charge. Meals can be supplied at from 2½ to 3 annas per meal.

Road Conveyance.—Bullock-carts are available at a charge of from 1½ to 2 annas per mile, according to season.

Local Manufactures and Products.—Rice is largely grown, and mats are manufactured. Salt is imported in large quantities from Seyyur and Soonampet.

Local Officials.—The Village Munsiff, Revenue Inspector, Sub-Inspector of Salt and Abkari and a Vaccinator.

Missions, Churches, etc.—There is a Roman Catholic Church near the railway station.

Objects of Interest.—A big Siva temple at Sothuppola, some 2 miles north of the station, contains inscriptions. Festivals are held here during March and April.

Sport.—Snipe shooting can be had during the cold weather. The wage of a shikary is from 8 annas to one rupee, and of coolies 4 annas *per diem*.

PERAMBAIR.

Perambair (pop. 600) is situated in the Madurantakam taluq of the Chingleput district, on the main line 62¾ miles from Madras (Egmore).

The village is about ½ mile, north-west of the station, and has an old Siva temple dedicated to Subramanya.

OLAKUR.

Olakur (pop. 2,767) is situated in the Tindivanam taluq of the South Arcot district, on the main line 68 miles from Madras (Egmore).

Local Manufactures and Products.—Rice and varagu are grown.

Local Officials.—The Village Munsiff and Kurnam.

TINDIVANAM.

Tindivanam (pop. 9,191), the station for Wandiwash, is the chief town of the taluq of the same name in the

South Arcot District. It is on the main line 75¼ miles from Madras (Egmore), and consists of the hamlets of Avarapaukam, Cauverypauk, Gidangal, Jaffarabad, Moorangapaukam and Tindivanam. Gidangal was formerly fortified. The ruins of the ramparts and ditch still exist, and the place most probably was once of considerable importance, being situated close to the large Gidangal tank, where it would afford a secure granary for the rice crops grown under the tank.

Local Accommodation.—For Europeans a fully furnished travellers' bungalow is kept up under the charge of a butler, but there is no cook, and travellers must make their own arrangements for food. Rent 8 annas per day.

For natives, a choultry is maintained close to the station, where meals are supplied at 2½ annas per head. There are besides a number of small hotels in the town.

Road Conveyance.—Bullock-carts can be hired at 2 annas per mile.

Railway Facilities.—There is a Waiting-room at the station for first and second class passengers.

Local Manufactures and Products.—Rice cultivation, weaving and tanning are the principal industries.

Local Officials.—The Sub-Collector, P. W. D. Sub-Divisional Officer, District Munsiff, Tahsildar and Sub-Magistrate.

Missions, Churches, etc.—There is a Protestant as well as a Roman Catholic Church, while the American Mission have established a station.

Clubs.—A small Reading-room for natives is maintained.

Historical.—Tindivanam itself possesses but little of interest. Gingee, however, was formerly of great importance.

Gingee.—From the Tamil Chenji, probably meaning a fortified place, is situated 18 miles from Tindivanam station with which it is connected by an excellent metalled road.

The distance is covered by a pony-jutka in two hours by day and three by night, and by bullock-cart in about 4¼ hours. The Station Master at Tindivanam can usually arrange for transport, if given a few hours' notice, at 2¼ annas for a jutka. and 1¾ annas for a bullock-cart per mile. The road is sufficiently good throughout to permit of the journey being made by bicycle. Close to Gingee is a Local Fund Rest-house, but as it only contains a bedstead, one chair and two tables, it is necessary to take bedding, furniture, and cooking utensils. Milk, butter, eggs, poultry are procurable locally, and it is advisable to take a supply of small change to pay for such purchases. The charge for the bungalow is 8 annas for each 24 hours or shorter period per person, or 12 annas for 2 persons sharing the same room.

Visitors to this ancient and almost impregnable stronghold will be amply repaid for any trouble taken in reaching it, and if they desire to thoroughly investigate the stupendous ruins, should devote at last three clear days to the trip. Gingee comprises a group of three strongly fortified hills rising from 400 to 600 feet above the surrounding plain. The hills with their connecting massive granite walls of circumvallation enclose an irregular triangle whose area, according to Orme, exceeds seven square miles. The citadel is on the summit of Rajagiri, the highest peak, and is absolutely unapproachable, except from the north side, where a frail bamboo bridge spans a natural chasm artificially enlarged to 24 feet in width and 60 feet in depth. This bridge, some idea of which is given in plate 9, is reached by a staircase of rough hewn granite blocks winding from the base to the summit by a fairly easy gradient. The ascent is admirably commanded by the strong gateways of the three inner walls, and the bridge is dominated at 30 yards range by another masonry gateway, the flanking walls of which are pierced with embrasures and loopholes. The remaining hills, Kistnagiri or the English

BRIDGE TO CITADEL GINGEE

Mountain, and Chandrayan Drug or St. George's Mountain, form suitable outworks to the citadel with which they are connected by the outer wall. Space will only admit of the most interesting objects being enumerated and which the visitor should not miss seeing. These are briefly the two unfailing springs on the summit of Rajagiri, the two pagodas, the Kaliyana Mahal, the Gymkhana, the Granaries, the Edgahs, the Prisoners' Well, and the Devil's Gate and Tank. The great gun of Gingee bearing the figures 7560 stamped in the breach and made of a metal which has successfully resisted oxidation should be seen, as also a granite slab 15 feet square and 4 or 5 inches thick and known as the Rajah's bathing stone. If possible, the visitor should endeavour to secure the services of an obliging village official in the capacity of cicerone. Many of them speak English very well, and they have a never-failing fund of fable and anecdote relating to the by-gone glories of Gingee. At the present time the forts are practically deserted, a casual devotee or cooly being the only living persons to be seen.

The construction of the fortress is generally attributed to the Vijayanagar rajahs, an hypothesis which receives some support from the marked similarity of the ruins to those of Vijayanagar at Humpi. Gingee was in possession of these rajahs from the close of the 13th century until A.D. 1564, when it was captured by the Bijapur troops during the struggle between Vijayanagar Viceroys of the south and the combined forces of Bijapur, Golconda and Ahmednagar. In 1661-62 famine and pestilence caused the Muhammedans to evacuate Gingee, with the result that five years later Sivaji was able to obtain possession of the place by treachery. In 1689, Ram Raja, a brother of Sivaji, fled to Gingee for refuge when it became a rallying point for the Mahrattas. The Mogul army, under Zulfikar Khan, is said to have besieged the fortress for eight years, though it seems doubtful whether he was not in secret communication with the enemy during the greater part of the time. However, in January 1698, news reached Madras that he had captured the place by escalade, and it remained in possession of the Moguls until taken by the French in 1750, by a night attack. Two years later, a small English force attempted to capture the fortress, and in 1761 a second investment by the British resulted in a successful escalade.

Objects of Interest.—At Perumukal, six miles from Tindivanam, is an isolated rock, which was a fortified post during the 18th century, and was captured and re-captured by the French and English on several occasions.

MAILAM.

Mailam (pop. 1,505) is situated in the Tindivanam taluq of the South Arcot district, on the main line 81 miles from Madras (Egmore). The village is about 3 miles, south-east of the station, to which there is a good metalled road. Mailam stands at the foot of a hill, on the top of which is a Siva temple dedicated to Subramanya Swami, the eldest son of the god.

Local Accommodation.—There are ten chuttrams for natives, in nine of which free lodging is allowed for three days, and food is supplied at $2\frac{1}{2}$ annas per meal. In the remaining chuttram (known as Vencataramana Iyer's) free meals are served to Brahmins.

Road Conveyance.—Bullock-carts are available.

Charges—

To the village	..	..	.. 4 annas.
Elsewhere	..	..	.. $1\frac{1}{2}$ annas per mile.

Local Manufactures and Products.—Some three miles, east of the station, are important stone quarries which are largely worked for religious purposes.

Local Officials.—The Village Munsiff and Kurnam.

Objects of Interest.—At Chittanur, four miles north of the station, is an old Jain temple containing inscriptions and a stone car said to have been brought from Tanjore.

VIKRAVANDI.

Vikravandi (pop. 2,734) is situated in the Villupuram taluq of the South Arcot district, on the main line 90¼ miles from Madras (Egmore). The village is about a mile south of the station.

Local Accommodation.—A travellers' bungalow having accommodation for two persons, but containing only one cot, two chairs and two tables, and unprovided with either crockery or servants, is situated near the station. Charge 8 annas *per diem*. Fowls, eggs and milk are the only eatables suitable for Europeans procurable locally. Two chuttrams are maintained—one for Brahmins only, the other for Brahmins and other natives which travellers may use free of rent for three days. The charge for meals varies from 2 to 3 annas, but occupants may do their own cooking if they wish.

Road Conveyance.—Bullock-carts are available on previous notice at 2 annas per mile.

Local Manufactures and Products.—Indigo, rice, gingelly seeds and tamarind are grown.

Local Officials.—The Village Munsiff, Kurnam, Sub-Registrar and Sub-Inspector of Salt and Abkari.

Missions, Churches, etc.—There is a Roman Catholic Church.

Objects of Interest.—Two miles, south-east of the station, is an old Siva temple dedicated to Nethrotharakar, embellished with good sculptures and some inscriptions. Festivals are held in January and April. The legend with regard to this temple is that once a Raksha did penance for a long time. Siva appeared before him and asked him what he wished for. The Raksha thereupon requested Siva to grant him power to destroy by fire any one upon whom he placed his hands. This request was granted and the Raksha immediately desired to test the supernatural powers thus conferred. Finding no human subject for the experiment, he attempted to lay his hands on the head of

Siva himself, but the god Siva being afraid ran away pursued by the Raksha and entered into a creeper where he disappeared. The name of this creeper is given to the village, and its blossom, if opened, is said to shew a lingam on close examination.

VILLUPURAM JUNCTION.

Villupuram (lat. 11·57°; long. 79·32°; pop. 7,950) situated in the Villupuram taluq of the South Arcot district is an important Junction station on the main line 98 miles south of Madras (Egmore). Branch lines to Pondicherry, Dharmavaram and Gudur take off at this station. Though the place is low lying it is healthy, and is liked by its European and large Eurasian population of railway employés.

The distances to the principal stations on the South Indian Railway are—

Chingleput	..	63 miles.
Arkonam (for Madras Railway)	..	103 ,,
Pondicherry	..	24 ,,
Mayavaram (for Negapatam and Mutupet)	..	75 ,,
Peralam (for Karaikkal)	..	85 ,,
Tanjore	..	119 ,,
Trichinopoly Junction (for Erode)	..	150 ,,
Ammayanayakanur (for Kodaikanal)	..	221 ,,
Madura	..	246 ,,
Tuticorin	..	345 ,,

Local Accommodation.—About 1½ miles from the station is a travellers' bungalow which can accommodate two persons. It is fully furnished; but occupants must make their own arrangements for cooking. Provisions are not procurable locally. Rent one rupee each person *per diem.*

Close to the station are two choultries for native travellers. Charge 2½ annas per meal.

Road Conveyance.—Bullock-carts are available at the station.

Charges—

To the town	..	1 anna.
Neighbouring villages	..	1½ annas per mile.

Railway Facilities.—A Waiting-room for first and second class passengers, and a Refreshment-room is provided at the station. The butler in charge of the refreshments has usually a small stock of travellers' requisites for sale.

For native passengers a Refreshment-room, under Brahmin management, is given at the north end of the waiting shed, the charges being—

Meals	..	..	.. 3 annas each.
Coffee or Tea	..	..	.. 1 anna 3 pies per glass.

Near this Refreshment-room is a small enclosed bathing place for the use of natives.

On the first floor of the station building are two bed-rooms and a sitting-room fully furnished for Europeans, which may be occupied on payment of the following charges :—

For periods not exceeding three hours ..	.. 8 annas.
Exceeding three and not exceeding twenty-four hours..	1 rupee.

Local Manufactures and Products.—Rice, ragi, ground-nuts and indigo are the chief products.

Local Officials.—The Tahsildar, Sub-Magistrate, District Munsiff, Sub-Registrar, Forest Ranger and Police Inspector. The East India Distilleries Company have an office here.

Missions, Churches, etc.—There are several schools, a Protestant Church of the Lutheran Mission near the Travellers' bungalow, and a Roman Catholic Church near the station.

Historical.—On the 24th July 1752, this place was captured from the French, and in the same year the fort was retaken by Dupleix. The English regained possession on the 3rd April 1760.

Objects of Interest.—At Villupuram itself there is little to see ; but about 2½ miles north-west is the village of Tiruvamathur, held sacred by the Hindus on account of an ancient temple dedicated to the god Abhi Rameswarer, and where the great Rama and the seven recognised sages of old are said to have worshipped. A festival takes place

25

annually in April. The name of the village which means " sacred milk, " is accounted for in the following legend :— When first created, cows were without horns, and, finding themselves helpless against ferocious animals, they prayed to Siva for some weapons of defence. The god presented himself before them in this village and blessed them with horns. About 3 miles east of Villupuram is a place called Kolianur which contains a Mariammen Temple, dedicated to Puttalayi Ammen, and is visited by pilgrims on Fridays.

Sport.—Good snipe shooting can be had from November to February at the Anangur and Kondangi tanks, 2 and 3 miles, respectively, south-east of the station when the water is not too high. In the reserved forests of Adanur and Kandambulyur, 3 and 6 miles, respectively, north of the station, deer may be found in abundance ; and in Aryatore, Odyanatham and Gangarambolum, 12, 13 and 17 miles, respectively, west, leopards and hyænas may be shot. To shoot in these forests, passes must first be obtained from the local Government Forest Officers.

SERNDANUR.

Serndanur (pop. 1,489) is situated in the Villupuram taluq of the South Arcot district on the main line 105¼ miles from Madras (Egmore). The village is about ¾ mile east of the station.

Local Officials.—The Village Munsiff and Kurnam.

PANRUTI.

Panruti (pop. 8,956) is a union town situated in the Cuddalore taluq of the South Arcot district, 110¼ miles from Madras (Egmore).

Local Accommodation.—A Travellers' bungalow fully furnished and having accommodation for two persons is situated at the Salem Frontier Road next to the Local Fund Dispensary. No cook is kept, and a charge of 8 annas per day for each person using the bungalow is levied. Provisions to a limited extent can be obtained in the local bazaar.

Two choultries are maintained, the one close to the station and the other in the town, where native travellers of all classes can put up for three days without charge. Meals are served if required at a charge of 2½ annas each.

Road Conveyance.—Jutkas and bullock-carts are procurable at the station.

Charges—

Jutkas	{ to the town	..	..1½ annas.
	{ elsewhere	..	..2 „ per mile.
Bullock-carts..	{ to the town	..	..1 anna „
	{ elsewhere	..	..1½ annas „

Railway Facilities.—A waiting-room is provided at the station for first and second class passengers.

Local Manufacture and Products.—Weaving, the manufacture of toys, and tanning are the principal industries. The chief products are ground-nuts, jaggery, rice, cereals, cashunuts and jack-fruit, oil and oil cake.

Local Officials.—The Deputy Tahsildar, Union Chairman, Police Inspector, Hospital Assistant. The East India Distilleries Company have an office, where banking is carried on.

Missions, Churches, etc.—The Church of Scotland have established a Mission centre at Panruti, and there is a Roman Catholic Church about 1¼ miles south-west of the station.

Objects of Interest.—An old Siva temple with a fine gopuram, an ancient mosque and two Siva temples about 1 mile south-east of the station at Thiruvethe.

NELLIKUPPAM.

Nellikuppam (pop. 1,112) is a union town in the Cuddalore taluq of the South Arcot district, on the main line 118¾ miles from Madras (Egmore).

Local Accommodation.—There are three Brahmin hotels and two choultries, where meals are supplied at a charge of 2½ annas each. At one of the choultries, travellers may make their own arrangements for food if they prefer to do so.

Road Conveyance.—Bullock-carts can be had at the station at a charge of 1¼ annas per mile.

Local Manufactures and Products.—The East Indian Distilleries Company have a large Sugar Factory and Distillery connected with the station by a private siding. Betel leaves are grown at Nellikuppam in large quantities.

Local Officials.—The Sub-Registrar, Union Chairman, and Inspector of Salt and Abkari.

Missions, Churches, etc.—About three miles, west of the station, is a Protestant Church.

CUDDALORE.

Cuddalore (lat. 11·43°; long. 79·49°; pop. 47,355) is the chief town of the taluq of the same name and the headquarters of the South Arcot district, 127¼ miles from Madras (Egmore). The Municipality is a large one comprising an area of about 13 square miles. It embraces the old town or Cuddalore proper, Fort St. David, Bandipolliem, Devanampatnam, Munjacoopam, Puthupolliem, Tirupapuliyur, and nine smaller villages. The mouth of the Gadilam river having silted up, only native craft and lighters can come up to the town; but good anchorage can be obtained in the roads 1½ miles from the shore. The Ponniar and Gadilam rivers run through Cuddalore, and afford an abundant water-supply. The old town, however, depends more or less on the reservoir close to the Railway station, which is fed by a channel from the Capper Hill.

Local Accommodation.—There is a furnished Travellers' bungalow on the Napier Road at Munjacoopam, which can be occupied on payment of one rupee per day. The butler in charge can supply meals if required, or occupants may make their own arrangements. Liquor, if required, must be privately purchased. There are two choultries close to the Railway station at Tirupapuliyur (new town) both intended for the accommodation of Hindus. Meals

are supplied gratis at the former. In addition to these
are half a dozen hotels for Brahmins, in which meals are
supplied at 2½ annas each; and about 20 small hotels
scattered about the town for the accommodation of other
caste than Brahmins, where the cost of meals varies according to quality.

Road Conveyance.—Jutkas and bullock-carts are procurable at 2 annas per mile; and coaches can be hired at
Rs. 1-8-0 per drive within the town.

Railway Facilities.—Waiting-rooms are provided at
Cuddalore (new town and old town stations) for first and
second class passengers. At the latter station a Refreshment-room is maintained by Messrs. Spencer & Co., where
a small stock of travellers' requisites is usually kept. Fruit
and native refreshments are available at both stations.

Shipping Arrangements.—The British India Steam
Navigation Company's and the Asiatic Company's coasting
steamers running between Calcutta and Bombay regularly
call at this port (old town), also steamers and native
vessels plying between the Madras Coast and the Straits
Settlements and Ceylon ports.

Local Manufactures and Products.—Weaving and dyeing
are the principal industries, and the chief products are
paddy and sugarcane.

Local Officials.—Cuddalore (new town) being the head-
quarters of the district, all the chief offices are located
there. The principal officials are the Collector and Political
Agent, the District and Sessions Judge, the Head Assistant
Collector and Assistant Collector, the Treasury Deputy
Collector, the Head-quarters Deputy Collector, the
District Superintendent of Police, the Government
Chaplain, the Executive Engineer, the P. W. D. Sub-
Divisional Officer, the Assistant Commissioner of Salt,
Abkari and Customs, the Superintendent of Post Offices,
the District Medical and Sanitary Officer, the District
Munsiff, the Tahsildar and the Sub-Magistrate. It is the

head-quarters of the Resident Engineer of the Railway, and the East India Distilleries Company maintain an agency here.

Churches, Missions, etc.—At Old Town the Government Church is situated; and in New Town, in charge of a European minister under the Pondicherry Mission, is a Roman Catholic Church, which has a large congregation of native Christians.

Clubs.—There are three clubs in the town, one for Europeans, another for Eurasians, and the third for natives.

Historical.—In 1682, the Company opened negotiations with the Khan of Gingee for a factory at Cuddalore. The first building was erected in 1683, and, during the next ten years, trade increased so rapidly that the Company erected Fort St. David and rebuilt their warehouses. In 1702, the whole of the fortifications were rebuilt. On the fall of Madras in 1746, the British Administration withdrew to Cuddalore, which was soon afterwards twice unsuccessfully besieged by the French under Dupleix. In 1752, the head-quarters of the Presidency were removed to Madras, and, six years afterwards, the French occupied the town and stormed and destroyed the fort. After the battle of Wandiwash in 1760, Cuddalore was retaken by a British detachment; but twelve years later it again fell into the hands of the French and their ally, Tippoo Sultan, by whom the fortifications were renewed sufficiently to enable it to stand a siege the following year. On the 1st February 1785, Cuddalore was formally restored to the British under the treaty of Versailles and in 1801 included in the cession of the Carnatic.

Objects of Interest.—Fort St. David, the ruins of which still exist, (plate No. 10) the old garden house built in 1738, where the Governors and Deputy Governors of Fort St. David formerly had their residence, now occupied by the Collector, and the Dutch cemetery at old town, which contains many old European tombs. About a mile to the west of

RUINS OF FORT St DAVID, CUDDALORE

Cuddalore is Capper Hill, named after Colonel Capper, of the Commissariat Department, who received permission from Government in 1796 to enclose a piece of ground on the hill and built himself a house there. The property has since reverted to Government.

ALAPAKAM.

Alapakam (pop. 736) is situated in the Cuddalore taluq of the South Arcot district, 7¼ miles from Cuddalore (O. T.), 16¼ from Chidambaram, and 134¼ from Madras (Egmore).

Local Accommodation.—At Shonagam Chavady about two miles south-west of the station, is a travellers' bungalow, which can accommodate two persons. It has only a table and a few chairs and no servants, so travellers should make their own arrangements for cooking, furniture, crockery, etc. Provisions are not procurable. The charge for the use of this bungalow is—

Single persons	..	..	8 annas per diem.
Married couples	..	..	1 rupee do.

In the same village are two hotels, where meals are served at 2½ annas each to natives of all classes.

Road Conveyance.—Bullock-carts can be had on previous notice at a charge of 2 annas per mile

Local Manufactures and Products.—Salt is manufactured at the Kambali Madu Factory about a mile from the Railway station. The chief products of Alapakam are paddy and firewood.

Local Official.—The Village Munsiff.

Fairs.—A fair is held every Sunday in the village of Kulen Chavady, three miles from the station.

PORTO NOVO.

Porto Novo (pop. 14,061) is a union town in the Chidambaram taluq of the South Arcot district, 17 miles from Cuddalore (O. T.), 29½ from Mayavaram, and 145 from Madras (Egmore). This place, known also as Parangipett and Muhammed Bunder, received its name from the Portuguese, by whom the settlement appears to have been established during the sixteenth century. The town is about a mile east of the Railway station.

Local Accommodation.—There is neither hotel nor tra-vellers' bungalow for Europeans. But for natives, there are three Brahmin and two other hotels, where meals are served at a charge of 2½ annas per meal.

Road Conveyance.—Jutkas and bullock-carts are usually available at the station, the fares being—

Jutkas ..	..	..	..	2 annas per mile.
Bullock-carts	..	..	..	1¼ do. do.

Shipping Arrangements.—The port carries on a busy trade with Ceylon, Acheen, Penang and Singapore, and is largely frequented by native craft. The B. I. S. N. Co.'s steamers for Singapore also call about once a fortnight, anchoring two miles from the shore in from 4½ to 5 fathoms of water. Cargo is shipped and landed at the Government Jetty opposite the Custom House, for which purpose about 20 boats are available.

Local Manufactures and Products.—Weaving of coarse cloth, and the production of a species of mat made from the leaves of the wild pine-apple, in imitation of similar mats of a very soft make imported from Acheen, are the chief manufactures. Salt is made at the Government Factory at Manambodi about two miles south-west of the Railway station. The chief agricultural produce is paddy.

Local Officials.—The Assistant Engineer, P. W. D., Assistant Inspector of Salt, Sea Customs' Superintendent, Sub-Registrar and Hospital Assistant.

Fairs.—A fair is held every Thursday.

Historical.—A cowle for founding a settlement was obtained by the English from Harjee Rajah, Subbadar of Gingee, in 1681 ; but, before trading was commenced in 1682, the Danes and Portuguese were already established. In 1748 the Factory being in a ruinous condition, a good

NEGATIVE BY A. D. G. SHELLEY

house was purchased for 500 pagodas and a Resident appointed. Nine years later Porto Novo, together with Fort St. David and Cuddalore, were captured by the French; but they were driven out in 1760 by Coote after his victory over Lally at Wandiwash. The town was burnt down by Hyder Ali in July 1780; but was, to some extent, rebuilt almost at once, as a year afterwards Sir Eyre Coote marched out of Porto Novo with 8,000 men to meet the whole army of Mysore, some 60,000 strong. In the battle which ensued at Mettupolliem the English won the most signal victory of the war. The French landed a large force at Porto Novo in 1782 and marched thence with Tippoo and captured Cuddalore. The settlement was restored to England under the treaty of Versailles on the 1st February 1785.

Objects of Interest.—In 1824 efforts were made to establish an iron foundry for the working of Salem ore, and the Porto Novo Iron Company built a large factory, which, after many years of patient endeavour, had to be abandoned. Nothing of the works remains now, but the ruins of one or two buildings, while the chimney, once a conspicuous object from seaward, has been destroyed.

KILLE.

Kille (pop. 3,105) is situated in the Chidambaram taluq of the South Arcot district, 20 miles from Cuddalore (O. T.), 26¼ from Mayavaram, and 147½ from Madras (Egmore). The village is about two miles north-east of the station.

Local Accommodation.—In the village is a chuttram where natives of all classes can find accommodation free of charge, but must make their own arrangements for food. In addition are two hotels where meals are served to all classes of natives at a charge of 2½ annas per meal.

Road Conveyance.—Bullock-carts can be obtained at 2 annas per mile, provided previous notice is given.

26

Local Manufactures and Products.—The chief produce
is paddy.

Local Official.—The Village Munsif.

CHIDAMBARAM.

Chidambaram (lat. 11·25°; long. 79·46°; pop. 18,640) is
situated in the Chidambaram taluq of the South Arcot
district, the town lying about half a mile west of the station. The following are the distances to the principal
stations on the South Indian Railway :—

To Madras (Egmore)	..	151 miles.
„ Chingleput (for Conjeeveram and Arkonam)	..	117 „
„ Villupuram (for Pondicherry, Dharmavaram and Gudur branches) ..	..	53 „
„ Katpadi (for Madras Railway) ..	..	153 „
„ Mayavaram (for Mutupet, Karaikkal, etc.)	..	28 „
„ Tanjore	..	67 „
„ Trichinopoly (for Erode)	..	98 „
„ Ammayanayakanur (for Kodaikanal) ..	..	169 „
„ Madura	..	194 „
„ Tuticorin or Tinnevelly	..	293 „

Local Accommodation.—A furnished travellers' bungalow, which can accommodate two persons, is situated about
1½ miles south-west of the station. It has no cook, but
provisions can be obtained in the local bazaar. The charge
for the use of this bungalow is :—

	RS. A. P.	
For single person	.. 1 0 0	} per diem.
For married couple	.. 1 8 0	

For natives there are over 60 chuttrams, maddams and
hotels in the town. In one of these (the Natukkottai
chuttram) free meals are given to all caste people throughout the year. In 25 other chuttrams free meals are given
on the occasion of festivals, and in 27 others, free lodging
only is given.

Eleven hotels supply food to all classes of Hindus at
from 2½ to 3 annas per meal.

Road Conveyance.—Jutkas and bullock-carts are available at the station, the fares being :—

Jutkas	.. 2 annas	} per mile.
Bullock-carts	.. 1½ „	

Railway Facilities.—Waiting accommodation is provided at the station for first and second class passengers.

Local Manufactures and Products.—Weaving of silk and cotton cloths is carried on, and paddy is largely grown.

Local Officials.—The Municipal Chairman, Tahsildar, Sub-Magistrate, District Munsif, Sub-Registrar, Sub-Engineer, P.W.D., Hospital Assistant and Police Inspector.

Fairs and Festivals.—Two festivals are held annually, one in July, called the " Ani Thirumanjanam," and the other, in December, called the " Aruthira Darsanam." These festivals last for ten days each, and from 30,000 to 40,000 pilgrims attend from all parts of the Presidency.

Missions and Churches.—About two miles north of the station is a Lutheran Mission Church.

Historical.—In 1749, the ill-fated expedition under Captain Cope against Devikotta, halted at Chidambaram on its retreat to Fort St. David, and in the following year the armies of Morari Rao and Moozuffer Jung met here. In 1753, the French took the neighbouring fort of Bowanigiri and occupied the Chidambaram pagoda on its being evacuated by the small English garrison which then held it, and in the same year the French and Mahratta forces united at Chidambaram before marching against Trichinopoly. In 1759, an attempt to capture the pagoda by the English failed, chiefly through mismanagement, but it was not strong enough, however, to withstand a regular siege and the garrison surrendered to Major Monson in 1760. A few years later, Hyder Ali improved the defences slightly and placed a garrison in the pagoda to maintain his line of communication with Pondicherry. An unsuccessful attack probably directed against the western entrance was made by Sir Eyre Coote in 1781.

Objects of Interest.—The Siva temple, about ten minutes' drive from the Railway station, is famous as being one of the few religious buildings in India, where both Siva and Vishnu have shrines in such close proximity that their respective followers may worship in the same place and view both deities at the same time ; and where, moreover, is reputed to exist the Akasa Linga (the Air Linga), one of the five great Lingas of India, sometimes known as the "Chidambaram Rahusiyam" or the secret of Chidambaram. The temple premises are situated in the centre of the town and cover an area of about 40 acres. They have four enclosures protected by high walls, one within the other. The outer enclosure consists merely of unkempt gardens or waste-land covered with scrub. The next enclosure contains the hall of 1,000 pillars, the golden tank, colossal figures of Siva's bull (Nandi) and several temples of more or less importance. The third enclosure contains a temple to Lukshmi, the wife of Vishnu, the "Coach-house" for the gods' vehicles, the Sreemoolastanam (the temple containing the stone image of Siva), Parvati's temple, mantapams, colonnades, and resting places for pilgrims ; and the fourth or innermost enclosure contains the audience and dancing chambers of Siva locally called Nattaraja and a temple to Vishnu locally called Perumalkoil.

There are four main entrances to the temple enclosures on the south, north, east and west sides. The entrances in the outermost wall are mere gateways, but those in the second wall, immediately in front of the outer ones, are conspicuous by fine gopurams.

The south entrance being nearest the station, is the one most convenient for visitors. Entering here and passing under the gopuram into the second enclosure, the visitor is recommended to inspect first the innermost enclosures. These are best reached by turning to the right and entering the third enclosure, nearly opposite to the east gopuram. Passing straight through the halls, which occupy the third enclosure, the visitor arrives at the entrance to the fourth enclosure, i.e., the cella of the temple containing the audience chamber of Siva and temple of Vishnu. The former

TEMPLE GOPURAM & TANK CHIDAMBARAM

NEGATIVE BY W. A. CROSS

is in front of the entrance and at once attracts attention by
its gorgeous golden roof, with 9 golden finials, the silver
staircase and silver mounted doorways, leading to the
dais, where stands Siva in the image of a naked giant with
four arms, in the attitude of dancing. Roofed with copper,
surmounted with 9 golden finials, and, standing slightly to
the left on a raised platform, is the temple of Vishnu. It
is in front of this sanctuary that devotees worshipping can
see the images of Siva and Vishnu at the same time.
Passing between the dancing chamber and the temple of
Vishnu, the visitor sees in the peristyle several small
apartments containing images of minor deities and a very
beautiful structure of polished black granite, the " bed
room " of the god Siva. Close by is the pretended " Air
Lingam." No Lingam exists, but a curtain is hung before
a wall, bearing an inscription, and, when visitors desire to
see the Lingam, the curtain is withdrawn and the bare
wall is shown, the explanation being that air is invisible.
Returning to the third enclosure, the visitor should now
pass half-way up the hall or mantapam and turn to the
right passing on his left a number of Brahman kitchens and
store-rooms. The next building of interest is the temple
dedicated to Lukshmi, the wife of Vishnu. This temple
being admired for its beautiful carving, the visitor next
passes the west (the only other) entrance to this enclosure
on his left and proceeds to the north corner, where is the
Vahanamantapam or shed already mentioned for stabling
the vehicles of the gods. The adjacent building on the left
is the Sreemoolastanam (or holy original place) of Siva
containing a stone image of the god. This is really the
holy of holies. Here also is a small temple to Parvati
remarkable for its elegant porch. All the way along are
springing up new colonnades and mantapams, now in the
hands of the builders. Having thus finished the two innermost enclosures, the visitor returns to the second enclosure.
Facing him as he emerges is the east gopuram which is

distinguished from the others by being the one through which Siva enters on his car on occasions of festivals. Proceeding northward on the left is a small temple containing a huge image of the bull Nandi as though richly caparisoned and ornamented with bells attached to necklets and saddle cloth, and to the right is the hall of 1,000 pillars. This is a very interesting structure, measuring 340 feet by about 190 feet, in front of which are rows of cylindrical granite monoliths, about 70 in all, evidently intended for a building which has never been finished and which are now used for supporting a pandal roof on ceremonial occasions. The visitor ascends by a grand stone staircase to a fine portico and by further flights of steps at intervals to an immense hall with elliptical roof and rows of columns on either side, at the north end of which is a dais fenced off to accommodate Siva on festival occasions in full sight of the crowds in the hall. The roof over this dais is frescoed with religious scenes. Using the steps on the left, nearly opposite to a second stone bull, the Sivagangay or the golden tank is reached. This is a fine deep tank measuring 160 feet by 100 feet, and is said to have derived its name "Golden" from the ancient King Verma Chukra who, after bathing in it, was cured of the leprosy from which he suffered, and thereafter assumed a golden colour. It has a mantapam and flights of dressed stone steps at the north end, a similar flight at the south-east and south-west corners, and a colonnade running all round it for the use of bathers with steps down to the water. Passing round by the north end of the tank, the next structures that attract attention are the north gopuram on the right and the Pandianayar Subramanya temple close by in the corner facing east. Just within the enclosure is a large stone figure of a peacock on a pedestal, and a stone altar. The temple itself is entered by a flight of stone steps flanked by stone elephants. The pillars of the hall are carved and the plinth all around the temple is covered with figures of musicians and devotees in various attitudes. Continuing the circuit, the next building on the right is a temple dedicated to the goddess Sivakami or Parvati. The cella of this temple is much below the level of the open courtyard. After passing through the portico and arriving at the great door ornamented with brass spikes or knobs, the visitor descends a flight of stone steps bearing inscriptions in Tamil and sees a massive ornamented golden flagstaff said to be made of sandalwood covered with gold-plated metal. The roof of the hall of the temple is frescoed and decorated with tapestry representing scenes in the lives of devotees, saints and deities. The pillars of the hall are carved; and running all round the cella is a sculptured stone gallery. Ascending again to the open courtyard, the next building on the right is the 100 pillar hall, a dilapidated structure which is now closed. Alongside is a small temple dedicated to Sundaraswara, a minor deity and disciple of Siva and on the left is the west entrance to the third enclosure. The walls of this enclosure have many ancient inscriptions in Tamil. On the right is the west gopuram with a smaller temple dedicated to Subramanya already mentioned. The space hereabouts is occupied by shops for the sale of food during festivals. The building in the south-west corner of the enclosure is the temple of Mukuruny Arisi Pilliyar or the "three-measure-of-rice-eating Ganasha." This temple is said to contain the largest idol of Ganasha in India. The hall of entrance has some well carved columns and the walls near the door of the sanctuary are ornamented with body-guards of the god and other figures carved in stone. The roof is surmounted with a small gopuram with coloured stucco figures in bas-relief. Another small temple dedicated to Dekshanamoorthy, the god who looks to the South, and another image of the bull Nandi situated in front of the south entrance exhaust the programme, and the visitor has returned to the gopuram by which he entered, having occupied in the round little more than two hours.

COLEROON.

Coleroon (otherwise called Aunikkaran chuttram), (pop. 2,431) is situated in the Shiyali taluq of the Tanjore district, 29 miles from Cuddalore (O. T.), 19 from Mayavaram, and 156½ from Madras (Egmore). The village is about a quarter of a mile south of the Coleroon river, after which it is named.

Local Accommodation.—On the north bank of the Coleroon, about half a mile from the station, is a choultry where lodging is given and meals served free to Brahmans. Close to it is a native hotel where meals are served to all classes of Hindus, except Pariahs, at 2½ annas per meal.

Road Conveyance.—Bullock-carts can be had if previous notice is given at 2 annas per mile.

Railway Facilities.—Waiting accommodation is provided at the station for first and second class passengers.

Local Manufactures and Products.—Korray mats and rattan baskets are made, and paddy, kumboo and raggi are the chief products.

Local Official.—The Village Munsiff.

Fairs.—A fair is held every Monday at a place about half a mile south-east of the station.

Missions and Churches.—The Lutheran Mission have a church at Achapuram, 3½ miles from this station.

Objects of Interest.—The Railway crosses the Coleroon on a bridge of 14 spans of 150 feet.

SHIYALI.

Shiyali (pop. 6,715) is a union town in the taluq of the same name in the Tanjore district, 34½ miles from Cuddalore (O. T.), 12¼ from Mayavaram, and 162 from Madras (Egmore).

Local Accommodation.—About a mile east of the station is a travellers' bungalow, which is fully furnished and can accommodate two persons. A cook is in charge, who can

supply meals if required. Liquor must be privately purchased. The charge for the use of this bungalow is :—

	RS.	A.	
For single person	1	0	} per diem.
For married couple	1	8	

For natives there are 4 Brahman hotels, 3 other hotels
and 2 chuttrams: in the hotels meals are served at 2½ annas
each, and in the chuttrams free accommodation is given to
all classes and free meals to Brahmans. Iyengar Brahmans
can also obtain free meals in the Vishnu temple.

Road Conveyance.—Bullock-carts are procurable at the
station at 2 annas per mile.

Railway Facilities.—Waiting accommodation is provided
at the station for first and second class passengers.

Shipping Arrangements.—Tirumalavasal, 7 miles east of
this station, is a small port, whence large quantities of rice
are exported annually to Colombo, the British India
Coasting Steamers calling as cargo offers.

Local Manufactures and Products.—Korray mats of good
quality are made, and some 8 miles south-east of this
station is the Nidavasal Salt Factory, which sends large
quantities of salt into Shiyali for export to the interior.
The chief produce of Shiyali is paddy.

Local Officials.—The Tahsildar, Sub-Magistrate, District
Munsiff, Sub-Registrar, Police Inspector and Apothecary.

Fairs and Festivals.—In the local Siva temple festivals
lasting 10 days are celebrated annually during the months
of April and May, when a large crowd of worshippers
assemble from all parts of the district.

Missions and Churches.—The Lutheran Mission has a
church about three-quarters of a mile south-east of the
station, and in the same locality is a Roman Catholic
Church.

Objects of Interest.—The Siva temple above referred to
is perhaps worth seeing.

VAITHISVARANKOIL.

Vaithisvarankoil (pop. 4,155) is situated in the Shiyali
taluq of the Tanjore district, 38 miles from Cuddalore

27

(O. T.), 8½ from Mayavaram, and 165 from Madras (Egmore). It is a place of pilgrimage for those who are sick as implied by its name which is derived from the Sanskrit "Vaidya" a physician, "ishvara" lord, and the Tamil "kovil" a temple, or the lord of Physician's temple.

Local Accommodation.—For natives, there are 15 hotels and 2 choultries. At the hotels meals are served at 2½ annas each, and at the choultries free accommodation is given, but travellers must make their own arrangements for food.

Road Conveyance.—Bullock-carts are procurable at the station, the fare being 2 annas per mile.

Local Manufactures and Products.—Paddy is the chief produce.

Local Official.—The Village Munsiff.

Fairs and Festivals.—A fair is held every Saturday at Thirupangar, a small village 2 miles west of the station.

The festival of "Kirthigai" is celebrated monthly, and the "Brahmautsavam" in February and March annually at the temple.

Missions and Churches.—In the village is a Lutheran Mission Church, and at Attengudi, a small village close by, the Roman Catholics have a church.

Objects of Interest.—The Siva temple at which a favourite offering to the god by sick persons is the hair of their heads; and it is a common sight to see natives, both male and female, leaving the temple with clean shaved heads.

ANTANDAVAPURAM.

Antandavapuram (pop. 1,617) is situated in the Mayavaram taluq of the Tanjore district, 43 miles from Cuddalore (O. T.), 4 from Mayavaram, and 170 from Madras (Egmore).

Local Manufactures and Products.—Paddy is the chief product.

Local Official.—The Village Munsiff.

PROCESSIONAL CAR

MAYAVARAM JUNCTION.

Mayavaram (lat. 11° 6'; long. 79° 43'; pop. 23,765) is a municipal town in the taluq of the same name in the Tanjore district, situated on the south bank of the river Cauvery, and is one of the chief seats of the Brahmanical religion in the district. The town is about 2¼ miles east of the station.

Passengers for stations on the Mayavaram-Mutupet and Peralam-Karaikkal Railways and Negapatam change here. The distances to the principal stations on the South Indian Railway are as under :—

To Madras (Egmore)	.. ..	.. 174 miles.
Chingleput (for Conjeeveram)	..	.. 140 ,,
Villupuram (for Pondicherry, etc.)		.. 76 ,,
Tiruvannamalai	.. ..	.. 118 ,,
Pondicherry	.. ..	.. 99 ,,
Vellore	.. .. ..	.. 169 ,,
Pakala	.. .. ..	.. 214 ,,
Dharmavaram (for S. M. Railway)	..	.. 356 ,,
Gudur (for East Coast Railway)	..	.. 298 ,,
Cuddalore	.. .. ..	.. 47 ,,
Tanjore	.. .. ..	.. 44 ,,
Trichinopoly (for Erode)	..	.. 75 ,,
Madura	.. .. ..	.. 171 ,,
Tuticorin or Tinnevelly	..	.. 270 ,,

Local Accommodation.—About a quarter of a mile south of the station is a travellers' bungalow which is fully furnished and can accommodate two persons. A cook is in charge who can supply meals if required ; but liquor must be privately purchased. The charge for the use of this bungalow is :—

		RS.	A.	
For single person	.. ..	1	0	} per diem.
For married couple	.. ..	1	8	

For natives, 3 choultries, 5 chuttrams, 4 Brahman hotels and 10 other hotels exist in the town. In one of the choultries (that maintained by the Natukottai Chetties) Brahmans can obtain both accommodation and food free. In the other 2 choultries free accommodation is given to all classes of natives but not food. In the 5 chuttrams Brahmans are fed free during the Tulakaveri festival only. At other times they, in common with other classes of natives, can get free accommodation only at the chuttrams. At all the hotels meals are served at from 2½ to 3 annas per meal.

Road Conveyance.—Jutkas and bullock-carts can be had at the station, the fares being :—

Jutkas	..	..	..	2 annas per mile.
Bullock-carts	..	..	1½ „ „

Railway Facilities.—Waiting accommodation is provided at the station for first and second class passengers, and also a refreshment stall under the management of Messrs. Spencer & Co., where light refreshments, such as tea, coffee, aerated waters, &c., can be obtained. The Railway Company maintain an Officers' Rest-house within the station compound and have also a dispensary at the station.

Local Manufactures and Products.—Kornad, a suburb of Mayavaram, is noted for the production of native female cloths, known all over the Presidency as " Kornad cloths." Paddy, cocoanuts and plantains are the chief products of Mayavaram.

Local Officials.—The Tahsildar, Municipal Chairman, Sub-Magistrate, District Munsiff, Sub-Registrar, Police Inspector and Apothecary.

Fairs and Festivals.—A fair is held every Monday and Friday. Festivals attended by from 30,000 to 40,000 persons are held in the Siva and Vishnu temples in October and November annually. These festivals last for 30 days, though the last 10 days are considered the most important. Ablutions in the Cauvery are considered to confer special spiritual benefit.

Missions and Churches.—The Lutheran Mission and the Roman Catholic community have churches in the town.

Clubs.—The Native officials maintain a reading-room.

Objects of Interest.—The Siva and Vishnu temples, the jewels and the silver bedstead for the god at the latter temple, are worth seeing.

KUTTALAM.

Kuttalam (pop. 3,537) is situated in the Mayavaram taluq of the Tanjore district, 6 miles from Mayavaram Junction, 14 from Kumbakonam, 39 from Tanjore, and 179 from Madras (Egmore). The village, which is on the south bank of the river Cauvery, is about a quarter of a mile from the station.

Local Accommodation.—Native travellers of all classes, except Pariahs, can find free accommodation in two chuttrams in the village, where, however, they must make their own arrangements for food. Besides these chuttrams are 3 hotels where natives of all classes can obtain meals at $2\frac{1}{2}$ annas each.

Road Conveyance.—Bullock-carts can be had if previous notice is given, the fares being 2 annas per mile.

Local Manufactures and Products.—Cloths of the best quality (for native women) are manufactured and the chief agricultural produce is paddy, cocoanuts and plantains.

Local Official.—The Village Munsiff.

Fairs and Festivals.—The " Brahmautsavam" festival is held in May and June annually at the Vishnu temple at Teralunthur, about 3 miles from here. It lasts for 10 days and attracts many pilgrims.

Objects of Interest.—Two Siva temples which are in a decayed state, but contain some good stone carving.

NARASINGANPET.

Narasinganpet (pop. 2,018), named after an ancient Rajah " Narasinga," is situated in the Kumbakonam taluq of the Tanjore district, 10 miles from Mayavaram Junction, 10 from Kumbakonam, 35 from Tanjore, and 183 from Madras (Egmore).

Local Accommodation.—About a quarter of a mile east of the station is a travellers' bungalow which is furnished, but has no crockery or a cook. It can accommodate two persons and the charge for occupying it is 12 annas each person per diem.

Road Conveyance.—Bullock-carts can be obtained at the station, the fares being 2 annas per vehicle per mile.

Local Manufactures and Products.—Cloths of the best quality for natives are manufactured at Thugili, about a a mile north of the station. The chief products are paddy, cocoanuts and plantains.

Local Official.—The Village Munsiff.

Fairs and Festivals.—At a village called Thiruvaduthorai, about a mile east of this station, lives the Mahunt of Thiruvaduthorai, a high priest of the Sudras, of the Siva sect. In the month of January annually the "Brahmautsavam" is celebrated in the Siva temple attached to the Mutt (high priest's residence), on which occasion he goes round the four main streets of the village attended by thousands of his disciples who bow down before him and make him offerings of money, jewels, fruit, flowers, &c., and receive in return his blessing accompanied by a present of a shawl or a cloth. On the occasion of this festival, meals are supplied free to all Hindus, bonfires are lighted and fireworks are let off. The high priest is very wealthy, as, in addition to receiving presents from rajahs and zemindars, a large quantity of land is set apart in various districts, the revenue derived from which belongs to this office. Some 3,115 people live in Thiruvaduthorai, practically the whole of whom are dependent on the high priest for their livelihood.

ADUTURAI.

Aduturai.—186 miles from Madras on the main line and 12½ miles from Mayavaram Junction. The public road which crosses the railway line is connected with the two trunk roads, *viz.*, Kumbakonam-Karaikkal road on the south and Madras road on the north.

There are several rivers, *viz.*, Palavar, Kauveri, Veerasholan and Pooratti, all of which are bridged.

Local Accommodation.—There is a choultry for Brahmans only, where free meals are served and supplies given to religious mendicants. There is a Brahman hotel, also hotels in the neighbourhood, where native travellers of other castes can find accommodation. Two annas per meal.

Road Conveyance.—Bullock-carts can be hired, the charge being one anna per cart per mile.

Local Manufactures and Products.—Weaving cloth for native women. The chief products are plantains, cocoanuts, and paddy.

Objects of Interest.—In the vicinity there are Siva and Vishnu temples.

TIRUVADAMARUDUR.

Tiruvadamarudur (pop. 2,580) is a union town on the south bank of the river Cauvery, situated in the Kumbakonam taluq of the Tanjore district, 15 miles from Mayavaram Junction, 5 from Kumbakonam, 30 from Tanjore, and 188 from Madras (Egmore). It formed the centre of the four sacred places of the Chola Kingdom, *viz.*, Trivadi in the west, Chidambaram in the north, Mayavaram in the east, and Tiruvallur in the south.

Local Acommodation.—In the town are 3 chuttrams, where Hindus of all classes, except Pariahs, can find free accommodation. In one of them, meals are served gratis to Brahmans and supplies given to Bairagis for 3 days. In the other two, meals are served at $2\frac{1}{2}$ annas each. Besides these there are two hotels, where all classes can obtain meals at $2\frac{1}{2}$ annas each.

Road Conveyance.—Single and double bullock-carts are usually procurable at the station, the fares being $1\frac{1}{2}$ and 2 annas per mile, respectively.

Local Manufactures and Products.—Native cloths are manufactured, and the chief products are paddy, cocoanuts and plantains.

Local Officials.—The Deputy Tahsildar and Sub-Magistrate, Sub-Registrar, Police Inspector and Hospital Assistant.

Fairs and Festivals.—No fairs are held, but festivals are frequent. In January annually a large " Pushyam " festival takes place which lasts 10 days, when the cars of the temple are dragged round the streets. The large car (one of the biggest in India) has attached to it, at the time of this festival, life-sized representations of three white horses, and is decorated with flags, flowers and fruit, while inside are seated a band of musicians. The dragging of this car is generally reserved for the concluding days of the festival, when ropes, quite 5 inches in diameter and about a quarter of a mile in length, are attached to it. The car, which is shewn in plate No. 2, is generally dragged by from 7,000 to 8,000 men. Cocoanuts are broken on the wheels, lighted camphor placed in front of the god and other ceremonies performed before commencing to pull it, and, as soon as it moves, fowls are sacrificed under the wheels. In May and June the " Tirukkalyanam " (marriage festival) takes place, and in October and November the " Navarathri " is celebrated. The " Unjal " festival, lasting 10 days, is held in December and January.

Objects of Interest.—The old Siva temple, which is well sculptured and has a fine gopurum. On the east gateway is a carving of Brahmahatti. The legend regarding this is as follows :—A Chola King is said to have committed the sin of Brahmahatti, *i e.*, murdering a Brahman. To cleanse himself of the sin and obtain salvation, he went on pilgrimage to many sacred places, but all to no purpose, as he could not shake off the ghost of his victim. At last he by chance entered this temple, and, to his surprise, found that the spirit of the murdered man did not follow him into the temple, but waited at the gateway for his return. The king knowing this did not go out of the temple the way he came in, but made a hole in the western wall and fled towards his capital of Tanjore. When he was a mile off the temple and found that the spirit (also called Brahmahatti) did not follow him, he there built a temple and founded a village named Terupuvanam in honour of the deity and in gratitude for his salvation. The temple remains to this day, and is well sculptured, containing inscriptions in Tamil, Grantha, Malayalam and Nagari characters.

KUMBAKONAM.

Kumbakonam (lat. 10° 57′; long. 79° 25′; height 85 feet above sea-level; pop. 54,307) is a municipal town situated in a taluq of the same name in the Tanjore district, in a low level tract between two considerable branches of the river Cauvery. It extends about 3 miles in length from east to west and 1½ miles in breadth from north to south, and is one of the most ancient towns in the Madras Presidency, having been at one time the capital of the Chola Kingdom. It is the centre of the Brahmanical religion and literature, and is sometimes called the Indian "Cambridge." A branch mutt of Shunkaracharry, the founder of the Adweitam philosophy, is presided over by a chief guru belonging to the Smartha Brahmans. It is the head-quarters of the Sub-Collector of the district, and was the seat of the Zillah Court from its first establishment in 1806 until 1863, when it was removed to Tanjore. The following are the distances to the most important stations on the South Indian Railway :—

Tanjore Junction (for Negapatam)	..	..	..	25 miles.
Trichinopoly Junction (for Erode)	..	..	56	,,
Madura ..	..	..	..	152 ,,
Tuticorin	..	..	..	251 ,,
Tinnevelly	..	..	..	251 ,,
Mayavaram Junction	..	..	20	,,
Villupuram Junction	..	..	95	,,

Chingleput (for Conjeeveram) ..	..	.. 159 miles.
Madras (Egmore) ..	..	.. 194 ,,
Tiruvannamalai ..	..	.. 137 ,,
Vellore ..	..	.. 189 ,,
Pakala Junction ..	..	.. 234 ,,
Gudur Junction (for East Coast Railway)		.. 328 ,,
Dharmavaram (for Southern Maharatta Railway)		.. 323 ,,

Local Accommodation.—About a mile north of the station is a travellers' bungalow, which is furnished, and can accommodate two persons, but has neither a cook nor crockery. The charge for the use of this bungalow is :—

	RS. A.	
For single person ..	..	.. 1 0 } per diem.
For a married couple ..	..	.. 1 8 }

Provisions are procurable in the local bazaar. For natives, there are 13 chuttrams, where free accommodation can be obtained by all classes of Hindus, except Pariahs; but private arrangements must be made for food. In addition are 2 chuttrams, where free accommodation is obtainable and meals are served gratis to Brahmans and supplies given to Bairagis. Brahmans can also get free meals in the Shunkaracharriar mutt, the Sarangapani Swami and the Chakrapani Swami temples. Supplementary to these institutions are more than 50 hotels, where natives of all classes can obtain meals at from 2½ to 3 annas per meal.

Road Conveyance.—Jutkas and single and double bullock-carts are usually procurable at the station, the fares being :—

For jutkas and double bullock-carts .. 2 annas per mile.
For single bullock-carts .. .. 1½ ,, ,,

Railway Facilities.—Waiting accommodation is provided at the station for first and second class passengers, and a refreshment room under the management of Messrs. Spencer & Co. The butler in charge of the latter has usually a small stock of travellers' requisites for sale. Wines and spirits are not supplied.

Local Manufactures and Products.—Native cloths, brass, copper and bell-metal vessels are manufactured in large quantities. The chief products are paddy, cocoanuts, betel leaves and plantains.

GOPURAM SARNGAPANI TEMPLE KUMBAKONAM

Local Officials.—The Sub-Collector, Municipal Chairman, Sub-Judge, Tahsildar, two District Munsiffs, Town Sub-Magistrate, Stationary Sub-Magistrate, Sub-Registrar, Police Inspector, Civil Apothecary and two Hospital Assistants.

Fairs and Festivals.—The "Brahmautsavam" festival is celebrated in the Sarangapani Swami, Kumbaiswara Swami, Chakrapani Swami and Rama Swami temples in February, March and April, when as many as 15,000 worshippers attend from different parts of the district.

Missions, Churches, &c.—In the town are two Christian Churches, one of which belongs to the Lutheran Mission, and one to the Roman Catholics, both of which have large congregations.

Clubs.—The native officials have a Club in the Porter Town Hall and a reading-room in the Gopalrao Library.

Objects of Interest.—There are 16 temples, 12 dedicated to Siva and 4 to Vishnu. The following are the most important :---

The Sarangapani Swami (Vishnu) Temple in the centre of the town which is entered through an enormous gopurum 147 feet in height, richly ornamented with figures and other devices. The back view of this temple with its 5 smaller gopurums and the Potamarai tank, is particularly fine. Attached to this temple are two processional cars of carved wood of elaborate design, one of the cars being of a very large size.

The Kumbaiswara Swami Temple, a Siva temple close by, is approached by a corridor 330 feet long by 15 feet wide. The principal gopurum is 128 feet high and leads to a court 83 feet by 55 feet. This temple is remarkable for the variety of its silver vahanams (conveyance for the idols) which are well worth seeing. The five cars, which stand in a row in front of the temple, belong to it and are of the same design as those mentioned above.

The Rama Swami Temple, which is also close by, has only

one small gopurum leading into the muntapam, but in it
are to be found the finest carvings in all the Kumbakonam
temples, the pillars having upon their faces splendid
sculptured figures representing the various incarnations of
Vishnu and the feats of Rama, the hero of the Ramayana.
Each pillar is carved from one large stone and the delicacy of the execution is most remarkable. The interior
of this mantapam is illustrated in plate No. 12.

The Chakrapani Swami Temple near the river Cauvery
is another temple much resorted to by pilgrims.

The Mahamagam Tank is one of the most sacred in
Southern India ; and to bathe in it, pilgrims come from the
remotest parts of the country. It covers about 20 acres
in area, has flights of steps on the four sides, and is surrounded by many small temples. An annual bathing
festival is held here in February, but once in twelve years
is held the celebrated Mahamagam festival, at which it is
estimated from 400,000 to half a million persons are present. This festival takes place when Brihaspati (Jupiter)
is in conjunction with Simham (Leo) and if this occurs on
the day of full moon, it becomes an exceptionally auspicious
time for bathing. Plate No. 1 (frontispiece) illustrates the
Mahamagam festival which was held in February, 1897,
and shows the crowd beginning to collect in the tank on the
principal day of the feast. Previous to the festival the
tank is emptied until the depth of water is reduced to $2\frac{1}{2}$
feet, a precaution very necessary as the entry of many
thousand persons into the tank causes the level of the
water to rise considerably. During the most auspicious
time for bathing, the crowd in the tank is so dense that
nothing but a mass of heads is visible, and the spectacle
is decidedly impressive. On the gods being exhibited,
the worshippers raise their hands in prayer, and dip
their heads beneath the surface of the water. Soon after
the festival commences, the water is transformed into a
black viscous fluid of the consistency of thick peasoup,

and judging from the hesitation displayed by the more educated bathers in submerging their heads, the act is one which nothing but intense religious devotion would induce them to perform. After bathing in the tank the worshippers proceed to the Cauvery and in its waters are relieved alike of their loads of sin and black oily sludge. Superstition attributes the efficacy of this bathing festival to the fact that once in every twelve years the holy waters of the Ganges find their way into the Mahamagam tank at Kumbakonam.

A unique temple is the *Brahma temple* which is dedicated to the sun, being the only one so dedicated in the whole of Southern India. Besides the above temples and tank, the following are objects of interest :—

The Government College has a good library and excellent play grounds attached to it. This institution has played an important part in the educational annals of the Presidency, many of the most cultured natives of the south having studied there, a result due in great measure to the labours of Mr. W. A. Porter and Rao Bahadur T. Gopalrao.

The "Town High School" and *the "Native High School"* are both old institutions and educate up to the Matriculation standard. The former has 500 scholars and the latter 300.

The Municipal Hospital, a deservedly appreciated institution, treats daily about 150 out-door and many in-door patients.

The Municipal Office has a very well kept up garden much resorted to by the public for recreation.

The Sub-Court, a fine building, where all the Magistrates hold their Courts.

The Porter Town Hall and *the Gopalrao Library* erected in memory of the two great educationalists of this city.

SUNDARAPERUMALKOIL.

Sundaraperumalkoil (pop. 2,689) is situated in the Kumbakonam taluq of the Tanjore district, 6 miles from Kumbakonam, 19 from Tanjore, 25 from Mayavaram, and 199 from Madras (Egmore). The village is about half a mile from the station on the south bank of the river Arasalar.

Local Accommodation.—In the village is a choultry where Hindus of all classes, except Pariahs, can find accommodation free; but must make their own arrangements for food. At Darasathiram, about 3 miles east of the station, is a choultry maintained by the late Tanjore Rajah's family, where meals are served gratis to Brahmans and supplies given to Bairagis. Besides these there are two hotels in Sundaraperumalkoil, where meals are served to natives of all classes at 2½ annas per meal.

Road Conveyance.—Bullock-carts can be had if previous notice be given, the fares being 2 annas per vehicle per mile.

Local Manufactures and Products.—Weaving is carried on, a very good description of native cloth being manufactured. The chief produce is paddy.

Local Official.—The Village Munsiff.

Fairs and Festivals.—At Swamimalai, 3 miles north-east of the station, is a Subramanya temple, at which every month a festival is held, a large crowd generally attending.

Objects of Interest.—An old temple built by a Chola King and dedicated to Sundaraperumal (Vishnu).

The brick remains of the palace of a Chola Rajah, which are situated about one mile south of a village called Tiruvalanjooly, itself a mile away from the station, possess antiquarian interest.

PAPANASAM.

Papanasam (pop. 1,688) is situated in the Kumbakonam taluq of the Tanjore district, 9 miles from Kumbakonam, 16 from Tanjore, 28 from Mayavaram and 202 from Madras (Egmore). The village is on the south bank of the river Kodamuruty.

Local Accommodation.—About a quarter of a mile from the station is a choultry, where Hindus of all classes, except

Pariahs, can obtain free lodging, but must make their own
arrangements for food. There is also an hotel in the
village, where meals are served to all classes at 2½ annas
per meal.

Road Conveyance.—Bullock-carts are usually procurable
at the station, the fares being 2 annas per vehicle per mile.

Local Manufactures and Products.—Weaving is carried
on at two villages about two miles from this station called
Conjemedu and Venkarampet, a coarse kind of country
cloth being made. The chief product is paddy.

Local Officials.—The Sub-Registrar and Hospital Assistant.

Fairs and Festivals.—In March and April annually the
" Brahmautsavam " festival is celebrated in the Vishnu
temple. At Rajagheri, about 1½ miles west of the station,
a Muhammedan festival is held at the Peerali mosque
annually in September.

Mission and Churches.—In the village is a Roman
Catholic Church.

Objects of Interest.—An old Siva temple which contains
108 lingams. It was here that Rama on his return from
Ceylon, after killing Ravana, performed poojah (worshipped
god) to cleanse himself from the sin he committed in
killing the rakshasas.

AYYAMPET.

Ayyampet (pop. 7,695) is situated in the Tanjore taluq
of the Tanjore district, 11 miles from Tanjore, 14 from
Kumbakonam, 33 from Mayavaram and 207 from Madras
(Egmore). The village, which is 114 feet above sea-level,
is about three-quarters of a mile north of the station.

Local Accommodation.—In the village are 3 chuttrams,
in one of which meals are served gratis to Brahmans and
supplies given to Bairagis. In the other two, Hindus of
all classes, except Pariahs, can find free lodging and can be
supplied with meals, if they wish, on payment of 2½ annas

per meal, or they may make their own arrangements for food. There are also 2 Sudra hotels, where meals are served at 2¼ annas each.

Road Conveyance.—Bullock-carts are usually available at the station, the fares being 2 annas per vehicle per mile.

Local Manufactures and Products.—Silk cloths, carpets of silk floss, and korray mats are largely manufactured. The chief produce is paddy.

Local Official.—The Village Munsiff.

Missions and Churches.—At Regunathapuram, 1½ miles east of the station, is a Roman Catholic Church.

Objects of Interest.—About 3 miles north of the station is an old Vishnu temple with inscriptions, where free meals for 12 Brahmans are supplied daily.

TITTE.

Titte (pop. 971) is situated in the Tanjore taluq of the Tanjore district, 6 miles from Tanjore, 18 from Kumbakonam, 38 from Mayavaram, and 212 from Madras (Egmore). The village, which is 128 feet above sea-level, is one mile west of the station.

Road Conveyance.—Bullock-carts can be had if previous notice is given, the fares being 3 annas per vehicle per mile.

Local Manufactures and Products.—The chief produce is paddy.

Local Official.—The Village Munsiff.

TANJORE JUNCTION.

Tanjore (lat. 10° 48′ N. ; long. 79° 11′ E. ; height above sea-level 193 feet ; pop. 54,390) is the principal town of a Collectorate of the same name. The district has an area of 3,654 square miles and contains the fertile deltaic lands of the Cauvery, the irrigation of which is controlled by the important anicuts " Upper " and " Grand " near Trichi-

nopoly. The town of Tanjore derives its name from
"Tanjan," a mythological giant, who haunted the neighbourhood and was slain by the god " Vishnu," who granted
the dying request of the giant that the place should be
called after him.   The European and East Indian quarters
are in the suburb of Manamboo Chavady, south-east of the
fort, while the native town outside the fort extends
northward for about 2 miles to the Jamboo Cauvery
channel.   The greatest length of the town south and north
is about 4, and its greatest breadth east and west about 3
miles.   The station is the junction for the Negapatam
branch line.   The following are the distances to the
principal stations on the South Indian Railway :—

Kumbakonam	24 miles.
Mayavaram Junction	44 ,,
Cuddalore	90 ,,
Villupuram Junction	119 ,,
Pondicherry	143 ,,
Chingleput Junction (for Conjeeveram)	183 ,,
Madras (Egmore)	217 ,,
Tiruvannamalai	165 ,,
Vellore	212 ,,
Pakala Junction	257 ,,
Renigunta Junction (for Madras Railway)	290 ,,
Gudur Junction (for East Coast Railway)	341 ,,
Dharmavaram Junction (for Southern Maharatta Ry.)	400 ,,
Tiruvallur Junction (for Mutupet)	34 ,,
Negapatam	48 ,,
Trichinopoly Junction	31 ,,
Erode Junction (for Madras Railway)	118 ,,

Local Accommodation.—Close to the station is a travellers'
bungalow, which can accommodate 4 persons, is furnished,
and has a cook, who will supply meals, if required.   The
charge for the use of this bungalow is, for single persons,
one rupee each, and for married couples Rs. 1-8-0 per
diem.   For natives there are 4 chuttrams, where all classes
can find accommodation, making their own arrangements
for food ; and about 50 hotels, where meals are served at
from 2½ to 3 annas each,

Road Conveyance.—Hackney carriages, jutkas and bullock-carts are obtainable, the fares being :—

		RS. A. P.
Hackney carriages	.. ..	(3 8 0 per diem. { 2 0 0 for half a day or less.
Jutkas	.. ..	(2 0 0 per diem. { 1 0 0 for half a day or As. 2 per mile.
Bullock-carts	.. ..	0 2 0 per mile.

If a hackney carriage be required, previous advice should be sent to the Station Master. A guide is generally at the station to meet trains, whose services can be obtained to shew the sights of the town at Rs. 1-8-0 per diem.

Railway Facilities.—Waiting accommodation is provided at the station for ladies, and a refreshment room is maintained by Messrs. Spencer & Co., the butler in charge of which has usually a small stock of travellers' requisites for sale. A new station is about to be built, in which sleeping accommodation and good waiting-rooms will be provided.

Local Manufactures and Products.—Tanjore is noted for its artistic manufactures, including silk cloths and carpets, jewellery, repoussé work, and models of temples, etc., in pith and other materials. At the Central Jail weaving is carried on, and carpets, mats, coir rope and other articles made by the prisoners may be purchased cheaply. The chief produce is paddy.

Local Officials.—The Collector (who lives at Vallam 6 miles from Tanjore), the Judge, the Superintending and Executive Engineers, P. W. D., the Superintendent of Police, the District Surgeon, the Local Fund Engineer, District Traffic Superintendent, Municipal Chairman, Deputy Tahsildar, District Munsiff and Sub-Judge.

Fairs and Festivals.—An annual festival is held at the temple in April which attracts many pilgrims.

Missions, Churches, etc.—The Tanjore district was the scene of the earliest labours of Protestant missionaries

in India. In 1706 a Lutheran Mission was established in
Tranquebar. The Mission at Tanjore was founded in 1778,
by the Rev. C. F. Schwartz, of the Tranquebar Mission,
who, having previously transferred his services to the
Society for the Promotion of Christian Knowledge, came
to Tanjore from Trichinopoly. The Tanjore Missions were
taken over in 1826 by the Society for the Propagation of
the Gospel, under which Society they are at present. St.
Peter's Church, which belongs to this Mission and is used
by the Church of England congregation, was built in 1780.
It was re-constructed in 1829 in accordance with the last
wishes of Bishop Heber.

In the Little Fort is situated the church built by Mr.
Schwartz in 1779, which contains the monument to his
memory. This church is not used now, except for an
annual service on New Year's day. The Leipzig Evangelical Lutheran Mission formed a congregation in Tanjor
in 1856, and they also have a church here. The Roman
Catholic Missions in Tanjore were established long before
the Protestant, and this city is still one of their principal
seats, their church being near the Club.

Clubs.—The European Club is very close to the Railway
station. It has a good library, two tennis courts and golf
links. Gentlemen received in society are eligible for
membership. Visitors may become honorary members
on being proposed and seconded, and are required to pay
8 annas per diem or Rs. 7 per mensem. The "Union" Club,
where educated natives associate. The upper storey of the
building is called the "Marsh Memorial Hall" to perpe-
tuate the memory of a distinguished educationalist of the
district.

Historical.—The early history of Tanjore is buried in
antiquity; but there are fair grounds for presuming that, in
the eleventh century A. D., it was made the capital of the
Kola dynasty by Rajah Kulottunga, and that probably it
was the seat of Kola kings in the second century A. D.

From about 1530 the city has been successively the seat of two Hindu dynasties, the Nayak and Maharatta. There were only four Nayak princes in all, and their dominion lasted till about 1665 A. D. These rulers were at first but Viceroys of the monarchs of Vijayanagar (the modern Bijanagar in the Bellary district), but seem to have been virtually independent later on, in consequence of the decline of the Vijayanagar Empire. The first Nayak built the Sivaganga Fort, generally known as the " Little Fort," which forms a projecting square at the south-west angle of the larger fort of Tanjore, and also the tank outside the fort called Sevappa Nayakkan kulam. The larger fort was constructed by Vijaya Raghava Nayak the last king. During this dynasty the first European settlements on the Tanjore coast were formed by the Portuguese at Negapatam and by the Danes at Tranquebar. Vijaya Raghava is said to have been a brave prince, but too much occupied in religious devotion to pay attention to affairs of State. He was killed in action together with his son Mannaru when endeavouring to repulse an attack on the town by Alagiri the General of the then Nayak of Madura. To prevent any member of his family or zenana from falling into the hands of his enemies, Vijaya Raghava directed his son to fill the zenana with gunpowder, to set fire to it at a given signal, and then to join him sword in hand, so that they might die together. This programme was duly carried out and the tragedy is commemorated to this day by the shattered tower over the Nayak's zenana at the south-west corner of the Tanjore palace and which is still supposed to be haunted by the ghosts of the unfortunate women. The crown Rani of Vijaya Raghava contrived, however, to save her male baby, who, afterwards, with the assistance of the Pathan King of Bijapur, ascended the throne. The young sovereign seems never to have been independent, and, on the death of the ruler of Bijapur, was deposed by Ekoji, the Mahratta General, who had placed him on the throne, and who thus founded the Mahratta dynasty. Ekoji came of a respectable family surnamed Bhonsale and was half-brother of the great Sivajee, founder of the modern Mahratta Empire in the Deccan. The history of this dynasty from the accession of Ekoji in 1674 to the first connection of the British with this principality in 1749 presents but few events of historical importance. In the early portion of this year the deposed Rajah Saiyaji requested the aid of the English in regaining his kingdom from the then reigning Rajah, Pratapsing, and promised to give them, in the event of success, the fort of Divikottei and certain contiguous territory. In response to this application a small force was despatched in April 1749 from Fort St. David at Cuddalore. The expedition was unsuccessful; but a second, which was despatched the following month, captured Divikottei and enforced the terms demanded. In 1754 and 1758, the district was overrun by the French, but they were finally compelled to evacuate the country on the English coming to the assistance of the rajah. At the instance of the Nawab of the Carnatic, two English expeditions were undertaken against Tanjore in 1771 and 1773, respectively, resulting in the city being entirely reduced, the rajah and his family taken prisoners, and the country being handed over to the nawab. This prince extracted all the money and jewels he possibly could from the inhabitants of the country; but his career of extortion was cut short by the Court of Directors of the East India Company disapproving of the action of the Governor of Madras, and ordering the reinstatement of Rajah Tulzaji. In 1781 the district was invaded by Hyder Ali and, with the exception of the town of Tanjore, remained in the occupation of his troops for some six or seven months. The decisive victory of Porto Novo, coupled with the capture of Negapatam from the Dutch allies of Hyder Ali, and the surrender to the British of other places of minor importance, compelled the invaders to withdraw from the district.

Rajah Tulzaji died in 1787 and was succeeded ultimately by his adopted son Sharabhogi, who was at first set aside for Amarsing, half-brother of Tulzaji. The history of Rajah Sharabhogi is intimately associated with the career of Mr. Schwartz, of the German Mission, a man who was not only honorably associated with the spread of Christianity, but also with the political history of Tanjore. A mural monument to Schwartz, by Flaxman, was erected by Sharabhogi in the small church situated in the little fort. Sharabhogi made an extensive collection of books, chiefly English and Sanskrit, and the library in the Tanjore palace is perhaps the largest and most valuable in the whole of Southern India. This rajah consented to resign the Government of his country to the East India Company, provided they made a suitable provision for his maintenance, and, in consequence, under a treaty made on the 25th October 1799, Tanjore became a British province.

Sharabhogi was succeeded by his son Shivaji, who died in 1855 without male heirs, when the titular dignity became extinct. The British Government made liberal provision for the family of the rajah, some of whom are still in occupation of the palace.

Objects of Interest.—The ruins of the old fort, which was originally formed of thick masonry walls 15 feet high, and a moat some 3 miles long and 15 feet deep. The walls, however, are being gradually removed by the Municipality and used for filling up the moat.

The little fort south-west of the main fort contains *The Great Temple*, the centre of attraction for all travellers in Southern India. This temple, generally called Brahadeeswaraswami koil, was built during the reign of Chola King Rajaraja, who reigned from A. D. 1023 to 1064, under the superintendence of the Rajah's Commander-in-Chief, by a man from Conjeeveram named Samavarma, and, as appears from the inscriptions which cover the walls, was endowed by the Rajaraja and his son Rajendra Raja by grant of

BRAHATHISVARAR TEMPLE — TANJORE

lands, money and golden jewels set with precious stones. The entrance is by a small bridge over the fort moat, whence an avenue leads through a small arched gateway, ornamented with brilliantly coloured stucco representations of some prominent members of the Hindu pantheon. A few yards beyond the gateway, the path leads under a gopuram 90 feet high, a little beyond which is a second gopuram of smaller dimensions (60 feet high) opening directly on to the courtyard of the temple. Immediately facing the gopuram is a large raised platform, the first structure on which is a " Balipeedam," or place of feeding crows. In front of this is a stone mantapam sheltering an enormous monolithic bull, and to the left, and somewhat in advance of the latter, is a small stone bull, and another " Balipeedam." To the right of the large bull is a small temple dedicated to Parvati under the name of Periya-nayagiammal. A flight of steps from the platform leads to the mantapam in front of the great vimanah. Separated from the Periyanayagiammal temple by a narrow pathway, and lying immediately to the right of the main temple, is a garden in which are grown the flowers used for decorating the idols. Returning to the second gopuram, and taking a route along the left side of the courtyard, the first structure to be observed is a raised railed platform known as the " Astakodi," where the dancing girls perform during festivals. Further on is a colonnade containing lingams, and another platform on which dancing also takes place. Outside the wall, on the left side of the courtyard, are the cooking room for the god, the temple stables, store-rooms, a garden, and a house in which Brahmans are fed. When passing the main tower of the temple, a small cell projecting from its base and reached by a flight of steps should be noticed as being the mantapam of Dakshnamurti, or the god who faces the south. In the left-hand corner of the enclosure is the Ganapati mantapam—an insignificant building—and a thatched shed for repairing cars. Commencing from this corner and running round the west and north sides of the enclosure is a colonnade containing 108 lingams, the walls of which are decorated with pictures of the gods and the 64 miracles. A margosa tree, under which is said to be buried the body of an extremely holy priest, is situated immediately to the west of the tower. Returning by the right side of the courtyard, the beautiful Subramanya temple is the first structure of note and attached to it is the Maha mantapam containing pictures of the Mahratta Rajahs. The Sabapathy mantapam, which is being extended, is on the right-hand side of the raised platform near the entrance gopuram, and the Oma-kuntam mantapam and the colonnade near it complete the buildings on the east side of the yard.

The outer-enclosure of the pagoda measures 415 feet by 800 feet.

The huge bull (Nandi), said to be of black granite, measures 16 feet in length, 12 feet in height, and 7 feet across, and is estimated to weigh 25 tons. It was popularly supposed by the natives that this bull was growing and, as they feared it might become too large for the mantapam erected over it, a nail was driven into the back of its head, and, since this was done, the size of the monolith has remained stationary.

The Chandikeswaran kovil is the shrine of the god who reports to the chief god the arrival of worshippers.

The great tower of the temple is 216 feet high, *viz.*, 168 feet from the base to the storey, on the four corners of which are nandis or bulls (each 6 feet by 4 feet), 33 feet from there to the top of the building, and 15 feet thence to the top of the gilded kalasam (spiked ornament). This ornament stands on a single block of granite, $25\frac{1}{2}$ feet square, estimated to weigh 80 tons, which was elevated to its present position by means of an inclined plane com-mencing at a village called Sarappullam (scaffold hollow) about 4 miles north-east of Tanjore. According to a

NEGATIVE BY A. D. G. SHELLEY

SUBRAMANIA'S TEMPLE, TANJORE

local legend, this tower took 12 years to build. On the north, against one of its outer walls, is placed a waterspout. The water which flows from it, being the washings of the idol (god Siva), is sprinkled over their heads by worshippers as a purifying act. On the south side of the tower, about half-way up, is a figure said to represent an Englishman; and tradition has it that, at the time of building the tower, the supremacy of the English was foretold and the prophecy recorded by representing an Englishman among the other sculptured figures. A more probable version is that the builders of the tower were aided by a Dutch architect, whose services were in part rewarded by thus perpetuating his memory. At any rate the figure more resembles a Dutchman than an Englishman. The Subramanya temple is " as exquisite a piece of decorative architecture as is to be found in the south of India." (*Fergusson*.) Though built behind an older shrine, which may be coeval with the great temple as originally designed, Subramanya's temple is certainly a century or two more modern than the great pagoda. It consists of a tower 55 feet high raised on a base 45 feet square adorned with pillars and pilasters, which ornament is continued along a corridor 50 feet long communicating with a second building 50 feet square lying to the east. The beautiful carving of this temple, which is as clear and sharp as the day it left the sculptor's hands, seems to be in imitation of wood.

The great temple at Tanjore is one of the very few temples in Southern India which have been built at one time and on one plan, most of the other temples having been originally very small buildings, which were subsequently added to, with the result that there is no uniformity in their design.

A little to the north of the temple enclosure is a garden, which was formerly the pleasure resort of the Mahratta Rajahs of Tanjore. It contains a tank of excellent water which, before Tanjore had a Municipal supply, was the only good water in the place. A larger reservoir, called the "Old Sivagunga Tank," lies to the west of the garden and close to the *Schwartz Church* (above described). Near the southern gate of the small fort is a gigantic "Arasu" tree with enormous branches around the trunk of which many images of "Naga" or representation of the cobra have been placed by childless religious Hindus.

The Palace, situated within the great fort, bears unmistakable signs of being a very old structure, which has been added to from time to time. The entrance is on the east side of the palace enclosures about three-quarters of a mile from the railway station. After passing through two quadrangles a third is reached, on the south side of which is a gopuram-like building of stucco some 90 feet in height. The palace itself is 5 storeys high, and the apartments, many of which are now locked up unused, are huge. On the east of the quadrangle is the Durbar Hall, in which, on a platform of black granite, stands the statue of Rajah Sivajee, executed by Flaxman in white marble, and representing the rajah standing with the palms of his hands joined as if in welcome to his courtiers. The reproduction in marble of the curious triangular pointed turban formerly used by the Tanjore princes is so heavy that it has been removed from the head of the statue and lies on a cushion near its base. In this hall is a fine bust of Lord Nelson presented to Sivajee by the Hon. Anne Seymour Damer, whose work it is, and a portrait of Lord Pigott.

The library is in the "Saraswati Mahal" and contains, among other works, 18,000 Sanskrit manuscripts, of which 8,000 are written on palm leaves. In another quadrangle is a building known as the Mahratta Durbar Hall, on the walls of which are portraits of the Mahratta Rajahs. The throne seems to have disappeared, and there is only a big chair placed under a canopy to shew where the throne was. In this hall is a large picture representing Sivajee, the last

INTERIOR OF THE PALACE AT TANJORE

Rajah of Tanjore with his Chief Secretary on his right and his Dewan on the left.

In the Armoury within the palace are many curious weapons, the greater number of which are more suited for display at a pageant than for use in war. Gold and silver handled swords, miniature guns, out of date rifles and pistols, howdahs, gold caps for ornamenting elephants and various dresses for men and animals worked up in lace are exhibited in considerable profusion.

Near the eastern gate of the fort is a *tower* called the " *Tasa Modu,*" which has a curious device on it for showing the time, and near to which is an old cannon, 25 feet in length and 2 feet in bore.

Outside the fort is a *clock tower* constructed in 1883 at the expense of one of the Tanjore Princesses. North of the clock tower is the *Rajah Mirasdar Hospital*, which is under the management of the District Surgeon.

About 7 miles south-west of Tanjore lies the small town of Vallam originally containing a strong fort surrounded by a deep moat and said to have been constructed in the sixteenth or seventeenth century. The fort was taken by the English Army from the Nawab of the Carnatic in 1771 and remained in British possession until its restoration to Rajah Tulzaji in 1776. Except the ditch and a few ruined walls but little now remains of the old fort. Quartz pebbles, rock crystals and other similar stones are found at Vallam and are cut into various ornamental and useful articles, among which may be mentioned brooch stones and spectacle lenses.

Tiruvayar or *Tiruvadi* is a small town on the north bank of the Cauvery, 7 miles from Tanjore and is one of the centres of the Brahmanical religion and contains a large well-sculptured temple dedicated to Siva. Aged Brahmans retire to this town to spend the evening of their lives and terminate their existence in view of the beatification which is considered to follow death at this place. In consequence of this belief, nearly one-third of the population are Brahmans.

ALAKKUDI.

Alakkudi.—Six and half miles from Tanjore Junction and 224 miles from Madras. It is on the south side of the Railway line where the Vallam road crosses, and, being nearer to Vallam than Tanjore, those wishing to see the Collector should alight at the station. There are two roads, one going to Vallam on the south, and one going to Perambur, &c., on the north.

Local Produce.—Varagu, kambu, thuvarai (dholl), raggy, cotton and coriander seeds.

BUDALUR.

Budalur (pop. 2,054) is situated in the Tanjore taluq of the Tanjore district, 11 miles from Tanjore Junction, 20 miles from Trichinopoly Junction and 229 from Madras (Egmore). The village is 188 feet above sea-level.

Local Accommodation.—If previous notice is given, natives of all classes can obtain meals at an hotel in the village, the charge being 2½ annas per meal.

Road Conveyance.—Jutkas and bullock-carts are usually to be had at the station, the fares being 2 annas per mile for the former and 1½ for the latter. There is a good metalled road to Tirukattupulli, a village 5 miles from this station.

Local Manufactures and Products.—The chief produce is dholl-gram and paddy.

Local Official.—The Village Munsiff.

Fairs and Festivals.—A fair is held every Thursday at Tirukattupulli.

Historical.—Colonel Smith took possession of the pagoda in 1773 when marching from Trichinopoly against Tanjore.

Objects of Interest.—At Tirukattupulli are the remains of an old fort and a Siva temple. The latter was built by Chola King and contains inscriptions.

TIRUVERUMBUR.

Tiruverumbur (pop. 1,042) is situated in the Trichinopoly taluq of the Trichinopoly district, 7 miles from Trichinopoly Junction, 25 from Tanjore Junction, and 242 from Madras (Egmore). The village is 230 feet above sea-level.

Local Manufactures and Products.—The chief product is paddy.

Local Official.—The Village Munsiff.

Historical.—This was formerly an important place as commanding the road from Trichinopoly to Tanjore.

Objects of Interest.—A strongly built Siva temple on a low rock with a rock-cut cave below it. Six miles north of this station is the Grand Anicut, which, though making no pretensions to architectural merit, is remarkable for its great utility.

Sport.—Good snipe shooting can be had here in the season.

TRICHINOPOLY.

Trichinopoly (lat. 10'49; long. 78'46; pop. 90,609) is a large Municipal town situated in a taluq of the same name in the Trichinopoly district, on the right bank of the river Cauvery. The town is divided into two parts, one called the "Cantonment," which contains the residences of the European and Eurasian community and the barracks of the native troops; the other, the "Fort," a densely populated locality occupied by natives. The "Cantonment" was formerly garrisoned by European and native regiments, but in 1878, when the fourth Afghan War broke out, the whole of the European troops were removed, and the garrison subsequently reduced to two native regiments. The "Fort" was rectangular in trace, measuring about a mile by half a mile, and was originally surrounded by ramparts and a ditch, but the walls have now been completely levelled and the ditch filled in. The streets in this part of the town are narrow, but have been, on the whole, regularly laid out. Inside the Fort is the Trichinopoly Rock, which rises abruptly out of the plain to a height of 273 feet above the level of the street at its foot. Trichinopoly has two railway stations, "Trichinopoly Junction" which serves the Cantonment and "Trichinopoly Fort," 2½ miles distant on the Erode branch, which accommodates the native town.

The South Indian Railway Company's head-quarters are in the Cantonment, the "General offices" being close to the Junction station.

The following are the distances from this Junction to the principal stations on the South Indian Railway :—

Erode Junction (for Madras Railway)	..	.. 87 miles.
Ammayanayakanur (for Kodaikanal)	..	.. 71 .,
Madura	..	.. 96 ,,
Tinnevelly	..	.. 195 ,,
Tuticorin	..	.. 195 ,,
Tanjore Junction (for Negapatam)	..	.. 81 ,,
Negapatam	..	.. 79 ,,
Mayavaram Junction ..	..	.. 75 ,,
Villupuram Junction ..	..	.. 151 ,,
Pondicherry	..	.. 174 ,,
Chingleput Junction (for Conjeeveram)	..	.. 215 ,,
Madras (Egmore)	..	.. 249 ,,
Tiruvannamalai	..	.. 193 ,,
Vellore	..	.. 244 ,,
Pakala Junction	..	.. 282 ,,
Gudur Junction (for East Coast Railway)		.. 373 ,,
Dharmavaram (for Southern Mahratta Railway)		.. 430 ,,

Local Accommodation.—About a mile from the Junction station is a travellers' bungalow which is fully furnished and can accommodate two persons at one time. The butler in charge can supply meals, if required, but wines and spirits must be privately purchased. The charge for the use of this bungalow is one rupee for each person per diem. Close to the river Cauvery, about three-quarters of a mile from the "Fort" station, are 4 choultries, where natives of all classes can find free lodging, but must make their own arrangements for food. Besides these, in the Fort there are 2 Brahman and about 27 other hotels, where meals are served at 2½ annas per meal.

Road Conveyance.—At the Junction station hackney carriages, jutkas and bullock-carts are procurable, the fares being :—

	For a Day.			For half Day.		
	RS.	A.	P.	RS.	A.	P.
Palanquin carriage	2	12	0	1	8	0
Broughams	3	0	0	1	8	0
Victoria (single)	3	8	0	1	12	0
Do. (pair)	6	8	0	3	0	0
Jutkas	1	4	0	0	12	0
Bullock-carts	0	10	0	0	6	0

A guide is generally at this station, who will show the sights of the town. His charge is Rs. 3 per diem.

At the Fort station, jutkas and bullock-carts are usually available, the fares being 2 annas and 1 anna per vehicle per mile, respectively.

Railway Facilities.—At the Junction station, waiting accommodation is provided for first and second class passengers. There is also a refreshment room under the management of Messrs. Spencer & Co., the butler in charge of which has usually a few copies of the *Madras Mail* and *Madras Times* for sale, as well as a small stock of travellers' requisites. On the first floor of the station building are two rooms furnished for sleeping, each of which contains two beds. The charges for the use of these rooms are as under :—

Not exceeding 3 hours, for each adult	.. 8 annas.
And for each child of 12 years and under	.. 4 „
Exceeding 3 hours and not exceeding 24 hours, or one night only, for each adult	.. 1 rupee.
Do. do. for each child of 12 years and under	.. 8 annas.

Punkah-pullers, and hot and cold water baths, are charged as extras. At the Fort station, waiting accommodation is provided for first and second class passengers.

Local Manufactures and Products.—The most important local industry is the manufacture of cigars, for which Trichinopoly is famous. Articles in silver and gold are excellently made by the local gold and silversmiths, who are very successful with their filagree and repoussé work. The cost of well-made silver articles is usually double the value of their weight in rupees. Hardware and native shoes are largely manufactured and weaving is carried on. At the Central Jail many useful articles are made by the prisoners. The chief products are paddy, plantains, cocoanuts and mangoes.

Local Officials.—The Collector and District Magistrate, Deputy Collector, District Judge, Sub-Judge, Superintendent of Police, District Surgeon, Deputy Commissioner of Salt and Abkari, Salt and Abkari Inspector, Forest Officer, Tahsildar, Town and Stationary Sub-Magistrates, District and Sub-Registrars and District Munsiff. The Agent, Chief Engineer, Traffic Manager, Chief Auditor, Superintending Physician, and many other officers of the South Indian Railway also reside in the Cantonment.

Fairs and Festivals.—A market is held daily in the centre of the town, about a mile east of the Fort station. In December-January of each year, a large cattle fair is held at Srirungam, and in March annually a similar fair is held at Samayapuram. Every year, in December-January, the Yekadasi festival takes place at Srirungam, and in March a festival is celebrated at Samayapuram. In August annually a large festival is held at the Fort temple, when the gods and goddess, Siva, Parvati, Ganesh and Subramanya are carried in procession round the four main streets of the temple.

Missions, Churches, &c.—Close to the Junction station is St. John's Church, used by the European and Eurasian Protestant community of Trichinopoly, which contains the remains of Bishop Heber. There are several Roman Catholic Churches, the finest being one recently built by the Jesuit fathers near the Fort station. The Society for the Propagation of the Gospel, the Wesleyans, Lutherans and Jesuits, all have Missions, the S. P. G. and the Jesuits each maintaining first-grade colleges affiliated to the Madras University.

Clubs.—The Trichinopoly Club is a well known institution and has over 50 local members. In connection with it is the "Gymkhana Club," which maintains the tennis courts, golf links, racquet courts, &c. Visitors making a short stay in Trichinopoly may join either of these clubs, the following rules being applicable to honorary members :—

Visitors and gentlemen holding acting appointments, whose stay in the station or district is not likely to exceed one month, may alone be admitted as honorary members of the club without ballot during their stay in Trichinopoly on being proposed by one member and seconded by two other members.

Honorary members pay a subscription of Rs. 6 a month. Half-subscription to be paid for any part of a month not exceeding 15 days.

In the Town Hall in the Fort is a reading-room maintained by native officials.

Historical.—Worriur, now a suburb of Trichinopoly, was an early capital of the old Chola Dynasty, whose authority in the city seems to have been terminated by the Muhammedan incursion under Malik Kafur in A.D. 1310. The Musalmans governed the district until about 1372 when a Vijayanagar General, named Kampana Udeiyar, obtained possession of both Trichinopoly and Madura. In 1559, Visvanatha Nayakkan established the Nayakka Dynasty in Madura, and obtained Trichinopoly from the king of Tanjore in exchange for the fort of Vallam near Tanjore. Visvanatha is supposed to have fortified the town, constructed the large teppakulam, and built the walls and gopurams of Srirangam temple. The eighth king of the dynasty, Mutthu Krishnappa, made Trichinopoly the capital of his empire, but his successor, the great Tirumala Nayakka, re-transferred the seat of

31

Government to Madura. During the reign of the next monarch, Muttu Verappa, the country was constantly devastated by Muhammedan incursions necessitating the strengthening of the Trichinopoly fortifications. The succeeding king again removed his capital to Trichinopoly and erected in the city the building known as the Nawab's palace, obtaining the necessary materials by demolishing portions of Tirumala Nayakka's palace in Madura. In 1663, the Musalmans again invaded the south and besieged Trichinopoly without success, while four years later an incursion of Mysoreans took place. On the death of the last Nayakka, Vijaya Ranga Choka in 1731, his widow, Minakshi, attempted to gain possession of the kingdom. In this she was opposed by Vangaru Tirumala, the son of a prominent minister of the late king, and the contest for supremacy finally resulted in Nawab Dost Ali being applied to for assistance by Vangaru. The Nawab's son, Safdar Ali, marched to Trichinopoly, accompanied by his brother-in-law, Chanda Sahib, and, having summoned the rival claimants, decided in favour of Vangaru. Chanda Sahib was left in Trichinopoly to collect Safdar Ali's fee of 30 lakhs for the arbitration. Minakshi entered into intrigues with Chanda Sahib, who, finally, in consideration of the promise of a crore of rupees, took possession of Trichinopoly in the queen's name. Minakshi retained Trichinopoly for herself, and left Tinnevelly, Madura and Dindigul with the Ramnad and Sivagunga Zemindaries under the management of Vangaru Tirumala. In 1736, Chanda Sahib gained possession of Trichinopoly, apparently by treachery, deprived Vangaru of Madura, and confined the queen as a prisoner in her own palace. The unfortunate lady seems to have poisoned herself shortly after, and, as a last resource, Vangaru Tirumala invoked the assistance of the Mahrattas. This appeal resulted in the invasion of the Carnatic by a large force under Ragbuji Bhonslai, which, after defeating Nawab Dost Ali on the 20th May 1740, marched at once

on Trichinopoly. Chanda Sahib defended himself with
vigour, but, after a three months' siege, was obliged to surrender the town to the Mahrattas on the 26th March 1741.
He, his son, and his principal officers were sent as prisoners
to Sattara, and Morari Rao, a Mahratta General, was appointed Governor of Trichinopoly with a force of 14,000
men to assure his position. Two years later, the Nizam of
Hyderabad, Asaf Jah, entered the Carnatic with a large
army, and demanded the surrender of Trichinopoly. Morari
Rao refused to comply, whereupon the Nizam laid siege
to the place which soon surrendered, and in 1743 Morari
Rao with his Mahrattas retired from the Carnatic. In
1748 the Nizam Asaf Jah died, when a contest for succession arose between his son Nazir Jung and a favorite
grandson Muzuffer Jung. At this time Chanda Sahib, who
had been released by the good offices of the French, and
was a claimant to the nawabship of the Carnatic, then held
by Anwar-ud-din, associated himself with the cause of
Muzuffer Jung. These allies defeated and killed Anwar-
ud-din at the battle of Ambur in July 1749, when his son,
Muhammad Ali, fled to Trichinopoly, and solicited the
assistance of the English. The French and English, who
had been at war since 1744, took opposite sides, the latter
espousing the cause of Nazir Jung and Muhammed Ali.
A small detachment under Captain Cope was accordingly
sent to Trichinopoly in response to the latter's appeal, while
the French supplied 800 European soldiers to Muzuffer
Jung and Chanda Sahib, who immediately marched against
Trichinopoly. *En route*, being short of funds, they proceeded to squeeze the king of Tanjore, a delay which
proved disastrous to their plans as the arrival in the Carnatic
of Nazir Jung compelled them to return to Pondicherry.
Muhammed Ali and Cope's detachment joined Nazir Jung's
force at Voldore, some 16 miles from Pondicherry, where
they were confronted by Muzuffer Jung's army. No battle
was fought as, owing to dissatisfaction on the part of the

French Officers who resigned their commissions, Muzuffer
Jung surrendered and Chanda Sahib and the French retired
to Pondicherry.   In December 1750, Nazir Jung was assas-
sinated when the greater portion of his army went over to
Muzuffer Jung.   Muhammed Ali thereupon fled to Trichi-
nopoly, where he was reinforced in February 1751 by 280
Europeans and 300 sepoys under the command of Captain
Cope.   On receiving intelligence that Chanda Sahib was
about to besiege Trichinopoly. Muhammad Ali applied to
the English for further assistance, and in April 1751, 500
Europeans and 1,000 sepoys with eight field pieces under
Captain Gingen were sent from Cuddalore.   Near the
village of Valikandapuram, on the high road between
Trichinopoly and Madras, this force, which had been joined
by a detachment from Trichinopoly, came in sight of Chanda
Sahib's army, then encamped along the bed of the Vellar
river.   The French advanced the following morning, when
the English troops, after a smart skirmish, retreated in great
confusion on Trichinopoly by forced marches.   A company
of Grenadiers under Captain Dalton fought an unsuccessful
rear-guard action with the allied troops of Chanda Sahib
and the French near the village of Uttattur in the Perum-
balur taluq, and the retreat was continued as far as the
north bank of the Coleroon.   This river separates from
the Cauvery at Trichinopoly, but for several miles after
the division the two streams continue so close together
that their banks are never more than two miles apart,
and 15 miles east of Trichinopoly at Koviladi, the two
rivers are only separated by a strong embankment.   The
enclosed strip of land is known as the island of Srirungam
and is famous for its great temple.   The English force,
after first occupying the pagoda at Pichandarkovil on the
Salem road, crossed the Coleroon and located themselves in
the Srirungam temple.   This building, though well adapted
for resistance, was found to be too large for defence by so
small a body of men, and the English force, therefore,

crossed the Cauvery and took shelter under the walls of Trichinopoly on the west side of the city. On Srirungam being vacated by the English, the French and Chanda Sahib's force immediately occupied the island ; but, elated by their success in capturing the small mud fort at Koviladi, Chanda Sahib's army was shortly afterwards moved across the Cauvery, and encamped to the east of Trichinopoly, a garrison being left in Srirungam. At this juncture, Lieutenant Clive was despatched with a small force from Fort St. David to the assistance of the city, but even with this reinforcement the disparity between the opposing armies was so great that, on his return in August to Fort St. David, Clive was permitted to create a diversion by undertaking his now famous expedition against Arcot. The siege operations against Trichinopoly devolved on the French, who erected their principal battery of three 8-pounders and three mortars about 1,200 yards to the south of the north-east angle of the town. On a little eminence, now known as the French Rocks, situated near the spot where the Tanjore road crosses the Wyacondan channel, two 18-pounders were mounted, and another 2-gun battery was constructed on Srirungam island. Muhammud Ali, who was now reduced to great distress for want of funds, entered into a secret treaty with Mysore, under which, as the price of his surrender of the country from Trichinopoly to Cape Comorin to that State, an army under the Dewan Nundiraz, and 4,000 Mahratta horse under Morari Rao, were sent to his aid. In preventing the French from intercepting the arrival of these reinforcements, Captain Cope was killed. Shortly afterwards, the Rajah of Tanjore sent to Muhammud Ali's aid 3,000 horse and 2,000 foot under Monakji, and the Tondiman of Pudukottai supplemented the force with 400 horse and 3,000 men. In March 1752, 400 Europeans and 1,100 sepoys under Major Lawrence, after successfully opposing an attempt by the French to prevent their progress beyond Tiruverumbur, arrived at Trichinopoly. The garrison being now superior in numbers to the besieging force, offensive operations against the French and their allies were prosecuted with vigour. Lawrence determined to first attack Chanda Sahib's camp, but Captain Dalton, the officer entrusted with the duty, was misled during a night march by his guides, and at daybreak, on April 2nd, found himself in the centre of the French outposts between Erumbisvaram rock near Tiruverumbur and the French Rocks. This mistake, which should have resulted in the annihilation of Dalton's force, so far from being availed of by Law, the French commander, actually determined this incompetent officer to fall back on Srirungam and thus allow Erumbisvaram to be easily captured by the English. Clive, who was now serving under Lawrence, persuaded the latter to divide his army into two divisions, and to allow him to lead one to the north of the city so as to intercept any possible reinforcement from Pondicherry. Clive fought a series of minor actions at the village of Samaya-puram, 8 miles north of Trichinopoly on the Madras road, and on one occasion, being surprised at night by a body of French reinforcements, his force narrowly escaped disaster, and he himself nearly lost his life in the Mariyam-man temple at the hands of an Irish deserter, who treach-erously fired at him during a parley. M. D'Auteuil, who commanded the French troops was, however, prevented from reaching Srirungam, and, after halting some days at Uttattur, was driven back on Valikandapuram by Dalton. In the meantime Clive proceeded to the attack of Srirun-gum, but on the fall of Pichandarkoil and the consequent closing of communication with Pondicherry, Chanda Sahib's army dispersed, the majority going to their homes, but some joining the English. M. D'Auteuil hearing of this disaffection marched out of Valikandapuram was promptly defeated by Clive and compelled to surrender. Chanda Sahib shortly after gave himself up to the Tanjore General Monakji on the promise of a money reward and of his life being spared. This promise was immediately broken and Chanda Sahib brutally murdered.

Lawrence then called upon the French remaining in Srirungam to surrender, which, after some delay, they did. Prior to the murder of Chanda Sahib the English were in ignorance of the treaty between Muhammud Ali and Nandiraz, and it became necessary for an English detachment to remain in Trichinopoly to prevent rupture between the two, as the Nawab plainly evinced his reluctance to give up the town to the Mysore Dewan. Dupleix, who had received large reinforcements from Europe, after having appointed Reza Sahib, the son of Chanda Sahib, to be Nawab, entered into an alliance with the Mysore and Mahratta troops. This led to an early recommencement of hostilities by the French, but, after gaining a few trifling successes, they sustained a crushing defeat from Lawrence at Bahoor, near Pondicherry. This English victory at first inclined Nandiraz to give up any intention of keeping faith with Dupleix, but subsequent inaction on the part of Muhammud Ali, to whom the next campaign was intrusted, resulted in the Mysore and Mahratta troops siding definitely with the French. The Madras Government, therefore, declared war against Nandiraz, whereupon Dalton, who had been left in Trichinopoly, proceeded to attack the Mysore army in Srirungam. This engagement, which took place on the 23rd December 1752, was, on the whole, unfavorable to the English, so that Nandiraz was able to make arrangements for the starving out of the garrison by intercepting the supplies which were derived from the Pudukottai State. He stationed a strong detachment in the Fakir's tope, and the blockade thus established compelled Lawrence to march to the relief of the city. The news of his approach, however, caused the Mysoreans to retreat to Srirungam, so that he was able to reach Trichinopoly without molestation. The first move of Lawrence was to attack Srirungam, but in this he only obtained a negative result, and, as the enemy declined to be drawn into a general engagement in the open, he temporarily devoted himself to provisioning the city. Dupleix contrived to send large reinforcements to the Mysoreans, and in a short time Lawrence found himself with 500 Europeans and 2,000 sepoys opposed to 450 Europeans, 1,500 trained sepoys, 2 companies of topasses, 8,000 Mysore horses, 3,500 Mahrattas, and 15,000 irregular infantry. The Mysore General, on being reinforced again, left Srirungam and encamped on the plains three miles to the north of Fakir's Tope. Failure on the part of an English officer to maintain, as usual, a detachment on Fakir's Rock, led to its occupation by the enemy and the consequent cutting off of the Pudukottai supplies. On 26th June 1753, M. Astruc, the French commander, proceeded to attack a guard of 200 sepoys, who held a small eminence, half a mile to the south-west of Lawrence's camp, the possession of which would have enabled him to drive the English inside the city walls. This attack developed into the action properly known as the battle of Fakir's Rock and in which Lawrence gained a brilliant victory. After the battle, Lawrence left for Tanjore in order to procure some cavalry from the Rajah; and on his departure, Trichinopoly was again blockaded. After a month's absence he returned with reinforcements. The enemy opposed his advance near the Golden Rock, but were completely defeated, and Trichinopoly was reached without further trouble. Lawrence soon fought a minor successful action at Wyacondantirumalai, after which both sides remained passive awaiting reinforcements. At the end of September, Lawrence provoked a general engagement and gained a signal victory, capturing 11 guns, and the whole of the French tents, baggage and equipment. This action should properly be called after Golden Rock, near which it was fought, but occasionally it is incorrectly referred to as the battle of the Sugarloaf Rock. Trichinopoly was now virtually

out of danger, but in November the French made one
more despairing effort to capture the city. The attack
was delivered against that portion of the fortifications
known as Dalton's Battery and resulted in some 360
Frenchmen being taken prisoners. In February 1754 a
convoy of provisions, military stores, and cash *en route*
to Trichinopoly was captured and the guard cut to pieces
at Kiliyur, 10 miles from the city, by an overwhelming
force of French and Mahrattas, and the disaster was the
severest blow experienced by the English during the war.
The next item of importance was a dispute between Morari
Rao and Nandiraz, which resulted in the former being
bought off by the Rajah of Tanjore after he had defeated a
body of Tanjore troops, and retiring to his own country.
Hostilities between the French and English were suspended in September, and a provisional treaty concluded
on 31st December 1754. As the Mysore Dewan refused
to be bound by this treaty, he continued to direct futile
attacks from Srirungam, until the news of an invasion of
Mysore, by the Nizam, recalled him hurriedly to his own
country. The provisional treaty was ratified and the
French remained peacefully in Srirungam until war was
again declared between France and England in 1756.
Operations in the Trichinópoly district were commenced
by the French sending a detachment of 200 Europeans
and 2,000 sepoys under M. D'Auteuil to collect tribute
from the Poligars of Ariyalur and Udaiyapolayam. After
reinforcement by 800 Europeans and 1,000 sepoys,
D'Auteuil advanced to Srirungam and joined the garrison
of that island ; Captain Joseph Smith, who then commanded the small force of 150 Europeans and 700 sepoys forming the company's garrison in Trichinopoly, obtained 600
men from Tanjore and Pudukottai, and sent for assistance to
Captain Calliaud at the time in Madura with 120 Europeans
and 1,200 sepoys. Calliaud skilfully eluded D'Auteuil's
troops and after he joined the garrison the French Com-

mander withdrew to Pondicherry. In May 1758 with a view of strengthening the army besieging Fort St. David, the French Governor Lally recalled all the French troops in Srirungam, which was handed over to a detachment of Mysoreans from Dindigul. Fort St. David fell in June, but the Trichinopoly garrison was not immediately reduced, and soon after assisted in repulsing a French attack on Tanjore, when, however, the French had captured a number of outlying English posts, and were threatening Chingleput, Calliaud, with all the European troops, was recalled from Trichinopoly; and in November, when Madras was invested, the garrison was further reduced by 2,000 sepoys. In July 1759 the French captured Thiagar, an important fortress commanding the road through Valikandapuram to Trichinopoly, and proceeded to ravage the country as far as Uttattur. They re-occupied the Srirungam pagoda in the following October, but the disastrous defeat inflicted on them at Wandiwash by Colonel Coote soon necessitated the recall at first of a portion, and, finally, the whole of their troops in the island. In 1766 Trichinopoly was threatened by Hyder Ali, who occupied Thiagar in June; beyond the capture, however, of Karur, by Captain Smith, nothing further of importance occurred in the district during this war. In 1768-69 Hyder Ali again devastated the country round Trichinopoly, but made no move against the city itself. Once more in 1781, he appeared on the scene, and on this occasion proceeded to invest the town, but was compelled to raise the siege after his defeat at Porto Novo. In the later Mysore war of 1790, Tippoo Sultan marched through Karur on Trichinopoly, laid waste the island of Srirungam, and retired after making a few feints against the city. Since this time Trichinopoly has been free from hostile demonstrations, and it passed quietly into the possession of the English by treaty with the Nawab in 1801.

Objects of Interest—*Trichinopoly Rock.*—The ascent is

THE ROCH & TEMPLE TRICHINOPOLY

made by series of flights of steps commencing at an entrance close to the junction of the Main Bazaar street with the China Bazaar street. On each side of the gateway are stone figures of elephants, the passage itself being lined with pillars having carved capitals. The first three flights of steps terminate on a landing, at the four corners of which are granite monoliths, and which gives access to the high level street encircling the rock. This road is generally followed by religious processions and from it a hall is entered on the left of which is a small shrine to Ganesha and on the right the stable of the temple elephant. The second series of steps leads out of this hall through an exit ornamented with statues of Dwarapalagals on each side. After ascending three more flights of steps a second landing is reached, on each side of which is a large hundred-pillared mantapam, that on the right being used as a store, and that on the left being used twice a year for the reception of the idol belonging to the main temple. More steps lead to a third landing, to the left of which is a small room for the temple records and in front of which is a shrine to Ganesha. The ascent now turns sharply to the left and then to the right terminating on a fourth landing, giving access to the great temple, this the visitor cannot of course enter, but a view of a portion of the interior can be obtained from the landing. The steps now emerge into the open, passing on the left a chamber hewn out of the rock and covered with Sanscrit inscriptions of the Puranas. This chamber was used as a magazine by the British during the siege. Two short flights lead to a mantapam, to which the temple deity is taken once a year, and to a platform on the shoulder of the rock whence the final series of steps commences. These terminate on the top of the rock in a small temple dedicated to Ganesha, whose shrine is surrounded by a gallery from which a fine view of the town and the adjacent country is obtained. At the end of this gallery overlooking

the great temple is a narrow door (to open which the
visitor must secure the services of one of the custodians to
be found at the entrance to the great temple) leading on
to a small platform from which a good view is seen of the
" Kalasam " or golden covering over the god. Beneath
will be seen, sculptured in relief on the surface of the rock,
two foot-prints which the Hindus state to be those made
by a giant named Vibishna when engaged in carrying off
Rama. The Muhammedans, however, claim the foot-prints
as those of a great saint called Nattu, who took up his residence on the rock from which he was ejected by the god
of the place. At the foot of the rock, on the north-eastern
side, will be seen a row of low buildings with semi-circular
arched roofs said to be the old bomb-proof barracks, and
further on—more to the east—a portion of the outworks of
the fort, the line of the walls being indicated by the open
space surrounding the town. On the top of the shrine is
a flagstaff on which the British flag was flown when the
fort was garrisoned.

The visitor may be interested to know that a representation of the rock is sculptured on a tablet to Major Lawrence in Westminster Abbey.

The Teppakulam.—At the foot of the rock is a large
masonry tank or teppakulam in the centre of which a
small but graceful mantapam has been built. Overlooking the tank, at its south-east corner, is the house which
was once the residence of Clive, but is now occupied by
St. Joseph's College.

The Nawab's Palace, a part of which is at present used
as the Town Hall and part as offices for the Tahsildar,
District Munsiff, District Registrar, Town Magistrate and
other public officials, is situated close to Trichinopoly Rock.
It originally consisted of a suite of rooms, galleries and
inner apartments and had fountains playing in the garden
attached to it. Though not kept up in the manner it was
in days gone by, it is still worth a visit.

Chunda Sahib's Tomb.—Situated near the Trichinopoly Fort station contains the remains of Chunda Sahib, who himself built the dome of the edifice, which appears to be constructed from materials of Hindu temples.

The Central Jail.—Situated near the Golden Rock is built upon the radial principle, almost every part of it being commanded by the central tower. It is capable of accommodating nearly 1,000 prisoners. Visitors can see the jail on permission being obtained from the Superintendent who resides near the jail.

Sessions Court Bath.—Within the precincts of the Sessions Court is a small swimming bath in which the late Bishop Heber, the well-known author of the hymn " From Greenlands Icy Mountains " met his death. It is supposed that while bathing he had an apoplectic fit. To commemorate the sad event a tablet has been erected by Government at the side of the bath.

The Great Vishnu Temple at Srirungam.—A bridge of 32 arched openings of 49 feet span over the Cauvery joins the mainland to the island of Srirungam, which contains one of the largest and richest temples in Southern India. This temple can hardly be considered architecturally beautiful and is imposing simply on account of its enormous extent as is only too frequently the case with Dravidian temples. It is rather a fortuitous assemblage of walls, gopurams and mantapams, than a structure built to a well arranged and preconceived design. In all probability the temple is the work of many kings and originated in the central shrine, which successive monarchs left untouched while rivalling each other in surrounding it with walls and lofty gopurams. Be the explanation what it may, the fact remains that the architectural merit of the entire structure becomes less, the closer the proximity to the central shrine. This is to be the more regretted, as it must be admitted with Fergusson, that could the principle of design be reversed, Srirungam would be one of the finest temples in Southern India. The central shrine is dedicated to Runganadaswami, and is surrounded by no fewer than seven enclosing walls and 15 gopurams. The outermost wall, which is 20 feet 8 inches in height and 6 feet wide at the top, measures in plan 3,072 by 2,521 feet, and is built of fine cut stone. The entrance through it from the Trichinopoly side is by means of a magnificent but unfinished gateway, built of enormous blocks of granite, which is one of the finest structures in the whole temple, a narrow staircase gives admittance to the platform at the top, and the climb is well worth facing, not only for the view obtained, but also for the sake of examining the massive character of the building. The second enclosure measures 2,108 feet by 1,846 feet and the third 1,653 feet by 1,270 feet the intervening areas being occupied by separating streets and houses, each face of the three outer walls is surmounted by a gopuram, but the fourth wall has only three and the remaining walls none. The fourth enclosure wall measures 1,235 feet by 849 feet and among its three gopurams is that known as the vellai or " white gopuram," which is 146½ feet in height and is the finest in the whole temple. Rumour has it that there was originally a fourth gate in the west face of the enclosure, but that it was blocked up in consequence of the residents of the neighbouring houses having plundered the temple. After passing through the Vellai gopuram a mantapam is entered which is separated by an enclosed yard from the hall of 1,000 columns. The mantapam contains the best example of carving in the temple, but this is not high praise, as the work is decidedly inferior to that at Madura, Vellore, Chidambaram and many other places. The mantapam or hall of 1,000 pillars is in reality misnamed, as the number of columns is only 940. To remedy this deficiency, the yard is covered in on the occasions of the annual Yakadesy festival in December by a handsomely decorated bamboo structure or pandal, which is supported by the deficient number

GATEWAY SRIRUNGAM

of pillars. The fifth, sixth and seventh enclosure walls measure 767 feet by 503 feet, 426 feet by 295 feet and 240 feet by 181 feet, respectively; but Europeans are not permitted to pass them. The jewels and plate of this temple are well worth seeing and are worth many lakhs of rupees. Amongst them is a golden salver presented by H. R. H. the Prince of Wales on the occasion of his visiting India in 1875. In order to see the jewels prior notice must be given to the temple trustees as these valuables are in the custody of several persons whose joint presence is necessary before they can be shown. It is customary to pay at least five rupees to the trustees for making the necessary arrangements.

The Jambukeshwara Temple.—About half a mile to the east of the famous Vishnu temple at Srirungam is another remarkable temple dedicated to Siva and known as the Jambukeshwara temple. The name is a compound of the words " Jambu," a kind of a tree, and " Iswara " (lord), one of the names of Siva. The image of the deity in this pagoda, said to be a hundred years old, is placed under a Jambu tree and is much venerated. Mr. Fergusson considers the edifice to far surpass the larger temple in architectural beauty. The Jambukeshwara temple has five enclosures, of which the first and innermost contains the shrine or vimanah and is surrounded by a wall 30 feet in height and encloses a space of 126 feet by 123 feet. The second wall is 306 feet by 197 feet with a wall 35 feet high. There are several small mantapams in this enclosure the surrounding wall of which contains a gopuram 60 feet in height. The third enclosure is 745 feet by 197 feet and is surrounded by a wall 30 feet high containing two gopurams 73 feet and 100 feet in height. In this portion of the building is a cocoanut tope, a small tank and a temple to which the idol from the great Vishnu temple at Srirungam is brought for one day in each year. The fourth enclosure measures 2,436 feet by 1,493 feet, the wall surrounding it being 35 feet in height and 6 feet in thickness. The fifth or outer enclosure contains four streets of houses, and has a small gopuram over the western entrance, which is probably not more than seventy to ninety years old. There are numerous inscriptions in various parts of the building recording grants of lands made to the pagoda from time to time. This temple is not properly kept up and portions are falling into ruins.

KOLATUR SOUTH.

Kolatur South (pop. 2,525) is situated in the Trichinopoly taluq of the Trichinopoly district, 11¼ miles from Trichinopoly Junction, and 260 from Madras (Egmore). The village is about half a mile north-west of the station.

Local Accommodation.—Close to the station is a chuttram, where native travellers of all classes can find free lodging, but must make their own arrangements for food. In the village are two hotels, where meals are served to natives of all classes at 2½ annas per meal.

Road Conveyance.—Bullock-carts can be had at the station, the fare being 2 annas per vehicle per mile.

Local Manufactures and Products.—Not far from the station are granite quarries which yield excellent stone.

Local Official.—The Village Munsiff.

Fairs and Festivals.— A fair is held every Tuesday.

MANAPARAI.

Manaparai (pop. 3,158) is situated in the Kulitalai taluq of the Trichinopoly district, 23 miles from Trichinopoly Junction, 74 from Madura, and 271 from Madras (Egmore). The village is a quarter of a mile east of the station.

Local Accommodation.—Close to the station is a travellers' bungalow. This building has a lofty circular dome resembling the large hall in the Nawab's palace at Trichinopoly. It is said to have been built by the queen Mangammal, who acted as Regent during the minority of one of the Nayak kings in the sixteenth century. It is fur-nished and can accommodate three persons at one time, but no cook is entertained. The charge for the use of the bunga-low is 8 annas for each person per diem. In the village is a choultry, where natives of all classes can find free lodging, but must make their own arrangements for food. Besides this are 5 hotels, where meals are served to natives of all classes at 2½ annas per meal.

Road Conveyance.—Bullock-carts are usually procurable at the station, the fare being 2 annas per vehicle per mile.

Local Manufactures and Products.—The chief products are paddy, ragi, cholam, horse-gram, chillies, tamarind and firewood.

Local Officials.—The Deputy Tahsildar and Sub-Magis-trate, Sub-Registrar, Hospital Assistant, Police Inspector, Local Fund Overseer, Forest Ranger, Sub-Inspector of Salt and Abkari and the Revenue Inspector.

Fairs and Festivals.—A fair, the largest in the district, is held here every Wednesday.

Missions and Churches.—At Malayadiputti, about three miles west of the station, is a Roman Catholic Church, at which a large festival is held in Easter week.

Objects of Interest.—About seven miles north-east of this station in a village called Kuppanarpatti, are the remains of a small military station. The ruins consist of two buildings once used as barracks for European troops, quarters for their officers, stables, a magazine, a guard-room and three wells. The ground on which these buildings were erected rises considerably above the surrounding plain and is about 10 acres in extent. It is evident that the settlement was once fortified to some degree and it was probably an outlying station for the garrison in Trichinopoly, when it was necessary to awe the wild sur-rounding tribes into peaceful behaviour.

Sport.—Good shooting can be had close to the station, teal and duck being obtainable in the tanks during the cold

33

season, while, in the hills close by, wild pig may be found. Shikarries can be obtained at 8 annas and coolies at 4 annas per diem.

VAIYAMPATI.

Vaiyampati (pop. 1,544) is situated in the Kulitali taluq of the Trichinopoly district, 32 miles from Trichinopoly Junction, 64 from Madura, and 280 from Madras (Egmore).

Road Conveyance.—If previous notice be given, bullock-carts can be obtained, the fare being 2 annas per vehicle per mile.

Local Manufactures and Products.—The chief produce is firewood.

Local Official.—The Village Munsiff.

Fairs and Festivals.—A fair is held every Saturday, which is poorly attended.

AYYALUR.

Ayyalur (pop. 4,275) is situated 1,087 feet above sea-level in the Dindigul taluq of the Madura district, 43 miles from Trichinopoly Junction, 54 from Madura and 291 from Madras (Egmore).

Local Accommodation.—In the village is a chuttram, where native travellers of all classes can find free lodging, but they must make their own arrangements for food. Besides this are two hotels, where meals are served if previous notice is given, at 2½ annas per meal.

Road Conveyance.—If previous notice be given, bullock-carts can be obtained, the fare being 2 annas per vehicle per mile.

Local Manufactures and Products.—The chief products are horse-gram, ragi and kumboo.

Local Official.—The Village Munsiff.

Fairs and Festivals.—A fair is held every Thursday.

VADAMADURA.

Vadamadura (pop. 4,770) is situated in the Dindigul taluq of the Madura district, 48 miles from Trichinopoly Junction, 48 from Madura and 296 from Madras (Egmore). The village is about 969 feet above sea-level.

Local Accommodation.—In the village is a choultry, where natives of all classes can find free lodging, but must make their own arrangements for food. There are also four hotels, where meals are served to all classes at 2½ annas per meal.

Road Conveyance.—Bullock-carts can be obtained, the fare being 2½ annas per vehicle per mile.

Local Manufactures and Products.—The chief products are tobacco, tamarind, oil-seeds, gram and firewood.

Local Official.—The Village Munsiff.

Fair and Festivals.—A fair is held every Saturday.

DINDIGUL.

Dindigul (lat. 10°22′ ; long. 78°00 ; height 924 feet ; pop. 20,203) is a municipal town situated in a taluq of the same name in the Madura district. The town, which enjoys a comparatively cool climate, is in the middle of an extensive plain, bounded on the east by the Sirumalais, rising to 4,000 feet above sea-level and on the west by the Lower Pulneys. The following are the distances to the principal stations on the South Indian Railway :—

Madura ..	.. 88 miles.
Maniyachi Junction (for Tinnevelly)	.. 119 ,,
Tuticorin	.. 137 ,,
Ammayanayakanur (for Kodaikanal)	.. 13 ,,
Trichinopoly Junction	.. 57 ,,
Tanjore ..	.. 88 ,,
Negapatam	.. 136 ,,
Mayavaram Junction	.. 131 ,,
Villupuram Junction	.. 208 ,,
Chingleput (for Conjeeveram, etc.)	.. 271 ,,
Madras (Egmore) ..	.. 306 ,,
Pakala Junction ..	.. 346 ,,
Gudur Junction (for East Coast Railway)..	.. 446 ,,
Dharmavaram Junction (for S. M. Railway)	.. 489 ,,

Local Accommodation.—In the town, close to the Municipal Office, is a travellers' bungalow, which is furnished and can accommodate two persons at one time. A cook is in charge, who can supply meals if required. The charge for the use of this bungalow is one rupee per diem for each single person, and for a married couple Rs. 1-8-0. For natives there are 5 chuttrams and 23 hotels in the town. In two of the chuttrams, natives of all classes can find free lodging; but must make their own arrangements for food. The other 3 chuttrams are reserved for Brahmans. The hotels supply meals at 2½ annas each to all classes of natives.

Road Conveyance.—Jutkas and bullock-carts are usually procurable at the station, the fares being :—

Jutkas during daylight	..	.. 2 annas per mile.
Do. at nights ..	..	.. 4 ,, ,,
Bullock-carts ..	..	.. 2 ,, ,,

If a jutka is hired for the whole day, the charge is one rupee and a bullock-cart for the same period 12 annas.

Railway Facilities.—Waiting accommodation is provided for first and second class passengers, and there is also a refreshment room, under the management of Messrs. Spencer & Co., where light refreshments are obtainable.

Local Manufactures and Products.—The chief manufactures are cigars, safes, locks, bell-metal vessels, country cloth and leather, and the chief produce is paddy and dry grains. Coffee and cardamoms are received from the neighbouring hills.

Local Officials.—The Sub-Collector, Tahsildar, Sub-Magistrate, Sub-Registrar, District Munsiff, Public Works Department Sub-Divisional Officer, Inspector of Police, Salt and Abkari Inspector and Hospital Assistant.

Fairs and Festivals.—A fair is held every Monday close to the station. Two festivals are held annually, one called the Alagar festival, which is celebrated at Dindigul on the day of the full moon in the month of Chittrai (April or May), and the other takes place at a village Agaram, six miles from Dindigul in the month of Arpisi (October or November). Both of these festivals attract a large number of pilgrims.

Missions and Churches.—Dindigul possesses a very fine Roman Catholic Church, and the American Mission has a Church in the town.

Historical.—Dindigul was formerly the capital of an independent province, nominally part of the Madura Kingdom. As a strategical point of great natural strength, commanding the passes between Madura and Coimbatore, its possession was always keenly contested. Between 1623 and 1659 it was the scene of many encounters between Mahrattas and Mysore and Madura troops, the Poligar of Dindigul holding at that time feudatory authority over eighteen neighbouring chieftains. Chunda Sahib, the Mahrattas, and the Mysore troops occupied the fort in turn; and during the intervals in which no greater power was in possession, the strongest local chief made it his headquarters. It was attacked by troops of the Poligars in the reign of Moottoo Verappa Nayak of Madura, in 1609-1622, and three years later, during the reign of Tirumala Nayakka, was besieged by an army from Mysore which was driven back by the Dalavy Sethupati of Ramnad. In 1736 it was stormed by Chunda Sahib, and, nine years later, conquered by the Mysore Rajahs. In 1755 it was garrisoned by Hyder Ali and used by him as a base of operations against the Poligars of Madura, when he contemplated annexing the greater part of that district as well as of Coimbatore. From its position as commanding the route from Coimbatore to the south, the fort proved a serious obstacle to the operations of the British troops at Trichinopoly and Madura in the wars with Hyder Ali. Dindigul was taken by the British in 1767, but was lost again the following year. In 1783 it was retaken, and in the following year given up to Mysore by the treaty of Mangalore. It was recaptured in 1790 and finally ceded to the East India

Company by the treaty with Tippoo Sultan of the 18th March 1792.

Objects of Interest.—The fort is built on a remarkable wedge-shaped rock 400 feet in length and 300 in breadth, 1,223 feet above sea-level. The strong fortifications extending on all sides but the south-west (which is precipitous and inaccessible) were constructed in the times of the first Nayakkan Kings. Hyder Ali also added to the fortifications which are at the present day in a state of good preservation and well worth a visit.

Messrs. Spencer & Co's. Cigar Factory.—This includes the tobacco warehouse, rolling rooms and box making, packing and labelling department. Visitors can see the various processes to which the tobacco is subjected from the time it comes into the premises fresh from the fields, to the time it is turned out a finished cigar. Some hundreds of natives are employed in the industry and a visit to the factory will prove extremely interesting and instructive.

AMBATURAI.

Ambaturai (pop. 4,975) is situated in the Dindigul taluq of the Madura district, 32 miles from Madura, 65 from Trichinopoly Junction, and 313 from Madras (Egmore). The village, which is three-quarters of a mile north-west of the station, is 997 feet above sea-level.

Road Conveyance.—If previous notice is given bullock-carts can be obtained, the fare being 2 annas per vehicle per mile.

Local Manufactures and Products.—Country cloths are manufactured and the chief products are coffee, cardamoms and plantains, which come from the neighbouring hills.

Fairs and Festivals.—A fair is held every Thursday near the station.

Missions and Churches.—At Paiyamputti, about 4 miles north-west of the station, is a Roman Catholic Church.

ROCK FORT, DINDIGUL

GRAPHIC ART SOCIETY

NEGATIVE BY A. D. G. SHELLEY

AMMAYANAYAKANUR.

Ammayanayakanur (pop. 3,820) is situated in the Dindigul taluq of the Madura district, 25 miles from Madura, 71 from Trichinopoly Junction, and 319½ from Madras (Egmore). Passengers for Kodaikanal, the well known sanitarium on the Pulney Hills, alight here.

Local Accommodation.—Close to the station is a furnished travellers' bungalow, which can accommodate four persons at one time. The butler in charge can supply meals, if required, at the following rates :—

				RS.	A.	P.
Chota-hazri	..	..	..	..	0	12	0
Breakfast ..	..	..	..	..	1	0	0
Tiffin	..	..	..	..	0	12	0
Dinner	..	..	..	..	1	8	0

He is not authorized to sell liquor, and alcoholic drinks must be privately arranged for. The charge for the use of the bungalow is one rupee for each person per diem, provided, however, that, if a short stay not exceeding 4 hours is made, 8 annas only is charged. Native travellers of all classes can find free lodging in a choultry in the village, but must make their own arrangements for food. In the village are also 7 hotels, where meals are served at from 2½ to 3 annas each.

Road Conveyance.—Jutkas and bullock-carts are usually procurable at the station at 2 and 1½ annas per mile, respectively. In the case of passengers proceeding to Kodaikanal, however, it is advisable to write ahead to one of the Transit Agencies or Carrying Companies at Ammayanayakanur station informing them of the number of persons for whom transit is required and the manner the journey is proposed to be performed. From Ammayanayakanur to the foot of the hills, 33 miles, the journey is usually performed in a spring cart drawn by a pair of bullocks, the charge for which is Rs. 5. The ghat journey can either be made in a chair, a dhooly or on a pony. The charge for a chair is Rs. 5-4-0, dhooly Rs. 7-8-0 and for a pony Rs. 2.

A charge of 8 annas is made for each 50 lbs. of luggage. The journey from Ammayanayakanur to the tope or grove at the foot of the hill occupies from 7 to 8 hours, and up the ghat about 6 hours. At the tope is a travellers' rest-house, where light refreshments can be obtained, if prior notice is given to the butler in charge.

Railway Facilities.—Waiting accommodation is provided at the station for ladies and gentlemen.

Local Manufactures and Products.—The chief products are kumboo, cholam, ragi, and coffee and cardamoms from the surrounding hills.

Local Official.—The Village Munsiff.

Fairs and Festivals.—A fair is held every Wednesday.

Historical.—This was one of the five polliems, or estates, held by a military chieftain, which Hyder Ali failed to resume, but it was afterwards sequestered by Tippoo Sultan. On the British occupation it was restored as a tributary polliem. A battle fought here in 1741 decided the fate of Dindigul, which then fell into the hands of Chunda Sahib.

Kodaikanal.—This favourite hill station, situated on the upper ranges of the Pulney Hills, is 7,000 feet above sea-level, and is much resorted to by Europeans, during the summer months. It has a cool and bracing climate, and, the soil being gravelly, it soon dries up after the heaviest rain. The annual rainfall is about 60 inches, and the shade temperature ranges from a maximum of 76 in summer to a minimum of 42 in winter. There are a Club, Hotel and several boarding houses; the lake is very beautiful and good boating can be obtained on it through the Boat Club. In the vicinity of Kodaikanal are many lovely walks and rides, while good large game shooting may be obtained at no great distance from the settlement.

SHOLAVANDAN.

Sholavandan (pop. 2,885) is situated in the Madura taluq of the Madura district, 13 miles from Madura, 83 from

GRAPHIC ART SOCIETY

KODAIKANAL.

NEGATIVE BY J. A. D. LLOYD

Trichinopoly Junction, and 332 from Madras (Egmore). The village is 547 feet above sea-level.

Local Accommodation.—About a quarter of a mile from the station is a choultry, where native travellers of all classes can find free lodging, but must make their own arrangements for food. There are also 3 hotels in the village, where meals are served at 2½ annas each.

Road Conveyance.—Bullock-carts can be obtained if previous notice is given, the fare being 2½ annas per vehicle per mile.

Local Manufactures and Products.—The chief product is paddy.

Local Officials.—The Sub-Registrar and Hospital Assistant.

Fairs and Festivals.—A fair is held every Friday.

Missions and Churches.—There is a Protestant Church in the village.

Historical.—The old fort now in ruins was occupied by Mahomed Yoosoof in 1757 to cover the operations of Calliaud against Madura. In the same year it was captured by Hyder Ali and retaken by the British.

Objects of Interest.—Two temples containing inscriptions, and a Musjid or Muhammedan mosque.

Sport.—Good snipe shooting can be had about 2 miles from this station in the cold season. Coolies can be procured at a charge of 6 annas each per diem.

SAMAYANALLUR.

Samayanallur (pop. 976) is situated in the Madura taluq of the Madura district, 8 miles from Madura, 89 from Trichinopoly Junction, and 337 from Madras (Egmore).

Local Accommodation.—Close to the station is a chuttram, where native travellers of all classes can find free lodging, but must make their own arrangements for food.

Road Conveyance.—If previous notice is given, bullock-carts can be had, the fare being 2 annas per vehicle per mile.

Local Manufactures and Products.—The chief produce is paddy.

Local Official.—The Village Munsiff.

MADURA.

Madura (lat. 9°55'; long. 78°10') is situated 440 feet above sea-level and contains 87,428 inhabitants. It is the principal town of a collectorate of the same name and from time immemorial has been the political and religious capital of the extreme south of India. The ancient Pandyan kings made it their seat of Government and it remained the metropolis of the empire for many years. In the second century Vamsa Sekhara established in the city a celebrated college which existed until the eighth century and made Madura the great seat of Tamil learning. The town, which is situated on the Vaigai river, was well known to the Greeks and Romans, being mentioned by several classical writers. Commercial relations must have existed with the Western markets, as several Roman copper coins have been found in the bed of the river. The line to Pamban and Rameswaram takes off at this station. The following are the distances to the most important stations on the South Indian Railway :—

Tinnevelly or Tuticorin	..	..	..	99 miles.
Ammayanayakanur (for Kodaikanal)		..	..	25 ,,
Trichinopoly Junction	..	..	..	96 ,,
Tanjore ..	..	..	..	127 ,,
Mayavaram Junction	..	..	..	171 ,,
Villupuram Junction	..	..	..	246 ,,
Chingleput Junction (for Conjeeveram)	..		..	310 ,,
Madras (Egmore) ..	..	..	..	344 ,,
Pakala Junction ..	..	..	..	384 ,,
Gudur Junction (for East Coast Railway) ..		..	468 ,,
Dharmavaram Junction (for S. M. Railway)		..	527 ,,

Local Accommodation.—Close to the station is a travellers' bungalow, which is fully furnished and can accommodate

THE GREAT CORRIDOR — TEMPLE AT RAMESWARAM

NEGATIVE BY MESS^RS NICHOLAS & C^O MADRAS

4 persons at one time. The butler in charge can arrange to supply meals, if required, but wines or spirits must be privately arranged for. The charge for the use of this bungalow is one rupee for each person per diem. For natives many choultries and hotels exist in different parts of the town. Free lodging can be obtained at the former, and meals are served at from 2½ to 3 annas each at the latter.

Road Conveyance.—Hackney carriages, jutkas and bullock-carts can be procured at the station, but, if a hackney carriage is required, previous advice should be sent. The following are the charges :—

	RS.	A.	P.	
Landau with pair of horses	7	0	0	per diem.
Do. do.	4	0	0	for half a day.
Brougham with pair of horses	6	0	0	per diem.
Do. do.	3	8	0	for half a day.
Brougham with single horse	3	0	0	per diem.
Do. do.	2	0	0	for half a day.
Phaeton with single horse	3	0	0	per diem.
Do. do.	2	0	0	for half a day.
Jutkas or bullock-carts	0	3	0	per mile.

A guide can be procured at the station to shew the sights of the town. His charge is Rs. 3 per diem.

Railway Facilities.—Waiting accommodation is provided at the station for first and second class passengers. There is also a refreshment room in the station building under the management of Messrs. Spencer & Co., the butler in charge of which has usually a few copies of the *Madras Mail* and *Madras Times* for sale, as well as a small stock of travellers' requisites. Upstairs are two rooms each containing two beds, comfortably furnished for sleeping. The charge for the use of these rooms is—

	RS.	A.	P.
Not exceeding 3 hours for each adult	0	8	0
For each child of 12 years and under	0	4	0
Exceeding 3 hours and not exceeding 24 hours for each adult	1	0	0
For each child of 12 years and under	0	8	0

Punkah-pullers and hot and cold water baths are charged extras.

Local Manufactures and Products.—Muslins of a very delicate texture, into which gold lace is interwoven, are made, also turbans and puggrees embroidered with gold thread, and silk cloths. Madura is also noted for its wood carving and brass work. Handsome tables are carved in blackwood, and, in addition to the ordinary brass work, animals, insects, etc., are made in that metal. The goldsmiths and silversmiths also do excellent work, and the tourist will find here much Indian workmanship of great interest. The chief produce is paddy and plantains.

Fairs and Festivals.—Fairs are held every Thursday and Sunday; and festivals are frequent at the temple, the most important being the " Chittrai," which is celebrated in April or May annually, and the great floating festival, which is held in the month of January or February.

Local Officials.—The Collector, the Judge, Superintendent of Police, Executive Engineer, P.W.D., Local Fund Engineer, two Subordinate Judges, two District Munsiffs, the Treasury Deputy Collector, the District Registrar, the District Traffic Superintendent and the Assistant Engineer, S.I.R.

Missions and Churches.—Christianity is making rapid progress in the district of Madura. A Jesuit Church was founded about the beginning of the seventeenth century, when a Portuguese priest ministered to a small congregation of fishermen, converted by St. Francis Xavier in 1606. Robert de Nobilis came to Madura, adopted the life, diet and dress of a religious devotee. He founded the flourishing Mission which is now said to number 70,000 converts. The American Mission was established in 1834, and is at present in a very flourishing condition, having two Churches, one high school and a large hospital in the town of Madura itself, besides an important college at Pasumalai, 2½ miles from Madura. About three-quarters of a mile from the station is a Church belonging to the Church of England, in which service is held once a month by the Chaplain of Trichinopoly.

STATUE OF GANESHA IN THE TEMPLE MADURA

Clubs.—About two miles from the station is the European Club, attached to which are tennis and racquet courts, and a swimming bath. Gentlemen making a short stay in Madura may join this club as honorary members on being proposed by one member of the club, seconded by two others and approved by the Committee. The subscription for honorary members is Rs. 10 per mensem.

A club for native gentlemen is also maintained in the town.

Historical.—The history of Madura has been fully dealt with in the introductory chapter to this work, to which the visitor is referred for information regarding this most interesting city.

Objects of Interest.—The great temple, situated about one mile west of the railway station, is divided into two parts, the southern dedicated to Meenatchy, the consort of Siva, and the northern to Siva himself under the name of Sunderaswerar. The usual entrance is that leading from the Vittavasal Street into the portion dedicated to Meenatchy. At the entrance is the Ashta-Lakshmy Mantapam, or the mantapam of the eight Lakshmies (goddesses presiding over eight sources of wealth) the statues of which support the roof on either side. Above these are depicted scenes from the life of Meenatchy representing her birth, war with Siva, marriage with him, the birth of their son Subramanya, and the assumption of sovereignty by Sunderaswerar. At the end of this mantapam is a doorway, on the left of which is a statue of Ganesha, and on the right one of Subramanya as the six-faced deity. Passing through this door a passage is entered, having on the right hand side a statue of Siva as a hunter, and on the left one of his consort Meenatchy as a huntress. This passage gives access to a large mantapam built by Meenatchy Naick, a prime minister of one of the Naick kings, in which the temple elephants are stabled. The exit from this mantapam is through a handsome brass faced doorway with receptacles for oil lights which are lighted every night; this doorway is a gift of the Sivaganga Zemindar. A dark mantapam is now entered lined with statues representing Siva in various forms; passing through this mantapam the Pottamarai, or the golden lotus tank is reached, this is surrounded by an arcade on the walls of which is depicted the history of the sixty-four miracles wrought by Siva at Madura as well as other mythological stories and which are intended for the education of the masses who attend on festival occasions. Turning to the left and proceeding along the eastern arcade, the visitor will observe over the roof of the opposite side the golden covering, or Vimanam, over the shrine of the goddess, and from near the end of the southern arcade can be similarly observed the golden roof over the shrine of Sunderaswerar. At this end of the arcade is the southern temple gate, a fine example of workmanship. Turning to the right the western arcade is now traversed, the first portion being lined with handsome pillars, beyond which is the entrance to the shrine of Meenatchy. In this portion of the arcade there are statues of the five Pandava brothers, the heroes of the Mahabarata. Further on is the shrine of Subramanya with two statues on either side of the pathway in front of it, the first being statues of Sugriva and his brother Vali, and the two in the next group being king Harichandra and his queen Chandramathi. Passing by this shrine, a gateway through the tower dividing the temple of Meenatchy from that of Sunderaswerar is reached; this gateway (opposite to which is a shrine to Ganesha, containing a figure said to have been found when excavating the Teppakulam tank), gives entrance to a fine corridor encircling the Sunderaswerar shrine. This corridor was built by the Pandyan kings, and along the right hand wall of the northern corridor will be seen inscriptions in Tamil and Sanskrit, giving the history of the temple. At the end of the northern corridor is the hundred-pillared mantapam, containing a shrine to Sabapathy (Siva) who, instead of

GRAPHIC ART SOCIETY

NEGATIVE BY A. D. G. SHELLEY

GRAPHIC ART SOCIETY

PILLAR TIRUMALA NAYAKKA'S CHOULTRY MADURA

being invisible as at Chidambaram, is here represented by a figure. Adjacent to this mantapam is a small enclosure dedicated to the nine planets which are :—

Mercury,	Saturn,
Venus,	Moon,
Mars,	Rahu,
Jupiter,	Kathu,

with the Sun in the centre.

Turning to the right a large hall is entered, a doorway in the centre of its western wall giving access to the shrine of Sunderaswerar guarded on each side by colossal figures of Dwarapalagas or guardians. Opposite to the entrance is a fine mantapam enclosed by eight pillars ornamented with twenty-five representations of Siva, and containing a figure of the sacred bull, also a gold plated flagstaff. Opposite to this mantapam, and on each side of the exit from the hall, are four finely carved columns, the two on the right representing Siva overcoming Dakshan, a great demon, while on the left are figures of Siva and Kali in dancing attitudes; behind these four figures are situated the rooms containing the gold and silver-plated figures of various animals used in processions. Passing through this exit and turning to the right a handsome hall with a wooden ceiling, called the Marriage Mantapam, is entered; traversing this and turning to the left the Veeravasantharayar's mantapam is reached, in the centre of which is the thousand-pillared mantapam built by Ariyanayaga Mudaliar, a prime minister of the Nayakkan dynasty, whose statue will be seen on the left mounted on a horse. This mantapam contains some fine sculptures, and, after they have been seen, the temple is left by the road through the large eastern gate which gives access to the same street from which the entrance to Meenatchy's temple was made. Outside the temple, over the other side of the road, is the " Puthu Mantapam," otherwise known as " Tirumala's " choultry. This, had it been finished, would have surpassed in magnificence all the other buildings of this monarch. It was built as a guest house for Siva, who promised to pay the king Tirumala an annual visit for ten days on condition that a hall worthy of his dignity was built for his reception. The hall has four rows of pillars supporting a flat roof and on either side of the centre corridor five pillars representing ten of the Nayakkan dynasty. Tirumala is distinguished as having a canopy over him and several figures at his back, one being his wife, a Princess of Tanjore. This hall was erected in 1623—45, and is said to have cost a million sterling. The effect of this fine hall is greatly destroyed by its being rented to shopkeepers for the sale of cloths, etc.

The Palace of Tirumala Nayak is about a mile and a half west of the railway station. It covers a vast area of ground. It has pillars of rough granite cased with cement supporting scalloped arches, has been restored and is utilised for the Judges' Courts and other public offices. The entrance is on the east side by a granite portico built in honor of Lord Napier and Ettric, who first ordered the restoration. At each corner of the east face of the palace is a low tower. The Napier gateway gives entrance to a quadrangle 252 feet by 151 feet. On the east, north and south sides are corridors, the roofs supported by arches resting on granite pillars. On the west side the corridor is double and is 67 feet broad. The west side is occupied by a lofty hall. On one of the stones of the staircase which leads up to it is a Tamil inscription. Passing from the staircase to a corridor 25 feet broad, a court, under the grand dome which was the throne room, is reached. It is 61 feet in diameter and 73 feet high and is unsupported by pillars. Outside round the room are galleries, where ladies in Tirumala's time sat and watched the State receptions. To the west of the grand dome is another domed chamber used for the records and treasury. Passing north to the west of this is an apartment called Tirumala's bedroom. There

GRAPHIC ART SOCIETY

TIRUMALA NAYAKKA'S PALACE, MADURA

GRAPHIC ART SOCIETY

NEGATIVE BY A. D. G. SHELLEY

TEPPAKOLAM MADURA

are four holes in the middle of the roof, two on either
side, and between the two on the south side was a large
open hole. There is a legend that Tirumala's cot was
suspended from hooks fixed in the four holes and that the
large hole was made by a thief who descended from it by
the chain supporting that corner of the cot and stole the
crown jewels. Tirumala is said to have offered an hereditary estate to the thief if he would restore the jewels
adding that no questions would be asked. On recovering
the jewels he kept his word, but ordered the man to be
decapitated.

On the further side of the river Vaigai, north of the city
and about a mile from the bridge, is a building called *the
Tomkam* built by Tirumala for exhibiting fights between
wild beasts and gladiators. This is now the residence of
the Collector. Three miles east of the station and south of
the river Vaigai is a very fine *Teppakulam* (tank of the raft)
said to have been built by Tirumala. The walls are faced
with finely dressed granite surmounted with a handsome
parapet beneath which runs a continuous paved platform.
In the centre is a square island with a lofty pagoda in the
middle and dainty little shrines at the four corners. Once
a year at the floating festival, held in January or February,
the parapets and pagoda are outlined with lights numbering about 10,000, while the idols from the great temple are
drawn round in a raft (Theppem).

The Great Banyan Tree.—In the compound of the Judge's
bungalow is a very fine Banyan tree. The main stem is
70 feet in circumference and the ground shaded by this tree
has a diameter of 180 feet in whatever direction it is measured.

About five miles north-east of Madura is a rock called the
"*Elephant Rock*" for its remarkable resemblance to a
colossal figure of that animal couchant. It is a solid block
of gneiss two miles in length, a quarter of a mile in breadth,
and about 250 feet in height. On new moon days many,
chiefly silk weavers, resort to the place and make *poojah*.

TIRUPARANKUNDRAM.

Tiruparankundram (pop. 850) is situated in the Madura taluq of the Madura district, 4 miles from Madura, 100 from Trichinopoly Junction, and 349 from Madras (Egmore). It is otherwise known as " Skanda Mallai " (the hill of Skanda, the son of Siva).

Local Accommodation.—Close to the station is a chuttram, where native travellers of all classes can find free lodging, but must make their own arrangements for food.

Local Manufactures and Products.—Granite is quarried in large quantities from the hill near the railway. Grain is the chief produce.

Fairs and Festivals.—A "Karthigai" festival is held monthly, and annually in April the " Pangani" Utsavam is celebrated in the Siva temple attracting large number of pilgrims from all parts of the district.

Objects of Interest.—The Siva temple, which is fairly well sculptured, and contains a number of inscriptions. In the hill are some rock-cut caves adorned with carved figures, and on its summit a small lake well stocked with fish. Other objects worth seeing are the tomb of Secundra Batcha, a Mussulman saint ; the "Saravanapoigai," a large bathing tank, about quarter of a mile north of the temple, and the Teppakulam. The last, which has a small mantapam in the centre, is picturesquely situated near the line and has been selected for the illustration given on plate No. 28.

TIRUMANGALAM.

Tirumangalam (pop. 6,451) is situated in a taluq of the same name in the Madura district, 11 miles from Madura, 107 from Trichinopoly Junction, and 355 from Madras (Egmore). The town is 416 feet above sea-level.

Local Accommodation.—Close to the station is a travellers' bungalow, which is partly furnished, and can accommodate two persons at one time. It has neither crockery nor a cook. The charge for the use of this bungalow is one rupee for each

ROCK & TEPPAKOLAM TIRUPARANKUNDRAM

NEGATIVE BY A. D. G. SHELLEY

person per diem. In the town is a choultry, where natives of all classes can find free lodging. Brahmans are fed without charge and provisions given to other class pilgrims. Besides this are several native hotels, where meals are served at from 2½ to 3 annas each.

Road Conveyance.—Bullock-carts are usually procurable at the station, the fare being 2 annas per vehicle per mile.

Railway Facilities.—Waiting accommodation is provided at the station for first and second class passengers.

Local Manufactures and Products.—The chief industry is cloth dyeing. Cotton is extensively cultivated, and paddy, cholam, dhall and gingelly seeds are also grown.

Fairs and Festivals.—A fair is held every Friday.

Local Officials.—The Tahsildar, Stationary Sub-Magistrate, Police Inspector, Salt and Abkari Inspector, Sub-Registrar, Imperial and Local Fund Overseers, and the Hospital Assistant.

Missions and Churches.—The American Mission has established a Church and schools.

Clubs.—The "Union" Club in the town is a native institution, to which all the prominent residents belong.

Sport.—In the Saptur and Elumalai Zemindaries, some 24 miles from this station, good shooting can be had, deer, bison and wild boar being fairly plentiful. Permission to shoot must first be obtained from the Zemindars. Shikarries and coolies can be hired at the spot.

KALLIGUDI.

Kalligudi (pop. 3,327) is situated in the Tirumangalam taluq of the Madura district, 20 miles from Madura, 116 from Trichinopoly Junction, and 364½ from Madras (Egmore).

Local Accommodation.—Near the station is a choultry, where native travellers of all classes can obtain free accommodation for three days.

Local Officials.—The Sub-Registrar and Revenue Inspector.

Local Manufactures and Products.—Cotton is grown in considerable quantities.

VIRUDUPATI.

Virudupati (pop. 6,614) is situated in the Satur taluq of the Tinnevelly district, 27 miles from Madura, 123 from Trichinopoly Junction, and 371 from Madras (Egmore). The town is 336 feet above sea-level.

Local Accommodation.—About 1½ miles from the station is a travellers' bungalow, which can accommodate two persons at one time, but is unfurnished and has no cook. The charge for the use of this building is 8 annas for each person per diem. For natives the Local Fund Department maintains a choultry in which cooking utensils are supplied free to enable travellers to prepare their own food. In addition to these are several native hotels in the town, where meals are served at from 2½ to 3 annas each.

Road Conveyance.—Bullock-carts are usually available at the station, the fare being 2 annas per vehicle per mile.

Railway Facilities.—Waiting accommodation is provided for first and second class passengers, and light repasts can be had at the refreshment room in the station building.

Local Manufactures and Products.—Ordinary bed sheets of rough texture and dusters are manufactured. The chief products are cotton, chillies and dry grains.

Local Officials.—The Stationary Sub-Magistrate, Civil Apothecary, Sub-Registrar, Police Inspector and Station House Officer.

Missions and Churches.—In the town is a Protestant as well as a Roman Catholic Church.

Objects of Interest.—At Rosalpati, about a mile east of Virudupati, is a temple, where a large number of peacocks are kept. The only objects of interest in Virudupati itself are four cotton presses.

TULUKAPATI.

Tulukapati (pop. 850) is situated in the Satur taluq of the Tinnevelly district, 36 miles from Madura, 132 from Trichinopoly Junction, and 381 from Madras (Egmore). The village is about $2\frac{1}{2}$ miles south of the Railway station.

Local Accommodation.—Half a mile from the station is a chuttram, where Brahmans can find free accommodation.

Local Officials.—The Village Munsiff and Kurnam.

Fairs and Festivals.—A fair is held every Friday and Sunday at which sheep are principally sold. An annual festival takes place in July and attracts a large number of people.

SATUR.

Satur (pop. 2,887) is situated in a taluq of the same name in the Tinnevelly district, 44 miles from Madura, 140 from Trichinopoly Junction, and 388 from Madras (Egmore). The town, which was formerly the centre of a Zemindary of great antiquity, is on the north bank of the river Veippaur.

Local Accommodation.—About three-quarters of a mile from the station is a travellers' bungalow, which is furnished and can accommodate 3 persons at a time, and is provided with a cook, who can supply meals if required. Wines and spirits must be privately arranged for. The charge for the use of this bungalow is one rupee for each person per diem. For natives the Local Fund Department maintains a chuttram and supplies cooking utensils, so that all classes can find free lodging and do their own cooking. Besides this there are several hotels in the town, where meals are served at from $2\frac{1}{2}$ to 3 annas each.

Road Conveyance.—Jutkas and bullock-carts are usually available at the station, the fares being 3 annas per mile for the former and $2\frac{1}{2}$ annas per mile for the latter.

Local Manufactures and Products.—Bell-metal vessels are manufactured at Srivilliputur some 24 miles from this place. Cotton, tobacco, cotton-seeds and chillies are the chief products.

Fairs and Festivals.—Two festivals are held annually, one in January and the other in July.

Local Officials.—The Tahsildar, District Munsiff, Sub-Registrar, Stationary Sub-Magistrate, Police Inspector, and Civil Apothecary.

Objects of Interest.—On a mantapam, 4½ miles to the east of the station, are sculptured figures. Five miles north-east is an old temple on a rock built over a statue found at Coondalcoot, and near this is a temple of Chokalinga-swami.

KOILPATI.

Koilpati (pop. 3,000) is situated in the Satur taluq of the Tinnevelly district, 57 miles from Madura, 153 from Trichinopoly Junction, and 401 from Madras (Egmore).

Local Accommodation.—About three-quarters of a mile from the Railway station is a travellers' bungalow, which is furnished, and can accommodate 4 persons at one time. A cook is in charge, who can supply meals, if required, but wines and spirits must be privately arranged for. The charge for the use of this bungalow is one rupee for each person per diem. Besides this there is a bungalow belonging to the Ettiapuram Zemindar, which may be occupied on his permission being obtained. This bungalow is unfurnished and has no cook. Natives of all classes can find free lodging in two chuttrams, but must make their own arrangements for food. In the town are 5 Brahman hotels as well as several hotels for natives of other castes, where meals are served at from 2½ to 3 annas each.

Road Conveyance.—Jutkas and bullock-carts can be procured, if previous notice is sent, the fares being 3 annas per mile for the former and 2 annas per mile for the latter.

Railway Facilities.—Light meals can be obtained at a small refreshment room at the station managed by Messrs. Spencer & Co.

Local Manufactures and Products.—The Koilpati Weaving

Company manufacture twist yarn, fine colored cotton carpets, country cloths, checks, blankets, etc. The chief products are cotton, chillies and coriander seeds.

Fairs and Festivals.—A fair is held every Monday..

Local Officials.—The Sub-Registrar and Station House Officer.

Missions and Churches.—In the town is a Roman Catholic Church.

Objects of Interest.—The Siva temple, in the tank of which is a perennial spring known as the Agastya teertam. About a mile south-west is a remarkable rock containing a cavern. The Spinning and Weaving Mills.

Sport.—Seven miles to the south of Koilpati is Kuru-malai, a small range of hills belonging to the Ettiapuram Zemindar, where there is good shooting (deer, wild boar and hares). Permission must be previously obtained, when the Zemindar will cause all necessary arrangements to be made.

Ettiapuram (pop. 7,000), the residence of the Zemindar, is about 8 miles from Koilpati. On a copper-plate attached to the wall of the temple close to the Zemindar's palace is an inscription containing a proclamation issued to the people of the Zemindary, on the 20th October 1799, urging them to submit to British authority and deliver up their arms to Major Bannerman.

Kalugumalai.—Twelve miles south-west of Koilpati con-tains a celebrated rock-cut temple, and also Jain sculptures and inscriptions.

Sankaranainarkoil.—Twelve miles west of Kalugumalai is a taluq town famous as a place of pilgrimage.

KUMARAPURAM.

Kumarapuram (pop. 400) is situated in the Ottapidaram taluq of the Tinnevelly district, 63 miles from Madura, 159 from Trichinopoly Junction, and 408 from Madras (Egmore).

Local Accommodation.—Three miles west of the station at Chatrapati is a chuttram, where natives of all classes can obtain free lodging and the loan of cooking utensils.

Local Manufactures and Products.—The chief produce is cotton.

Sport.—Kurumalai (described under Koilpati) is only 1¼ miles east of this station. It is best for sportsmen to make Koilpati their head-quarters on account of the bungalow accommodation there available.

KADAMBUR.

Kadambur (pop. 2,421) is situated in the Ottapidaram taluq of the Tinnevelly district, 10 miles from Maniyachi Junction, 71 from Madura, 167 from Trichinopoly Junction, and 415 from Madras (Egmore).

Local Accommodation.—Three-fourths of a mile from the station is a choultry, where natives of all classes can find free lodging, but must make their own arrangements for food. In addition there are 4 hotels, where meals are served to all classes of natives at from 2½ to 3 annas each.

Fairs and Festivals.—A fair is held every Wednesday.

Local Manufactures and Products.—Cotton, chillies, kumboo, cholam and ragi are the chief produce.

Local Official.—The Village Munsiff.

MANIYACHI JUNCTION.

Maniyachi (lat. 8°52′; long. 77°56′; height above sea-level 206 feet; pop. 1,396) is situated in the Ottapidaram taluq of the Tinnevelly district. It is the Junction for Tinnevelly, from which station the proposed line to Quilon will start. The following are the distances to the principal stations on the South Indian Railway :—

Tinnevelly	..	..	..	..	18 miles.
Tuticorin	..	..	..	..	18 ,,
Madura ..	..	..	..	..	81 ,,
Ammayanayakanur (for Kodaikanal)		..		..	106 ,,
Trichinopoly Junction (for Erode)		..		..	177 ,,

Tanjore Junction (for Negapatam)	 208	miles.
Mayavaram Junction	 251	,,
Villupuram Junction (for Tiruvannamalai)	.. 327	,,
Chingleput Junction (for Conjeeveram)	 391	,,
Madras (Egmore)	 425	,,
Pakala Junction	 465	,,
Gudur Junction (for East Coast Railway)	.. 559	,,
Dharmavaram Junction (for S. M. Railway)	.. 608	,,

Local Accommodation.—Close to the station is a chuttram, where natives of all classes can find free lodging for 3 days, but must make their own arrangements for food. In the village are several native hotels, where meals are served at from 2½ to 3 annas each.

Road Conveyance.—If previous notice is given, bullock-carts can be procured, the fare being 2 annas per vehicle per mile.

Railway Facilities.—Waiting accommodation is provided for first and second class passengers.

Local Manufactures and Products.—Cotton, cotton seeds, kumboo, gram, and coriander seeds are the chief produce.

Missions and Churches.—A Roman Catholic Church has recently been built in the village.

TATAPARAI.

Tataparai (pop. 1,386) is situated in the Ottapidaram taluq of the Tinnevelly district, 9 miles from Maniyachi Junction, 9½ from Tuticorin, and 434 from Madras (Egmore). This is the Emigration Depôt of the Ceylon Government, the coolies for the tea estates breaking their journey here before undertaking the sea voyage from Tuticorin to Colombo.

Local Accommodation.—About 1½ miles from the station are two chuttrams, where natives of all classes can find free lodging, but must make their own arrangements for food.

Road Conveyance.—Jutkas and bullock-carts can be had at the station in the morning, the fares being for jutkas 3 annas per mile and bullock-carts 2 annas. If required in the evening, previous arrangements must be made with the Transit Office at Ottapidaram.

Local Manufactures and Products.—At Puthiamputhur, 3 miles from this station, net towels are manufactured. Cotton, kumboo, chillies, onions and coriander seeds are the chief products.

Objects of Interest.—At Panchalamkurichi, 7 miles from this station, are the remains of an old Poligar fort and the tombs of the European officers and men who were killed in the assaults on the fort.

Ottapidaram (pop. 3,631), the head-quarters of the taluq of the same name, is about 6 miles from Tataparai. A fair is held every Tuesday, and the Tahsildar, Sub-Magistrate, Sub-Registrar and Hospital Assistant reside here.

TUTICORIN.

Tuticorin (lat. 8°48'; long. 78°12'; height above sea-level 6 feet; pop. 25,107) the southern terminus of the main line is a municipal town in the Ottapidaram taluq of the Tinnevelly district situated on the north-west shore of the Gulf of Manaar and between the mouths of the Tambrapurni and the Veippaur. Tuticorin is the chief port of the district, affording good shelter for small boats, but, owing to the extreme shallowness of the water, steamers of even moderate draught have to anchor from 5 to 6 miles from the shore. The distances to the principal stations on the South Indian Railway are :—

Maniyachi Junction (for Tinnevelly)	18	miles.
Madura	99	,,
Ammayanayakanur (for Pulney Hills)	124	,,
Trichinopoly Junction (for Erode)	195	,,
Erode Junction (for Madras Railway and Nilgiri Mountains)..	282	,,
Tanjore Junction (for Negapatam and Mutupet) ..	226	,,
Villupuram Junction (for Vellore and Katpadi) ..	345	,,
Katpadi Junction (for the Madras Railway) ..	444	,,
Chingleput Junction (for Conjeeveram and Arkonam)..	409	,,
Madras (Egmore)	443	,,

Local Accommodation.—The British India Hotel, imme-diately opposite the station, has accommodation for 3 first class and 2 second class visitors. The charge for board and lodging is—

				RS.	A.	P.	
First class	..	..	..	4	8	0	} per diem.
Second class	..	..	..	3	0	0	

There are three Brahman hotels at Melur, about a mile from the station, and some twenty small hotels in the vicinity of the station, where native travellers of other castes can find accommodation. A Local Fund choultry is provided at Melur, where free lodging for three days is allowed to all classes, except Europeans and Eurasians. There is also a choultry for Brahmans only, about half a mile from the station on the Melur road, where free meals are served, and supplies given to religious mendicants.

Road Conveyance.—Carriages and jutkas are usually procurable at the station, the fares being 8 and 2 annas per mile, respectively. Bullock-carts can be hired in the town, the charge being 2 annas per mile.

Railway Facilities.—First and second class carriages are run to and from the pier in connection with the departure and arrival of the mail steamers to and from Colombo. Waiting accommodation is provided at the station for ladies and gentlemen, and there is also a refreshment room under the management of Messrs. Spencer & Co. The butler in charge has usually a few copies of the *Madras Mail* and *Madras Times* for sale, as well as a small stock of travellers' requisites. In case of the late arrival of the Colombo steamer, Messrs. Spencer & Co. can generally arrange to serve breakfast in the train. Ice and aerated waters are carried by all main line mail trains during day journeys, and can be purchased at the rates published in the Company's Guide.

Shipping Arrangements.—A British India Steam Navi-gation Company's steamer leaves daily (Sundays excepted) at 5 P.M. for Colombo, and one arrives from Ceylon daily (Mondays excepted) at about 8 A.M., the passage occupying about 16 hours. The journey between the pier and steamer is made in a steam launch belonging to Messrs. Adamson, Mactaggart & Company, the British India Agents at Tuticorin, and occupies about three-quarters of an hour. For further particulars, in connection with the launch service, the Company's Guide should be consulted. The B. I. S. N. Company's coasting steamers between Calcutta and Bombay touch at Tuticorin once a week and their other vessels as occasion offers. The Asiatic Company's steamers and those of the Japanese line also call at the port. A large number of sailing boats of 20 tons burden are always procurable on an average payment of Rs. 12-8-0 per trip to steamer and back. The pier belongs to Government and is under the control of the Port Officer. There are also several private jetties belonging to the various mercantile firms.

Local Manufactures and Products.—There is a large Government salt factory about a mile and a half from the station with which it is connected by a siding. In the town are several cotton presses and an important spinning mill. Tuticorin is the centre of very ancient pearl and conch shell fisheries, but since the deepening of the Pamban channel between India and Ceylon the yield has greatly decreased. The Manaar pearl, which is not of good colour, is usually fished for in March, April and May under Government management.

Local Officials.—The officials having offices in Tuticorin are the Sub-Collector, Deputy Tahsildar, Sub-Registrar, Assistant Superintendent and Inspector of Police, Assistant Commissioner of Salt and Abkari, Customs Superintendent and the Port Officer, who is also the Superintendent of Pearl Fisheries. The Bank of Madras and the National Bank of India have branches, and British India and Asiatic Steam Navigation Companies, Agencies in the town.

Missions, Churches, etc.—The Society for the Propagation of the Gospel maintains a training school, and a college named after the late Bishop Caldwell. Within easy reach of the station are a Protestant and two Roman Catholic Churches. The native fishing community profess Christianity to a large extent and are almost entirely Roman Catholics.

Club.—A club for Europeans is situated on the sea front.

Historical.—Tuticorin was orginally a Portuguese settlement and was founded about 1540. In 1658 it was captured by the Dutch, and in 1782 by the English. It was restored to the Dutch in 1785 and again taken by the English in 1795. During the Poligar war of 1801, it was held for a short time by the Poligar of Panchalamkurichi and was ceded to the Dutch in 1818. It was finally handed over to the English in 1825.

Objects of Interest.—The old Dutch cemetery containing several tomb stones, on which are carved armorial bearings and raised inscriptions, is worthy of a visit. Twenty miles south of Tuticorin on the sea lies the village of Trichendur, which contains a large and important temple dedicated to Subramanya, the god of war, and second son of Siva. The temple contains some excellent sculpture and several inscriptions. A few miles further south is a group of 16 columns each bearing an inscription. There is a good road to Trichendur, and carts can be hired for the journey there from Tuticorin at Rs. 5 each.

ARKONAM BRANCH.

VILLIYAMPAKKAM.

Villiyampakkam (pop. 500) is situated in the Chingleput taluq of the Chingleput district, on the Chingleput-Arkonam branch, 7 miles from Chingleput, and 41½ from Madras (Egmore).

Local Accommodation.—A travellers' bungalow close to the station can be used free of charge. It has neither furniture, crockery, nor cook. There is also a choultry, capable of accommodating 15 persons, which is in charge of a cook, who supplies meals at from 2½ to 4 annas each.

Road Conveyance.—Bullock-carts can be obtained, if previous notice is given, at 2 annas per mile.

Local Manufactures and Products.—Rice is the staple product of the surrounding country.

Local Officials.—The Village Munsiff and Kurnam.

Objects of Interest.—About 2½ miles west of the station is a temple, where the three rivers Palar, Cheyyar and Vegavathy meet.

Sport.—Duck and teal can be found in the cold season on a large lake to the south of the station, and snipe are also procurable. The wages of shikarries are from 8 annas to one rupee daily, according to sport shown. Coolies 4 annas per diem.

WALAJABAD.

Walajabad (pop. 4,534), 14 miles from Chingleput, and 48 from Madras (Egmore) *via* Chingleput, is situated on the left bank of the Palar river in the Conjeeveram taluq of the Chingleput district. It received its name from Nawab Wallajah in 1776, and became a British Cantonment about 1786. It was garrisoned for many years by a European regiment, a regiment of native cavalry, and two or three regiments of native infantry. A race course was laid out on the plain which lies to the north of the place. Walajabad up to 1860 continued to be the head-quarters of a native veteran battalion, but is now quite given up as a military station.

Local Accommodation.—There is a Brahman hotel, where meals are supplied at 2½ to 3 annas per head. No travellers' bungalow or chuttrams.

Road Conveyance.—Bullock-carts can be had, if previous notice be given, at a charge of 2 annas per mile.

Railway Facilities.—Waiting accommodation at the station for first and second class passengers.

Local Manufactures and Products.—Chintz, for which Walajabad was formerly famous, is still manufactured. Rice and ragi are the chief crops.

Local Official.—The Sub-Registrar has an office here.

Missions, Churches, &c.—The Free Church of Scotland has two schools, inclusive of an industrial school in which carpentry is mainly taught, and a hospital.

Objects of Interest.—The ruins of the Grand Stand, two of the officers' houses, a few gate posts, and the cemetery are all that now remain of this once bustling cantonment. The last is in a very good state of preservation, the oldest tomb is that of Ensign Edmund Bacon, who died in October, 1802.

Tenneri, 5 miles north of Walajabad, has a large tank, some stones in the dam of which bear inscriptions. One in Tamil records that a man named Tettacharayar dug the tank.

Sport.—Good snipe shooting can be had in the season. Shikarries available at a charge of from 8 annas to one rupee daily, according to sport shown. Coolies 4 annas per diem.

CONJEEVERAM.

Conjeeveram (pop. 42,800) was formerly known as Kanchi, or Kanjipuram (the golden city) and is a large municipal town on the Chingleput-Arkonam branch, 22½ miles from Chingleput.

It is one of the seven holy cities of India and is called the Benares of the South. The town is five or six miles long, the streets are usually broad and are planted on both sides with cocoanut and other trees, and there are many gardens and topes, under the shade of which weavers erect their looms. The town is divided into Great Conjeeveram and Little Conjeeveram, the latter being two miles south-east of the Railway station. The Municipality supplies the whole town from its water-works.

Local Accommodation.—There are five Brahman and one Sudra hotels, which charge from 2½ to 4 annas per meal, and also 10 chuttrams and 25 maddams, where natives can find accommodation, but to which they must bring their own provisions and cook. During festivals, meals are supplied free to all Brahmans.

Road Conveyance.—Jutkas and bullock-carts are procurable at the station. Charge to the town :—

Ordinary days	Jutkas		4 annas.
	Bullock-carts		2 „
During festivals	Jutkas		1 rupee.
	Bullock-carts		8 annas.

Railway Facilities.—Waiting accommodation is provided at the station for first and second class passengers.

Local Manufactures and Products.—Cotton handkerchief and native cloths are woven, also silk sarries. The artificers of the town are clever workers in brass and copper, and also expert at fashioning native jewellery.

Local Officials.—The Tahsildar, Sub-Magistrate, District Munsiff, Police Inspector, Sub-Registrar, Municipal Chairman, P. W. D. and Local Fund Overseers.

Missions, Churches, etc.—The Scottish Free Church has a Mission in the town. There is also a High School maintained by Patcheyappa's charities.

Historical.—A great deal has yet to be learnt of the history of Conjeeveram. Poolikeshy, of the Chalukyan dynasty, conquered a Chola king and burned Conjeeveram. The date of this ruler is about 489 A.D. It was the residence of the Palava kings in the eleventh century. In the fourteenth century, it became the capital of Tondaimundalam. After the fall of the Vijianagar family in 1644, it was subject to the Golcondah Princes, and, afterwards, passing under Mahomedan rule, became part of Arcot dominions. Captured by Clive from the French in 1751, it was in the same year taken by Raja Sahib, but re-captured by Clive in 1752. In 1757, the French, beaten off in an attack upon the pagoda, set fire to the town; in 1758 British garrison was temporarily withdrawn on account of the expected advance of the French on Madras, but was soon sent back with reinforcements; retaken from the French in 1759, and plundered by Hyder Ali in 1780.

Hwenthsang, the Chinese traveller, makes Conjeeeveram as old as Buddha, for he states that Buddha himself converted the people, that Dharmapala was born in Kancha, and that Asoka built many stupas there.

Objects of Interest.—Conjeeveram is full of temples and sculptures, many of considerable antiquity, the great Siva temple being the most conspicuous. This temple is dedicated to Ekambaranatha, and the lingam is one of the five principal lingams in Southern India. The temple grew from small beginnings and is very irregular in shape. The great gopuram was built by Krishnadeva Ranja, of Vijianagar. It bears the mark of Hyder Ali's cannon balls. The principal festival takes place in April annually and lasts 15 days. Its origin is given in the following fable :—Siva was conducting the united offices of the Hindu trinity (creating, preserving and destroying). His consort, Parvati, giving way to a levity unworthy of her exalted position, went behind her husband and put her hands over his eyes, with the result that the whole world was enveloped in darkness. Siva cursed and deposed her, but of course immediately regretted what he had done. Being unable, however, to cancel his act, he advised her to sit for 6 months in the Kambanadi tank in Ekambaram's temple meditating on the deity, and at the end of this period he appeared before her and took her back. This is symbolised on the tenth day of the feast, by placing images of the god and goddess together in one chamber for the night.

The next most important shrine is the Vishnu temple at Little Conjeeveram. There is some splendid carving here, notably in the mantapam of the hundred pillars.

The alleged origin of this temple is as follows:—Brahma once upon a time had great trouble with his wife, Saraswati, the goddess of learning, because, on her putting the question, he was compelled in truth to answer that he preferred Vishnu's wife, Lutchmi, the goddess of riches. Saraswati then ran away from Brahma and lived apart. The latter, meanwhile, went to Conjeeveram to perform the "Aswamathayagam," or horse sacrifice. He chose Conjeeveram on the score of economy, as one sacrifice there was equivalent to 1,000 performed anywhere else. While he was performing his sacrifice on the spot on which the temple now stands, his wife, assisted by goblins and devils, appeared in the form of a flood, which threatened to carry the whole thing away. Vishnu, being invoked to come to Brahma's assistance, was eventually obliged to take the form of a naked man and lie across the course of the torrent. This was too much for the modesty of the irate lady, and she gave in on condition of being held more sacred than the Ganges everywhere south of the Deccan. Brahma's sacrifices were successfully offered, when the delighted common people standing round asked Vishnu to dwell permanently among them, and, on his agreeing to do so, the temple was constructed.

In a part of the town called Yathatakari is a small Vishnu temple with a recumbent nude statue, probably of Jain origin.

The Kamatchi temple is the third in importance.

Besides these Hindu temples, there is the Jain temple in the hamlet of Tiruparattikundram about two miles from Conjeeveram, which is well worth a visit, and a mosque of considerable size, the result of the Muhammedan occupation. This building is said to mark the burial place of a fakir from Bijapur called Hajarath Sahib Amir Avalya.

HALL OF 100 COLUMNS CONJEEVERAM

The tanks of the town are considered scarcely less sacred than the temples.

The hospital is a fine building.

PALLUR.

Pallur (pop. 1,572) is a village situated in the Walajabad taluq of the North Arcot district on the Chingleput-Arkonam Branch, 30 miles from Chingleput. The village is about half mile north-west of the station.

Road Conveyance.—Bullock-carts can be obtained on previous notice, at a charge of 2 annas per mile, or to the Pullalur cemetery and back 8 annas.

Local Manufactures and Products.—Rice of the finest quality is grown here.

Local Officials.—The Village Munsiff and Kurnam.

Objects of Interest.—About 1½ miles north of Pallur Railway station is a village called Pullalur, remarkable only as being the scene of the most grievous disaster which ever befel the British arms in India, namely, the total defeat of Colonel Baillie's force by Hyder Ali in 1780.

A tombstone was erected in 1781 on the field of battle in memory of those slain, and is still in good preservation.

ARKONAM JUNCTION.

Arkonam (pop. 4,236), situated in the Walajabad taluq of the North Arcot district, is the terminus of the South Indian Railway Company's Chingleput-Arkonam Branch, and is an important Railway Junction with the Madras Railway, where passengers change for the Madras Railway Company's north-west and south-west lines.

Local Accommodation.—There are two chuttrams and 15 hotels for natives of all classes in the village close to the station, where meals can be had at 2½ to 4 annas per head.

Road Conveyance.—Bullock-carts can be had. Charge 2 annas per mile.

Railway Facilities.—Waiting accommodation is provided

at the station for first and second class passengers. On
the Madras Railway platform is a refreshment room and
comfortable upstairs quarters, where passengers can find
accommodation on payment of the following charges :—

	RS.	A.	P.
Not exceeding 3 hours	0	8	0
Above 3 and not exceeding 24 hours	1	0	0

The charges for meals at the refreshment room here
are :—

	RS.	A.	P.
Breakfast	1	0	0
Dinner	1	8	0

when previous notice has been given, or tickets purchased, otherwise :—

	RS.	A.	P.
Breakfast	1	8	0
Dinner	2	0	0

The Madras Railway also maintain a native refreshment
room. The scale of charges being :—

	RS.	A.	P.
Superior meals	0	3	0
Sweet pongul (one cake)	0	2	6
Pongul	0	2	0
Puliyotharai	0	1	9
Thathiothanam	0	1	6
Coffee (per tumbler)	0	1	3
Tea do.	0	1	0

Local Officials.—The Sub-Magistrate and Sub-Registrar.

Clubs.—The Madras Railway have a reading room in
their station compound, where passengers can see the
papers at a charge of 4 annas per diem.

PONDICHERRY BRANCH.

VALAVANUR.

Valavanur (pop. 3,527) is a union village on the
Villupuram-Pondicherry Branch, 5½ miles east of Villupuram, and 103¾ from Madras (Egmore), in the Villupuram
taluq of the South Arcot district.

Local Accommodation.—There are two Brahman hotels and two choultries near the station for natives of all classes, where meals are supplied at a charge of 2½ annas per meal. At the choultries travellers may make their own arrangements for cooking, when no charge is made.

Road Conveyance.—Both single and double bullock-carts are available, if previous notice is given. Charge 1 anna and 1½ annas per mile, respectively.

Local Manufactures and Products.—Oil and oil-cake are manufactured here. At Siruvanthadu, 3 miles south of the station, a good description of cloth is manufactured, which is exported to different parts of the district. The chief articles of produce are ground-nuts, paddy, ragi, indigo, kumbu, gingelly seeds and onions.

Local Officials.—The Sub-Registrar, Chairman of the Union and Messrs. Parry & Co.'s agent here.

Objects of Interest.—Two old temples bearing inscriptions are situated here.

Sport.—Snipe shooting can be had close to the station in the cold season. Shikarries are not available, but coolies can be hired at a charge of 4 annas per diem.

KANDAMANGALAM.

Kandamangalam (pop. 718) is situated in the Villupuram taluq of the South Arcot district, 14 miles east of Villupuram, and 112 miles from Madras (Egmore). It is the frontier station for French territory (Pondicherry). The British Customs authorities here inspect all luggage coming out of French territory, and levy duty usually at 5 per cent. on goods of every description, except wearing apparel, which has been used, and food-grains.

Passengers, possessing dutiable articles when going into French territory on a short visit, should declare them, depositing such articles as are not required for immediate use with the British Customs Superintendent, who will deliver them on the return journey without collecting duty.

Road Conveyance.—Bullock-carts can be had, if previous notice is given, at a charge of 2 annas per mile.

Local Manufactures and Products.—Indigo is produced at the village of Nallathur, about 4 miles south of this station·

Local Officials.—The British Customs Superintendent, Salt Sub-Inspector, Village Munsiff and Kurnam.

Objects of Interest.—At Sannasikuppam in French territory, about 3 miles north-west of this station, is a colossal stone bull elaborately sculptured. At Valadavur, 4 miles north, are the ruins of an old fort, containing several subterranean cells, which is said to have been the residence of one Mahud Khan, the Prime Minister of a ruler of Gingee. On the west side of the fort stand three stone figures well sculptured and larger than life, which are supposed to represent Rama, Lakshmana and Sita. As there is a better road from Villianur than from Kandamangalam to this place, passengers, who wish to see the above, are advised to go from that station, though the distance is longer.

VILLIANUR.

Villianur (pop. 4,900) is a municipal town in French territory on the Pondicherry Railway, 19¾ miles from Villupuram, and 118 from Madras (Egmore).

Local Accommodation.—There is a choultry about quarter mile south of the station for native travellers, where meals are served at 2½ annas each.

Road Conveyance.—Jutkas and bullock-carts are available at a charge of 2 annas per mile.

Railway Facilities.—Waiting accommodation is provided at the station for first and second class passengers.

Local Officials.—Chief of Police, Health Officer, the Mayor and the Notary.

Missions, Churches, etc.—A fine Roman Catholic Church has been built close to the station and is attended by large numbers of worshippers during the festival held annually in April.

GRAPHIC ART SOCIETY

PONDICHERRY

NEGATIVE BY W. A. CROSS

PONDICHERRY.

Pondicherry (lat. 11° 56'; long. 79° 53'; pop. 50,000) is the capital of the chief settlement of the French in India and the residence of the Governor. It is the terminal station of the Pondicherry Branch and is 24 miles from Villupuram, and 122½ from Madras (Egmore).

Until the middle of the last century, Pondicherry was the largest European city in India and it now extends along the sea-coast for a distance of about a mile and a quarter, and inland for about three-quarters of a mile. The town is well built, and is divided into two parts, separated by a canal. Its streets, lined with trees, are systematically laid out and cut each other at right angles, while its water-supply is excellent, owing to the successful artesian wells which have been sunk in recent years. The town lies on a flat sandy coast, off which good anchorage is obtained, but this open roadstead can hardly be considered a satisfactory port in the north-east monsoon.

The distances of the principal stations from Pondicherry are as under :—

Chingleput Junction	88 miles.
Katpadi Junction (for Madras Railway)	123 ,,
Mayavaram Junction (for Negapatam and Mutupet)	99 ,,
Tanjore	148 ,,
Trichinopoly Junction (for Erode)	174 ,,
Ammayanayakanur (for Kodaikanal)	245 ,,
Madura	270 ,,
Maniyachi Junction (for Tinnevelly)	350 ,,
Tuticorin	368 ,,

Local Accommodation.—The principal European hotels are the Grand Hotel d'Europe and the Hotel de Paris et Londres. The former is in the European part of the town close to the station, and has accommodation for 8 persons. The charges for board and lodging per head are :—

	RS.	A.	
First floor	4	0	} per diem.
Ground floor	3	0	

The Hotel de Paris et Londres is situated near the lighthouse and the sea, about 10 minutes' drive from the station. It has accommodation for 14 persons at the following tariff per person for board and lodging:—

			ns. a.	
First floor (double rooms)	..	..	5 0	per diem.
First floor (single rooms)	..	..	4 0	
Ground floor ..	..	..	8 0	

In addition to these hotels, a fully furnished travellers' bungalow for Europeans is maintained by a native gentleman. Travellers are allowed to reside in the bungalow, which is close to the station, for three days, free of rent, and meals can be supplied at the occupant's expense. About half a mile from the station are 7 Brahman hotels, and in the town, some 15 small hotels for native travellers of other castes. There are also 5 choultries, where free lodging is allowed to all natives.

Road Conveyance.—The means of conveyance most generally adopted by Europeans and Eurasians is the pousse-pousse, a kind of bath chair pushed by one or more coolies, the rate of hire being one rupee per day. Jutkas and carts are also procurable at the station at a charge of one rupee per day for the former, and 2 annas per mile for the latter.

Railway Facilities.—There is a waiting room at the station for first and second class passengers and a Customs office, where passengers for British Territory must submit their luggage for examination, and pay duty on such articles as are liable.

Shipping Arrangements.—The British India Steam Navigation Company's steamers between Negapatam and Rangoon call here once a week, and the same Company's steamers between Madras and Singapore fortnightly. In addition, the French mail steamers and the Asiatic Company's steamers touch at the port every alternate week. There is an exceedingly neat iron screw pile pier, from which passengers are embarked and landed in surf boats. The journey to and from the steamers takes about 10 minutes in fair weather.

Local Manufactures and Products.—Three mills for the manufacture of cloth for shipment to France and the French Colonies are in operation, and a fourth (a very large one) is under construction.

Local Officials.—His Excellency the Governor and staff, the General Secretary, Commander-in-Chief, Mayor, British Consul, Chief of Control, Captain of the Port, Chief Justice, Judges of the Civil and Magistrates Courts, Procureur-General, Procurator of the Republic, Commissioner of Police, City Treasurer, Agent of the Indo-China Bank, and the Agents of Messageries Maritimes, British India and Asiatic Steam Navigation Companies.

Missions, Churches, etc.—Pondicherry is the head-quarters of the French Roman Catholic Mission, and the seat of an Archbishop, and contains one Protestant and five Roman Catholic Churches. The Cathedral, built in 1855, is called " Notre Dame des Anges."

Clubs.—There is a club for Europeans, as well as for natives.

Historical.—Pondicherry was purchased by the French from the Vijianagar Rajah in 1672. In 1693 it was captured by the Dutch, but was restored at the peace of Ryswick in 1699. It was besieged unsuccessfully by the English in 1748, but it was, however, captured by Sir Eyre Coote in 1761 to be restored to the French some 2 years later. In 1778, Sir Hector Munro laid siege to and captured the town which was given back in 1785. It was again captured by Colonel Braithwaite in 1793, and finally restored in 1816, since which time it has remained under French rule. The old fort, which was built 500 feet from the sea with bricks and covered with fine plaster resembling marble, was demolished by the English in 1761.

Objects of Interest.—Government House, a handsome building, situated on the north side of the Place Dupleix within 300 yards of the sea. The pier 150 metres long, which is the fashionable promenade in the evenings; the

Marina extending from the pier to the south end of the
European town; the statue of Dupleix standing on a
pedestal of stones brought from the temple at Gingee; the
Place de Government, where the band plays twice a week;
the Lighthouse, about 90 feet high; the High Court, a
handsome square building; and the Library, Hospital, and
Public Gardens. The Roman Catholic cemetery, with its
numerous carved tomb stones, is very interesting. Three
miles south of Pondicherry on the coast lies the village of
Veerampatnam, which contains an ancient temple dedicated to the goddess Sangalaniammal, and which attracts
numerous pilgrims annually in August. Four miles south
of Pondicherry is the village of Aryankuppam, where there
is a very ancient Roman Catholic Church.

VILLUPURAM—GUDUR SECTION.

VENKATESAPURAM.

Venkatesapuram (pop. 362) is situated in the Villupuram
taluq of the South Arcot district, 5 miles west of Villupuram, and 94¼ from Katpadi Junction.

Local Accommodation.—About a mile north-west of the
station is an old Vishnu temple in which meals are served
free to Brahmans, and which constitutes the only public
accommodation for travellers.

Road Conveyance.—If previous notice is given, bullock-
carts can be had at the station, at a charge of 2 annas per
vehicle per mile.

Local Manufactures and Products.—Common cloth is
manufactured, and paddy, ragi, kumboo, indigo and
jaggery are the chief products.

Local Officials.—The Village Munsiff and Kurnam.

Fairs.—A fair is held every Friday near the Railway
station.

Objects of Interest.—The great Ahobela Swami, the

Jaiyar or Chief Priest of the Vadagalay branch of the Vaishnava sect in South India, resides at Vittalai Perumbakam, about a mile from the station, where he is visited by his numerous disciples.

MAMBALAPATTU.

Mambalapattu (pop. 1,758) is situated in the Villupuram taluq of the South Arcot district, 10 miles west of Villupuram, and 89¼ from Katpadi Junction.

Local Accommodation.—There is a small choultry about a quarter of a mile west of the station, where natives of all classes can obtain accommodation, but private arrangements for food must be made.

Road Conveyance.—If previous notice is given, bullock-carts can be had at the station, at a charge of 2 annas per vehicle per mile.

Local Manufactures and Products.—The East Indian Distilleries Company possess a sugar factory at Tiruvanna-nullur, some seven miles south of this station. The chief products of Mambalapattu are paddy, ragi, kumboo, cholam, indigo, ground-nuts and gingelly seeds. About 1½ miles west of the station are two granite quarries.

Local Officials.—The Village Munsiff and Kurnam.

Fairs.—A fair is held every Thursday at the village.

Sport.—Snipe shooting can be had in the season. Shikarries are procurable at one rupee and coolies at 4 annas per diem.

MUGAIYUR.

Mugaiyur (pop. 1,259) is situated in the Tirukoilur taluq of the South Arcot district, 15¾ miles west of Villupuram, and 83½ from Katpadi Junction. The village is about three-quarter mile from the station.

Local Manufactures and Products.—Mats and country cloths are manufactured, and paddy, gram and gingelly seeds grown.

Local Officials.—The Village Munsiff and Kurnam.

TIRUKOILUR.

Tirukoilur (pop. 5,732) is a Union town situated in the Tirukoilur taluq of the South Arcot district, 21 miles north-west of Villupuram, and 79 miles from Katpadi Junction. The town is on the south bank of the Pennar river, which has to be crossed to reach the station.

Local Accommodation.—In the town are 4 Brahman hotels and a choultry, where native travellers of all classes can find accommodation. Meals are served at from 2½ to 4 annas each according to quality.

Road Conveyance.—If previous notice is given, bullock-carts can be hired at the station, at a charge of 2 annas per mile in the fair season, and 6 annas per mile in the rainy season.

Local Manufactures and Products.—The chief products are jaggery, paddy and stone.

Local Officials.—The Deputy Collector, Assistant Superintendent of Police, Hospital Assistant, Forest Ranger, District Munsiff, Salt Inspector, Local Fund Sub-Engineer, Tahsildar, Sub-Magistrate and Sub-Registrar.

Fairs.—A fair is held in the town every Wednesday.

Missions, Churches, etc.—There is a Danish Mission establishment at Kiloor, about a mile from the town.

Objects of Interest.—Tirukoilur possesses an elaborately sculptured Vishnu temple containing inscriptions and dedicated to Thiruvikrama Gopalmoorthy or Krishna. Large numbers of worshippers attend the great festivals which are held in April and December annually. In the bed of the Pennar is a large boulder supporting a temple dedicated to Ganesha. The suburb of Kiloor contains an old Siva temple, and on a small hill on the opposite side of the river is a deserted temple, neither of which possesses architectural merit. In Kiloor is also a Siva temple with a gopurum eight storeys in height which a century ago was partially used for storing Government salt. At Arikandanallur near to the station and built on a rocky eminence is an ancient Siva temple the walls of which bear numerous inscriptions and below which are three caves. Below the temple in a depression of the hill is a small lake which has never been known to dry up.

TANDARAI.

Tandarai (pop. 666) is situated in the Tiruvannamalai taluq of the South Arcot district, 31½ miles north-west of Villupuram, and 67¾ miles from Katpadi Junction. The village is about half a mile west of the station.

Local Manufactures and Products.—Common cloths are manufactured, and paddy, ragi, kumboo, and gram are produced.

Local Officials.—The Village Munsiff and Kurnam.

TIRUVANNAMALAI.

Tiruvannamalai (lat. 12°15′; long. 79°07′; pop. 12,155) is the head-quarters of the taluq of the same name in the South Arcot district, 41¾ miles north-west of Villupuram and 57½ miles from Katpadi Junction. The name Tiruvannamalai, which means the sacred red mountain, has been given to the town from the red appearance before sunrise of the hill below which it lies. It is the first town on the road from the Baramaha in the Salem district, through the Chengam Pass and from it roads diverge to the north, south and to the coast. It is thus a trade centre for South Arcot and the country above the ghats, while its hill with three fortified peaks has always been considered an important military point. The main peak is covered with jungle accessible only on foot and from its summit rises a natural vertical column held by Siva Brahmans to be a sacred lingam. The peak is 2,668 feet high and the town, which is situated at the foot of it, is about three-quarter mile south-west of the Railway station.

The following are the distances to the principal stations on the South Indian Railway :—

Vellore	..	..	..	..	52 miles.
Pakala	..	..	..	..	97 ,,
Gudur	..	..	..	..	181 ,,
Dharmavaram Junction (for S. M. Railway)			..	239 ,,
Pondicherry	..	..	..	..	66 ,,
Chingleput	..	..	..	..	105½ ,,
Cuddalore	..	..	..	..	70¾ ,,
Tanjore	..	..	..	..	161 ,,
Trichinopoly Junction (for Erode, etc.) ..			..	192 ,,
Madura	..	..	..	..	288 ,,
Tinnevelly	..	..	..	..	386¾ ,,
Tuticorin	..	..	..	..	386¾ ,,

Local Accommodation.—A travellers' bungalow close to the station, which contains two rooms fully furnished, is in charge of a butler, who can supply meals, if required ; but spirits and aerated waters must be privately purchased. The daily charge for the use of this bungalow is one rupee for each person, but if two persons share one room, only Rs. 1-8-0 per diem is charged. There are 5 chuttrams and 37 maddams in the town, where free accommodation is allowed to all classes of Hindus. In two of the chuttrams, meals are supplied gratis for three days, but in the others travellers must make their own arrangements. There are also more than a dozen hotels, in which meals are served to all classes at from 2½ to 3 annas per meal. The Municipality maintains a dispensary.

Road Conveyance.—Jutkas and bullock-carts are procurable at the station. Charges :—

				A. P.	
Jutkas	..	...	..	.. 2 0	per mile.
Bullock-carts..		..	..	.. 1 6	,,

Railway Facilities.—There is a refreshment room at the station, where light refreshments and aerated waters may be obtained. The butler in charge keeps a small stock of travellers' requisites for sale. The Railway Company has an officers' rest-house near the station, which, when not in use by railway officers, may be occupied by any European gentleman with the previous sanction of the Resident Engineer residing at Vellore. If gentlemen are accompanied by their families, the prior sanction of the Agent, South Indian Railway, must be obtained. The charge for the use of this bungalow is for each person :—

Per diem   ..   .. 12 annas.

For a stay not exceeding 8 hours   ..   .. 8 ,,

This rest-house is partially furnished, but travellers must make their own arrangements for food while staying there.

Local Manufactures and Products.—The chief products are jaggery, paddy, ragi, kumboo, cholam, sugarcane, soapnuts, myrabolams, tobacco, bamboos and granite obtained from four large quarries around the foot of the hill.

Local Officials.—The Tahsildar, Sub-Magistrate, Sub-Registrar, Municipal Chairman, Forest Ranger, Police Inspector, Salt Inspector and Hospital Assistant.

Fairs.—A fair is held in the town every Tuesday, and, during the yearly Karthigai festival, a large cattle market is also held.

Missions, Churches, etc.—About two miles south of the station is a Church of the Danish Mission.

Clubs.—A reading room for natives is maintained in the town.

Historical.—Between 1753 and 1791 Tiruvannamalai was besieged on ten separate occasions and was six times taken, thrice by assault. The temple and the town adjoining it were on several occasions the scene of severe fighting, the marks of cannon balls being visible on these temple walls to this day. In 1753 it was closely besieged by Murtiz Ali Khan and Morari Row and very gallantly defended by Barkat Ulla Khan on behalf of the Nawab of the Carnatic, until on reinforcements from Arcot being sent to his assistance the siege was raised. In 1757 the garrison abandoned the place on the approach of a French army under Soupires, but in August of the following year it was recaptured by Krishna Row, the Killadar of Tiagar. A month later, however, a strong detachment under Saubinet attacked and captured it after three assaults when the garrison was put to the sword. In 1760 it was taken by Captain Stephen Smith, and in August of the same year was attacked by the Mysore troops which, after two unsuccessful assaults, withdrew to Tiagar. On the outbreak of the First Mysore War the allied forces of Hyderabad and Mysore invaded the Carnatic by the Chengam Pass. A desperate fight took place on 3rd September 1767, near Chengam, 16 miles from Tiruvannamalai, when some 6,000 men under Colonel Smith totally routed the invading army. A second battle was fought at Tiruvannamalai which lasted two days and resulted in the allies losing 4,000 men and 64 guns. In 1790, after being repulsed from Tiagar, Tippu captured Tiruvannamalai.

Objects of Interest.—The large Siva temple at the foot of the hill dedicated to the "Tejo" or "Fire" lingam. It has four large gopurums from nine to eleven storeys high, and five minor ones. The temple contains many inscriptions and several fine structures, among which may be specially mentioned the small temple of Ganesha (see plate No. 32), and the hall of 1,000 columns. The Nattukottai Chetties, a wealthy mercantile community, are at present erecting a fine mantapam containing 24 columns of polished granite, and are about to undertake extensive restorations. The temple is famous on account of the Karthigai festival celebrated in honour of the completion of Parvati's penance and her reconciliation with Siva, who then appeared to her in the form of a flame of fire spouting from the top of Tiruvannamalai Hill, and thus terminating the darkness which had enveloped the world. The festival continues 10 days, and on the evening of the last day, just before the rising of the full moon, is performed the ceremony of the "Dipam." This consists in the temple Brahmans removing a large

NEGATIVE BY A. D. G. SHELLEY

covered vessel of blazing camphor from before the lingam within the Mulastanam or "holy of holies," and carrying it to a mantapam in the centre of the temple courtyard, when the cover is suddenly removed and the flaming camphor dashed on the ground in front of the idol Aruna-chelleshwara (Siva), which has been previously placed in the mantapam. This is the signal for a party of temple Brahmans to light up on the top of the hill a large torch built up in a huge bowl containing the camphor and ghee which have been offered by pilgrims during the festival. The blaze generally lasts for 48 hours, and the worshipper who first sees it, after having witnessed the ceremony in front of the idol, is supposed to secure great good fortune for the future. The rush of pilgrims to view the flame on the hill-top is so great that only by careful police control are accidents prevented. The number of persons attending the festival has been estimated at the high figure of 100,000.

Behind the temple on the hill above is a tank known by the name of Mulaippal theertham and which is noted for the remarkable purity of its water. In the hills about Tiruvannamalai are several rock-cut caves, and on a low eminence, quarter mile west of the station, is a small temple dedicated to Subramanya, the eldest son of Siva.

Sport.—About two miles south of the station, hares, partridges, quails and antelope can be shot. Shikarries can be engaged at a charge of 8 annas, and coolies at 4 annas per diem.

AGARAM SIBBANDI.

Agaram Sibbandi (pop. 159) is a small village situated in the Tiruvannamalai taluq of the South Arcot district, 52¾ miles north-west of Villupuram, and 47 from Katpadi Junction.

Local Official—The Village Munsiff.

POLUR.

Polur (pop. 8,631) is a Union town in a taluq of the same name in the North Arcot district, 61½ miles north-west of Villupuram, and 38 miles from Katpadi Junction. The whole of this taluq is mountainous, the Javadi Hills rising to 2,800 feet in height, occupying a large portion of it. The town is 544 feet above sea-level, and lies 2 miles west of the Cheyar river, which irrigates the surrounding country.

Local Accommodation.—There is a travellers' bungalow, which can be occupied on payment of 10 annas per diem; but is provided with neither furniture, crockery nor servants. Fowls, eggs and milk are the only items of food procurable locally. There are three hotels and a chuttram for natives. Travellers can live rent free at the chuttram, but must make their own arrangements for food. The charge at the hotels is from 2½ to 3 annas per meal.

Road Conveyance.—Jutkas and bullock-carts are procurable at the station. Charges :—

Jutkas	..	..	..	.. 2 annas per mile.
Bullock-carts ..	..	..	.. 1½ ,, ,,

Local Manufactures and Products.—Weaving and shoe-making are the principal industries, and paddy, ragi, kumboo, cholam, gram, tamarind, karanai root, bamboos, jungle-wood, myrabollams, soapnuts and tanning bark are the chief products.

Local Officials.—The Tahsildar, Union Chairman, Sub-Magistrate, Sub-Registrar, Forest Ranger, and Hospital Assistant.

Fairs.—A fair is held every Wednesday.

Missions, Churches, etc.—A Roman Catholic Church has been built about a mile north-east of the station.

Historical.—The history of the taluq can be traced back as far as the year 1596, when Bungauroo Yatusama Naidoo, the 22nd Zemindar of Venkatagiri, who had obtained the title of Rajah Bahadur from the Court of Hyderabad, having

suddenly died, his three young sons, and an adopted
Brahman boy, Rama Row, were summoned to Hyderabad
to receive their shares of the ancestral property. The
adopted son, who was given the taluq of Polur, dying
without issue, Polur returned to the eldest branch of
the family.

Objects of Interest.—The only objects of interest are a
temple on a hill near the town dedicated to Narasimmaswami, or the lion incarnation of Vishnu, and a small
ruined fort, about which nothing is known. The following
is the legend regarding the River Cheyar :—Many years ago
the river was called the Skandanadi, because Skandaswami
or Subramanya, when fighting against the demon Taraka-
suran, requiring water for his army, ordered his peacock to
procure it by picking a hole in a hillside and this formed
the source of the present river. After the lapse of ages, two
brothers, the sages Vasadu and Sumati, took up their abodes
upon opposite sides of the river. They were both so deeply
engaged in meditations that they only opened their eyes
once in 12 years to eat what fruits they found to hand.
Upon one of these rare occasions the brother, who lived on
the southern side of the river finding the country desolated
with famine and impelled by hunger, crossed the stream and
plucked fruit within his brother's domain without the
latter's knowledge. This crime, which rendered the offender
liable to punishment, both in his present and future existence, was atoned for by the loss of a hand. The other
brother advised the mutilated man to worship at Polur and
after that to bathe in the Skandanadi. The remedy proved
efficacious, the hand was restored and the river became
known as the Bahudanadi or "hand-giving river," the
Telegu equivalent for which is "Cheyar."

Tirumalai, 6 miles north-east of Polur, contains two
Jain temples, and in it reside many Jain families. In this
village is a most striking representation of a Jain figure, $16\frac{1}{4}$
feet high, which is roughly cut on the face of a cliff near

the summit of the hill. Close to the lower temple are some rock chambers constructed in a natural cave formed in a scarp of the mountain side. The walls of the caverns are decorated with numerous frescoes, on the whole very well executed, the most interesting being a circular design, having a Jain figure seated in the centre, with the surrounding partitions filled with nagas, monks, white-hooded nuns and others.

Sport.—Good shooting is obtainable in the Reserved Forests on the Javadi and Karnatighur Hills with the permission of the Forest Department. Wild buffaloes, cheetahs, bears, hyænas, sambur, deer and wild pigs are common, while tigers are occasionally seen.

KALAMBUR.

Kalambur (pop. 570) is situated in the Polur taluq of the North Arcot district, 72¼ miles north-west of Villupuram, and 28 miles from Katpadi Junction. Passengers for Arni, 6 miles east of Kalambur, alight at this station.

Road Conveyance.—Jutkas and bullock-carts are procurable at the station. Charges :—

Jutkas	..	..	..	2 annas per mile.
Bullock-carts		..	..	1¼ „ „

Railway Facilities.—A waiting room is provided at the station for first and second class passengers.

Local Manufactures and Products.—Paddy and gram are the chief products.

Local Officials.—The Village Munsiff, Kurnam, Revenue Inspector and Salt Sub-Inspector. At Arni the local officials are the Deputy Collector, Deputy Tahsildar, District Munsiff and Sub-Registrar.

Objects of Interest.—About 6 miles west of this station at Padaved are the ruins of a great city probably of Pallava origin, but now for the most part buried or covered with scrub-jungle. The following are the principal remains at present visible :—The Rumkambalana temple, at which a festival is still held annually in July, and the Ramaswami kovil. These two temples are about three-quarters of a mile apart and the road between them was originally floored with stone ; a portion of the pavement is still existent. In olden days the festival car used to be dragged from one temple to the other along this road, on the sides of which are several small temples all in ruins and overgrown with prickly-pear and shrubs. In one of these temples is a stone image of the monkey god, Hanuman, well carved and in a good state of preservation, and near the roadway the foundations of some of the old houses are still to be seen. Traces of a large fort are also visible, which evidently contained many buildings, though only a ruined temple, known as the Peria Varatha Rajah Perumal, is now left as a relic of the past. A small fort is still in existence ; but the structures which were in it have all disappeared with the exception of a small temple called Chinna Varatha Rajah Perumal. There are rumours that ryots occasionally find ancient coins while tilling the land ; but such finds have always been kept secret.

KANNAMANGALAM.

Kannamangalam (pop. 2,500) is situated in the Arni Jagir of the North Arcot district, 80¼ miles north-west of Villupuram and 19 from Katpadi Junction. The village is about half a mile east of the station.

Road Conveyance.—Bullock-carts can be obtained, if previous notice be given. Charge 1½ annas per mile.

Local Manufactures and Products.—Paddy, ragi and cholam are the chief items of produce.

Local Officials.—The Village Munsiff and Kurnam.

Fairs.—A fair is held here every Monday.

KANIYAMBADI.

Kaniyambadi (pop. 2,467) is situated in the Vellore taluq of the North Arcot district, 85¾ miles north-west of Villupuram, and 13¼ from Katpadi Junction. The village is about three-quarters of a mile from the station.

Local Accommodation.—A travellers' bungalow, having neither furniture, crockery nor servants, can be occupied free. Fowls, eggs and milk are procurable. For natives there is a choultry, where meals are served to all classes at 3 annas per meal.

Road Conveyance.—Single and double bullock-carts are available at the station, if previous notice is given. Charges:—

Single bullock-carts .. .. .. 1½ annas per mile.
Double bullock-carts .. .. .. 2 ,, ,,

Local Manufactures and Products.—From the Thellai and Amirithi forests, 8 to 12 miles south of this station, bamboos, myrabollams, pungam seeds, kabili powder, tamarind and gunia are procured.

Local Officials.—The Village Munsiff and Salt Sub-Inspector.

Fairs.—At Amirithi a market is held every Monday, Wednesday and Friday, and at Thellai every Thursday and Sunday.

VELLORE.

Vellore (lat. 12°55'; long. 79°11'; pop. 44,925) is an important municipal town in the taluq of the same name in the North Arcot district, 93¼ miles north-west of Villupuram, and 6 miles from Katpadi Junction. More than a fourth of the total population are Musalmans, the descendants of the soldiery brought down by the Muhammedan invaders from Bijapur and Golconda. The town stands about a mile south of the Palar river and is about 700 feet above the level of the sea. The original settlement was Vellappadi, now a suburb, which derived its name from the circumstance of its being situated in the midst of a forest of " Vela " or babool trees. Vellore is often called Royavellore to distinguish it from Ellore in Godavery, known as Uppuvellore, or Salt Ellore. It contains a large masonry fort which is considered to be one of the most perfect specimens of military architecture in the south of India and was formerly a cantonment, but no troops are quartered here now. A Station Staff Officer is, however, still maintained for the disbursement of payments to the families of sepoys serving elsewhere. Overlooking the town on the east is a range of hills from which rise three peaks, Murtizghar, Gajjaraoghar and Sajjaraoghar, which were formerly fortified. The defences on the first named and most northern eminence were constructed by the last Governor of Vellore; while the other two, of which Sajjaraoghar is the more southerly, were due to the Mahrattas. The town at the foot of the hills was surrounded by a wall and connected by lines of fortification with the hill forts, from which another defensible wall was constructed to the banks of the Palar river. The station is very healthy, though the heat is great, owing to radiation from the rocky hills which surround it.

The mileages to the principal stations on the South Indian Railway are as under :—

Pakala Junction	.. 45 miles.
Gudur (for East Coast Railway) ..	.. 129 ,,
Dharmavaram Junction (for S. M. Railway)	.. 187 ,,
Pondicherry	.. 117 ,,
Cuddalore	.. 123 ,,
Negapatam	.. 208 ,,
Tanjore	.. 218 ,,
Trichinopoly (for Erode, etc.)	.. 244 ,,
Madura	.. 340 ,,
Tinnevelly	.. 439 ,,
Tuticorin	.. 439 ,,

Local Accommodation.—A fully furnished travellers' bungalow, capable of accommodating two persons, is maintained. Meals can be supplied by the butler in charge, if required; but beer, spirits, etc., must be privately arranged for. The charge for the use of the bungalow is for a single person, one rupee per day, and for a married couple,

Rs. 1-8-0. No charge is made for children. Provisions of all sorts are procurable in the local bazaar. For natives there are two chuttrams, where travellers of all classes may put up, making their own arrangements for food and cooking. In addition to these, there are 5 Brahman, 8 Sudra and 4 Muhammedan hotels, where meals are served at 2½ to 4 annas per meal, according to the quality. There is a hospital under the supervision of a District and Assistant Surgeon close to the station, and a Military Hospital within the fort.

Road Conveyance.—Jutkas and bullock-carts are available, the fares being :—

Jutkas	..	..	..	.. 1	anna per mile.
Double bullock-carts	..	..	.. 1¼	,,	,,
Single bullock-carts	..	..	.. ¾	,,	,,

Railway Facilities.—A waiting room is provided at the station for first and second class passengers.

Local Manufactures and Products.—At Saidapet, 1¼ miles north-east of the station, brassware is made in large quantities. Native boots, shoes and slippers, and wooden toys are made in the local bazaar. At the Central Jail, about 2½ miles south of the station, much excellent work is done by the prisoners, such as brass and copper work, weaving, carpentry, shoe-making, carpet-making, tent manufacture, etc., etc. Tourists should make a point of seeing the goods exhibited at the sale room, where all articles made by the prisoners such as carpets, blankets, sheets, towels, napkins, tablecloths, furniture, tents, fancy tables, purdahs, mats, etc., can be purchased cheaply.

The chief produce of Vellore is paddy, kumboo and ragi, and it is the most important centre of the grain trade of the district.

Local Officials.—The Sub-Collector, District Forest Officer, District Medical Officer, Chaplain, Executive Engineer, Assistant Engineer, Deputy Inspector-General and Assistant Superintendent of Police, Tahsildar, Sub-Registrar, Assistant Commissioner of Salt and Abkari, Jail Superintendent and Staff Officer. The Resident Engineer and Assistant Engineer of the South Indian Railway also reside here.

Missions, Churches, etc.—There is a Protestant Church within the Fort, and a Church belonging to the American Mission, quarter of a mile to the east of the station, close to the hospital. The town also possesses two Roman Catholic Churches, one close to the station, the other about a mile and a half east of it. The American Mission supports a college for the education of all classes of children, and Government maintains a girls' school and a Native High School. A fourth school is under the management of the Chaplain of the district.

Clubs.—The Local European residents have established a small club about three-quarters of a mile from the station, and the natives possess a reading room.

The following are the rules with regard to the honorary members of the former.

A candidate for honorary membership shall be proposed by one member and seconded by another, and then be elected or rejected by the Committee.

An honorary member shall cease to be such at the expiration of three months from date of election.

The subscription of an honorary member shall be Rs. 7 per mensem. He shall not be required to pay any entrance donation.

Historical.—According to the tradition, the fort was built in 1295 by a native of Bhadrachalam on the Kistna named Bommi Reddi or Naidoo, who obtained permission to settle in Vellore from a Chola Rajah. The designer is said to have been a son of Bommi Reddi, but it is not improbable that the fort was laid out by early Italian Engineers; at any rate, it is obvious that the upper brick parapets, which are pierced with embrasures, is a work of European and much later construction than the remainder of the fortifications. From an inscription on the walls of

40

a temple in the Gudiyattam taluq, it would appear that neither the fort nor the temple inside it, could have been built before the middle of the fourteenth century, and that their antiquity must have been locally exaggerated. About A.D. 1500, Vellore passed into the possession of Narasinga Rayar, of Vijayanagar, from which dynasty it was taken by the Sultan of Bijapur in the middle of the seventeenth century. The Musalmans ruled in Vellore until ousted by the Mahrattas under Tukoji Row, to whom the fort was surrendered in 1677 by Abdulla Khan, the then Commandant. Towards the close of the seventeenth century, Zulfikar Khan, a celebrated General of the Moghul Emperor Aurungzeb, beseiged the fort for two years, but was ultimately bought off by the Governor Sinkoji on payment of 1,50,000 pagodas. In 1708 Daud Khan, another Moghul General and Nabob of the Carnatic, drove the Mahrattas out of this strong hold after a siege of four and a half months, and two years later, his successor, Sudat-Ulla Khan gave Vellore and the surrounding country in jagir to his brother Ghulam Ali Khan, whose grandson Mortiz Ali held the fort for many years until dispossessed by the combined forces of the English and the Nabob Muhammad Ali after a three months' siege in 1763. In 1779 Hyder Ali, during the second Mysore War, surrounded Vellore with a circle of desolation by burning down the villages and crops within a radius of ten miles, and two years later, he proceeded to regularly besiege the place, but, after his failure to capture Wandiwash, was obliged to restrict his operations to a blockade. The troops in Vellore, who were commanded by Colonel Ross Lang, were reduced to dire straits for want of food until November 3rd, 1781, when Sir Eyre Coote succeeded in throwing in a fresh supply of provisions. The relief was, however, only temporary, as, after news of the reverse at Palupet, near Sholinghur, and, in consequence of the approach of the rainy season, the English troops were compelled to retire to Madras, and thus allowed the blockade to be renewed. On January 2nd, 1782, the English again took the field and on the 11th a convoy with three months' provisions was passed into the fort, which had again been reduced to extremities. On the outbreak of the Third Mysore War in 1790, the British troops were massed at Vellore, and except for the Vellore Mutiny in 1806, the military history of the fort then closed. During the operations of 1780—81, the value of the hill forts which could command the main work with artillery fire was recognised and they were accordingly held with great stubbornness against attacks, directed by skilled French officers. The most determined attempts were made to capture Sajjaraoghur, now known as " Sayers Hill," but all proved ineffectual against the courage and skill of Lieutenant Parr, who commanded the fort. On the 10th July 1806, at 2-30 A.M., the native troops in Vellore rose against the European portion of the garrison consisting of two companies of the 69th Regiment now the 2nd battalion of the Welsh Regiment. Ten officers and 115 men were killed besides others wounded. The immediate cause of the rising was the introduction of a new turban and a cross-shaped turnscrew which superstition translated into a design to convert the sepoys to Christianity, though it was proved that the dissatisfaction had been encouraged by the members of Tippu Sultan's family who had been permitted to live in Vellore under scarcely any restraint. The native garrison consisted of six companies of the first battalion of the 1st Regiment and the second battalion of the 23rd Regiment of Infantry numbering upwards of 1,500 men. On the night of July 9th, the guards were furnished by the 1st Regiment who were the principal conspirators. In the early morning a band of mutineers marched silently to the main guard which was composed principally of Europeans, and with the native sepoys on guard turned on their English comrades and killed them. A party of mutineers then ran to the parade ground where the 23rd Regiment had formed up and induced them to join in the rising. These men allowed themselves to be marched to the European barracks (now the Civil dispensary) and after surrounding the building poured, under the orders of their native officers, volley after volley upon the sleeping and defenceless soldiers. A party of the 1st Regiment then proceeded to massacre the European officers and their families many of whom were killed in bed. In the meantime the Europeans who had escaped managed to collect and offered a most gallant resistance. They succeeded in securing possession of the main entrance to the fort, and by so doing, prevented the drawbridge from being raised. While these events were progressing the leaders of the mutiny proclaimed Futteh Hyder, the second son of Tippu Sultan as Rajah and hoisted the Mysore banner on the fort flag-staff. The Europeans then sallied, and a man of the 69th Regiment succeeded in climbing the pole and removing the flag. News of the mutiny had in the meantime reached Colonel Gillespie, commanding the 19th Dragoons at Ranipet, and at 9 A.M. he reached Vellore with a squadron of his own corps and a troop of the 7th Native Cavalry. These reinforcements quickly put a different complexion on the struggle and in a short time the mutiny was effectually extinguished. About 350 sepoys were killed in the fort, the ringleaders were blown away from guns, and the 1st and 23rd Native Regiments were struck off the strength of the army.

Objects of Interest.—The fort, which is of an irregular four-sided trace, is one of the most perfect specimens of military architecture to be found in Southern India, and consists of a main rampart broken at irregular intervals by round towers and bastions. Below the ramparts is a fausse-braie with machicolated turrets and separated from a solid masonry counterscarp by a broad wet ditch of varying width. A covered way surrounds the fort, except on the north side, where the main road to Salem now occupies the glácis. The old entrance was by a winding

VELLORE FORT

GOPURAM OF THE TEMPLE AT VELLORE

roadway with massive gates, and protected by a draw-bridge. The ditch is supplied with water by a subterranean drain connecting with the bathing tank of Sooryagoonta. The main walls are built of massive granite stone, admirably cut to join and fitted together without mortar. The upper parapets are of brickwork in which the embrasures are cut. Within the fort in the north-east angle stands the temple, which for many years was used as an arsenal, and is a most interesting structure. Two centuries ago the temple was defiled by the shedding of blood in it and has since never been used regularly for religious purposes. The entrance is topped by a fine gopurum, of seven storeys, about 100 feet high with massive gates and rich carvings. It is sacred to Siva under the title of Jalakanteswara, or Siva " residing in the water." There are two dwarpals or door-guardians of blue granite at the entrance of the gopurum. The sides of the passage through the gopurum are lined with pilasters ornamented with medallions containing groups of figures. Among them is a representation of Bommi Reddi, who built the fort and temple. On the left hand after entering, within a distance of a few yards, is a stone pavillion called the Kaliana muntapam, in which, formerly the idol was placed when his marriage was yearly celebrated. It contains monolithic sculptures of marvellous beauty. On either side of the steps of the muntapam, there are pillars carved to represent various animals and monsters, one above another, in a way, which shews enormous labour and great skill. In the mouth of one of the animals was a ball of stone which could be freely turned within its jaws, but could not be extracted. This has, however, been lately destroyed by some mischievous person. The two ornaments of the roof are particularly striking, representing three circles of parrots hanging heads downwards and holding in their beaks and claws the open petals of a lotus flower. Each is carved from one large stone and the delicacy of execution is most remarkable. The centre of

the hall is supported upon huge monoliths, cut into groups
of fine pillars, joined by thin stone panels, fretted with
graceful patterns, the pillars and the four panels joining
being carved out of a single stone.   Each pillar has upon
its faces, figures from one to two feet in height, well
proportioned and magnificently chiselled, in very high
relief the limbs standing clear away from the background.
In fact, every stone in this wonderful building is well worth
notice.   A corridor runs round the temple enclosure
supported by many pillars, all with carvings on them.
There is a muntapam at each corner of the enclosure which
have some carvings also.   Opposite the muntapam, in the
north-west corner, is a well which is worthy of notice from
the fact that below the usual water-level it has a pivoted
stone doorway.   This leads to a spacious subterranean
muntapam supported on stone pillars, and from which a
passage leads probably to the Palar.   Rumour has it that
the temple jewels are concealed in this muntapam under
the guard of malignant evil spirits.   The supply of water
in the well is too copious to allow of it being emptied for
the investigation of this curious muntapam which was
viewed by the station staff officer's clerk during the exceptionally dry season of 1877-78.   Around the church, inside
the fort, are the Mahals which were the residence of the
family and descendants of Tippoo.   The old cemetery is a
little to the south-east of the fort and contains the tombs
of European officers and soldiers of the 69th Regiment
who fell during the Mutiny of 1806.   Hazrat Makam, the
tomb of a Muhammedan saint is in a street of the same
name about 250 yards west of the fort.   The tombs of
Tippoo's family, consisting of ten chiefs and about 400
minor ones are about three-fourths of a mile, west of the
fort, in an enclosure which is not well kept up though out
of 15 acres of land granted by Government in 1805, three
acres only are now covered by these tombs, the rest of the
land being rented for up-keep of the place.

COLUMN VELLORE TEMPLE

COLUMN VELLORE TEMPLE

Half a mile from the fort lies the tomb of a dancing girl who was murdered in the temple by a Muhammedan Governor about the end of the 17th century Service at the temple was discontinued in consequence of this murder, the temple jewels disappearing about the same time. The jewels have never been found and were either seized by Muhammedans, or concealed in the underground muntapam.

There is a ruined temple at Vellappadi said to have been in existence at Vellore before the construction of the fort. Native tradition asserts that this was the residence of a Chola Chief at the time that Bommi Reddi came from the north and built the fort.

KATPADI JUNCTION.

Katpadi (lat. 12°58'; long. 79°11'; pop. 2,511), 696 feet above sea-level is a junction station with the Madras Railway, 99¼ miles from Villupuram in the Gudiyattam taluq of the North Arcot district. Passengers for Madras, Arkonam, Jalarpet, Bangalore, Salem, Erode and Calicut change here. Two miles from the station, the river Palar is crossed by a masonry bridge about half a mile in length.

The mileages to the most important stations on the South Indian Railway are as under :—

Pakala ..	..	..	..	..	39 miles.
Gudur (for East Coast Railway)		..	..	123	,,
Dharmavaram (for S. M. Railway)		..	..	181	,,
Pondicherry	..	..	..	..	123	,,
Cuddalore	..	..	..	..	129	,,
Negapatam	..	..	..	..	214	,,
Tanjore ..	..	..	..	..	219	,,
Trichinopoly (for Erode, &c.) ..		..	..	250	,,
Madura ..	..	..	..	..	346	,,
Tinnevelly	..	..	..	..	445	,,
Tuticorin	..	..	..	..	445	,,

Local Accommodation.—Near the station is a travellers' bungalow which is fully furnished and can accommodate two persons. Meals can be supplied by the butler in charge, if required, but liquor must be privately purchased. The charge for the use of the bungalow is for single persons, one rupee per diem; and for married couples, one rupee eight annas. Children free. Fowls, eggs and milk can be purchased locally.

There are two chuttrams and 5 hotels, where native travellers of all classes can find accommodation. The charge for meals is from $2\frac{1}{2}$ to 3 annas each.

Road Conveyance.—Jutkas and single bullock-carts are procurable at the station   Charge—

Jutkas	..	..	..	.. 2 annas per mile.
Bullock-carts	..	..	.. $1\frac{1}{2}$ „ „

Railway Facilities.—A waiting room is provided at the station for 1st and 2nd class passengers, and a refreshment room under the management of the Madras Railway Company.

Local Officials.—The Village Munsiff, Kurnam and Sub-Registrar.

Fairs.—A fair is held every Saturday near the station.

RAMAPURAM.

Ramapuram (pop. 275) is situated in the Chittoor taluq of the North Arcot district, 109 miles north-west of Villupuram, and $9\frac{3}{4}$ miles from Katpadi Junction.

Local Manufactures and Products.—Kumboo, ragi, and cholum are the chief products.

Local Official.—The Village Munsiff.

MOGARALAPALLI.

The station is situated at mile G. 212/3, at a distance of two furlongs from the village. It is 14 miles from Vellore and 6 miles from Chittoor.

Road Conveyance.—Bullock-carts available at a charge of 2 annas per mile.

Products.—Paddy, ragi, cholum, kumboo, dhall-gram, horse-gram, ground nuts and chillies.

Local Officials.—Monigar and Kurnam.

Fairs.—A weekly fair is held every Sunday, at Nararipet Village, 2 miles south of the station, and one every Monday, at Narasinganrayanpet, 3 miles east of the station.

CHITTOOR.

Chittoor (pop. 9,965) is a union town, situated in the Chittoor taluq of the North Arcot district, 119¾ miles north-west of Villupuram and 20¼ miles from Katpadi Junction. It is not only the Head-quarters of the taluq but of the district, though it is by no means the most important town in North Arcot. It was chosen as the Collector's residence not merely on account of its central position, but because it was close to the estates of the principal Poligars, whose lawless conduct caused Government considerable anxiety for many years. These people have, however, long ceased to be troublesome. The scenery of the neighbourhood is very picturesque, low ranges are seen to rise on every side as far as the eye can reach, the shapes of some of the peaks being very fantastic. A magnificent view may be had from the summit of one of the highest hills called Chase's Folly, to which there is a good road.

Several miles of roads have been made between the hills by convict labour, forming pleasant drives for the residents and from the town, excellent roads branch to all parts of the district.

Local Accommodation.—There are two travellers' bungalows, about half a mile south-west of the station. One (maintained by the Local Fund Department) is furnished and can accommodate four persons. A cook is in charge, who can supply meals if required, but liquor must be privately purchased. The charge for this bungalow is 12 annas for each person per diem. The other rest house (maintained by the Forest Department) is unfurnished and has no cook and can be occupied free of charge. Travellers

41

must make their own arrangements, but provisions of all descriptions are procurable in the local bazaar. For natives, accommodation is procurable in 4 chuttrams 3 Brahman hotels and 5 other hotels. In the chuttrams, lodging is free, but travellers must make their own arrangements for food. In the hotels, meals are served at 2½ to 4 annas each. There is a fine hospital about a mile west of the station.

Road Conveyance.—Jutkas and bullock-carts are procurable at the station if previous notice given. Charges :—

| Jutkas | .. | .. | .. | .. 2 annas per mile. |
| Bullock-carts | .. | .. | .. | .. 1½ ,, ,, |

Railway Facilities.—A waiting room is provided at the station for first and second class passengers.

Local Manufactures and Products.—The soil is particularly suitable for mangoes and large quantities of this excellent fruit, are grown and exported.

Local Officials.—The Collector and District Magistrate, District Judge, Superintendent of Police, Assistant Surgeon, Treasury Deputy Collector, District Munsiff, District Registrar, Tahsildar and Sub-Magistrate.

Missions, Churches, etc.—About half a mile south-east of the station is a Protestant Church, and about the same distance south-west an American and a Roman Catholic Church.

Clubs.—The Native officials have a club, within the town and also maintain a Reading room.

Historical.—Chittoor was formerly the private estate of the Arcot family, and in 1781 was occupied by British troops under Sir Eyre Coote, and remained a military station until 1874. There was a small fort here, the residence of the Chittoor Jaghirdar, to whom the Poligars were subordinate, but nothing remains of it now.

Sport.—At Palmanair, about 25 miles west of the station, good shooting is obtainable. Deer, wild pig and panthers are fairly common and both tigers and bears are occasionally seen in the jungle at the foot of the hills. On the slopes, hares, pea-fowl, jungle-fowl and pigeons are plentiful and in the season excellent duck, teal and snipe shooting are to be had in the neighbourhood of the station. Shikarries are available at a charge of one rupee to two rupees per diem, according to sport shown. Coolies 4 annas.

PUTALAPATTU.

Putalapattu (pop. 2,337) is situated in the Chittoor taluq of the North Arcot district, 128¼ miles north-west of Villupuram and 29¼ from Katpadi Junction. The village is about 1½ miles north of the station on the Cuddapah road, at the confluence of the rivers Eiraula and Poyney.

Local Accommodation.—In the village is a Travellers' bungalow, which can accommodate four persons, but occupants must make their own arrangements for furniture, crockery and food, as the bungalow is very poorly furnished and has no cook. Fowls, eggs and milk only are procurable. Rent 8 annas per diem. For natives, there is a choultry which provides accommodation free of charge. Travellers using this must make their own arrangements for food.

Road Conveyance.—Bullock-carts are procurable at the station, if previous notice given. Charge 2 annas per mile.

Local Manufactures and Products.—Paddy, ragi, and sugar-cane are the chief products.

Local Officials.—The Village Munsiff and Kurnam.

Fairs.—A fair is held every Tuesday.

Objects of Interest.—Putalapattu and Kalavagunta 5 miles south of it, are both regarded as somewhat sacred places. A Brahman was, the local legend says, many years ago, carrying the bones of his mother to the Ganges. Halting at Kalavagunta one night, where the rivers above mentioned meet, he found that the bones had all mysteriously changed into the buds of the " Kalava " or blue water lily. At Putalapattu, next morning he again examined them and found the bones had opened into flowers. He did not look at them again until he got to Benares when he found them bones. He therefore concluded that the river near Putalapattu was more sacred than the Ganges, and retracing his steps, cast his mother's bones into the river near a rock in its bed, on which is seen the print of Siva's foot. The bones of deceased persons are even now brought from all parts of the taluq and deposited in the river near this rock.

PAKALA JUNCTION.

Pakala (pop. 5,192) is situated in the Chandragiri taluq of the North Arcot district, 1,208 feet above sea-level, is an important Junction on the Villupuram-Dharmavaram-Gudur Sections, 138¼ miles from Villupuram, 142½ miles from Dharmavaram, and 84 miles from Gudur.

Passengers to and from Vayalpad, Madanapalle *viâ* Chinna Tippa Samudram, and the Southern Mahratta Railway Junction at Dharmavaram change here.

The distances to the principal stations on the South Indian Railway are as under :—

Renigunta (for Madras Railway)	.. ..	33 miles.
Vellore	..	45 ,,
Tiruvannamalai	..	97 ,,
Cuddalore	..	168 ,,
Mayavaram (for Mutupet and Tiruvallur)..	..	214 ,,
Negapatam	..	253 ,,
Tanjore	..	258 ,,
Trichinopoly Junction (for Erode)	..	289 ,,
Madura	..	385 ,,
Tinnevelly	..	484 ,,
Tuticorin	..	484 ,,

Local Accommodation.—There is a Native hotel, where meals are served to all classes of natives at 2½ annas per meal.

Railway Facilities.—About ¼ mile from the station there

is a rest house, belonging to the South Indian Railway Company. When not in use by the Company's officers, European gentlemen not belonging to the Railway may occupy it on obtaining the previous sanction of the Resident Engineer, Vellore. Charge Rs. 1-8 per day. The house is fully furnished for two persons, but travellers must make their own arrangements for food while staying there. The station contains a Ladies' Waiting Room and a Refreshment Room, under the management of Messrs. Spencer & Co. The butler in charge has usually a small stock of travellers' requisites for sale.

Local Manufactures and Products.—The chief products are sugar-cane, tamarind and dry grains.

Local Officials.—The Village Munsiff and Sub-Registrar and the District Traffic Superintendent.

Fairs.—A fair is held every Monday.

Missions, Churches, etc.—Service is held in the Railway Recreation Room, the Chaplain coming from Vellore periodically for this purpose. There is a small Roman Catholic Church near the station, and the American Mission is just commencing to build a church near the station.

Object of Interest.—Pakala is essentially a " Railway " village. There is a large number of Railway buildings here, but nothing to interest the traveller.

PANAPAKAM.

Panapakam (pop. 2,465) is situated in the Chandragiri taluq of the North Arcot district, 7½ miles from Pakala Junction, and 145¾ miles from Villupuram. The village is about half a mile south-east of the station.

Local Accommodation.—Free accommodation is given in a chuttram in the village to all classes of Hindus, who must make their own arrangements for food. There is also a Native hotel where on previous notice, meals are served to all classes of natives at 2½ annas per meal.

Road Conveyance.—Bullock-carts can be obtained at

the station, on previous notice, **at a charge of 2 annas**
per mile.

Local Manufactures and Products.—Sugar-cane and
tamarind are the chief products.

Local Officials.—The Village Munsiff.

CHANDRAGIRI.

Chandragiri (pop. 4,790) is a union town, situated in a
taluq of the same name of the North Arcot district, 18¼
miles from Pakala Junction, 14 miles from Renigunta and
156¾ miles from Villupuram. The town, which is 675
feet above sea-level is 2½ miles south of the station on the
right bank of the River Swarnamukhi and east of the hill,
on which the fort stands.

Local Accommodation.—A portion of the old Palace is
now used as a travellers' bungalow. It has only a table
and a few chairs and as no cook is on the establishment,
travellers should make their own arrangements for everything. Fowls, eggs and milk can be purchased locally.
The charge for the use of the bungalow is one rupee each
person per diem. There are 2 Brahman, and 5 Sudra,
hotels in the town, where meals are served to all classes
of Hindus at 2½ annas per meal.

Road Conveyance.—Bullock-carts are available at 2 annas
per mile.

Local Manufactures and Products.—The chief products
are sugar-cane, paddy, myrabollams, bamboos, avaram
bark and firewood.

Jaggery and gingelly oil are manufactured.

Local Officials.—The Tahsildar, Sub-Magistrate and
Forest Ranger.

Historical.—The fort was originally built in A. D. 1,000
by a Yadava Rajah named Immidi Narasinga, the first of
a line of 11 kings, who reigned in Chandragiri until ousted
by Krishna Deva Roya of Vijayanagar in 1314. On the
fall of the Vijayanagar dynasty in 1565, the deposed king

NEGATIVE BY A. D. G. SHELLEY

first retired to Penukonda and twenty-seven years later
the seat of Government was removed to Chandragiri. In
1639 Shree Runga Royer of Vijayanagar signed in this
palace the treaty by which the site of the Presidency town
(Madras) was made over to the English. The fort fell
in 1646 into the power of the Sultan of Golconda from
whom it was wrested a century later by the Nawab of
Arcot. In 1758, it was held by Nawab Abdool Wahab
Khan, who assumed the protection of the sacred town of
Tirupati. In 1782, it was captured by Hyder Ali and
remained subject to Mysore until the Treaty of Siringapa-
tam in 1792, when it came into possession of the British.

Objects of Interest.—There are several very interesting
remains in Chandragiri, among which may be mentioned
the old forts and the two mahals or palaces within the
lower one. The hill fort is constructed on an isolated
rounded mass of gneiss rising some 600 feet above the
surrounding country and dominating the lower fort and
palaces. The hill is surrounded by two walls of enormous
blocks of granite, the outer of which is the more pretentious
both in massive strength and defensive merit. The fortifications are discontinued where the steepness of the hill
side renders ascent impracticable. Upon the summit are
the remains of some small buildings and a pool of water,
while upon the eastern side of the hill is an old gong stand.
A similar stand was erected upon the Tirumalai cliff near
the holy temple, and by means of these gongs the rajahs
used to be informed when the idol had dined after which
they partook of food themselves. The lower fort is divided
into three portions by two inner walls, the latter of which
inclosed the two mahals. One of these was the residence
of the Ladies and is believed to be connected with the
larger building by a subterranean passage. The main
building which faces south is about 150 feet long and has
an imposing and well balanced facade of three storeys.
The sky line is pleasingly broken by Hindu terminations,

the largest of which surmounts the Durbar hall an apartment of about 21 feet square and noted as being the room in which the Deed granting the site of Madras was signed. The lower portion of the building is of stone and the upper of brick in mortar. The illustration shows the front elevation of the building and brings into prominence a lack of ornamentation which suggests the conclusion that the structure was never fully completed. In close proximity to the place are several small temples and mantapams now in ruins. Upon the eastern slope of the hill is a somewhat remarkable boulder, known as the bell rock which when struck produces a clear metallic sound. About a mile east of Chandragiri on the north of the road leading to Tirupati is a decayed temple, once of considerable size and grandeur. The ruins are exceedingly picturesque, the stone sculptures being extensive and well executed while judging from the height of its lower portion the gopurum must have been of great elevation. The Head Works of the Tirupati water supply are situated within a mile of Chandragiri station at the foot of the Railway embankment at the Kalian River crossing.

Sport.—Good shooting (cheetahs, deer, etc.,) can be had in the Reserved Forest, on permission from the Forest Department. Coolies can be hired at 6 annas per diem.

TIRUPATI.

Tirupati (pop. 14,292) is a Municipal town, 514 feet above sea-level, in the Chandragiri taluq of the North Arcot district, 25 miles from Pakala Junction, 6½ miles from Renigunta and 163¼ miles from Villupuram. It is served by two railway stations "Tirupati East" and "Tirupati West," a mile apart, the former being open for passenger traffic only and the latter for both passengers and goods. Tirupati proper is a very old town with some interesting temples and is sometimes called "Lower Tirupati" to distinguish it from Upper Tirupati or Tirumalai.

Tirumalai is about 6 miles from the Tirupati West station, and contains one of the most sacred Hill Pagodas in India. The scenery about Tirupati is very picturesque, the steep cliffs of the Tirumalai range looking down upon it from a distance of about a mile on the north, while to the south and west innumerable ranges of hills rise one above the other as far as the eye can reach. The principal water-supply of the town derived from springs near Chandragiri, is brought to the town through pipes, which deliver the water into two large stone reservoirs.

Local Accommodation.—There is a travellers' bungalow about 1½ miles from Tirupati West, and ½ a mile from Tirupati East stations, which can accommodate two persons, but travellers using it should make their own arrangements for everything, as it contains practically no furniture and there is no cook. Provisions are procurable in the local bazaar. The charge for use of the bungalow is 8 annas per room per diem. Natives can find lodging in 5 chuttrams where accommodation is given free to all classes, but they must make their own arrangements for food. Besides these, there are 3 chuttrams, where meals are served gratis to Brahmans and supplies for 3 days given to Bairagis. Accommodation can also be procured in 5 Brahman hotels and 8 hotels for other classes, the charges being from 2½ to 3 annas per meal. The Local Fund Board maintains a dispensary and the Municipality a hospital in the town.

Road Conveyance.—Jutkas and bullock-carts are available. Charge :—

Jutkas	..	..	.. .. 2 annas per mile.
Bullock-carts	..	..	.. 1½ ,, ,,

Railway Facilities.—There are waiting rooms at both stations for first and second class passengers.

Local Manufactures and Products.—Very good work is locally executed in brass, copper and in red wood (Petrocarpus santalinus). On brass and copper plates, are skilfully engraved, floral devices or pictures illustrating the

42

religious fables of the Hindus; and in red wood, images of the gods are carved. Brass and copper vessels are also made in considerable quantity. The chief products of Tirupati are paddy, ragi and castor seed.

Local Officials.—The Deputy Tahsildar, District Munsiff, Sub-Registrar, Assistant Engineer, P. W. D., Inspector of Police and Hospital Assistant.

Fairs and Festivals.—Pilgrims and religious devotees flock from all parts of India throughout the whole year to Tirupati, but the most important festival is the "Brahma-utsavam" held on the hill annually in the month of September. In April or May, in Lower Tirupati, a feast is celebrated called the "Gangajatra" which is largely frequented by people of the district. At this festival, a large number of buffaloes, sheep, goats and fowls are sacrificed.

Missions, Churches, etc.—About a mile to the north of Tirupati East station are a Lutheran Church and a connected High School.

Clubs.—The native officials of the town have a reading room and library, which is situated about quarter of a mile north of Tirupati East station.

Objects of Interest.—There are about 12 temples in the lower town, many of which are insignificant, the most important being those of Govindarajaswami and Rama-swamy, the former having an imposing gopurum. A mile north of the town is the "Kapila Tirtam" or bathing pool, where all pilgrims bathe before ascending the sacred hill. This pool is a picturesque spot fed by a waterfall and surrounded by muntapams and shrines. Those who can swim are expected to sit upon a figure of Hanuman, the monkey-god, over which the water falls. The most generally adopted ascent to the sacred hills is from Lower Tirupati and commences from a large gopurum at the foot, called "Alipiri" whence the pilgrim proceeds up a long flight of broad steps to the "Gali Gopurum" at the summit. From this a walk of 5 miles over a rough granite pavement provided with resting places and muntapams at intervals, leads through the forest to the town and temple of Tirumalai or Upper Tirupati. The view from the Gali Gopurum or "Wind Tower" which is built on the very edge of the cliffs is magnificent.

Tirumalai (pop. 2,712) is situated at the top of the range, about 6 miles from Lower Tirupati. The range has 7 separate peaks, each of them sacred and each bearing a distinct name. Near one of them named Seshachalum, stands the temple and the whole range is frequently called after this peak. The hills are said to have originally formed part of Mount Meru, the paradise of Siva, and their change of locality to have arisen from a dispute between Adi Sesha, the thousand-headed serpent, and Vayu, the god of the winds as to which of them was the more powerful. To exhibit his strength, Adi Sesha lifted one of the peaks of Mount Meru upon one of his heads, when Vayu raised so terrible a tempest with his breath that the peak was blown away and falling to the earth formed the Tirupati Hills. Near the temple is a large tank surrounded with cut-stone steps called the Swamipushkarani. Every pilgrim bathes in this as the act is a sure purification from sin though the green, stagnant liquid filth which it contains is most uninviting. About 3 miles from the temple is a waterfall and pool known by the name of Papavinasam. Bathing in this is even more morally purifying than bathing in the Swamipushkarani. By standing under this fall, murder and every other sin under the sun may be washed away. The extent of the bather's sinfulness is even by educated Hindus said to be revealed by the water becoming dark and foul in proportion to the wickedness of his life. Besides these, there are many other Tirtams or pools of water all more or less sacred, and to which pathways lead from the town of Tirumalai. They are generally paved with flat stones which bear rudely cut inscriptions to the effect that a certain person came and visited the swami, the idea being that if the dust from a really pious man's foot should chance to fall upon the name, the salvation of the person named is assured. All classes of people may go as far as the "Alipiri Gopurum," but beyond this, none but caste natives can proceed. European officers are allowed to visit Tirumalai, but the desecration has to be removed by ceremonies costing Rs. 105, and prior permission must be obtained from the District Magistrate at Chittoor, who will arrange matters with the temple authorities. The town of Tirumalai is said to be squalid and mean in extreme, most of the buildings being modern choultries erected by native chiefs and small shops. The only structure worthy of notice is a thousand-pillared muntapam on the skirts of the town, which, though much inferior to similar buildings at Madura, Tiruvannamalai and Rameswaram, is still a fine piece of architectural work.

The temple which no European has yet entered is surrounded by three stone walls on the outer one of which are inscriptions. In the centre of the enclosed space is seen a dome. While an inferior gopurum marks the entrance to the enclosure. The size of the outer enclosure is 137 yards by 87 yards. The shrine has a small chamber, lighted only by lamps, which contains the idol, a standing representation of Vishnu in stone, seven feet in height. This idol was originally worshipped as Siva and the ornament of the hair, the cobras carved upon the body, and other peculiarities, prove that Siva and not Vishnu was intended to be represented. In front of the holy of holies is an ante-room, before which is a muntapam having in the centre a brass vessel containing a bag, for the reception of the money and jewels offered by the pilgrims. On either side of it hangs a gong. When struck on the left side it is said to distinctly utter the name "Govinda" and when struck on the right "Narayana."

Sickness and the desire of male offspring are the chief causes which induce persons to make a vow to the Tirupati idol.

A very common oblation by women is the hair of their heads, and there is a spot near the large muntapam where barbers shave these votaries in such numbers that the hair forms an enormous pile.

The temple is one of the richest in Southern India and is controlled by two Jiyengars and the Mahunt. The latter is the secular head and is always a north country Brahman. The Jiyengars are the religious heads and are so holy as to almost rank as divinities. The conduct of the Mahunts has not always been above reproach, one having been ejected from his office by his disgusted disciples, and another having in recent years been sentenced to imprisonment for misappropriating money.

Tiruchanur.—Three miles south-east of Lower Tirupati is Tiruchanur, celebrated for its temple dedicated to Lutchmi.

RENIGUNTA JUNCTION.

Renigunta (lat. 13°38'; long. 79°33'; pop. 781) situated in the Chandragiri taluq of the North Arcot district, 368 feet above sea-level, is a Junction station with the Madras Railway, 32½ miles from Pakala, 51½ miles from Gudur and 170¾ miles from Villupuram.

Passengers for Arkonam, Madras, Cuddapah, Raichur and Northern India change here.

The distances to the principal stations on the South Indian Railway are as under:—

Dharmavaram (for S. M. Railway)	..	..	175	miles.
Vellore	..	..	78	,,
Tiruvannamalai	..	..	130	,,
Cuddalore	..	..	201	,,
Mayavaram (for Mutupet)	..	..	247	,,
Negapatam	..	..	286	,,
Tanjore	..	..	291	,,
Trichinopoly Junction (for Erode)	..	..	322	,,
Madura	..	..	418	,,
Tinnevelly	..	..	517	,,
Tuticorin	..	..	517	,,

Local Accommodation.—There are two chuttrams, where Hindu travellers of all classes, except Pariahs, can obtain free accommodation. They must make their own arrangements for food. Besides these, are 2 Brahman and 4 other native hotels, where meals are served at from 2½ to 3 annas each.

Road Conveyance.—Jutkas and bullock-carts are procurable at the station. Charge :—

Jutkas ..	..	..	.. 2 annas per mile.
Bullock-carts	..	..	.. 1¼ ,, ,,

Railway Facilities.—A waiting-room is provided at the station for first and second class passengers and also a refreshment-room under the management of the Madras Railway. Besides this retiring and sleeping accommodation is available for both Europeans and natives. The charge for the rooms are :—

For Europeans—

Not exceeding 3 hours	..	..	.. 8 annas.
Exceeding 3 and not exceeding 24 hours	..		.. 1 rupee.

For Natives—

Not exceeding 3 hours	..	..	.. 4 annas.
Exceeding 3 and not exceeding 24 hours	..		.. 8 ,,

Local Officials.—The Railway P. W. Inspector and Apothecary.

Missions, Churches, etc.—A Roman Catholic Church has been built near the station.

YERPEDU.

Yerpedu (pop. 598) is situated in the Kalahasti taluq of the North Arcot district, 6 miles from Renigunta, 38½ miles from Pakala and 176¾ miles from Villupuram. The village is about one mile north of the station.

Local Accommodation.—There is a travellers' bungalow about a mile east of the station which can accommodate two persons, but travellers using it must make their own arrangements for everything, as it contains practically no furniture and there is no cook. Provisions are not procurable. The charge for the use of the bungalow, 6 annas per room per diem. For natives, accommodation can be obtained in a choultry in the village, which may be used free of charge, but travellers must make their own arrangements for food.

Local Manufactures and Products.—The only industry is the manufacture of bangles. Paddy, bamboos and firewood are the chief products.

Objects of Interest.—At the foot of a hill to the west of the village is a small temple dedicated to Oottaleswara, where a perennial stream issues from the ground, and being believed to flow from Benares, is called "Kasiboogga."

KALAHASTI.

Kalahasti (pop. 11,754) is the chief town of a taluq of the same name in the North Arcot district. The town, which is 215 feet above sea-level, is built upon the right bank of the Swarnamukhi river, at the extremity of the Nagari hills. These hills are considered so holy in the neighbourhood that it is not permitted to quarry stone or gravel from them.

Local Accommodation.—There is no travellers' bungalow, but H. H. the Rajah of Kalahasti provides a hill-tent with furniture to European travellers and officials, on previous application, for which, of course, no charge is made. Provisions are procurable in the local bazaar. The Rajah maintains a choultry in the town, where meals are supplied free to Brahmans and supplies given to Bairagis, additional accommodation can be obtained in two choultries attached to the temple, where respectable natives may put up, making their own arrangements for food. There are two hotels in the town, where meals are served to all classes of Hindus, except Pariahs, at 2½ to 3 annas per meal.

Road Conveyance.—Jutkas and bullock-carts are procurable at the station. Charges:—

To the Town—
(Fair season) Jutkas ..	..	..	.. 6 annas.
Bullock-carts	..	..	.. 3 „
(Wet season) Jutkas ..	..	..	.. 8 „
Bullock-carts	..	..	.. 4 „

If previous application is made, the Rajah will kindly send a Palanquin to cross the river and in the case of Europeans and native gentlemen, a carriage to drive about in.

Railway Facilities.—A waiting room is provided at the station for first and second class passengers.

Local Manufactures and Products.—Fine lace cloths, bangles and wooden combs are made and indigo is manufactured. Paddy is the chief produce.

Local Officials.—The Deputy Tahsildar, Sub-Magistrate, Sub-Registrar, Police Inspector and Hospital Assistant.

Fairs and Festivals.—The Shivaratri festival which takes place here annually in February is a most important one. The Rajah sends his elephants, horses and retainers to take part in the various processions. As many as 15,000 persons attend this festival; and on the 7th day, a most gorgeous torchlight procession takes place. All the Zemindar's elephants gaily caparisoned and carrying gilded and silver howdahs take part in the pageant, as well as horses with gold and silver trappings, spearmen, torchbearers and the like. This spectacle is worth seeing.

Missions, Churches, etc.—There is a Lutheran Mission Church about 3 miles north-east of the station.

Historical.—The Rajahs of Kalahasti appear to have always belonged to the Velama caste and to have come south with the Vijayanagar kings who made them menkavalgars or minor custodians, from which position they rose to be Poligars. The first man of note seems to have been one Jabbi Naidu, who assisted in raising the siege of Warangal in the 12th century. The next person of whom tradition speaks was Damara Javi Rayanivaru, the first Poligar, and an ally of a local King named Orontangi Pratapa Rudra. The Damarala Varus or Kalahasti Poligars might be described as free lances in the early history of the Zemindari, but in the 15th century having helped the Gajapatti rajahs, they were given large tracts of land, a considerable portion of which was lost on the fall of the

Vijayanagar Dynasty. Kalahasti Poligars had possession of the country as far as Madras and Conjeeveram and from one of them named Damerala Vencatadri Naidu, Mr. Francis Day in 1639 obtained the grant of the site on which Madras now stands. A sanad was obtained from Sree Runga Royal, Rajah of Chandragiri, but it was the Poligar who first invited Mr. Day, the chief of the Armoogam Factory to move to Madras.

In 1790 when the Company's troops were absent in Mysore, the Kalahasti Poligar's son took up arms against his father, who was forced for a time to resign his authority, until the Commandant of Chandragiri marched up and suppressed the disturbance. A few years later, the two Poligars of Kalahasti and Karvetnagar waged a small war against one another, a contest which resulted in many lives being lost. In 1799, two brothers contested the right to possession of the Matta Zemindari in Cuddapah and each invoked the assistance of these Poligars, who, accordingly took opposite sides and both intrigued with the Fouzdar of Cuddapah for considerable sums of money. They took the field with some 6,000 men each and Kalahasti was defeated losing two guns. He, however, reinforced his little army, and, in spite of the remonstrance of Government seized Matta and placed his ally in possession of the estate. In 1801, both Poligars were forced to disband their armed retainers and in the following year obtained permanent sanads as " Zemindars."

Objects of Interest.—The temple, which stands at the foot of the hill, about half a mile from the station is said to have been created by Brahma, and to have been extended and improved by the Cholas and by the Rajah of Vijayanagar. If is dedicated to Siva, and is one of the five " Lingams of the Elements," this being the " Air Lingam." The sacred lamp suspended over the idol though entirely shut off from the breeze is in perpetual motion, the swaying being attributed to Siva manifesting himself in the form of a

43

mysterious and imperceptible current of air. As a matter of fact, the movement of the lamp is due to the rising of the air heated by a lower lamp, but of course, this natural explanation is not accepted by the Hindus. To the south-east of this temple is a rock-cut muntapam, which is called "Manikanniaghattam" in memory of a woman who prayed steadfastly to Siva until he whispered into her right ear the "taraka muntram" or dying prayer. The bodies of those who are at the point of death are often brought to this place, and placed upon their right side, the ear resting upon the ground. At the moment of death, it is asserted, the body turns round upon its left side, while the spirit passes out of the right ear and attains everlasting bliss.

YELLAKARU.

Yellakaru station is situated in the Venkatagiri taluq of the Nellore district, 54½ miles from Pakala, 22 from Renigunta, 29½ from Gudur and 192¾ from Villupuram. There is no village of the name and the station is the boundary dividing the Kalahasti and Venkatagiri Zemindaries.

Sport.—There are said to be panthers in this jungle, but to shoot them it would be necessary for the sportsman to bring with him the beaters and shikarries he requires.

VENKATAGIRI.

Venkatagiri (pop. 9,623) is situated in the Venkatagiri taluq of the Nellore district, 286 feet above sea-level. The Rajah of Venkatagiri resides in the town, about 2 miles from the station, which is 62 miles from Pakala, 22 from Gudur, 29½ from Renigunta and 200¼ from Villupuram.

Local Accommodation.—Two travellers' bungalows are maintained by the Rajah, one close to the Railway station and the other in the town, the former being unfurnished. The latter is fully furnished, but there is no cook. Either bungalow may be occupied without charge, on permission from the Rajah. Provisions can be procured in the local bazaar.

In the town are two choultries, where accommodation can be had, free of charge, by all Hindus, except Pariahs. Travellers must make their own arrangements for food. In another choultry, 50 poor persons are fed daily by the Rajah. Besides the above, are three native hotels, where meals are served at a charge of two annas per meal. Native gentry are accommodated in the Town Hall, free of charge.

Road Conveyance.—Bullock-carts are procurable at the station at a charge of two annas per mile. If European travellers wish to see the town, the Rajah will kindly send a carriage. For this, of course, no charge is made, but previous advice should be sent.

Local Manufactures and Products.—Fine lace cloths and bangles are made and indigo is manufactured. The chief products of Venkatagiri are dry grains and tobacco.

Local Officials.—The Deputy Tahsildar, Sub-Registrar, Apothecary and Police Inspector.

Fairs and Festivals.—In June of every year, a great Car Festival takes place which lasts ten days.

Missions, Churches, etc.—The Lutheran Mission has a church in the town.

Clubs.—There is a reading room in the town, where the *Madras Mail* and the *Illustrated London News* can be seen.

Historical.—The Zemindary was formerly held on military tenure under the Nawab of Arcot. The house of Venkatagiri was founded by Chevy Reddy, 28 generations ago, whose great-grandson, Yerra Yautsama Naidu, a noted warrior, assisted in driving the Pandyan Rajahs of Madura from Conjeeveram. His successors distinguished themselves in all parts of Telingana as far north as Rajahmundry and as far south as Madras. In 1751, the Zemindar asssisted the English against Hyder Ali, who destroyed the town in retaliation. The family has always been distinguished for its loyalty to the British, and, in recognition of this, a sanad was forwarded to the Zemindar with a complimentary letter by Lord Clive, dated 24th August 1802. The present Rajah who is the chief of the Velama caste is the 28th of the line.

Objects of Interest.—The palace of the Rajah and his garden, two temples (one Siva and the other Vishnu) and the water-supply tank.

YENDOD.

Vendod (pop. 1,187) is situated in the Gudur taluq of the Nellore district, 72¼ miles from Pakala, 39¾ from Renigunta, 11¾ from Gudur and 210½ from Villupuram. The village is about two miles north of the station.

Local Manufactures and Products.—Indigo is manufactured, and paddy and mica are the chief products.

Local Official.—The Village Munsiff.

Missions, Churches, etc.—There is a Lutheran Mission Church in the village.

GUDUR JUNCTION.

Gudur (lat. 15°46'; long. 77°51'; pop. 5,749), situated in the Gudur taluq of Nellore district, is a Junction station with the East Coast Railway, 51 miles from Renigunta, 84 from Pakala, and 222¼ from Villupuram. The following are the distances to the most important stations on the South Indian Railway :—

Vellore ..	..	..	..	.. 129 miles.
Tiruvannamalai	..	..	..	.. 181 ,,
Pondicherry	..	..	..	.. 216 ,,
Mayavaram (for Mutupet)	..	..	.. 298 ,,
Tanjore ..	..	..	..	.. 342 ,,
Trichinopoly Junction (for Erode)	..	.. 373 ,,
Madura ..	..	..	..	.. 469 ,,
Tinnevelly	..	..	..	.. 568 ,,
Tuticorin	..	..	..	.. 568 ,,

Local Accommodation.—About quarter of a mile east of

the station is a furnished travellers' bungalow which can
accommodate two persons. It has neither cook nor crockery, so occupants must make their own arrangements for
food. Charge one rupee each person per day. For natives,
a large choultry is provided in the village, where all classes
may put up, free of charge. They must, however, make
their own arrangements for food. Besides the above, are
two hotels, where meals are served to all classes of Hindus
at 2½ to 3 annas per meal.

Railway Facilities.—Waiting accommodation is provided
at the station for first and second class passengers.

Local Manufactures and Products.—Mica is obtained in
moderate quantities, and it is thought that before long, the
industry will largely develop.

Local Officials.—The Head Assistant Collector, Tahsildar, Sub-Magistrate, Sub-Registrar, Police Inspector and
Hospital Assistant.

Missions, Churches, etc.—There is a Lutheran Church
near the station.

PAKALA-DHARMAVARAM SECTION.

DAMALCHERUVU.

Damalcheruvu (pop. 3,581) is situated in the Chandragiri
taluq of the North Arcot district, 4¾ miles from Pakala,
142½ from Dharmavaram and 143 from Villupuram. The
village, which is about quarter of a mile north-east of the
station, is surrounded by lofty granite hills, covered with
low jungle, and lies near the mouth of a valley leading by
the Kallur Pass to the Mysore plateau.

Local Accommodation.—There are two native hotels,
where meals are served on previous notice being given, to
all classes of Hindus. Charge 2½ annas per meal.

Road Conveyance.—Bullock-carts can be had, if previous notice be given, at a charge of 2 annas per mile.

Local Manufactures and Products.—Brown sugar is made in two small factories owned by natives. The chief products are tamarind, sugarcane, paddy, ground-nuts, ragi, dhall, gram and castor seeds. In the reserved forest—soap-nuts, avarum bark, myrabolams and honey are procured.

Local Officials.—The Village Munsiff and Police Inspector.

Fairs.—A fair is held every Sunday in the village.

Historical.—Damalcheruvu is noted for the great battle fought in 1740, some two miles to the north between an invading force of Mahrattas under Raghoji and the Carnatic Nabob, Dhost Ali. The Mahrattas descended from the Mysore plateau by the Kallur Ghaut and were hurriedly opposed by the Nabob who utilized an old earthen embankment which crosses the road as a screen for his artillery. This bund is said to extend from Tirupati to Yelagiri in the Salem district and to mark the frontier between the ancient Chola Kingdom and the more northern Empires. The Mahratta leader succeeded in corrupting the Pulicherla Poligar who allowed his forces to gain the rear of the Nabob's lines under the cover of darkness. By this stratagem, the Nabob's artillery was useless, and after a stubborn fight, the Mahrattas gained a complete victory, both the Nabob and his son being amongst the slain. During Hyder Ali's invasion of the Carnatic in 1780-81, the Kallur Ghaut formed the main route by which the supplies for his troops were drawn from Mysore.

Sport.—Wild boar can be shot in the neighbouring hills.

MANGALAMPETA.

Mangalampeta (pop. 867) is situated in the Chandragiri taluq of the North Arcot district, 11¼ miles from Pakala, 131 from Dharmavaram and 149¾ from Villupuram.

Local Manufactures and Products.—Jaggery is manufactured, and tamarind is exported.

Local Official.—The Village Munsiff.

Fairs.—A fair is held in the village every Saturday.

Sport.—Panthers and deer may be got on the surrounding hills.

PULICHERLA.

Pulicherla (pop. 152) is situated in the Chandragiri taluq of the North Arcot district, 16¼ miles from Pakala, 126¼ from Dharmavaram, and 152¼ from Villupuram.

Local Accommodation.—There is a choultry near the station, where all classes of Native travellers may put up without charge. They must make their own arrangements for food. Provisions can only be obtained on the weekly market day.

Local Manufactures and Products.—Jaggery is manufactured and the chief products are tamarind, paddy, kumboo, ragi and castor seed.

Fairs.—A fair is held here every Wednesday.

PILER.

Piler (pop. 1,781) is situated in the Vayalpad taluq of the Cuddapah district, 25¾ miles from Pakala, 116¾ from Dharmavaram, and 164 from Villupuram. The village is about a mile south of the station.

Local Accommodation.—A two-roomed travellers' bungalow is situated close to the station, which only contains a few chairs, a table and one cot, so travellers should make their own arrangements for furniture and supplies. There is no cook. Charge 8 annas each person per day. Fowls, eggs and milk can be procured locally.

Local Manufactures and Products.—Jaggery is manufactured and the chief products are tamarind, paddy, kumboo and castor seeds.

Local Officials.—The Deputy Tahsildar and Hospital Assistant.

Fairs.—A fair is held every Tuesday.

KALIKIRI.

Kalikiri (pop. 638) is situated in the Vayalpad taluq of Cuddapah district, 34½ miles from Pakala, 108 miles from Dharmavaram, and 172¾ from Villupuram.

Local Manufactures and Products.—The chief products are tamarind, paddy, cheakoy, soapnuts and avarum bark, and the only manufacture is that of woollen carpets.

Local Official.—The Village Munsiff.

Fairs.—A fair is held every Monday.

Objects of Interest.—The scenery about here is very pretty, but beyond this there is nothing noteworthy.

VAYALPAD.

Vayalpad (pop. 4,016) is a union town in a taluq of the same name in the Cuddapah district, 46½ miles from Pakala, 95½ from Dharmavaram, and 184½ from Villupuram. The town is about quarter of a mile north-east of the station.

Local Accommodation.—A travellers' bungalow is situated close to the station, which can accommodate two persons. It contains a few chairs and a table, but no crockery and has no cook, so travellers must make their own arrangements for food and kit. Charge 8 annas for each person per day. Fowls, eggs and milk can be procured locally. For natives of all classes there is a choultry in the town. Occupants must, however, make their own arrangements for food. There are also 4 hotels, where meals are supplied to all classes of natives at 2½ annas per meal.

Road Conveyance.—Bullock-carts are available on previous notice. Charge 2 annas per mile.

Local Manufactures and Products.—There are two large tanneries in the town, and the chief products are tamarind, castor seeds, cholam and tanning bark.

Local Officials.—The Tahsildar, Sub-Registrar and Police Inspector.

Fairs and Festivals.—A fair is held every Wednesday, and there is a ten days' festival in March annually at the temple.

Clubs.—The native officials have a reading room in the town.

Objects of Interest.—Near the station is a hill called "Ancaulamma Konda" crowned by a tall square rock, which is a very conspicuous landmark for 10 miles round. Gurram Konda, 10 miles north of this station, was once an important hill fortress and is situated in a commanding position on an isolated rock. It was built by a Pathan Nawab after the fall of Vijayanagar and remained one of the principal Muhammedan strongholds till the fall of Seringapatam in 1799. Near the fort are several sculptured Muhammedan buildings and the tomb of Mir Rajah Ali Khan, uncle of Tippoo. There is a Persian inscription on this tomb embodying an epitaph, and the date of Ali Khan's death in 1780. Gurram means a horse and Konda a hill, and the current story is that a horse, which was supposed to be the guardian of the fort, was always kept on the top of the hill that, as long as the horse remained there, the fort would be impregnable. It is said that for generations this horse, or, at all events, a descendant of it, was kept in a stable in the upper fort. At length a Maharatta thief made the attempt to steal the horse. He climbed up the bare perpendicular rock by making steps with long iron nails, and, on reaching the top, gained the stable, and, wonderful to relate, conveyed the horse down the cliff in the same way that he had ascended. The upward climb must have been perilous enough, but was nothing compared to this miraculous descent. He reached the foot of the hill in safety, but, while stopping in a tope to rest, was captured together with the horse. The Governor of the fort, astonished at the boldness and skill of the thief, contented himself with inflicting the comparatively lenient punishment of cutting off both his hands. The

44

spell had, however, been broken, the divine horse had been carried away, and, when next the fort was attacked, it was taken. At Targonda, 4 miles north of Vayalpad, is an old Vishnu temple of some importance.

CHINNA TIPPA SAMUDRAM.

Chinna Tippa Samudram (pop. 2,642) is situated in the Madanapalli taluq of the Cuddapah district, 51½ miles from Pakala, 90½ from Dharmavaram, and 189¾ from Villupuram. As it is about 2,000 feet above sea-level the climate is very cool and pleasant. Passengers for the small hill station of Madanapalli alight here.

Road Conveyance.—Jutkas and bullock-carts are available at the station. Charges :—

Jutkas	..	..	.. 2 annas per mile.
Bullock-carts	..	..	.. 1½ ,, ,,

Railway Facilities.—There is a waiting room at the station for first and second class passengers, and also a refreshment room, under the management of Messrs. Spencer & Co., where light refreshments are procurable. A rest house belonging to the Railway Company, within the station compound, when not in use by the Company's officers, may be occupied by European gentlemen not belonging to the Railway on obtaining the previous sanction of the Resident Engineer, Vellore. The bungalow can accommodate 2 persons at a time and is fully furnished, but travellers using it must make their own arrangements for food. The charge for use of bungalow is Re. 1 for each person per diem.

Local Manufactures and Products.—The chief products are tamarind, oil seeds and ragi, and near Madanapalli jaggery is manufactured.

Local Official.—The Village Munsiff.

Sport.—Excellent duck shooting can be had here in the cold season.

Madanapalli.—About eight miles south-west of Chinna

Tippa Samudram is Madanapalli, the sanitarium of the Cuddapah district. It was once the residence of a Poligar, whose family is now extinct, but the remains of his old fort still exist. This town is the favourite resort of the pensioned officials of the district. The Sub-Collector, Assistant Superintendent of Police, District Forest Officer and Executive Engineer have their head-quarters in Madanapalli. An European Club and an American Mission Depôt are among the institutions of the place.

KURABALAKOTA.

Kurabalakota (pop. 3,836) is situated in the Madanapalli taluq of the Cuddapah district, 57½ miles from Pakala, 85 from Dharmavaram, and 195¾ from Villupuram. The village is about 1½ miles south-east of the station. For travellers coming from the north, this is the station to alight at for Madanapalli.

Road Conveyance.—Jutkas and bullock-carts are procurable at the station. Charges :—

Jutkas	..	..	..	.. 2 annas per mile.
Bullock-carts	..	..	..	.. 1½ ,, ,,

Local Manufactures and Products.—Jaggery is made, and castor seeds, tamarind, kumboo, avarum and konnam bark produced.

Local Official.—The Village Munsiff.

Fair.—A fair is held every Monday.

Horsleykonda.—About seven miles to the west of Kurabalakota is the highest peak in the district, called Horsleykonda after a Collector, who was the first to build on it. The hill rises to 4,100 feet above sea-level, and is free from fever. It is ascended by a ghaut-path about 4 miles in length. The climate is from 10 to 12 degrees cooler than that of the plains below. The bungalow built by Mr. Horsley now belongs to the Forest Department and can only be occupied with the permission of the Forest Officer. Travellers, obtaining permission to occupy, have to pay a charge of 8 annas per diem, and must take with them servants, provisions and such furniture as they require. The American Mission also possess a bungalow on this hill.

TUMMANAMGUTTA.

Tummanamgutta (pop. 679) is situated in the Madanapalli taluq of the Cuddapah district, 66¾ miles from Pakala, 75¾ from Dharmavaram, and 205 from Villupuram. The village is about a mile east of the station.

Local Accommodation.—About two miles east of the station is a travellers' bungalow, which can accommodate two persons. As it contains only a table and a few chairs and no cook, and no provisions are procurable, occupants must make their own arrangements for food and lodging. Charge for use of bungalow :—

				RS.	A.	P.	
For single person	..	..	..	1	0	0	} per diem.
For a family	..	..	..	1	8	0	

Road Conveyance.—Bullock-carts can be had, if previous notice is given, at a rate of 2 annas per mile.

Local Manufactures and Products.—The chief products are paddy, kumboo, ragi, gram and castor seeds.

Local Official.—The Village Munsiff.

Fairs.—A fair is held every Saturday at Burnkayakotta, about two miles from the station.

Missions, Churches, etc.—There is an American Mission Church about a mile from the station, and one close to the travellers' bungalow.

Sport.—Good shooting can be got in the adjacent hills, in which tigers and bears are frequently seen, and sambur and deer occasionally met with. Shikarries can be engaged at 8 annas, and coolies at 4 annas per diem.

Horsleykonda.—Although about three miles nearer this station than Kurabalakota, Horsleykonda is better reached from the latter station, as pony-jutkas are there available.

Objects of Interest.—Alongside the line at mile 304, near Tummanamgutta station, is a granite stone some 14 feet

COBRA STONE NEAR TUMMANAMGUTTA

in height which has weathered into an extraordinary resemblance to the head of a cobra with expanded hood. It is, at first, difficult to believe that the stone has not been shaped by the hand of man, but a close inspection of plate No. 37 will show that this is not the case.

BATTULAPURAM.

Battulapuram (pop. 365) is situated in the Madanapalli taluq of the Cuddapah district, 72¼ miles from Pakala, 70¼ from Dharmavaram, and 210¼ from Villupuram. The village is about 1½ miles north-east of the station.

Local Manufactures and Products.—The chief products are tamarind, ragi, kumboo and cholum.

MULACALACHERUVU.

Mulacalacheruvu (pop. 1,073) is situated in the Madanapalli taluq of the Cuddapah district, 77 miles from Pakala, 65¼ from Dharmavaram, and 215¼ from Villupuram.

Road Conveyance.—Bullock-carts can be had, if previous notice is given, at a rate of 2 annas per mile.

Local Manufactures and Products.—Jaggery is manufactured, and the chief products are paddy, cholum, kumboo, beans, gram, castor seeds and tamarind.

Local Official.—The Village Munsiff.

Fairs.—A fair is held every Friday at Soampulli, about four miles from this station.

Objects of Interest.—About three miles south-east of the station, on a hill called Kanukonda, is a temple dedicated to Tiruvenketanathaswami (Vishnu), but by the side of the image of the deity is a Siva Lingam. The god is therefore called Harihara, *i.e.*, the conjoint deity. The temple is said to have been founded by Nandana Chakravati Roya and to have been subsequently enlarged. One mile south-east of this, and four from the Railway station, is a place of pilgrimage called Soampulli, where there is also a very fine old Vishnu temple with some very good stone-carving.

In front of the pagoda stands a sculptured monolithic pillar 50 feet high. About 1½ miles east of this is the fort of Causincote, the age of which is approximately 800 years.

TANAKALLU.

Tanakallu (pop. 3,236) is situated in the Kadiri taluq of the Cuddapah district, 86½ miles from Pakala, 56 from Dharmavaram, and 225 from Villupuram.

Local Manufactures and Products.—The chief products are gram, tamarind, avarum and konnam bark and castor seeds.

Local Official.—The Village Munsiff.

Fairs.—A fair is held here every Saturday.

NALLACHERUVU.

Nallacheruvu (pop. 2,472) is situated in the Kadiri taluq of the Cuddapah district, 94½ miles from Pakala, 48½ from Dharmavaram, and 232¾ from Villupuram. The village is about 2½ miles south-east of the station.

Local Manufactures and Products.—The chief products are cholum, beans, tamarind and avarum bark.

Local Official.—The Village Munsiff.

Sport.—Good shooting is obtainable on the surrounding hills, antelope and wild boar being found, as well as larger game.

KADIRI.

Kadiri (pop. 6,059) is a union town in the Kadiri taluq of the Cuddapah district, about 2,000 feet above sea-level, 100½ miles from Pakala, 42¼ from Dharmavaram, and 238½ from Villupuram. The whole taluq is very rocky and barren and is cut up by detached rocky hills perfectly destitute of vegetation. Though so high above sea-level, Kadiri is hot during the summer season. The ryots are then entirely dependent on wells for water, the rivers and almost all the tanks being quite dry. The wells are constructed at great cost and with considerable labour, being often from 30 to 40 feet in depth and requiring four pairs of bullocks for drawing water. The Muduleru rises in the taluq and the Paupugnee passes through it, but they are of little advantage as far as the supply of water is concerned.

Local Accommodation.—There is a travellers' bungalow about a mile north-west of the station, which has two rooms, but neither furniture, crockery nor servants. Travellers occupying this must make their own arrangements for everything. Fowls, eggs, milk and vegetables can be purchased in the bazaar, but bread cannot be obtained. The charge for the use of the bungalow is 8 annas per day of 24 hours or part of it. For natives of all classes, except Pariahs, a choultry is kept up in the town, where accommodation is supplied free of charge. Travellers must make their own arrangements for food. There are also two Brahman and 8 other hotels, where meals are served at from 2½ to 3 annas per meal.

Road Conveyance.—Bullock-carts are procurable at a charge of 2 annas per mile.

Railway Facilities.—Within the station compound is a rest house belonging to the South Indian Railway Company. When not in use by the Company's officers, European gentlemen, not belonging to the railway, may occupy it, on obtaining the previous sanction of the Resident Engineer, Vellore. This bungalow is partially furnished (no cots), and there are no servants. The charge for its use is 12 annas for each person per day.

Local Manufactures and Products.—There is a tannery about a mile east of the station where skins are dressed and tanned. The chief products of Kadiri are wheat, cholum, horse-gram, kumboo, castor seeds, tamarind, chillies and avarum bark.

Local Officials.—The Tahsildar, Sub-Magistrate, Sub-Registrar, Police Inspector and Apothecary.

Fairs and Festivals.—A fair is held every Sunday. During February and March, a festival is held in the temple, to attend which people come from Bellary, Mysore and other distant places. Two days after the car procession, Pariahs are allowed to enter the temple, after bathing in the river Muduleru.

Missions, Churches, etc.—There is an American Mission Church about three-quarters of a mile from the station.

Objects of Interest.—Kadiri possesses a large pagoda dedicated to Narasimmaswami, or the boar incarnation of Vishnu, and which has two stone columns 40 feet in height in front of it. An image of the god is said to have been found in an ant-hill under a Chendra tree, whose Sanskrit name is " Khadri," and when the jungle was cleared by Renga Naidu, a Poligar of Patnam, and the pagoda built, this name was given to the town which arose round it. It was for a long time the practice to let loose a tiger at the Pongul festival, which tiger was at once shot. On one occasion, however, an ill-directed shot resulted in loss of human life, when this dangerous practice was stopped by Mr. Smith, a late Collector of the district. Kadiri shews signs of having been at one time a Mussalman town for, though the building shews no signs of Muhammedan architecture, there are a very large number of tombs and mosques, mostly decayed around the town within a two-mile radius.

KALASAMUDRAM.

Kalasamudram (pop. 1,069) is situated in the Kadiri taluq of the Cuddapah district, 109 miles from Pakala, 33¾ from Dharmavaram, and 247¼ from Villupuram. The village, which is about half a mile from the station, is surrounded by hills on all sides.

Road Conveyance.—Bullock-carts can be had, if previous notice is given, on payment of 2 annas per mile.

Local Manufactures and Products.—The chief products

are cholum, ragi, wheat, kumboo, horse-gram and castor seeds.

Fairs.—A fair is held every Monday at Patnam village, about a mile from the station.

Objects of Interest.—About four miles east of the station are some caves in the hills, which are said to have been occupied by Rama and his wife Seeta.

Sport.—Good shooting can be obtained on the surrounding hills, where deer, wild boars and cheetahs are found.

MALAKA VEMALA.

Maluka Vemala (pop. 727) is situated in the Kadiri taluq of the Cuddapah district, 114 miles from Pakala, 28¾ from Dharmavaram, and 252¼ from Villupuram, and is surrounded by a range of lofty hills.

Local Manufactures and Products.—The chief products are wheat, ragi, cholum, horse-gram and dhall gram.

Local Official.—The Village Munsiff.

Fairs.—A fair is held every Thursday at Reddipally, and one every Monday at Patnam, 5 and 3 miles, respectively, from this station.

Sport.—Excellent duck shooting can be had in the cold season, but as the tanks are large, it is advisable to come provided with a collapsible boat or some other means of getting within range of the birds. Wild boars, deer and cheetahs can be found in the surrounding hills.

MUDIGUBBA.

Mudigubba (pop. 422) is situated in the Kadiri taluq of the Cuddapah district, 120¾ miles from Pakala, 22 miles from Dharmavaram, and 259 from Villupuram. The village is about half a mile south of the station.

Railway Facilities.—About a quarter of a mile from the station is a rest house belonging to the South Indian Railway Company. When not in use by the Company's officers, European gentlemen, not belonging to the Railway, may occupy it, on obtaining the previous sanction of the Resident Engineer, Vellore. This bungalow is unfurnished and there are no servants. The charge for occupancy is 12 annas for each person per diem. Provisions are not procurable, so travellers must make their own arrangements for everything.

Local Manufactures and Products.—The chief products are cholum, ragi, kumboo and horse-gram.

Local Official.—The Village Munsiff.

Sport.—Good shooting can be had in the surrounding hills, bear and deer being the chief game.

MUKTAPURAM.

Muktapuram (pop. 400) is situated in the Kadiri taluq of the Cuddapah district, 125½ miles from Pakala, 17¼ from Dharmavaram, and 263¾ from Villupuram.

Local Manufactures and Products.—The chief products are cholum, ragi and kumboo.

Fairs.—A fair is held every Monday at Kodavanlapulli, about 6 miles from this station.

Sport.—Excellent duck shooting can be had here in the season, and bears, cheetahs, deer, etc., can be obtained on the surrounding hills.

CHINNEKUNTAPALLI.

Chinnekuntapalli (pop. 1,162) is situated in the Dharmavaram taluq of the Anantapur district, 133¾ miles from Pakala, 9 from Dharmavaram, and 272 from Villupuram. The village is about half a mile from the station.

Local Official.—The Village Munsiff.

DHARMAVARAM JUNCTION.

Dharmavaram Junction (pop. 6,836), situated in the Dharmavaram taluq of the Anantapur district, 142½ miles from Pakala, and 280¾ miles from Villupuram, is the terminal station of the Pakala-Dharmavaram section and the Junction station with the Southern Mahratta Railway.

Passengers for Bangalore, Anantapur, Guntakul, Bellary, etc., change here.

The following are the distances to the most important stations on the South Indian Railway:—

Kadiri ..	.. 42 miles.
Renigunta (for Madras Railway)	.. 175 ,,
Vellore ..	.. 187 ,,
Tiruvannamalai ..	.. 239 ,,
Pondicherry ..	.. 304 ,,
Mayavaram (for Mutupet)	.. 356 ,,
Tanjore ..	.. 400 ,,
Trichinopoly Junction (for Erode)	.. 431 ,,
Madura ..	.. 527 ,,
Tinnevelly ..	.. 626 ,,
Tuticorin ..	.. 626 ,,

Local Accommodation.—There are two chuttrams, where natives of all classes (except Pariahs) can find accommodation free of charge. They must make their own arrangements for food. Additional accommodation is also obtainable in 3 Brahman and 5 other hotels near the station, where meals are served at from $2\frac{1}{2}$ to 3 annas per meal.

Road Conveyance.—Bullock-carts are procurable at the station at a charge of 2 annas per mile.

Railway Facilities.—A waiting room is provided at the station for first and second class passengers, and also a refreshment room maintained by the Southern Mahratta Railway.

Local Manufactures and Products.—Silk cloths of superior quality are manufactured, and the chief products are paddy, ragi and cholum.

Local Officials.—The Tahsildar, Sub-Magistrate, Sub-Registrar, Police Inspector and Apothecary.

Historical.—The town was founded by Kriyashacty Wodeyar, of Mysore, and was formerly fortified. The fort walls have been demolished, and only the ruins now remain.

Sport.—Good duck shooting can generally be obtained on the large Dharmavaram tank, but to properly cover the water several guns are required.

MAYAVARAM-MUTUPET BRANCH.

MANGANALLUR.

Manganallur (pop. 1,124), on the Mayavaram-Mutupet Branch line, is situated in the Mayavaram taluq of the Tanjore district, 5 miles from Mayavaram, 49 from Mutupet, and 179 from Madras (Egmore). The village, which is on the north bank of the river Arasilar, is about three-fourths of a mile from the Railway station.

Local Accommodation.—In the village is a choultry, where native travellers of all classes (except Pariahs) can find accommodation free of charge. They must, however, make their own arrangements for food.

Road Conveyance.—Bullock-carts can be obtained at the station, if previous notice is given, the fare being 2 annas per vehicle per mile.

Local Manufactures and Products.—Paddy is the chief product.

Local Official.—The Village Munsiff.

Objects of Interest.—At a place called Valavoor, about a mile and a half north of this station, is a Siva temple with inscriptions, which attracts a large number of worshippers during the time of its annual festival, held in the months of April and May. The legend with regard to this temple is as follows :—

In remote ages many Rishis with their families lived in the Darakavanam (sacred forest) at Valavoor, where they passed their days in penance and meditation. The god, Siva, in order to test their honesty of purpose, disguised himself as a beggar and appeared naked before them holding in his hand a " Thiruvasee " (cocoanut shell for alms) and singing sacred songs very melodiously. The wives of the Rishis, hearing the music, came out of their houses, and, being attracted by his beauty and his sweet songs, followed him for a considerable distance, some of them throwing

their bangles down and otherwise showing they could not
control themselves.   They wanted to embrace the Swami,
but he replied that he would embrace them at Madura in
the form of a Chetty (bangle-seller), and so saying picked
up all the bangles and disappeared.   The Rishis, having
heard of their wives' behaviour, determined to kill the supposed beggar, and, for this purpose, made a big yagam or
sacrifice and thus raised several devils, giants and other
monsters, whom they ordered to destroy Siva.   This they
could not do, and the Rishis then procured an elephant
which they directed to swallow Siva.   This it did to the
grief of Parvati and her son Skandar, who witnessed the
scene.   Siva, however, soon burst the body of the animal,
which he afterwards wore as a garland round his neck,
and his deliverance is thus represented in the temple to
the present day.

PERALAM JUNCTION.

Peralam (pop. 961) is situated in the Nannilam taluq
of the Tanjore district, 10 miles from Mayavaram, 44
from Mutupet, 15 from Karaikkal, and 184 from Madras
(Egmore).   This station is the Junction for the Peralam-
Karaikkal Railway and that at which the Customs examination takes place on goods, luggage or parcels arriving
from French territory.   No duty is levied on goods going
into French possessions.   Passengers going on a short
visit beyond the English frontier are advised to declare
the contents of their baggage to the Customs (Sayer)
Superintendent at Peralam, depositing with him such
articles as would be dutiable if brought from French territory and which will be returned free when they again
reached British soil.

The scale of charges for dutiable articles are 5 per cent.
ad valorem.   Piece-goods are charged at $3\frac{1}{2}$ per cent., and
food-grains are passed free.

Local Accommodation.—A travellers' bungalow near the

station. Close by is a choultry for natives, where all classes can find accommodation free of charge, but they must make their own arrangements for food. There are also two native hotels in the village, where meals are served at 2½ annas each.

Road Conveyance.—Bullock-carts are usually procurable at the station, the fare being 2 annas per mile.

Railway Facilities.—Waiting accommodation is provided at the station for first and second class passengers.

Local Manufactures and Products.—Paddy is the chief product.

Local Officials.—The Customs (Sayer) Superintendent, Sub-Registrar and Revenue Inspector.

Objects of Interest.—Two miles south-east of this station is Tirumalappathu, a place of pilgrimage, containing a Siva temple. At the time of the annual festival, during the month of Vyasi (May or June), large numbers of worshippers assemble from all parts of the district.

AMBAGARATTUR.

Ambagarattur (pop. 390) is situated in French Territory, 5 miles from Peralam, 10 from Karaikkal, 15 from Mayavaram, and 189 from Madras (Egmore).

Local Manufactures and Products.—Paddy is the chief produce.

Local Officials.—There is a Customs (Sayer) Superintendent here for examining the road traffic between French and British territory.

TIRUNALAR.

Tirunalar (pop. 9,186) is situated in French territory, 10 miles from Peralam, 5 from Karaikkal, 20 from Mayavaram, and 194 from Madras (Egmore). The town, which possesses several tanks with good drinking water, is about half a mile north of the station.

Local Accommodation.—In the town are 4 chuttrams, where accommodation can be had free by all classes of native travellers, except Pariahs, but those using it must make their own arrangements for food. In addition there are two native hotels, where meals are served to all classes at 2½ annas per meal.

Road Conveyance.—Bullock-carts can be had at the station, if previous notice be given, the fare being 2 annas per mile.

Local Manufactures and Products.—Paddy is the chief product.

Local Officials.—The Adjutant de Police Notaire, Ecrivain de l'etat, Receveur Adjoint.

Fairs and Festivals.—The " Vasanta Utsavam " festival lasting 20 days is held annually in the Siva temple here during April and May. Five cars are then drawn round the main streets by the large number of worshippers who attend from surrounding parts. Another festival called " Swamy Paythi " is celebrated once in every 2½ years, when about 30,000 pilgrims attend.

Missions and Churches.—About 2 miles north of the station is a Roman Catholic Church.

Objects of Interest.—The Siva temple, the shrine in which is dedicated to " Darbaraniaswaraswami."

KARAIKKAL.

Karaikkal (lat. 10°55′ N.; long. 77°24′ E.; pop. 34,770), the chief town of the French province of the same name and the terminal station of the Peralam-Karaikkal Railway, is situated on the Coromandel Coast about 1½ miles from the mouth of the river Arasilar, one of the branches of the Cauvery. This place, which is in charge of an Administrateur, who is subordinate to Pondicherry, is a nicely laid out healthy little town, the streets being for the most part broad and straight and, in some cases, planted with trees.

The distances to the principal stations on the South Indian Railway are as under :—

Peralam Junction ..	..	..	..	15 miles.
Mayavaram Junction	..	..	..	25 ,,
Villupuram (for Pondicherry) ..	..	..	101 ,,
Chingleput (for Conjeeveram) ..	..	..	165 ,,
Madras (Egmore) ..	..	..	..	199 ,,
Tanjore ..	..	..	..	69 ,,
Trichinopoly	..	..	..	100 ,,
Madura ..	..	..	..	196 ,,
Tinnevelly or Tuticorin	..	..	295 ,.

Local Accommodation.—For European travellers there is no accommodation, except the waiting rooms at the station, as the only travellers' bungalow in the place is reserved for the use of French officials travelling on duty. For natives, there are 4 chuttrams, where free accommodation can be obtained by all classes, who must, however, make their own arrangements for food ; and 2 hotels, where meals are served at from 2½ to 3 annas each.

Road Conveyance.—To Negapatam and Tranquebar, 12 and 7 miles distant, respectively, are good metalled roads. Jutkas and bullock-carts can be had at the station, if previous notice be given, the fares being 2 annas and 1½ annas per vehicle per mile respectively.

Railway Facilities.—There are two Railway stations, one at the north end of the town called "Porear Road" and the other Karaikkal near the European quarter of the town. At the latter station, in addition to a waiting room for first and second class passengers, is sleeping accommodation (one bed), a lavatory, and a saloon reserved.

Shipping Arrangements.—The port carries on a considerable trade in rice with Ceylon ; and in betel-nuts, sandalwood, camphor, spices and crackers with the Straits Settlements. There is also a large passenger traffic with Penang and Singapore, the B. I. S. N. and Asiatic Companies' steamers calling here regularly every fortnight. The port is in charge of a Harbour Master (Maitre de Port), and there is a well-organised boat service. In front of the Port office, which is about a quarter of a mile south of Karaikkal station, is a jetty at which passengers land and embark, and cargo is shipped. The charge for a boat from the jetty to the steamer is Rs. 3, the journey occupying about an hour.

Local Manufactures and Products.—The weaving of country cloth is the principal industry, and paddy is the chief local production.

Local Officials.—The Administrateur (Administrator) Juge President (Judge), Procureur de la Republique (Public Prosecutor), Lieutenant de Juge (Sub-Judge), Medecin des Colonies (Doctor), Percepteur (Treasurer), Recevur de l'enregistrement, (Collector), Conducteur dos ponts et chausse's (Sub-Engineer), Maitre de Port (Port officer), Juge de Paix (Justice of the Peace), Commissaire de Police (Commissioner of Police), Directeur d'Ecoles (Director of Schools), Superieur de College (Principal of the College), and Maire (Mayor).

Fairs and Festivals.—On the 14th of July is celebrated annually the "Fête Nationale." In October, the annual "Kandiri" festival is held at the Muhammedan mosque and in June the Mango festival at the Hindu temple. The legend with regard to this last festival is as follows:—

On a certain occasion an individual in Karaikkal sent to his wife, Kariamman, two mangoes of a special kind, with strict orders that they should be kept and served to him at his meals. In the meantime a sanyasi (recluse) came to the woman's house and begged for meals, whereupon she, in accordance with custom, invited the recluse into her house and served him with the best she could. After the recluse had had the meal, he asked for dessert. The woman having no other fruit than the two mangoes sent by her husband, deliberated, but thinking that her husband would no doubt give her one and take one for himself, gave hers to the visitor. He finding the fruit delicious begged for another. She was then puzzled, fearing her husband's

46

anger if she gave away the other mango, and the maledictions of the recluse if she refused. Finally her devotion for the aged recluse prevailed and she gave him the other mango and he, after pronouncing his benediction, departed. The husband shortly afterwards returned and asked for the mangoes, whereupon the wife with implicit belief in god went to the place where the mangoes had been kept and there found two others resembling those she had parted with. She gave these to her husband who, on tasting them, found them unusually delicious, but detected that they were not those he had sent. After taxing his wife for an explanation, she finally confessed what had occurred, when the husband overjoyed prostrated himself at her feet. She could not bear this and prayed that she might be destroyed. This request was granted and her body immediately crumbled into dust, but divine honours have ever since been paid to her memory. On festival occasions mangoes are thrown on the ground in front of the temple, the crowd scrambling for them.

Missions and Churches.—The Church of " Notre Dame des Anges " is a fine building of the Gothic order of architecture, the steeple of which was recently re-erected at the expense of Madame Laforgue, a munificent lady of the town.

Historical.—The French seized the town in 1736 and constructed a fort, which was taken by the English on the 5th April 1760. Five years later it was restored, but it was seized again in 1778 and finally restored by treaty in 1814, on condition that no fortifications should be erected therein. By the terms of the treaty, no military are to be retained, but such as are required for police duties. Karaikkal formed the base of Lally's operations against Tanjore.

Objects of Interest.—The " Hotel du Gouvernement," the residence of the " Administrateur " a fine building close to Karaikkal Railway station ; the Church of " Notre Dame des Anges," the "Hospital Colonial" near the Church; and the "Petit Seminaire" containing about 300 scholars and controlled by 4 European and 7 native professors.

Tranquebar.—About 6 miles to the north of Porear Road station lies the old fortified town of Tranquebar, an ancient Danish settlement, which was at one time a busy port and the head-quarters of the Tanjore collectorate. Tranquebar was the first seat of the Protestant Missions in India and even now is one of the principal stations of the Lutheran Evangelical Mission. Many of the former European houses are now in ruins, but there is an old-world restfulness about the place which makes it a favourite resort for those desiring a few days' quiet. The former residence of the Danish Governors, a large furnished house close to the sea belongs to Mr. Ponnusami Nadar, who is kind enough to place it at the disposal of European gentlemen with whom he is acquainted. He has a residence in Porear, a populous native town, some two miles from Tranquebar, and in the grounds surrounding his house is a tank, which affords excellent labeo fishing. In Tranquebar is a large Government Salt Factory, and some old graves of pioneer European Missionaries.

NANNILAM.

Nannilam (pop. 2,758) is a union town in a taluq of the same name in the Tanjore district, 15 miles from Mayavaram, 9 from Tiruvallur, and 189 from Madras (Egmore). The Railway station is at Sennavur, Nannilam being 3 miles west of it.

Local Accommodation.—A travellers' bungalow, which contains a table and a few chairs only and has two rooms, is maintained by the Local Fund Board at Nannilam. The charge for the use of the bungalow is :—

		RS.	A.	P.	
For single person	..	.. 0	8	0	} per diem.
For a married couple	..	.. 1	0	0	

Fowls, eggs and milk are the only articles of food which

can be procured locally. There is no cook at this bungalow.
Close to the Railway station is a chuttram for natives,
where free accommodation can be had by all classes and in
Sennavur are 2 hotels, where meals are served at 2½ annas
each. In Nannilam there are 3 chuttrams, 2 Brahman
hotels and 3 other hotels. Free accommodation is given
to all classes at the former, and meals are served at 2½
annas each at the latter. At Enangudi, a village 2 miles
east of the station, a wealthy cultivator maintains a chuttram, where free meals are given to Brahmans and supplies
to bairagis. The Local Fund Board maintains a dispensary
at Nannilam.

Road Conveyance.—From the Railway station to the town
of Nannilam is a good metalled road. Jutkas and bullock-
carts are usually procurable at the station, the fare being
2 annas per mile.

Railway Facilities.—Waiting accommodation is provided
at the station for first and second class passengers.

Local Manufactures and Products.—Paddy is the chief
product.

Local Officials.—The Tahsildar, Sub-Magistrate, Sub-
Registrar, Police Inspector and Hospital Assistant.

Missions and Churches.—One mile south of Nannilam
is a Wesleyan Mission Church.

Objects of Interest.—At Nannilam is an old Siva temple,
and within 3 or 4 miles are several places of pilgrimage,
among which may be mentioned :—

Thiruppugalur, which contains a famous Siva temple,
where a large festival is held in the Tamil month of Chittrai
(April and May) ; *Thirukkanapuram*, where there is a
Vishnu temple as important as the large one at Srirungam
(Trichinopoly) ; *Thiruchungattangudi* or Rakta aranaiyam
(Red forest) at which an annual festival is held in April
and May ; *Srivanjium* (so called because Vishnu here
recovered his separated wife Lukshmi) where there are
tanks so sacred that bathing in them removes all sin, even
so great a sin as Brahmahatti (the murder of a Brahman) ;
and *Tiruppanayur* containing a Siva temple.

VETTAR.

Vettar (pop. 654) is situated in the Nannilam taluq of the Tanjore district, 20 miles from Mayavaram, 5 from Tiruvallur, and 193 from Madras (Egmore). The station is named after the river Vettar, on the north bank of which it stands, Kangalancheri being the name of the village.

Local Accommodation.—Near Kangalancheri is a P.W.D. free rest house, which can accommodate one person. Travellers wishing to use this bungalow should bring everything with them, as it is unfurnished and has no cook. For natives there is a chuttram, where all classes can find free accommodation, and 2 hotels, where meals are served at 2¼ annas each.

Road Conveyance.—Bullock-carts can be had, if previous notice be given, the fare being 2 annas per mile.

Local Manufactures and Products.—Paddy is the chief produce.

Local Official.—The Village Munsiff.

Missions and Churches.—At Karaiyur, 3 miles east of the station, is a Roman Catholic Church.

TIRUVALLUR JUNCTION.

Tiruvallur (lat. 10°47'; long. 79°41'; pop. 9,415) is a union town situated in the Negapatam taluq of the Tanjore district. It was formerly the chief town of a taluq of the same name. The station is an important Junction on the Tanjore-Negapatam and Mayavaram-Mutupet branch lines. The following are the distances to the principal South Indian Railway stations :—

Negapatam	15 miles.
Mutupet	30 ,,
Tanjore	34 ,,
Trichinopoly	65 ,,
Madura	161 ,,
Tuticorin or Tinnevelly	260 ,,
Mayavaram	24 ,,
Villupuram (for Tiruvannamalai, etc.)	100 ,,
Chingleput (for Conjeeveram, etc.)	164 ,,
Madras (Egmore)	198 ,,

Local Accommodation.—The old Rajah's palace near the temple tank has been converted into a travellers' bungalow and the building is sufficient to accommodate 3 families at one time. It is unfurnished and intending visitors should take their own furniture, crockery and servants. Fowls, eggs and milk can be procured locally. The charge for the use of the bungalow is :—

	RS.	A.	
For single person	0	8	} per diem.
For a married couple	0	12	

For natives there are 4 choultries, where free accommodation is given to all classes, except Pariahs, free meals in addition being given to Brahmans and supplies to Bairagis, and 21 hotels, where meals are served to all classes at from 2½ to 3 annas per meal.

Road Conveyance.—Bullock-carts are usually available at the station, the fare being 2 annas per mile.

Railway Facilities.—Waiting accommodation is provided for first and second class passengers. The Railway Company also maintains a rest house, which can accommodate two persons, and which, when not being used by Company's officials, may be occupied by other European gentlemen, on sanction being first obtained from the Resident Engineer, Cuddalore. The charge for the use of this building, which is partially furnished, is :—

	RS.	A.	
Under 8 hours	0	8	} each person.
Over 8 hours and not exceeding 24 ..	0	12	

Local Manufactures and Products.—The weaving of Native cloths is the principal industry, and paddy is the chief product.

Local Officials.—The Deputy Tahsildar and Sub-Magistrate, Sub-Registrar, Police Inspector, District Munsiff, and Hospital Assistant.

Fairs and Festivals.—A fair is held every Thursday near the Railway station. In March and April, a large festival is held at the Siva temple, which attracts pilgrims from all parts of the district.

Missions and Churches.—The Wesleyan Mission has a small Church in the town.

Clubs.—The Native officials maintain a reading room.

Objects of Interest.—The Siva temple with its 4 large gopurams, and sacred tank in front on an island, in the centre of which is a small pagoda. North of the temple is a stone car, having under one of its wheels the figure of a child. Near the car is a cow with a dead calf, also sculptured in stone.

Within the temple is a 1,000-pillared muntapam, the roof of which is decorated with pictures, now much dilapidated, illustrating stories from Hindu mythology. Outside this muntapam are many stone pillars which are roofed in during the time of festivals. There is but little carving to be seen inside the temple, the best work being the small stone figures placed in the niches of the gopurams. There are five wooden cars belonging to the temple, the largest of which is a fine example of its kind. The group of stone figures to the north of the temple is intended to commemorate a legendary incident in the career of a Chola king named Manuneethekanda, who was noted for his goodness of heart and sense of justice. The god Siva wishing to test the king's reputation for justice, after having disguised himself as a cow and "Yamadarma" (the destroyer) as a calf, went to Tiruvallur to graze in the streets. The king's only son, Veethevidangan, who happened to be driving at this time ran over the calf and killed it. The Prince trembling at the terrible sin he had committed in killing so sacred an animal as a calf and, fearing his father, went to the Brahmans for advice as to how he should free himself from the sin. Meanwhile the cow, being unable to bear her grief, went to the king's palace to inform him of the matter, and, having reached the Palace, she rang the bell with her horns. The king, who was with his ministers at the time, was informed of what had occurred. After consulting with them how best to render his son guiltless he decided that

as all the ceremonies in the world would not restore the calf
to life, it would only be just if he himself experienced the
same grief that the cow had suffered. He therefore ordered
one of his ministers to cause his son to be run over by his
car, but the minister, afraid of executing so dreadful a task,
committed suicide. The king then decided to do the deed
himself and, having ordered his son before him, crushed
him to death under his chariot wheels. Siva, being much
pleased with the king's justice, resumed his proper form,
and, accompanied by Parvati, visited the city, after embracing the monarch, he restored to life the calf, the Prince and
the minister and took them all up with him to heaven.
Four miles west of Tiruvallur is *Tirukkannamangai*, where
there is an important Vishnu temple dedicated to "Bak-
thabaksalar" and the goddess "Abishekavalli" his wife.
An annual festival is held in April and May.

TIRUNATTIYATTANGUDI.

Tirunattiyattangudi (pop. 463) is situated in the Tiruturaipundi taluq of the Tanjore district, 6 miles from Tiruvallur Junction, 25 from Mutupet, 30 from Mayavaram, and
203¼ from Madras (Egmore). The village is about three-
quarters of a mile north-west of the station and is a place of
pilgrimage. Its name is a compound of the words Tiru+
Natti+Yattan+Gudi meaning Holy+Holding+Receiv-
ing+Temple. The legend connected with the place is as
follows :—A General of one of the Chola Kings reigning
at Tanjore had a country seat at this village. Being a
religious man he spent his time, when not in the field, in
worshipping the presiding deity Ruthnapureswara and
Mangalanayaki, his divine spouse. On a certain occasion,
war having broken out, he was called away to the command
of his Sovereign's army. He anticipated the war would
last two years and, before leaving, he provided a store of
grain for his family and for the daily offerings to the deity
sufficient to last the time he would be away. During his

absence a severe famine broke out and the wife finding her store of grain exhausted made use of that set aside for the deity, considering the god would think it no sin on her part to appropriate it for such a purpose. On the termination of the war, the General returned home filled with pleasure at the prospect of resuming his devotions. Great, however, was his horror at finding how the grain had been disposed of and so great was his rage that he at once slew his wife and pursuing his three sons, who on seeing the fate of their mother, had fled for their lives, he caught one up and slew him at a place called Kumaramangalam (place of the son), a second was overtaken and killed at Puttamangalam (a place of the same meaning), the third he killed at Virkunnam (Perspiration Hill). He now returned to put an end to his youngest son and notwithstanding the intercession of his neighbours who pleaded that so young a child could not be guilty of a crime, he threw him up in the air with the intention of receiving him on the point of his sword in the fall, when, lo, the sword was turned into a soft flower wreath and the child was miraculously stayed in the air. The astonished father on looking upward saw the god robed in light with the forms of his slain wife and children standing on either side of him and heard that what had been done had been but to test his faith. He then rising in the air was translated with his wife and children to Kylasa (Heaven). The General was known as Kotpali Nayanar and the village from this time was called Tirunattiyattangudi.

Road Conveyance.—Bullock-carts can be obtained, if previous notice be given, fare 2 annas per mile.

Local Manufactures and Products.—The chief product is paddy.

Local Official.—The Village Munsiff.

TIRUNELLIKAVAL.

Tirunellikaval, 32½ miles from Mayavaram Junction, and 206¼ miles from Madras (Egmore), is situated on the boundary limit of the three taluqs of Negapatam, Tiruturaipundi, and Mannargudi, near the Junction of the

Nannilam to Tiruturaipundi, and the Mannargudi to Negapatam roads.

Produce.—Large quantity of paddy is available for export.

Objects of Interest.—The village of Tirunellikaval is a place of pilgrimage, and in its vicinity there are several Siva temples.

PONNIREI.

Ponnirei (pop. 397) is situated in the Tiruturaipundi taluq of the Tanjore district, 12 miles from Tiruvallur Junction, 19 from Mutupet, 36 from Mayavaram, and 209¼ from Madras (Egmore). The village is three-quarters of a mile east of the station.

Local Accommodation.—Close to the station is a chavadi (resting place), where natives of all classes can find accommodation. They must, however, make their own arrangements for food.

Road Conveyance.—Bullock-carts can be obtained, if previous notice be given, fare 2 annas per mile.

Local Manufactures and Products.—The chief product is paddy.

Local Official.—The Village Munsiff.

TIRUTURAIPUNDI.

Tiruturaipundi (pop. 2,666) is situated in a taluq of the same name in the Tanjore district, 14 miles from Mutupet, 16 from Tiruvallur Junction, 40 from Mayavaram, and 213¾ from Madras (Egmore). The town is about half a mile south-east of the station. Passengers alight here for Kodikary, where sea-baths are taken in January, August and September on new moon days.

Local Accommodation.—In the town are three chuttrams, where accommodation can be had by natives of all classes, except Pariahs, but private arrangements for food must be made. Besides these there are 2 Brahman and 3 other hotels, where meals are served at 2½ annas each.

Road Conveyance.—Bullock-carts are usually procurable at the station, the fare being 2 annas per mile.

Local Manufactures and Products.—The chief products are paddy and cocoanuts.

Local Officials.—The Tahsildar, Sub-Magistrate, District Munsiff, Sub-Registrar, Police Inspector, Sub-Divisional Officer, P. W. D., and Hospital Assistant.

Fairs.—A fair is held every Friday, which is well attended.

Missions and Churches.—In the town is a Roman Catholic Church.

Objects of Interest.—The old Siva temple, which has inscriptions.

PANDI.

Pandi (pop. 444) is situated in the Tiruturaipundi taluq of the Tanjore district, 10 miles from Mutupet, 20 from Tiruvallur Junction, 44 from Mayavaram and 218 from Madras (Egmore). The village is about a mile north-east of the station.

Road Conveyance.—Bullock-carts can be obtained at the station, if previous notice be given, the fare being 2 annas per mile.

Local Manufactures and Products.—The chief product is-paddy.

Local Officials.—The Village Munsiff.

TILLAIVILAGAM.

Tillaivilagam (pop. 2,715) is situated in the Tiruturai-pundi taluq of the Tanjore district, 5 miles from Mutupet, 25 from Tiruvallur Junction, 49 from Mayavaram, and $222\frac{1}{2}$ from Madras (Egmore). The village is about $2\frac{1}{2}$ miles south-west of the station.

Local Accommodation.—At Gopalasamudram, about one mile south-west of the station, is a choultry, where all classes of native travellers, except Pariahs, can find accommodation free, but must make their own arrangements for food. In Tillaivilagam is an hotel, where meals are served to natives of all classes at 2½ annas each, if previous notice be given.

Road Conveyance.—Bullock-carts can be procured on previous notice, the fare being 2 annas per mile.

Local Manufactures and Products.—The chief products are cocoanuts and paddy.

Local Official.—The Village Munsiff and Kurnam.

Fairs and Festivals.—Festivals are held in the Vishnu temple in January, July, September and October.

Objects of Interest.—About 30 years ago, large sized idols of Rama, Lutchmanan, Seetay, Hanuman and Natesan were unearthed. They appear to be made of a mixture of metals in which gold predominates and are worth seeing. A small temple has been constructed for them, and pilgrims from distant places now come there to worship.

MUTUPET.

Mutupet (lat. 10°23'; long. 79°32'; pop. 5,381) is a busy trading port on the river Korayar, 7 miles from the sea and situated in the Tiruturaipundi taluq of the Tanjore district. It has a large Muhammedan (Lubbay) community, who trade principally with Ceylon.

The station is the terminus of the Mayavaram-Mutupet Railway.

The following are the distances to the principal South Indian Railway stations :—

Tiruvallur Junction	30 miles.
Negapatam	45 ,,
Mayavaram Junction	54 ,,
Villupuram Junction	130 ,,
Pondicherry	153 ,,
Chingleput Junction (for Conjeeveram, etc.).. ..	194 ,,
Madras (Egmore)	230 ,,
Tiruvannamalai	172 ,,
Vellore	223 ,,
Pakala	268 ,,

Gudur Junction (for East Coast Railway)	..		..	252 miles.
Dharmavaram Junction (for S. M. Railway)..			..	410 ,,
Tanjore ..	..	..	..	.. 61 ,,
Trichinopoly	..	..	..	.. 95 ,,
Madura ..	..	..	..	.. 191 ,,
Tinnevelly or Tuticorin	..	..	..	.. 290 ,,

Local Accommodation.—Close to the Railway Station is a travellers' bungalow maintained by the P. W. D., which has sufficient accommodation for two families, but is practically unfurnished, and has no cook. The charge for the use of this building is 8 annas for each person per day. Meat, eggs, fowls and milk can be procured locally. For natives there are two choultries, where free accommodation is given to all classes, except Pariahs, but travellers must make their own arrangements for food. Besides these, there are one Brahman and 3 other hotels, where meals are served at from 2½ to 3 annas each.

Road Conveyance.—Bullock-carts are usually procurable at the station, the fare being 2 annas per mile.

Shipping Arrangements.—The river Korayar runs through the town down to the sea 7 miles away. Cargo is shipped from the town into boats of shallow draught which sail down the river and out to sea, where the goods are transferred to large native vessels which ply between Mutupet and Colombo and are generally anchored some 6 to 7 miles from the shore. The journey down the river and out to the ships takes 12 hours in the fair season and 10 in the monsoon, the charge being Rs. 6 per boat. There are 35 boats in Mutupet and 9 large sailing vessels on the Colombo service. Rice is the chief export and 13,565 tons of it were sent to Ceylon in the year 1896-97; betel-nuts and timber are the chief import, but the trade in them is small. A Sea Customs' Superintendent is stationed at Mutupet to collect duty.

Local Manufactures and Products.—The chief products of Mutupet are cocoanuts and salt. The latter is manufactured at Adirampatnam about 8 miles west of the station, from which place salt-fish is also sent inland in large quantities.

Local Officials.—The Customs' Superintendent, Sub-Registrar, and Hospital Assistant.

Fairs and Festivals.—A festival is held in September annually in the Muhammedan mosque, large numbers assembling on the occasion from surrounding villages.

Objects of Interest.—About one mile west of the station is an old musjid, erected to the memory of one Shaik Dawood Avooliah, who died here many years ago.

NEGAPATAM BRANCH.

MARIAMMANKOVIL.

Mariammankovil.—Four miles from Tanjore Junction and 221¼ miles from Madras (Egmore). There is a public road from Tanjore to Negapatam, and its distance from the station is about 5 furlongs.

Objects of Interest.—There are two large temples, Mariamman temple, and Srikothandaramaswami temple, to which pilgrims from remote places resort during the festivals in April and August.

SALIYAMANGALAM.

Saliyamangalam (pop. 1,336) is situated in the Tanjore taluq of the Tanjore district, 8¼ miles from Tanjore Junction, 39 from Negapatam, 53 from Mayavaram Junction, and 226¾ from Madras (Egmore). The village is about 121 feet above sea-level.

Local Accommodation.—At Poondi, about 2 miles west of the station, is a furnished bungalow maintained by a wealthy Mirasidar, which European travellers may occupy free of charge on application. For native travellers of all classes there is a hotel in the village, at which, if previous notice be given, meals are served at 2½ annas each.

Road Conveyance.—To Tanjore (9 miles) and Papanasam (10 miles) is a good metalled road. Bullock-carts can be obtained, the fare being 1½ annas per mile.

Local Manufactures and Products.—Weaving is carried on and paddy and ground-nuts are the chief produce.

Local Officials.—The Village Munsiff and Kurnam.

AMMAPET.

Ammapet (pop. 3,804), 106 feet above sea-level, is situated in the Tanjore taluq of the Tanjore district, 12½ miles from Tanjore, 36 from Negapatam, 56¼ from Mayavaram Junction, and 230 from Madras (Egmore). The village is about a mile north of the station.

Local Accommodation.—In the village are 2 Sudra hotels, where meals are served to natives of all classes at 2½ annas each.

Road Conveyance.—Bullock-carts can be obtained, if previous notice be given, the fare being 1½ annas per mile.

Local Manufactures and Products.—Silk cloths for females and common country-cloths are woven, and paddy is the chief produce.

Local Officials.—The Village Munsiff and Kurnam.

Fairs and Festivals.—A fair is held every Sunday. About 3 miles south of the station is a place called Vaduvur, which contains an old Vishnu temple, at which a festival, attracting many pilgrims, is held during March and April, annually.

NIDAMANGALAM.

Nidamangalam (pop. 2,806) is situated in the Mannargudi taluq of the Tanjore district, between the rivers Vennar and Korayar, 19 miles from Tanjore Junction, 30 from Negapatam, and 236 from Madras (Egmore), and is 78 feet above sea-level.

Local Accommodation.—To Brahmans meals are supplied free of charge, and to bairagis supplies are given, at a well endowed chuttram built here in 1761, by Rajah Pratapa Singh in honour of his Rani Yamoonah Bye Sahiba. Besides this chuttram, there are 3 Brahman and 3 Sudra hotels, where meals are served at from 2½ to 3 annas each.

Road Conveyance.—To Mannargudi (9 miles) and Kumbakonam (15 miles) are good metalled roads. Jutkas and bullock-carts are available at the station, the fares being 1½ annas per mile.

Local Manufactures and Products.—Messrs. Arbuthnot & Co. have a Rice Mill near the station, under the management of a European. The chief produce of Nidamangalam is paddy.

Local Officials.—The Deputy Tahsildar, and Sub-Registrar.

Objects of Interest.—The Korayar head works, where three rivers discharge by means of a fine masonry sluice, is close to the town.

Mannargudi (pop. 20,395) on the southern bank of the Paumaniyar, a branch of the Vennar, has a considerable Brahman population. It contains a bathing tank called Haridranuddy, 1,158 feet long and 837 feet broad, and 9 old temples, 4 of which are Vishnu and 5 Siva. At the Rajah Gopalswami temple, the largest and most important, an annual festival is held in March, which lasts for 16 days. On the 7th day the image of the god is placed under an artificial "Pinnai" tree, the branches of which are hung with the garments and ornaments of females, and around which several nude female figures are represented in a standing attitude begging for their clothes. Krishna is seen seated on a branch playing a flute. This spectacle is one of the credas (plays) of Krishna, who, on a certain occasion, appeared and rebuked certain maidens, who, in observance of a vow, were bathing "*in puris naturalibus.*"

Mannargudi is the chief seat of the Wesleyan Mission in Southern India.

KORADACHERI.

Koradacheri (pop. 612) is situated in the Nannilam taluq of the Tanjore district, 24 miles from Tanjore Junction, 10 from Tiruvallur, 25 from Negapatam, and 241 from Madras (Egmore).

Local Accommodation.—Close to the station is a large travellers' bungalow, maintained by the P. W. D., which, though it can accommodate 4 persons at one time, is practically unfurnished. The charge for the use of this building is :—

For a single person .. .. .. 8 annas } per diem.
For a married couple .. .. .. 1 rupee }

For natives about a furlong north of the station is a chuttram, where all classes can find accommodation, but they must make their own arrangements for food. Besides this, in the village are 1 Brahman and 2 Sudra hotels, where meals are served at 2½ annas each.

Road Conveyance.—Jutkas and bullock-carts are usually available at the station, the fares being 2 annas and 1½ annas per mile respectively.

Railway Facilities.—Waiting accommodation is provided at the station for ladies.

Local Manufactures and Products.—The chief product is paddy.

Local Officials.—The Village Munsiff and Kurnam.

Kodavasal (pop. 7,785), 7 miles north of this station and connected with it by a good road, has two temples and a large Brahman population.

KULIKARAI.

Kulikarai (pop. 587) is situated in the Nannilam taluq of the Tanjore district, 4 miles from Tiruvallur Junction, 18 from Negapatam, 30 from Tanjore, and 247 from Madras (Egmore).

Road Conveyance.—Bullock-carts can be obtained, if previous notice be given, the fare being 1½ annas per mile.

48

Local Manufactures and Products.—The chief products are paddy and cocoanuts.

Local Officials.—The Village Munsiff and Kurnam.

ADIYAKKAMANGALAM.

Adiyakkamangalam (pop. 3,015) is situated in the Negapatam taluq of the Tanjore district, 3 miles from Tiruvallur Junction, 12 from Negapatam, 37 from Tanjore, and 200¾ from Madras (Egmore). The inhabitants are chiefly Muhammedans.

Local Manufactures and Products.—The chief products are paddy and cocoanuts.

Local Official.—The Village Munsiff.

Fairs and Festival.—A festival is celebrated annually in the local mosque in September.

KIVALUR.

Kivalur (pop. 2,108) is situated in the Negapatam taluq of the Tanjore district, 7 miles from Negapatam, 8 from Tiruvallur Junction, 41 from Tanjore, and 205¾ from Madras (Egmore). The village is about half a mile north of the station.

Road Conveyance.—Bullock-carts can be had on previous notice, the fare being 1½ annas per mile.

Local Manufactures and Products.—The chief product is paddy.

Local Officials.—The Village Munsiff and Local Fund Overseer.

Historical.—In 1758, this place was ransacked by Lally in the hope of finding treasure.

Objects of Interest.—An old Siva temple with inscriptions, one of which records a grant of lands to the temple by Tulzagi, Rajah of Tanjore.

SIKKIL.

Sikkil (pop. 2,648) is situated in the Negapatam taluq of the Tanjore district, 3 miles from Negapatam, 12 from Tiruvallur Junction, 45 from Tanjore, and 209¾ from Madras (Egmore).

Local Accommodation.—Near the station are 2 chuttrams, where free accommodation can be had by native travellers of all classes, except Pariahs, but private arrangements for food must be made. In addition, there is an hotel in the village, where meals are served to all classes of natives at 2¼ annas per meal.

Road Conveyance.—Bullock-carts can be had, if previous notice be given, the fare being 2 annas per mile.

Local Manufactures and Products.—The chief product is paddy.

Local Official.—The Village Munsiff.

Fairs and Festivals.—A festival called "Soora Samharam" (to kill a Raksha) is held in November annually at the Siva temple which is well attended. The festival was originated to commemorate the destruction of a demon named Tricira, who lived on the Trichinopoly rock, and with his followers ravaged the country along the Cauvery. Tricira, who was a three-headed giant, was killed by one Suravadhittan, who afterwards ruled as a local chief.

Sport.—Snipe-shooting is obtainable here in the season, and shikaries can be procured at 8 annas per diem.

NEGAPATAM.

Negapatam (lat. 10°46'; long. 79°53'; pop. 59,221) is one of the most important Ports in the Madras Presidency. It is called by the natives "Nagapattanam" or snake-town, and, according to Colonel Yule, is the Malefattan of Arab geographers. This important municipal town, which is situated in a taluq of the same name in the Tanjore district, was the city of Coromandel of the early Portuguese. About 20 per cent. of its population are Lubbays, a bold, active and thrifty race, in descent half-Arab and half-Hindu, who have established prosperous Colonies in Ceylon, Burma and the Straits Settlements. The town, which is divided into three parts, *viz.*, Negapatam proper (south), Velippalaiyam (central), and Kadambadi (north), is situated at the mouth of the river Cadoovaiyar on an open level sandy expanse having a gentle slope to the sea. The South Indian Railway Company has here its Locomotive and Carriage Workshops, employing several thousands of natives, and General Stores Depôt.

The distances to the principal stations on the South Indian Railway are as follows :—

Tiruvallur Junction ..	.. 15 miles.
Tanjore Junction ..	.. 48 ,,
Trichinopoly Junction (for Erode)	.. 79 ,,
Madura ..	.. 175 ,,
Tuticorin or Tinnevelly	.. 274 ,,
Mayavaram Junction ..	.. 39 ,,
Cuddalore ..	.. 85 ,,
Villupuram Junction (for Pondicherry, etc.)..	.. 114 ,,
Chingleput Junction (for Conjeeveram)	.. 178 ,,
Madras (Egmore) ..	.. 212 ,,
Tiruvannamalai ..	.. 156 ,,
Vellore ..	.. 208 ,,
Pakala Junction ..	.. 253 ,,
Dharmavaram Junction (for S. M. Railway) ..	.. 394 ,,
Gudur Junction (for East Coast Railway) ..	.. 336 ,,

Local Accommodation.—There are no hotels for Europeans, but at Kadambadi an unfurnished rest-house is maintained by the P. W. D. The charge for the use of the bungalow is 8 annas for each person per diem. For natives there are two choultries, where accommodation is given free to all classes, but occupants must make their own arrangements for food. In addition are 40 hotels, where meals are served at from 2½ to 4 annas per meal. In Velippalaiyam is a municipal dispensary in charge of an Assistant Surgeon.

Road Conveyance.—Jutkas and bullock-carts are usually available at the station, the fares being 2 annas per mile for jutkas and double bullock-carts, and 1 anna per mile for single bullock-carts. The following charges are, however, levied for journeys to Velanghanny :—

	RS.	A.
Jutkas ..	1	0
Double bullock-carts ..	1	0
Single do. ..	0	8

Railway Facilities.—There is a ladies' waiting room at the station for first and second class passengers, and sleeping accommodation is also provided, the room set apart for this purpose containing two beds. The charge for the use of the room is :—

	RS.	A.	P.
For periods not exceeding 3 hours for each adult	0	8	0
For each child of 12 and under ..	0	4	0
For occupation exceeding 3 hours and not exceeding 24 hours, or one night only for each adult	1	0	0
For each child of 12 and under ..	0	8	0

There is also a refreshment room under the management of Messrs. Spencer & Co., the butler in charge of which has usually a few copies of the Madras newpapers for sale, as well as a small stock of travellers' requisites. In the station compound is a railway dispensary.

Shipping Arrangements.—The Port carries on an active and increasing trade and a large passenger traffic with Ceylon, Burma and the Straits Settlements, and great quantities of cattle and other live-stock are exported annually. Both the B. I. S. N. and Asiatic Companies' steamers call regularly, and a large number of native brigs and barques are owned at and sail from this Port. Steamers lie from a half to one mile from the shore and some 160 boats are employed to take the cargo and passengers on board, the charge for a boat being Rs. 3 to 5, according to the weather. The Port is under the management of a Port Officer, who is also Superintendent of Mercantile Marine, Registrar of Shipping and Emigration Officer. Cargo is landed and shipped at the wharf (opposite the Customs House), on which there are two cranes, each of 3 tons lifting capacity. Government contemplate erecting a screw pile pier shortly which will greatly facilitate work.

The light-house, which is built of stone and painted white, is situated on the wharf and has a fixed white dioptric light of the fourth order, which is visible in clear weather to a distance of 14 miles.

The following is a list of steamer lines calling at Negapatam :—

British India Steam Navigation Company.

Coasting Steamers from Calcutta to Bombay ..   .. Weekly.

Coasting Steamers from Bombay to Calcutta..   .. Do.

  (These steamers also call at Colombo.)

To Rangoon, *via* Cuddalore, Pondicherry and Madras

  (voyage takes 6 days)   ..   ..   .. Weekly.

To Penang and Singapore   ..   ..   .. On alternate

                                                   Wednesdays.

  The voyage to Penang, Singapore and back occupies three weeks, and the steamers on this line are the finest in the Company's Coasting Service, the first and second class passenger accommodation being excellent.

To Colombo, *via* Ammapatam, Tondi and Pamban (voyage

  36 to 40 hours)   ..   .. Every Tuesday.

Asiatic Steam Navigation Company.

Coasting Steamers from Calcutta to Bombay ..   .. Fortnightly.

Coasting Steamers from Bombay to Calcutta ..   .. Do.

Local Manufactures and Products.—Piece-goods are dyed here, and soap is manufactured. The principal exports are rice, cattle, earthenware, ground-nuts and oil, copra, castor seeds, ghee, tamarind, coriander seeds, onions, chillies, tobacco and cigars and dyed piece-goods, while the imports are principally coal, timber, railway material, grains, pulse, turmeric, sandalwood and betel-nuts.

Local Officials.—The Head Assistant Collector, Port Officer, Assistant Superintendent of Police, Assistant Commissioner of Salt and Abkari, Executive Engineer, P. W. D., Assistant Surgeon, Tahsildar, Sub-Magistrate, Sub-Judge, District Munsiff, and Customs Superintendent.

The Madras Bank, and the B. I. and Asiatic S. N. Companies, have agents in the town, in which also reside the Locomotive and Carriage and Wagon Superintendent, the Deputy Locomotive Superintendent, and the General Storekeeper, of the South Indian Railway.

Fairs and Festivals.—A fair is held every Sunday at Velippalaiyam.

Missions and Churches.—St. Peter's, an old Dutch Church, is now used by the Church of England congregation, and the Wesleyan Mission also have a chapel.

Clubs.—At Kadambadi, about 2½ miles north of the station, is an European Club. Visitors may become Honorary Members, on being proposed by one member and seconded by one other. A visitor can remain an Honorary Member for a period not exceeding three consecutive months.

The Wesleyan Mission maintain a reading room near the station.

Historical.—This place was one of the earliest Portuguese Settlements on the Coromandel Coast, but was taken from the Portuguese by the Dutch in 1660, and became head-quarters of the latter. In 1781, it was taken from the Dutch by the English, and 18 years later, was constituted the principal station of the Collector of the District, an arrangement continued until 1845, when the Collector's head-quarters were removed to Tranquebar, and subsequently to Tanjore.

Objects of Interest.—The old Dutch cemetery (near the Railway Company's Workshops) with its quaint and bulky tombs, (two Hindu temples, one dedicated to Siva and the other to Vishnu, a wall of the former containing a stone which bears an epitaph in Dutch in memory of a Dutchman who died in A.D. 1777), the bastion (the sole remaining portion of the old Dutch fort).

NAGORE.

Nagore (pop. 16,000), 4½ miles from Negapatam and within the municipal limits of the latter, is situated on the Vettar River, which is deep enough in places for docking and repairing native craft from 300 to 400 tons burden. It is 7 miles south of the French Station of Karaikkal (see page 359).

Objects of Interest.—An old Hindu temple, which gives the place the name of Punnagavanam, and a large Muhammedan mosque, the latter with five minarets, one of which is of a fine architectural design and is 124 feet in height. This mosque is resorted to by pilgrims from Arabia, parts of India, Ceylon and the Straits Settlements, and is said to have been built about 300 years ago by the then Rajah of Tanjore, who endowed it with a large area of land in order to provide for the celebration of the annual festival (Kandiri) in honor of the saint who lies interred in the mosque, and who is said to have worked miracles here.

General Information.—A large number of wealthy Hindu and Muhammedan merchants reside at Nagore, who carry on trade with Burma and the Straits Settlements.

Local Official.—Sub-Registrar.

Road Conveyance.—

				RS.	A.
To Karaikkal—					
Jutka ..	..	..	..	.. 0	8
Double bullock-cart	..	..		.. 0	12
Single do. ..	..	..		.. 0	6
To Tranquebar—					
Jutka ..	..	..	..	.. 1	8
Double bullock-cart	..	..		.. 1	12

ERODE BRANCH.

ELAMANUR.

Elamanur (pop. 296) is situated in the Trichinopoly taluq of the Trichinopoly district, 35 miles from Karur, 12 from Trichinopoly Junction, and 75 from Erode Junction. The river Cauvery divides itself into the Coleroon, and the Cauvery, at this place, in consequence of which, is considered very sacred by the Hindus.

Local Accommodation.—On the south bank of the Cauvery, close to the station, is a bungalow belonging to the Forest Department, and about a mile from the station on the spot, where the Coleroon branches from the Cauvery, is another maintained by the P. W. Department. Either of these bungalows, when not in use by Officers of these Departments, may, on permission being obtained, be occupied by European travellers. At neither bungalow is there furniture nor cook. The charge made in each case is one rupee for each person per diem. The P. W. D. bungalow is a well built house, close to the anicut across the Coleroon, and is located charmingly in a shady situation. About a mile west of the station is a chuttram, where Hindus of all classes, except Pariahs, can find free accommodation, but must make their own arrangements for food. In the village is a hotel, where meals are served to all classes at from 2½ to 3 annas per meal.

Local Manufactures and Products.—Plantains are grown in large quantities.

Local Official.—The Village Munsiff.

Fairs and Festivals.—In October annually a large bathing festival is held.

Objects of Interest.—The Upper Anicut, which has been built across the Coleroon at the point where that river separates from the Cauvery. Shortly after Trichinopoly came into possession of the British Government, it was observed that the bed of the Coleroon was gradually deepening, while that of the Cauvery was silting up. The effect of the change was to cause a constantly increasing difficulty in securing sufficient water in the Cauvery for the irrigation of the Tanjore district. Colonel (now Sir) Arthur Cotton, one of the Madras Engineers, therefore proposed to build an anicut across the head of the Coleroon, and this work was carried out in 1836. The anicut, although situated in the Trichinopoly district, was designed for the benefit of Tanjore and has always remained under the supervision of the P. W. D. officers of that district. In its original form, the upper anicut consisted of a simple bar of masonry, 750 yards in length, divided into 3 parts, by the interposition of two small islands formed in the bed of the stream. The northern portion is 7 feet 4 inches and the remainder 5 feet 4 inches in height. The body of the dam is of brick masonry, coped with cut stone, there being 6 feet 4 inches or 4 feet 4 inches of the former, according to position. The thickness throughout is 6 feet. This bar, forming the portion of the dam, rests on a foundation of masonry 3 feet deep, built on three lines of wells, 6 feet in exterior diameter and sunk to a depth of 6 feet into the sandy bed of the river. In the rear of the bar, there is an apron of masonry, 21 feet broad, covered with cut stone, one foot in thickness, carefully laid in cement. Below the apron, a mass of rough stone from 9 to 12 feet broad and 4 feet deep has been formed to protect the junction of the apron and river bed. Twenty-two openings or sluices, 2 feet in width by $3\frac{1}{2}$ feet in length are distributed throughout the length of the dam, their sills being on the same level as the apron or bed of the stream. The object of this arrangement is to afford free passage to the sand, and, if possible, to prevent the bed of the Coleroon above the dam being raised by deposits. In consequence of the obstruction caused by the anicut, a greatly increased volume of water was thrown into the Cauvery during freshes and this led to great erosion of its banks and the deepening of its bed. Simultaneously with these changes in the Cauvery, the waterway of the Coleroon became contracted by heavy deposits, sand-banks were formed above the dam, and the deep channel which formerly followed the right bank of the river was thrown across to the left. In a word, the inversion of the former relations of the two branches became imminent, the Cauvery becoming the main stream, and the Coleroon ceasing to obtain its due share of water. This would have led to disastrous results in Tanjore and measures were accordingly adopted to obtain entire command over the bed of the Cauvery. The first of these measures, executed in 1843, on the recommendation of Colonel Sim of the Engineers, was to lower the central portion of the Coleroon dam by two feet. This was done on a length of about 700 feet, and, of course, added considerably to the volume of the Coleroon. Still, however, the enlargement of the head of the Cauvery continued; the banks were cut away, and there was great difficulty in preserving the narrow part of the island which separated the two branches. These effects were especially noted in 1844, and a masonry regulating dam across the mouth of the Cauvery was constructed. This work, consisting of a bar of masonry 650 yards in length, was executed in 1845. The level of the ground at the central portion was the same as that of the river bed, while 150 feet at each flank were raised from 1 foot to 18 inches above it, being protected by strong wing walls. The measures thus adopted proved sufficient to control the two rivers for some time, but it is now proposed to remodel the anicut and an estimate amounting to Rs. 5,34,000 has been sanctioned by Government for this purpose. The new work has been commenced.

Sport.—Good snipe shooting can be had near this station in the cool season, the charge for coolies being 4 annas each per diem.

PETTAIVAYTALAI.

Pettaivaytalai (pop. 170) is situated in the Trichinopoly taluq of the Trichinopoly district, 29 miles from Karur, 19 from Trichinopoly Junction, and 69 from Erode Junction. The village is on the east bank of the Vyacondan river, an important irrigation stream taken off the Cauvery.

Local Accommodation.—About half a mile, west of the station, is a bungalow maintained by the P. W. D., which, when not in use by Officers of that Department, may, on permission being obtained, be occupied by European travellers. This bungalow is unfurnished and has no cook, and the only articles of food for Europeans which can be purchased locally are fowls, eggs and milk. One rupee per diem is charged for the use of this bungalow.

Road Conveyance.—If previous notice is given, bullock-carts can be obtained at the station, the fare being 2 annas per mile.

Fairs.—A fair is held every Tuesday.

Sport.—Good snipe shooting can be had in the fields surrounding the station in the cold season, the charge for coolies being 4 annas each per diem.

KULITALAI.

Kulitalai (pop. 7,000) is situated in a taluq of the same name in the Trichinopoly district, 24 miles from Karur, 13 from Trichinopoly Junction, and 64 from Erode Junction. Kulitalai itself is only a small village (pop. 1,451), but it is the centre of three or four other villages, which almost adjoin and together form a small town. The greater part of the land around is highly cultivated and there are numerous clumps of cocoanut and other trees, which give the place a green and fresh appearance.

Local Accommodation.—About two miles, south of the station, at a place called Pudupolium, is a rest-house belonging to the Forest Department, which, when not in use by the Officers of that Department, may be occupied by European travellers, on permission being obtained. This bungalow, which can accommodate 2 persons at one time, is practically unfurnished and has no cook. The charge for the use of it is one rupee each person per diem. Close to the station is a chuttram, where natives of all classes can find free lodging, but they must make their own arrangements for food. In the town are 4 hotels, where meals are served at from $2\frac{1}{2}$ to 3 annas each.

Road Conveyance.—Jutkas and bullock-carts are usually procurable at the station, the fares being 3 and 2 annas per mile respectively.

Railway Facilities.—Waiting accommodation is provided at the station for first and second class passengers.

Local Manufactures and Products.—The weaving of country cloth is carried on, and paddy, cocoanuts and plantains are the chief products.

Local Officials.—The District Munsiff, Tahsildar, Stationary Sub-Magistrate, Sub-Registrar, Police Inspector, and Hospital Assistant.

Fairs and Festivals.—The most important festival held here is the " Pushyam " in January annually. On the day of the full moon, 8 Hindu gods are brought to the bed of the river and halt there for a whole day. These gods come from Kadambarkoil(½ a mile west), Karupattur(4 miles west), Tiruvangimalai (2 miles north), Musiri (1½ miles north), Sivayam (5 miles south), Rajendram (2⅓ miles south-east), Pettaivaytalai (4 miles east), and Vallur (3 miles south-west). It is estimated that 1,000 pilgrims assemble on the occasion, who, after bathing in the river, go in their wet clothes to receive holy waters from the priests in charge of the gods. Other minor festivals are the Magam, which takes place on the next full moon (February or March) and the floating festival on the tank near the railway station in the same month. These are, however, of purely local importance.

Missions and Churches.—The Roman Catholics have two churches, one close to the station, and the other at Musiri, 2 miles north of it.

Clubs.—The Local Fund Department maintains a reading room and library in the town.

Objects of Interest.—The Siva and Vishnu temples, the Taluq Cutcherry, the Courts of the District Munsiff and Stationary Sub-Magistrate.

Sport.—Good snipe shooting is to be had in the cool season, shikarries and coolies being obtainable at the rate of 12 annas per diem for the former and 4 annas for the latter.

Objects of Interest.—About 5 miles from Kulitalai is a place called Sivayam, noted for its temple situated on the top of a hill, and which can be seen from the station platform. There are about 1,000 steps to the top of the hill, and Cauvery water is carried up daily to bathe the god.

Musiri, a taluq town, is situated almost exactly opposite to Kulitalai, on the north bank of the river Cauvery. It is a fair sized town and possesses an old Siva temple.

LALAPET.

Lalapet (pop. 992) is situated in the Kulitalai taluq of the Trichinopoly district, 18 miles from Karur, 29 from Trichinopoly Junction, and 58 from Erode Junction. The village, which is about 317 feet above sea-level, is on the south bank of the river Cauvery.

Road Conveyance.—Single bullock-carts can be had, if previous notice be given, the fare being one anna per mile.

Local Manufactures and Products.—Weaving is carried on, country cloth being manufactured, and paddy and plantains are the chief produce.

Local Official.—The Village Munsiff.

KATALAI.

Katalai (pop. 2,110) is situated in the Kulitalai taluq of the Trichinopoly district, 11 miles from Karur, 36 from Trichinopoly Junction, and 51 from Erode Junction. The village is 346 feet above sea-level.

Local Accommodation.—Close to the station is a chuttram, where Hindus of all classes, except Pariahs, can find free lodging, but they must make their own arrangements for food, besides this, there are three hotels in the village, where meals are served at 2½ annas each.

Road Conveyance.—Single bullock-carts are usually available at the station, the fare being one anna per mile. Should a cart be engaged for the whole day, however, a charge of one rupee is made for that period.

Local Manufactures and Products.—The chief products are paddy, plantains, cocoanuts and firewood.

Local Official.—The Village Munsiff.

Fairs.—A fair is held every Monday.

Sport.—During the cold season there is very good snipe shooting, and coolies can be hired at 6 annas each per diem.

PULIYUR.

Puliyur (pop. 2,762) is situated in the Karur taluq of the Coimbatore district, 5 miles from Karur, 42 from Trichinopoly Junction, and 45 from Erode Junction. The village is about one mile west of the station.

Local Manufactures and Products.—Dry grains are the chief produce.

Fairs.—A fair is held every Sunday.

Sport.—During the cold season there is good snipe shooting about half a mile from the station, and coolies can be had at 4 annas each per diem.

KARUR.

Karur (lat. 10°58′; long. 78°07′; height 391 feet; pop. 10,750), the Karoora of Ptolemy, is situated in the Karur taluq of the Coimbatore district, on the left bank of the Amaravati near its confluence with the Cauvery. It is a place of great antiquity and during the struggle among the Chera, Chola and Pandiya dynasties, frequently changed hands. These troublous times were finally ended in 1790, when the British captured and dismantled the stone-built fort. Karur possesses considerable sanctity, being one of the seven sacred Sthalams or Sivalayams of the Kongu country. Its principal temple is dedicated to Pasu Pathiswara Swami (Siva) and is a large edifice, the walls of which are covered with inscriptions. The lingam is 5 feet high and is noted for a mark on it, the origin of which is explained as follows:—A cow originally discovered the lingam buried in the earth, and, being piously inclined, bathed it with milk. The owner of the cow discovering the animal, but not recognizing the holy act in which it was engaged, struck it a heavy blow, when the hoof of the startled animal coming in contact with the lingam, caused the mark in question. Many Roman coins have been found in Karur. The following are the distances to the most important stations on the South Indian Railway :—

Erode Junction (for Madras Railway)	..	.. 40 miles.
Trichinopoly Junction	.. ..	.. 48 ,,
Ammayanayakanur (for Kodaikanal)	..	.. 119 ,,
Madura ..	.. .. ..	.. 144 ,,
Tuticorin	.. .. ..	.. 242 ,,
Tinnevelly	.. .. ..	.. 242 ,,
Tanjore Junction (for Negapatam)	..	.. 79 ,,
Negapatam	.. .. ..	.. 127 ,,
Villupuram Junction	.. ..	.. 198 ,,
Chingleput Junction (for Conjeeveram)	..	.. 262 ,,
Madras (Egmore) ..	.. ..	.. 296 ,,
Katpadi Junction (for Madras Railway)	..	.. 297 ,,
Pakala Junction	.. .. ..	.. 336 ,,
Dharmavaram Junction (for S. M. Railway)		.. 478 ,,
Gudur Junction (for East Coast Railway)	..	.. 420 ,,

Local Accommodation.—About half a mile south-west of the station is a P. W. D. rest-house, which, when not occupied by the Officers of that Department, may be used by European travellers, on application to the Executive Engineer. This bungalow contains two rooms, which are practically unfurnished, and has neither crockery nor a cook. The charge for the use of the building is 8 annas per diem for each person. In the town are two chuttrams, where Hindus of all classes, except Pariahs, can obtain free lodging, but must make their own arrangements for food. Besides these, there are about 10 native hotels, where food is served to all classes at from 2 to 2½ annas per meal.

Road Conveyance.—Jutkas and bullock-carts are usually procurable at the station, the fares being 3 annas and 1½ annas per mile respectively.

Railway Facilities.—Waiting accommodation is provided at the station for first and second class passengers. A private room is also reserved for the use of Railway Officers.

Local Manufactures and Products.—The chief products are chillies and dry grains. For "Local Manufactures," see the paragraph under the head of "Missions,"

Local Officials.—The Tahsildar, District Munsiff, Stationary Sub-Magistrate, two Sub-Registrars, Apothecary, Local Fund Supervisor, P. W. D. Overseer, and Police Inspector.

Fairs and Festivals.—A fair is held every Saturday. In March and April annually a festival is held in the Pasu Pathiswara Swami temple, which draws a large number of worshippers.

Missions, Churches, etc.—Karur is one of the four chief stations of the Wesleyan Mission in the southern parts of the Madras Presidency. The Mission here was started about 1870 by the Rev. Henry Little, and, during the famine of 1877, a large orphanage was established, out of which has developed the present extensive Industrial School which employs about 100 men and boys and teaches carpentry, cabinet-making, smithing, weaving and rattan work. It is the largest establishment of the class in the Presidency, educates boys for the most advanced Government examinations, and is well worth a visit. The beautiful new church built of brick which stands close by is almost entirely the product of the school, which has also supplied the woodwork for the new cutchery on the West Road. Specimens of fine cabinet-making and wood-carving, as well as choice rattan work and woven goods, may be seen and purchased at the sale room. The Christian community connected with this Mission, which also has 4 girls' schools in the town, numbers about 500. On the north bank of the river Amaravati, about three-quarters of a mile from the station, is a Roman Catholic Church.

Clubs.—A very nice little building is situated in the town about half a mile from the station called the "Diamond Jubilee Reading Room." It was partly constructed in 1887 and added to in 1897.

Historical.—In 1736, Chanda Sahib besieged Karur unsuccessfully. In 1760, it was captured by the English after a short siege, and held by a British garrison for 8 years,

50

when it was taken by Hyder Ali, to whom its possession was confirmed by treaty in 1769. In 1783, Colonel Lang held the fort for a few months, and 7 years later, it was a third time captured (by General Meadows) and again restored in 1792. At the close of the Second Mysore War in 1799, it was finally ceded to the English and was abandoned as a military station in 1801.

Objects of Interest.—An obelisk, 3 miles from the station, which bears the following inscription :—

This obelisk commemorates the siege of the fort of Caroor and its evacuation on the 2nd April 1783, during which operations, there was sustained a loss of 1 officer Lieutenant Stanely, 102 regiment, killed 19 Europeans, 30 sepoys killed and wounded.

A small cemetery, which contains the tombs of the British soldiers who died at Karur on their way to Trichinopoly, is situated in the town near the Wesleyan Mission buildings.

The Siva temple described above.

The new cutchery.

The hospital.

At Thanthoni, about 1½ miles from Karur, on a small hill, is a Vishnu temple, one of the 108 Tirupatis in Southern India. Pilgrims who are unable to go to Tirumalai often resort to this shrine, treating it as equivalent to Tirupati. There is, however, nothing much to see at the temple.

PUGALUR.

Pugalur (pop. 4,757) is situated in the Karur taluq of the Coimbatore district, 31 miles from Erode Junction, 9 from Karur, and 56 from Trichinopoly Junction. The village, which is about 2 miles north of the station, is 504 feet above sea-level.

Local Accommodation.—Hindu travellers of all classes, except Pariahs, can find free lodging in two chuttrams in the village, but must make their own arrangements for food. There are also 5 hotels, where meals are served at from 2½ to 3 annas each.

Road Conveyance.—If previous notice is given, jutkas and bullock-carts can be obtained at the station, the fares being 2 annas and 1½ annas per mile, respectively, with a minimum charge of 4 annas for a jutka and 2 annas for a bullock-cart.

Local Manufactures and Products.—The chief products are paddy and dry grains.

Local Official.—The Village Munsiff.

Fairs.—A fair is held every Thursday.

Objects of Interest.—About two miles, north of the station, on a small hill, close to the Cauvery, is an ancient Siva temple, to which a large number of pilgrims go for the monthly " Kirthigai " festival.

NOYAL.

Noyal is situated in the Coimbatore district, and is 25 miles from Erode, à terminal station, and 15 miles from Karur.

Local Accommodation.—There are neither choultries nor hotels at this place, but there is a P. W. D. rest-house within half a mile of the station available for travellers at a charge of 8 annas per diem. The rest-house is very poorly furnished. It has only 2 tables, 2 chairs and a wash-hand stand, but no crockery. It can conveniently accommodate 2 persons, and there is no cook.

Provisions are not procurable, and persons intending to halt at the place will have to bring their own cook and provisions.

Road Conveyance.—Only common carts are procurable, for which the charge is 2 annas per mile.

Fairs and Festivals.—No fairs, but there is a temple named " Sellandiammankoil " about 100 yards from the station, where a feast is held every year in the month of March, and to which about two or three thousand people resort.

KODUMUDI.

Kodumudi (pop. 4,020) is situated in the Erode taluq of the Coimbatore district, 23 miles from Erode Junction, 17 from Karur, and 64 from Trichinopoly Junction. The village is 430 feet above sea-level.

Local Accommodation.—The nearest travellers' bungalow is 3 miles away close to Unjalur station, under which it is described. There is a chuttram for Brahmans close to Kodumudi station, where free accommodation and meals are given. For other classes of natives, a hotel in the village supplies meals at 2½ annas each.

Road Conveyance.—If previous notice is given, bullock-carts can be had at the station, the fare being 2 annas per mile.

Local Manufactures and Products.—The chief products are paddy and ragi.

Local Officials.—The Sub-Registrar, Hospital Assistant, and Salt and Abkari Sub-Inspector.

Fairs and Festivals.—A fair is held every Monday, which is much frequented by grain merchants.

Objects of Interest.—On the banks of the Cauvery is an ancient and well sculptured Siva temple, at which a car festival is held during Chittrai (April and May). Large number of pilgrims attend from all parts of the district.

UNJALUR.

Unjalur (pop. 4,399) is situated in the Erode taluq of the Coimbatore district, 19¼ miles from Erode Junction, 21½ from Karur, and 68 from Trichinopoly Junction. The village is 446 feet above sea-level.

Local Accommodation.—About a mile, north of the station, on the right bank of the river Cauvery, is a rest-house maintained by the P. W. D., which, when not in use by the Officers of that Department, may be occupied by European travellers on application to the Executive Engineer. This bungalow can accommodate 2 persons at one time, but is practically unfurnished, and has no cook. Eight annas per diem is charged to each person who occupies it. Close to the station is a well endowed chuttram, where high caste native travellers are provided with meals free. Besides the above, there are two hotels near the station, where natives of all classes can obtain meals at 2½ annas per meal.

Road Conveyance.—If previous notice is given, bullock-carts can be obtained at the station, the fare being 2 annas per mile.

Local Manufactures and Products.—The chief products are paddy and dry grains.

Local Official.—The Village Munsiff.

Fairs and Festivals.—A fair is held every Tuesday. About 3 miles west of the station, on the Karur-Erode road, at the village of Kolanalli, is a small modern temple of Kottai Mariamman, which is now in great repute amongst the ryots of this and the neighbouring taluqs; great numbers of fowls are sacrificed every Tuesday, and at the annual festival on the full moon of Masi (February and March) a large number of sheep and buffalo calves (male) besides fowls innumerable are sacrificed by ryots to bring good luck in the coming year, or in satisfaction of vows made in the past year. The fame of the temple is due to an alleged miracle upon the person of a blind man, a few years ago to whom the goddess is said to have appeared and restored sight.

PASUR.

Pasur (pop. 1,335) is situated in the Erode taluq of the Coimbatore district, 11¼ miles from Erode Junction, 29 from Karur, and 76 from Trichinopoly Junction. The village, which is half a mile east of the station, is 497 feet above sea-level.

Local Manufactures and Products.—The chief products are paddy and dry grains.

Local Official.—The Village Munsiff.

CHAVADIPALAIYAM.

Chavadipalaiyam (pop. 250) is situated in the Erode taluq of the Coimbatore district, 6½ miles from Erode Junction, 33½ from Karur, and 81 from Trichinopoly Junction. The village is about a mile south-east of the station.

Local Accommodation.—Native travellers of all classes, except Pariahs, can obtain free lodging at a choultry close to the station, but must make their own arrangements for food.

Road Conveyance.—If previous notice is given, bullock-carts can be obtained, the fare being 2 annas per mile.

Local Manufactures and Products.—The products are ragi, paddy and saffron.

Fairs.—A fair is held every Wednesday about two miles from the station.

ERODE JUNCTION.

Erode (lat. 11°20'; long. 77°46'; height 543 feet; pop. 12,339) is a municipal town, situated in a taluq of the same name in the Coimbatore district. The town, which is surrounded by paddy-fields, plantain and betel-nut gardens, has a very fertile and refreshing appearance, the country about here being irrigated by the Kalingarayan channel which runs close to the station. This channel, which takes off from the Bhavani river, is said to be of great antiquity and to have been constructed many hundreds of years ago by a Hindu prince named Kalingarayan. The river Cauvery also runs through Erode, which is situated on the south bank of it. The station is the terminal station of the Trichinopoly-Erode branch and a Junction with the Madras Railway. Passengers for Madras, Bangalore, Salem, Mettupalaiyam and Calicut change here. The following are the distances to the most important stations on the South Indian Railway:—

Trichinopoly Junction	..	..	..	88 miles.
Ammayanayakanur (for Kodaikanal)		..	..	159 ,,
Madura ..	..	..	..	184 ,,

Tuticorin	..	..	..	.. 282 miles.
Tinnevelly	..	..	..	.. 282 ,,
Tanjore Junction	..	..	..	.. 119 ,,
Negapatam	..	..	..	.. 167 ,,
Villupuram Junction		..	..	.. 238 ,,
Vellore ..	..	..	..	.. 331 ,,
Pakala Junction	..	..	..	.. 376 ,,
Chingleput Junction (for Conjeeveram)		..		.. 336 ,,
Madras (Egmore) ..		..	..	.. 331 ,,

Local Accommodation.—About three-quarters of a mile from the station is a P. W. D. bungalow, which can accommodate two persons, but is unfurnished. No charge is made for its occupation. Native travellers can find free accommodation in 3 chuttrams in the town, but must make their own arrangements for food. Besides these, there are some 17 native hotels, where meals are served at from 2½ to 3 annas each.

Road Conveyance.—Jutkas and bullock-carts are usually procurable at the station, the fares being 2 annas and 1½ annas per mile respectively.

Railway Facilities.—Waiting accommodation is provided at both the South Indian and Madras Railway Stations for first and second class passengers. In the Madras Railway building there is also a refreshment room (for Tariff, *see* their Guide) and (upstairs) two airy and comfortable rooms furnished for sleeping. Four persons can be accommodated in these sleeping rooms at one time, and, as they are let in the order of application, timely notice should be sent to the Madras Railway station master. The charges for these rooms, which include cold water baths, are :—

	Each Adult.			Each Child of 12 years and under.		
	RS.	A.	P.	RS.	A.	P.
Not exceeding 3 hours	0	8	0	0	4	0
Exceeding 3 hours and not exceeding 24 hours	1	0	0	0	8	0

Local Manufactures and Products.—The chief products are paddy, saffron, plantains, chillies, betel-leaves and cotton.

Local Officials.—The Sub-Collector, Municipal Chairman, Tahsildar, Sub-Magistrate, District Munsiff, Sub-Registrar, Assistant Superintendent of Police, Assistant Engineer, P. W. D., and the Apothecary.

Fairs and Festivals.—A fair is held every Thursday. A bathing festival in the river Cauvery takes place in October and November annually which draws a large number of pilgrims.

Missions and Churches.—The London Mission has a chapel near the station and the Roman Catholics a church in the centre of the town at which there is a European priest.

Clubs.—In the town is a reading room and small library maintained by natives, also a tennis court.

Historical.—In the time of Hyder Ali, this town contained about 3,000 houses with a population of 15,000 ; but in consequence of successive Mahratta, Mysore and British invasions, it eventually became almost deserted and fell into ruins. Until 1667 it formed part of the Madura Kingdom, but in that year was captured by Dodda Deo Rajah of Mysore. In 1768 it was taken and lost by the British, and 22 years later, finally recaptured. As soon as the treaty of peace was signed, the people returned to a place with so many advantages in position and fertility, and within a year, it had 400 houses and a population of over 2,000. The garrison was withdrawn in 1807 and the ruined fort levelled as a relief work during the famine of 1877, the space enclosed within the ramparts having long before been occupied by cotton presses and saltpetre warehouses.

Objects of Interest.—Two old temples with inscriptions, one dedicated to Siva and the other to Vishnu.

Bhavani (pop. 7,341), situated at the confluence of the Cauvery and Bhavani rivers, 8 miles north-east of Erode, contains a well sculptured Siva temple. It is related that 4 Asuras (giants) attempted to steal a vessel of nectar (Amirtham) presented by Vishnu to a devout Rishi. He thereupon prayed to Vishnu, when Kalis were sent to his assistance, who slew the Asuras and undertook the guarding of the nectar, which afterwards was found to be solid and was at once worshipped as the "Amirtha Lingam." Several Rishis are said to have attained salvation after bathing at the confluence of the Bhavani and Cauvery rivers and consequently numbers of pilgrims now patronize the place. There is a thriving industry in the manufacture of cotton and woollen rugs at this town.

TINNEVELLY BRANCH.

GANGAIKONDAN.

Gangaikondan (pop 2,971) is situated in the Tinnevelly taluq of the Tinnevelly district, 9 miles from Maniyachi Junction, 9 miles from Tinnevelly, and 434 from Madras (Egmore). The village is about two miles north of the station.

Local Accommodation.—Native travellers of all classes can find free lodging in a chuttram in the village, where, however, they must make their own arrangements for food. Besides this there are native hotels at which meals are served at from 2½ to 3 annas each.

Road Conveyance.—Bullock-carts are usually procurable at the station, the fare being 1½ annas per mile.

Local Manufactures and Products.—Cotton, paddy, cholum, and senna are the chief produce.

Fairs and Festivals.—An annual festival takes place in April, and during the time this is celebrated, a cattle fair is held.

Objects of Interest.—The large ancient Siva temple on the banks of the river Chittranadi, which is richly sculptured and contains several inscriptions.

TINNEVELLY.

Tinnevelly (lat. 8°44'; long 77°44'; height 213 feet; pop. 24,768), on the left bank of the Tambrapurni, is the largest town in the district of the same name, and the terminal station of the Tinnevelly Branch of the South Indian Railway. The administrative head-quarters of the district are at Palamcotta on the right bank of the same river about 2 miles distant, the two places being connected by a bridge of eleven arches of 66 feet span each, which was erected by the Naib Sheristadar, Soluchenam Mudeliar. Close to the bridge is a column erected by the East India Company to commemmorate this public-spirited act. The following are the distances to the principal stations on the South Indian Railway :—

Maniyachi Junction	18 miles.
Tuticorin	36 ,,
Madura ..	99 ,,
Ammayanayakanur (for Kodaikanal)	124 ,,
Trichinopoly Junction (for Erode)	195 ,,
Tanjore Junction (for Negapatam)	226 ,,
Mayavaram Junction	269 ,,
Villupuram Junction	845 ,,
Chingleput Junction (for Conjeeveram)	409 ,,
Madras (Egmore)	443 ,,
Pakala Junction	483 ,,
Gudur Junction (for East Coast Railway)	567 ,,
Dharmavaram Junction (for S. M. Railway)	626 ,,

Local Accommodation.—About 2 miles from the railway station (at Palamcotta) is a travellers' bungalow which is furnished and can accommodate 3 persons at one time. A butler is in charge, who can supply meals if required, but the traveller must provide his own wines and spirits. The charge for the use of this bungalow is one rupee for each person per diem. Hindu travellers of all classes can obtain free lodging for 3 days in a chuttram close to the station, and not far from this is a similar chuttram for Muhamedans. Besides these are many native hotels, where meals are served at from 2½ to 3 annas each.

Road Conveyance.—Jutkas, bullock-coaches and ordinary bullock-carts are always procurable at the station, the fares being :—

	RS.	A.	P.
Jutkas to Tinnevelly or Palamcotta	0	4	0
Bullock-coaches	1	0	0
Ordinary bullock-carts	0	3	0

If these vehicles are hired by the mile, the charge is :—

Jutkas	3 annas.
Ordinary bullock-carts	2 „

A transit goes daily to Trivandrum. The United Transit Company supply special vehicles for this journey, if required, the charge being :—

	RS.	A.	P.
Spring bullock-cart	15	4	0
Ordinary bullock-cart	12	4	0

Railway Facilities.—Public waiting accommodation is provided at the station for ladies and gentlemen, and also a private room for the use of the officers of the Railway.

Local Manufactures and Products.—Cloth is woven and cotton carpets are made in Melapolium, a village close to Tinnevelly, and metal utensils are made in Tinnevelly itself. The chief produce is jaggery, a large quantity of which is exported to the sugar factories at Nellikuppam. The local sugar mills also (one of which turns out as much as 7 tons of refined sugar per diem) are large consumers of jaggery.

Fairs and Festivals.—A fair is held every Thursday. In July a car festival is held at the Siva temple, which attracts numerous pilgrims from the surrounding villages.

Local Officials.—The Collector and District Magistrate, the Judge, the District Forest Officer, the Executive Engineer, the Local Fund Engineer, the District Sanitary and Medical Officer, the Superintendent of Police, Subordinate Judge, District Munsiff, Additional Munsiff, Deputy Collector and Magistrate, and Treasury Deputy Collector.

Missions and Churches.—Tinnevelly is now the most Christian district in India, and it was here that St. Francis

Xavier began his work as an apostle to the Indies. The converted fishermen of the coast (protected by the Portuguese against Mussulman oppressions) were formed by Xavier into churches and still speak of themselves as the children of St. Francis. The Church Missionary Society and the Society for the Propagation of the Gospel are also most successful with their mission work. The " Sarah Tucker " College belonging to the former society has some 400 pupils and several affiliated branch day and boarding schools, besides schools for the blind, deaf and dumb. It is estimated that there are about 175,000 Christians in the Tinnevelly district, of whom 100,000 belong to these two missions, the remainder being Roman Catholics.

Clubs.—At Palamcotta there is a European Club. A reading room and a tennis court are maintained by prominent native gentlemen at Vannarpet.

Historical.—During early times the history of Tinnevelly is practically a repetition of that of Madura. Both districts formed portion of the old Pandy's kingdom and both suffered from the Muhammedan irruption of 1310 and subsequently fell under the sway of Vijayanagar, and the Madura Nayakkas. The first Pandyan capital was at Koskai near the mouth of the Tambrapurni river, and was known to the Greeks as the seaport of Kolkoi. For sometime this emporium was the head-quarters of the pearl fisheries, but being gradually left by the sea was replaced by a port named Kayal, which was visited by Marco Polo, and in its turn deserted by the retreating sea. The earliest connection of the English with the district was due to the espousal of the cause of Nawab Mahamed Ali, to whom Tinnevelly and Madura belonged after the Nayak dynasty had been expelled by the Mussulmans. Tinnevelly was farmed out by the Nawab at a low rent ; but this generally ruined the renters partly because of the resistance of the Poligars, the feudal chieftains of the old dynasties, and partly because of the mismanagement

ENTRANCE TO TEMPLE TINNEVELLY

NEGATIVE BY A. W. CROS

GRAPHIC ART SOCIETY

and tyranny of the renters themselves. The Poligars kept about 30,000 peons, a rabble of ill-armed and ill-drilled soldiers, which secured their independence. Up to 1781 the history of the district is a confused tale of anarchy and bloodshed. In 1756 Mahamed Yoosuf Khan was sent by the Nawab of Arcot to settle the two countries of Madura and Tinnevelly. He gave Tinnevelly in farm to a Hindu at Rs. 11,00,000 a year, and invested him with civil and criminal jurisdiction. Mahamed Yoosuf was recalled from the south in 1758, and the country immediately relapsed into its previous state of anarchy. He returned in 1759 and undertook himself the farm of Madura and Tinnevelly. He ruled till 1763, but, as he could not or would not pay his tribute, an army was sent against him by the Nawab, and he was captured at Madura and hanged. In 1781 the Nawab of Arcot assigned the revenues of the district to the East India Company, whose officers then undertook the internal administration of affairs. In 1782, the strongholds of Choccaniputty and Panjalamkurichi were reduced by Colonel Fullerton, who also subdued some refractory Poligars. However, to the end of the century, some of the Poligars exercised civil and criminal jurisdiction in their territories. They rebelled in 1799, when the war with Tippoo had withdrawn our troops from the south and were therefore disarmed and their forts destroyed; but another rising took place in 1801. This was put down, and, in the same year, the whole Carnatic, including Tinnevelly, was finally ceded to the English. Since that time there has been no historical event worthy of notice.

Objects of Interest.—The temple contains many inscriptions and is dedicated half to Nelliappan (Siva) and half to Kanthimathi (Parvati). Though not so large as the Madura temple, it gives a good idea of the arrangement of the large Dravidian temples, having been built on one plan at one time without subsequent alteration or change. There are three towers to either half, those on the east being the principal, and having porches outside them. After entering there is in front an internal porch of large dimensions, on the right of which is a Teppakulam (tank) and on the left a 1,000-pillared mantapam, a mass of columns ten deep and extending to 100 in length which runs nearly the whole breadth of the enclosure. There are two entrances to the temple, both on the east face. This temple is certainly worth a visit, for it contains a good deal of excellent carving and sculpture, though some of the best work has been spoilt by yellow wash. At both entrances are porches, the roof and sides of which are carved in wood, a most unusual practice in Dravidian architecture.

The Hindu College, close to the Railway Station.

The Government Industrial Institution and Normal School, which produces some very good work in carpentry, etc.

The C. M. S. College, midway between the Railway station and Tinnevelly town, which has about 300 scholars and teaches up to the F. A. class.

The Sarah Tucker Institution.

The Jail at Palamcotta, at which weaving and carpet-making is done by the prisoners. The Sugar Mills, one owned by the East India Distilleries Company, and the other by the Tinnevelly Sugar Mills Company.

BATHING GHAT PAPANASAM

SPORT.

Although the country through which the South Indian Railway passes, lying, as it does, in a closely-populated region, fails to offer the same opportunities for big game shooting as the Madras Railway, it is far above that line in the facilities which it affords for sport, in the way of small game, particularly snipe. To obtain to a satisfactory extent, however, anything but this particular description of bird, one must go to places beyond the range within which it pays the native shikari, or trapper, to kill, or catch, game for the European market; but it is questionable whether it is always worth the trouble to go so far, as the shooting to be found is, chiefly, in the shape of partridges, which can give the French bird points in the way of running, and which, when tired of that, and marked, perhaps, into a bush, will squat there like a stone, not rise until poked out by a beater's pole, and then get up, generally, on the wrong side for the gun; and hares, which are not much larger than a good sized rabbit, and which lie almost as close as the partridges. Now and then, one comes upon them on favourable ground i.e., low scrub in small and pretty thick clumps, with open spaces between, in fair numbers and in the flying, or bolting, mood, and on such occasions, pretty good sport is to be had; but to get it, even then, requires a considerable experience, which is not to be gathered by a brief apprenticeship of the ways of the Indian partridge, or hare, and the chances are, as nothing but human retrievers can be used, that but little of what is not shot dead is brought to bag.

Duck and teal shooting is more satisfactory; but even this, frequently, proves disappointing, as, after a shot or two, which one does not, often, get within a really reasonable distance, except when far out of the beat of the native sportsman, the birds become exceedingly wary, and seem to be able to fix, with an accuracy, most satisfactory to themselves, but quite the reverse to the gunner, the exact effective range of the weapon used. It does not matter much what one shoots with, the quarry very promptly learns how far it carries, and the usual result of a day, devoted to duck and teal, is a lot of empty cartridge cases, with, by no means, a corresponding number of victims. I recollect a friend of mine, a hot sportsman of herculean proportions and strength, who, finding himself unable, after the first essay, or so, to circumvent the swarms of ducks on a large tank, not far from the station at which he was quartered, invested in a huge, single, 4-bore, shoulder gun, which carried a cartridge like a Bologna sausage, and an appalling charge of shot and which had been sold as firing it had broken the collar bone of its owner. It was a success for a while, and astonished the ducks, upon which it was used from a small canoe, very much, but the range of the new weapon was soon calculated, and the hand cannon became as useless as the ordinary gun had been. Sometimes, one stumbles on satisfactory sport in pretty shallow, moderately sized tanks, with a good lot of lilies, or weed, in them, such as that at Perambair, about two miles south-west of the Acharapakam station, on the line to Cuddalore. These, the cotton teal (*Netappus coromandelicus*), which is ornithologically a diminutive goose, loves. It is the only really stupid bird, in the web-foot game line, that I have ever seen, and will not, like the duck and true teal, which are to be found in the same localities, clear out for other quarters after having been shot at for a short time. A flock can, often, be driven backwards and forwards, past the gun, or guns, by three, or four, knowing beaters, until a large portion of it has been knocked over. The bird, though small, affords, not only good sport, as its flight is very rapid and it turns very quickly, but it is, during the winter, very good eating. I do not think it necessary to go into a dissertation on the different varieties of duck and teal which are obtainable in Southern India. They are numerous, and some are very handsome. There are two, however, which, for both sport and food, are utterly worthless; the Brahminy duck (*Casarca rutila*) and the whistling teal (*Dendrocygna awsuree*). There is one word of caution to be given, before quitting the subject of Indian wild fowl shooting, and that is, beware of tanks, in which a floating feathery weed grows. This is a most dangerous plant, and has been the cause of very numerous deaths from drowning, when bathing, or attempting to recover game which has fallen on its treacherous surface. It catches round and clings, as though it was some living, crawling, creature, to the limbs of the swimmer and, gradually enveloping him, draws him down. The only chance of getting out of the tangle is to turn on one's back and use only the arms. No sportsman should, unless a buoyant log, or raft of dry reeds, or bamboo, is used as a help, allow, under any circumstances, anyone with him to go, beyond his depth, into a tank, having in it weed of the kind described above, nor should he venture in himself, under like conditions, unless, on the emergency of trying to save life. Peafowl may be obtained in the jungles between Chingleput and Sadras, and near Tirukalikundram and Tiruporur, which are, respectively, 12 and 19 miles to the eastward of Chingleput; but the cover is, generally, very thick, and the birds are difficult to get out of it. The most successful method of obtaining them, is to ascertain their morning and evening feeding grounds. They come out into the open then, and may be picked up by lying in wait with a gun loaded with No. 1 or 2 shot, or a small gauge pea rifle. Shooting them can, hardly, be called sport, though a cock, when in full plumage, as he is in February and March, is a handsome trophy to anyone collecting birds. From the gastronomic point of view, the chicks, alone, are worth anything, and are, for table, something like an indifferent pheasant. During the cold season, the golden plover is, not infrequently, to be found, in large flocks, on the flats near the sea, which are accessible from the Buckingham Canal, between the Adyar river and Sadras, a village 19 miles east of Chingleput, with a good road to it. They occur, too, on open, grassy ground, often at some distance inland. One comes across them, also, now and then, on paddy-fields which are being prepared for cultivation. They are excellent eating ; but, as a rule, very wary, and the only way of getting at them satisfactorily, is for the sportsman, when a flock is observed, to make a long circuit, down wind of it, if possible, walk cautiously up to about 150 or 200 yards, and lie down, and then for three, or four beaters to make a like circuit in the opposite direction and walk, in a half circle, towards the shooter. The flock will, almost always, go down wind and, if properly driven, can be put over the gun. A winged bird will, generally, bring the flock circling back, and three or four shots may, then be had before it finally clears out. It is good enough sport, whilst it lasts, as the birds fly fast and wheel very unexpectedly.

The grey, and the black-breasted quail, (*Coturnix communis* and *Coturnix coromandelica*) are to be found, principally, in the fields of dry grain, and rice stubble in which a vetch, known as black gram, has been sown directly after the crop has been cut, and whilst the ground is still damp, but, as the season advances and reaping is pretty well over, they take to the scrub bordering on the cultivation. If only enough of them can be found, they afford nice sport, but, of late years, they seem to have disappeared, in a marked degree, from the areas anywhere within reach of the sportsman who cannot, or does not care, to go very far afield. This is, as in the case of the partridge and the hare, probably the result of the constant snaring and trapping, which, in the absence of any real effort on the part of Government to enforce the forest rules as regards close seasons and the snaring and netting of game, goes on, year in and year out, to supply the markets in Madras and the towns where there is any decent number of European inhabitants and which will lead, before many years are over, to the virtual extinction, for sporting purposes, of many of the game birds of the country. There is, at present, not a month in the year, during which one cannot go into the Madras market and buy live partridges and quail, and, very often, junglefowl, and this is the case, though the forest rules lay down that no netting, or snaring of these birds is permitted and make doing so, a punishable offence. The excuse of the captors of game of this sort, is, that it has been taken on private lands, not under the Government rules; but those who have been about the jungles, etc., under the care of the Forest Department, as much as I have, and who know anything about the native game-trappers arrangements, have no doubt as to the real truth.

The lesser florican (*Sypheotides auritus*) is to be had, all along the shooting grounds accessible from the South Indian main line, for, certainly, 100 miles from Madras, which is the distance along that line with which I have a more, or less, personal shooting acquaintance. The bird is, decidedly, rare anywhere near the railway, and shooting one is quite an event. It is, however, stumbled upon sometimes, in the most unexpected way, and in the most unexpected places. I have killed the florican along the railway line—chiefly about Chingleput, in the neighbourhood of which I have shot more constantly than elsewhere—in pretty high jungle (when looking for partridges and hares) in ripe paddy, in raggi stubble, in the grass at the head of tanks, in raggi and in varagu fields, in the long grass in young topes of trees and even in a damp, growing, paddy field. The Tamil name of

the bird is " Varagu kóli " (the varagu fowl) and it is so
called because it is, most frequently, found in fields of
this description of crop, which is a coarse millet, growing
usually, not very thickly and about knee high, on unirrigated lands. It lies, generally, very close and is apt to startle
the shooter, when flushed near him, as it springs up
suddenly and goes off with a peculiar, short, sharp, flap of
the wings, which gives it the appearance of flying much
faster than it really is. The result is, not infrequently,
especially when the bird, which is about the size of a hen
pheasant, is seen for the first time, a miss. It is, however,
very easily dropped, even with No. 8 shot, as the skin is
very thin, and the bones peculiarly fragile. As a bird for
the table, it is one of the best in India, and that is saying a
good deal: this, its beautiful plumage, and game appearance, and its comparative rarity in places within the reach
of civilization, render it a prize which most sportsmen
will take a good deal of trouble to obtain, though, from
the shooting point of view, alone, it is not of much
account.

The usual way of getting a florican up, when marked
down, as it, very frequently, is beforehand by one's shikari,
or one of his assistants, is with a line of beaters, as in
ordinary snipe shooting, but a very good way to make sure
of flushing the bird, is to have a long light rope along which
are fastened, at intervals of about 6 inches, narrow strips,
about half an inch wide and 18 inches long, of the inner,
blanched, young leaves of the palmyra palm. This
trailed between a couple of men, walking parallel to each
other, over anything in the grass, or crop line, will very
seldom fail to bring out any florican that may be in it.

There is a bird which is sometimes palmed off, on the
unknowing, as a florican. It is the golden-eyed plover, or
thick-knee. It is often called the bastard florican, but is
not found in the same class of country as the true florican.
It is something like the real bird, at first sight, and I have

more than once been put on to one, in my salad days, on the representation that it was a florican, but anyone who has even only a smattering of ornithology, would at once be able to detect the imposition. It, however, not infrequently, does duty at Madras dinner tables as a florican, as sandpipers do for snipe.

I have now mentioned all, save one, of the chief varieties of game available along so much of the South Indian line, as is within my ken as a sportsman. That one, though last, is not by any means the least, for it is the snipe—the bird which, wherever there is ground suited to it, is, in the pleasanter part of the year, to be found all over the Balmy East in varying quantities, according to locality and season, and one which, though, year after year, killed off, in thousands, by everyone who shoots small game, from the griff to the grey-headed oldster whose adieu to India is not very far off, and potted and snared by the hundreds of purveyors of game for the large towns, who make their living in this way, returns every cold season in apparently unabated numbers. Where the myriads of snipe, that we have, come from, is, I believe, not quite clear, but it seems to be agreed that they breed in the steppes to the north of Hindustan.

The South Indian Railway runs through country in which some of the best snipe-shooting in the Madras Presidency is to be had, and as I have pursued this amusement, pretty assiduously, from the time that I landed as a youngster, and am even still, though not so young as I was, given to it, when opportunity offers, I shall now go, as far as in me lies, into the how, when and where, to chase this blessing to the sporting exile, and give some hints connected therewith, which may be of use to those who have not had much experience of this class of shooting, though, perhaps, stale enough information to the many past masters in the art to be found in India. As what I have to say is however, not intended for them, I hope that they will acquit me of any attempt to teach my grandmother to suck eggs.

I shall commence with a statement of the varieties of snipe which may be brought to bag on the plains. The haunts of the woodcock (*Scolopax rusticola*) and wood snipe (*Gallinago nemoricola*) are too far from any portion of the existing South Indian line, and the birds, themselves, are, comparatively, too few in number, in the places where they are found, to render it worth while saying anything about them. The solitary snipe (*Gallinago solitaria*) does not, I believe, occur in Southern India. This name is frequently, incorrectly, applied to the wood snipe, which is, occasionally, met with on the Nilgherries and, I believe, Pulnies.

Three varieties of snipe are to be found in the plains :—

(1). The pintail snipe (*Gallinago stenura*).
(2). The common snipe (*Gallinago scolopacinus*).
(3). The jack snipe (*Gallinago gallinula*).

As far as I have seen, the first named of these is, by far, the most common. Its flight is slower than that of the common snipe, it, very frequently, rises without calling, which the common snipe never does, and it can be easily identified, when killed, by the dark barred lower wing-coverts, and six small stiff and pointed feathers in the tail, three on each side. Jerdon says that it is slightly smaller than the ordinary snipe; but my experience—and I have shot some thousands—is that exactly the reverse is the case. Lastly, the pintail snipe is much better eating than the other, a fact which it is as well to bear in mind when one has to eat what one shoots. The common snipe, which is often called the "fantail" by Europeans, on account of the shape of its tail, which one can easily open out, like a fan, and which is usually known to the shikaries as the "white snipe," from its colour, as contrasted with the other, which is very marked when on the wing, is the same bird as that met with at home and, notwithstanding the Eastern sun, is, usually, a remarkably free mover and quite up to the " Europe " standard. It is not of much use going out after this snipe in places where—as is sometimes the case—it is found, to the exclusion of the pintail, until certainly 9, or even 10, in the morning. Before that time, or on a showery day, or after heavy rain, or even in continuously cloudy weather, the bag where " white snipe " abound, will, even with good and practised shots, be comparatively small, and the empty cartridge cases and maledictions many.

The jack snipe is, to all appearance, the same as the bird found at home. It is comparatively rare. The largest bag of it that I have shot in one day, within reach of the South Indian Railway, was four couple ; but I once killed, on the Mysore plateau, in the course of an afternoon stroll with the gun round a grassy tank, double that number. In its flight, it looks like a drunken butterfly, and, once missed, it is very difficult to get up again. When bagged, it is a very pretty little fellow, and, as far as eating goes, is far superior to its cousins.

There is a bird which one sometimes comes across, occasionally in some numbers, especially in swampy ground with bushes and scrub interspersed, and which is, usually, called the " painted snipe," ornithologically known as *Rhynchæa bengalensis*, or *Rhynchæa ocellata*. The natives call it the " Rajah " (King) snipe, but it is not a snipe at all, though it looks something like one, and is not worth, either from the sportsman's, or the gastronomic point of view, a charge of powder and shot. The plumage is, however, very beautiful, though the colours are quiet. This bird, which is rather larger than a pintail snipe, can be easily identified by its slow, lumbering flight, and by the ocellations, on its olive green wings, which are, on a very reduced scale, rather like those of the argus pheasant. The pintail snipe affects the short, wiry grass and prickly weed to be found at the heads of many tanks, young paddy, particularly in the stage when it is unweeded,

and the stubble in the rice-fields in which grass and weeds
have grown up, and it specially loves the patches of uncultivated land which one, with feelings of gratitude towards
the lazy, or litigious native farmer, finds, not infrequently,
in the midst of cultivation, and which are usually covered
with short, brown, grass, ankle deep. In the early part of
the season, it favours the stubble of the raggi (millet)
which, during the dry season, is, in many parts of the country, raised, in patches, on irrigated lands. The ears are cut
off well up the plant, and the stubble, which is usually
knee high, is left to rot. When the rain comes, the ground
becomes thoroughly soaked, and the bird finds abundant
food beneath the decaying straw, which, at the same
time, affords good cover. A small patch of raggi stubble will,
under these circumstances, often hold a swarm of snipe, all
of the pintail variety, which lie well, do not get up " all
of a heap," but singly, or in couples, and afford excellent
shooting. The sportsman should never leave an uncultivated plot in the midst of, or partly surrounded by, cultivation,
or a patch of raggi stubble, unexplored. Later on, when
the crops are pretty well all cut, and the sun, towards the
close of the season, begins to grow strong, the pintail be-
takes itself to the neighbouring scrub, or jungle, if any,
and thence may be beaten out in considerable numbers.
It is quick shooting and, though bags are not often large,
the sport is, to my mind, the cream of snipe shooting,
as one has to look sharp and shoot straight. The birds
come fast and a miss means, as a rule, gone for good,
for, generally speaking, a driven snipe, if it escapes the
gun, clears out for some distant and ungetatable place, and
is not at all—as is the case with the bird flushed out of
grass, paddy, or stubble—inclined to give the shooter
another chance.

The common snipe, on the other hand, delights in the
swampy fields at the head of tanks and the half-mud, half-
water, which lies between the body of the tank and the

grass fringing its upper margin. A special haunt is the
head of a tank, with water just deep enough to make a
noise when one walks along, and with tussocks of grass, etc.,
which afford resting places for the birds, scattered about.
It also likes recently cut paddy-fields, particularly if there is
water in them, and then the proverbial hawk is a joke to
it in wildness. It does not frequent raggi stubble much, nor
is it, often, found in the short grass, with pretty nearly dry
ground underfoot, which is the usual haunt of the pintail.
It, however, often lies, mixed with *Scolopax stenura*, in
short, young, paddy and the mixture is a nuisance, as, not
only does the common snipe as a rule, rise wild, but its shrill
cry starts off its more phlegmatic cousin, which would,
otherwise, have remained where it was, until beaten up
decently and in due order, and its rapid and twisting flight
is apt to put the shooter off when he has it and the much
easier target, which the pintail affords, to deal with, and
does not know which will first offer. It is ever on the alert,
and is often aided by the sandpipers, which are dotted
about on every coign of vantage and which lose no opportunity of letting their friends know that a man with a gun,
whom they themselves do not, in the least, fear, is about.

It appears to migrate sooner than the other variety,
though it seems to arrive no earlier, and it seldom, if ever,
is found in the scrub, and jungle, to which the pintail be-
takes itself towards the close of the season, and in which I
have seen the latter so numerous, and come out so fast and
thick, that I have had to stop shooting to let the gun cool :
driven, then, as I have often had them, from the steep,
rocky, hills, clad with low jungle, which abound in the
neighbourhood of Chingleput, they afford sport unequalled
in the small game line by anything that I have seen in
India, or elsewhere. Both the pin and the fantail snipe,
begin to come in, in Southern India, about the end of
August, and their arrival is heralded by the appearance of a
very pretty little yellow white and brown wagtail ; but it is

not worth while going out for them until about the middle of September. The best of the shooting is from the middle of October to the middle of January, and, by the end of March, the snipe shooting may be said to be over. I have shot them, in the plains, in small numbers, up to the end of April, but they fly lazily then, and are abominably oily and fishy to eat. The latest date upon which I ever saw a snipe was the 8th May. On the Mysore plateau, however, the snipe are found, in considerable numbers, well into April. Many years ago, on the 22nd of that month, I bagged, not far from Oosoor with my friend the late Sir Penn Symons, who was shooting with a muzzle loader, 59 couple. We killed many more, which were not recovered, as they fell in long ripe crop. During February and March—sometimes earlier, if the season is a dry one—the snipe take to jungle, scrub and betel gardens, and, where there is sugarcane, to fields of that crop, and, when driven out of cover of this description, afford, as has been said before, excellent sport, though really big bags are, then, never attainable. The best time for these is November.

I shall now make some remarks regarding guns, dress, etc.

The usual weapon is a 12-bore, which has no doubt sundry advantages, the chief being that ammunition for it can be procured everywhere and that, if one runs out of cartridges when shooting with a companion, one has the chance of indenting upon him. It also carries a heavier charge than the smaller bores, and on that account is better for duck and teal shooting. But, to my mind, it is big to handle and feels clumsy. It is certainly, very appreciably, heavier than a small bore, if built, as every gun should be, to carry its largest effective charge without recoil, and the ammunition not only weighs more, but takes up more room. I prefer a 16-bore, with one barrel cylinder and the other modified choke. This requires straighter holding than a 12, but it is a lighter and handier weapon, which is a considerable advantage when one has to carry a gun about, in a tropical sun, pretty nearly all day. There is, practically, no difficulty in getting 16-bore ammunition, almost any-where, now-a-days. Having an ejector gun is a great pull in a warm corner with snipe, or when duck shooting.

It is desirable to, always, take out, even when snipe are all that one expects, some No. 6, 4 or 3 shot cartridges, in case of coming across, as one not infrequently does in the most unexpected manner, duck, teal, partridges, etc. No. 6 shot is rather too light for ducks or hares. No. 5 is, perhaps, the best size to carry, in addition to No. 8 if one does not care to be troubled with an assortment of cartridges with different grades of shot. The question of powder is a vexed one. There is, I think, but small doubt that a fine grained black powder combines evenness of shooting, with strength, to a degree not to be found in any smokeless powder, but there are the objections to it that, when a gun is fired, with black powder, rapidly, or in warm weather, it quickly fouls and kicks a good deal—sometimes very heavily—and that, in the morning and evening, and in damp cloudy weather, the smoke, which is always a nuisance, hangs so thickly that it is, occa-sionally, impossible to see to get in the second barrel. Added to this, the heavy report alarms the birds and, where they lie thick is, on this account, very objectionable. Lastly, it is, not infrequently, the cause of gun headache. I have never suffered from this myself, but I have known many who did, and severely. I have tried, in some cases fully, several smokeless powders and I consider that E. C. is the best, not only to shoot with, but for the gun. Cartridges charged with it remain good for a considerable time, and they seem to be affected by damp less than the others. The corrosive effect too seems to be less.

The cartridge bag should be of good water-proof mate-rial, to hold 50, with a pocket which will carry a dozen or so cartridges, with larger sized shot. The reserve can be carried in a bag, which will hold a hundred, or a " Payne

Gallwey " bag of stiff leather, which, if properly dressed, will keep out any amount of rain, which can be locked so as to prevent pilfering—a by no means uncommon occurrence—and which will contain 150 cartridges.

A stout, brown, water-proof canvas cover for the gun, tipped with leather at the muzzle, should always be carried in the field, as rain is not an infrequent feature of a day's snipe shooting, and nothing injures a gun like a thorough wetting. It should be made to slip on and off, easily. An oil rag should always be carried in a small tin, or a leather pouch, in order to rub the gun over as soon as the day's shooting is at an end. Two game carriers of some sort or the other, to hold twelve couple of birds each, should form part of the kit. I have always used the ordinary Indian snipe stick, the fashion, of which is well known to every shikari and which I think the handiest and best ; as it will carry any kind of game, which the English pattern will not.

As regards dress, I have in my time, tried all sorts of things ; thick and thin, cotton, wool and flax, and have come to the conclusion that the best is a suit of brown shikar káki, of the kind made at the Basel Mission Weaving Establishment, at Calicut and Mangalore. I do not believe in knickerbockers and stockings, or in leather, or water-proof canvas gaiters: the knees of the knickerbockers hold the moisture if one walks through water, or high wet grass, and stockings get heavy with water and chill one's legs, whilst, if one walks, as one often does, through spear grass, or prickly jungle, in them, the effect is anything but pleasant. Leather gaiters soon get sodden and are, then, very uncomfortable, and water-proof gaiters are exceedingly hot when one is out of the water and mud, and very cold when one is in them; as for keeping one dry, they do not, excepting for a very short time. I advocate pantaloons fitting easily and buttoning well down below the swell of the calf, and gaiters made of the same materials as the shooting dress and lined with holland, fitting tightly to the leg and over the top of the boot, and fastened to a button, at the back of the leg, just below the bend of the knee. The socks are pulled up over the bottom of the pantaloons, and the gaiter should fit as tightly as is compatible with comfort, over all. This arrangement will keep out spear grass and all thorns, excepting very special ones, will, completely, prevent mud and gravel getting into one's boots and will keep one's legs and feet dry much longer than anything else that I know of. The foot gear question is one on which opinions differ a good deal. My experience is that a stout, ordinary shooting boot, with plenty of nails, is, far and away, the best. If good and properly rubbed with dubbing, or some other like composition, they will keep one dry in all ordinary walking; stony ground does not hurt the feet, and the nails prevent slipping on muddy ground, or on paddy bunds. Weight is the general objection raised to boots, but one soon gets used to that, and the protection and general comfort which they afford, infinitely outweigh the pound, or two, extra to carry, which wearing them involves. The kit which I have worn, for years, when shooting, has been a thick flannel shirt, a soft silk handkerchief for the neck, a Basel Mission káki Norfolk jacket, pantaloons with gaiters, as described above, thick socks and stout boots. It is advisable to use, and I now always do, on the plains a light, tightly quilted, cotton pad, with tapes sewn at each angle which covers the shoulders completely and reaches to the top of the pelvis. This is tied to tapes inside the coat, corresponding with those on it; and should be allowed to hang fairly loose. It cannot be regarded as an absolute necessity, but it is a great relief in a blazing hot sun and makes a great difference when one has to walk all day: moreover, it acts as a considerable protection if one is, as is sometimes the case, caught, in a heavy shower, without umbrella, or water-proof; the rain will very soon go through káki and a flannel shirt, but it takes a long while to penetrate the cotton quilt. One thing that I have always worn, having picked up the wrinkle directly after I began to shoot in India, has been a belt of broad horse girthing, double the usual width and fastened by three small straps and buckles. This not only keeps one together, but serves as a very great protection to the abdominal region from the sun and chills. For a head covering, the safest thing to wear is a large and thick pith hat. The only drawback to this is that, if rain comes on, the pith is apt to become sodden and heavy. This can be obviated, to a considerable extent, by carrying a light water-proof cover, which can be slipped on, if there is a shower, or the day turns out wet. There are some men, with thick heads, who can wear ordinary hats, but it is as well not to try experiments, as doing so is, frequently, attended with serious results. Whatever is worn, the colour, or covering of the hat, must be brown or grey, as there is no bird sharper than a snipe at catching sight of anything white, or light coloured, and then promptly sheering off. A common bazaar umbrella, with a white cover, is a very useful adjunct to one's shooting kit. It is, very often, a particularly comfortable thing to have over one's head and face, when walking in the sun, from one patch of shooting ground to another, and equally so, if a shower, suddenly comes on. It can easily be carried by a beater, or one's shikari. An old light overcoat is useful too, when one sits down to tiffin, and there is a cold wind blowing. In the latter days of my shooting experiences, I took to carrying with me a small circular air cushion as a seat at tiffin and to put under me when riding in the very hard-bottomed carts of sorts, which one has to use very largely, when going out to distant and out-of-the-way spots. Like the overcoat, it is a luxury, no doubt, but it is one which occupies a very small space in the tiffin basket, on top of which the coat can easily be tied, and they both add very materially to one's case, especially when the day is over, the evening air is chill, and one does not feel at all disposed to have the tender spots in one's body emphasised by the hard frame of a native cart or a jutka and finds one's change of clothes not so warm as one could wish. A flannel shirt and suit, a spare set of under clothing, if usually worn, socks, a pair of light shoes and a thick silk neckerchief, should always be taken out and the sportsman, as soon as he has finished shooting and has reached a point beyond which he knows that there will be no further water, mud, or rough walking to encounter, should at once change into these and put on an overcoat. Doing this will save many an attack of fever and many a cold, to say nothing of the resulting comfort, which is very great, and which makes all the difference between feeling fagged and, often, shivery and appetiteless and being comparatively, if not quite, fresh and, very appreciably, hungry, when one gets back to dinner.

There are one or two things more, which are neither heavy nor cumbrous, and which are very useful articles to have when shooting. One is a light water-proof, to be carried in the early part of the season, as one may, at that time of the year, start with a cloudless and gloriously fine morning, to find it, by midday, raining " cats and dogs ;" another article is a small, light and sharp bill-hook, for many a bird is lost through dropping into thorny jungle, or a prickly-pear bush, which could easily have been recovered, if something to chop a way to it was at hand. If this is not carried, the sportsman should always have a sharp clasp knife with him, as one never knows when a cartridge may not jam, even with the best of guns, and the only way of getting rid of it is to cut a stick and push the offender out by thrusting this down the barrel.

What one should eat, and what one should drink, before going out, and when out shooting, is another point upon which opinions vary very much.

There is no doubt, I consider, that it is desirable, before starting out in the morning for a day's shooting, to have a good, solid meal, the best drink at which is unsweetened cocoa (Van Houten's being a particularly good one): this has a very sustaining effect when taking hard exercise, can be prepared in a minute or two, does not require absolutely boiling water, and can be drunk without milk. Whilst out, however, it is a mistake to eat meat of any kind. The best meal for one person is a half pound tin of preserved soup, of one of the thick varieties, with half an ordinary pound loaf of bread and, perhaps, where the appetite is large, a cuddy biscuit and cheese, with plantains, or a cold milk pudding of some sort or the other after it. The only drink that can safely be taken, is a very weak whisky, brandy, or gin, and soda water. Wine and beer are both, to my mind, absolutely pernicious. A pound tin of soup is quite enough for two persons. It should be diluted with half the tin full of water; salt, pepper, and a little sugar, which last takes all taste of tin off, should be added, and the mixture then heated up to the verge of boiling, which can be done either in a small enamelled saucepan, or, what is very much better, in the very handy cooking tin, used by the German soldiers, which stows into a very small space and can be made of brass or aluminium. The beaters can always pick up the few sticks necessary to boil the soup. Whether the weather is warm, or cold, hot soup, fairly thick (hotch-potch is one of the best) pulls one together in a most wonderful way, and the effect of it lasts for a considerable time. Whilst actually shooting, the best drink is, I believe, water, and drinking it, freely, is good, as it makes the skin act. I have tried pretty nearly everything, weak tea, with and without milk or sugar, tea, with a slice of lime in it, weak cocoa and weak coffee—the former of which produces a consuming thirst whilst the latter does not allay it—lime juice and water, lime cordial and water, and divers other concoctions including, once, when I knew no better, weak claret and water, and I have finally returned, and adhered to water. It is often difficult to get this good, on the spot, but, wherever obtained, it is always desirable to have it boiled before drinking. Filtered water is popularly supposed to be quite safe, but with the filters generally in use, this is, by no means, the case. The water should be procured from the best source available and the sportsman should *make sure* that, before being put into his bottle, it has been thoroughly boiled. He should, in this respect, take nothing on trust ; wherever natives have anything to do with the supply, boiled water means safety, and unboiled, the reverse. The best bottle to use is a half gallon vulcanite one, with a cup of the same material fitting on top of it, and fastened by a strap, fixed to the back of the vessel and running through a slot at the bottom of the cup. This is secured by an eylet to a hasp in front, and the whole thing can thus be padlocked so as to prevent a cooly helping himself to a drink, when other water is not handy. The bottle is covered with thick felt and if this is well soaked, before starting and wetted at intervals during the day, the water will remain agreeably cool during the hottest weather. It is desirable to have a stout rattan tiffin basket, which, unless the sportsman is prepared, when at the close of the day and after he has changed, he sets to work to mix for himself the peg which he has been longing for, but from which he has virtuously refrained, to find that the whiskey has evaporated, "God knows how," as the tiffin cooly will tell him, should be kept fastened with a good padlock. Ice is a very pleasant adjunct to a day's shooting, and if one is within, what an up-country friend of mine used to call "the glacial circle," it is as well to have it. It fully repays the cost of the extra cooly, necessary to carry it.

Having mentioned what has occurred to me as likely to be of use as regards preparations for snipe shooting,

I shall now proceed to give the outlines of a day out, say from Chingleput, which is the main centre from which the snipe shooter, residing in Madras, works. I shall then refer to some of the best shooting grounds in close proximity to the line of rail, and make less detailed mention of some others which are less easily workable from the railway itself. But, before doing so, I shall deal with an important point with regard to obtaining sport, and that is, the shikari.

This is the individual upon whom the sportsman must very largely depend, if, unless he is an old hand, he is to get any shooting worthy of the name, and even then, the bag is not likely to be always satisfactory, as it is quite on the cards that he may go over very good ground, which contains nothing, as Mr. X, or Mr. Y, has shot it a day or two before. He will be able to pick up a considerable assortment of empty cartridge cases, but only a bird or two, and the sole consolation—not at all an adequate one—for the empty bag, will be the knowledge that there were, very recently, plenty of snipe, on the ground and that his judgment, as to where he ought to have found them, was not wrong. As for the tyro, his chance, whether there are birds about or not, will always be a poor one, unless he has some one to show where they are. A shikari is, therefore, a necessity if sport is to be obtained anywhere near Madras. Further afield, of course, the sportsman, who knows the habits and haunts of snipe and the language of the country, can get on, but there is, frequently, a lot of time and temper lost looking about and enquiring for ground which snipe are likely to affect. All this is saved by keeping a shikari, who knocks about looking for birds. When he has found them, he informs his employer, who can then come out, be at once conducted to the spot and can promptly set to work. This makes matters pretty nearly a certainty, though not an absolute one, for, occasionally a " claim " is " jumped " either through ignorance, or very rarely, intentionally, by some-one else.

The difficulty is to get a good shikari, for the demand is much larger than the supply. The really good men, whose word can be trusted, who will give an amazingly close estimate of the number of birds in a particular place, who, when a snipe is dropped, will mark it with accuracy, and who are not afraid to tell the truth about a bird which has " gone on," but has really not been touched, are but few in number and are snapped up by the leading sportsmen of Madras, as permanent servants. There are, however, some good, though not first-class men, always to be had, and they will show sport which would satisfy most people.

As regards remuneration, 8 annas to an ordinary shi-kari, taken by the day, is ample ; a tip not amounting to more than Re. 1 at the outside being admissible where a good bag is made. If a regular shikari is employed, the best plan is to give him 5 or 6 rupees a month—certainly never more than 10—and then pay him by results, not exceeding Re. 1 for every 10 couple bagged.

We will now suppose that a permanent shikari is kept, that he brings, or sends, news of a find of birds, that Madras is the point of departure, and that Chingleput is the station from which the start for the shooting ground is to be finally made. It is desirable to go down the night before, if possible, as if one takes the earliest morning train, which is a slow one, there is considerable delay before breakfast at the station can be got through and a start made. The night train, on the other hand, takes one down, rapidly and comfortably, to dinner at the station at which, when not staying with friends, of whom I, fortu-nately, had, at Chingleput, a long succession of very kind ones, including one very well known shot and right good fellow, I always had my meals, which were good and served at any time that one wished, if ordered beforehand. There is a pretty fair public bungalow, not far from the station, which, thanks partly to my friends, and partly to my having rented, for two or three years, a small and handily situated house, I but seldom occupied. The friendless must use the bungalow as a halting place, but where this is done, it is desirable, for all commissariat matters, to go to the station, which is within easy reach. The sportsman should bring with him, besides his shooting paraphernalia and the materials for his tiffin, a couple of pillows and a rug, for not only are public bungalow pillows and blankets, not nice, but he will require them, next day, to ease his journey to and from the shooting ground. The shikari interviewed, beaters are ordered. Where there is only one gun, and the shooting does not involve any beating of scrub, or jungle, five men—four to beat and one to carry the tiffin—constitute, with the shikari, quite a sufficient number. With more than this, birds are constantly flushed out of range and ground uselessly disturbed. If ice is taken out, another cooly is required. If it is likely that there will be much scrub, or jungle beating, a couple more men, making eight at the outside, should be taken out, and two-thirds of the party should be provided with stout sticks. The day's wage, per cooly, is 4 annas. If one has an exceptionally good day, 2 annas extra, each, is not money thrown away. The shikari and beaters having gone out early in the morning to the point where the sportsman has to take to riding, if he has sent out a horse, or walking, if he has not, he has breakfast at about eight, and this over, gets into what is known, all over the shooting country, as a *jutka ;* not the square box, on wheels, with four generally much undressed natives closely packed inside it, so familiar to residents in Madras, but a little, light, tilted cart, long enough for one to lie down in, and classed by courtesy and Municipal Chairmen as " a *springed vehicle.*" This is drawn by a wretched looking pony, which, nevertheless, can get along at an astonishing pace, and thinks nothing of ten miles out and the same back. The harness is still more disreputable and wretched in appearance than its wearer, and it has often been a mystery to me how it held together for even a couple of minutes.

With pillows and the rug on top of the grass put in for the pony's day feed, one can be comfortable enough in this machine, into which the gun and other shikar impedimenta, are stowed. Cranky as it looks, and emitting, as it does during the journey, constant sounds as if its dissolution was imminent, it is safe enough, and, though I have used jutkas many scores of times on shooting trips, I have only once come to grief in one, and then all the damage done was the breaking of a gun-stock. It is on the return journey that the air cushion comes into play, as the pony has, by this time, finished the grass, and the thin cotton carpet and the rug which, then, cover the bottom of the cart, are but small protection to weary bones from the endless knobs and projections which beset the floor of the conveyance.

The proper hire of a jutka is, I believe, 12 annas a day. Re. 1 will be received, but not thankfully. I used to give Rs. 2, but I employed the same jutka for years and the driver was an expert valet, and did not care when, or where, I took him or how long I kept him out. Having driven between two and three miles, along the Conjeeveram road, to the eastward of Chingleput, the jutka pulls up and, is unpacked, and the sportsman, unless luxurious enough to bring out a horse, has to take to his legs for the rest of the day; a short walk westward, across dry fields, brings one to the bank of the Pálár, which is, at this point, more than half a mile wide and sandy, with, in ordinary weather, a small stream or two running along its bed. The trudge across is nothing much when one is fresh, but, when returning, especially after a hot day, constant walking and poor sport, it is an undertaking to which I have, many a time, looked forward with anything but pleasure, even though beyond was a change of dry clothes, a cold drink, a smoke lounging in the moonlight on a rug, and a chat over the day's doings with one or the other of the good shooting chums, who can shoot with me no more. The river passed, a walk of two or three hundred yards brings one to the first bit of shooting ground. This is the bed of the Kávitandalam tank around which grow mixed together a short wiry grass and a soft prickly weed, which, when the ground is fairly damp, hold a goodly number of snipe. I have seen this place, in the palmy days when Chingleput and its neighbourhood were unknown to any but a very few, swarm with birds. A few teal are, occasionally, to be found in the tank when pretty full, and, as the season draws on, and the water falls, grey quail are often to be picked up in the grass and stubble inside the tank. This bit of ground shot over, there is, about a mile and a half to the South-west, with paddy fields intervening, the Vichúr tank with, again, short grass and weed, and a good long stretch of it, in its bed; beyond and, practically adjoining it, there is, again, another tank (Tandiri) with yet more grass and weed. On this bit of water there are, very often, teal and sometimes duck, and I have, not infrequently, bagged a partridge or two in the prickly-pear and bushes which line a deep water channel, running along its western side. Both Vichúr and Tandiri are excellent grounds for snipe. A friend and I once, when, by some happy chance, it had not been disturbed for some little time, took 69 couple off the beds of the three tanks which I have mentioned, and I have, frequently, got over 30 couple off this ground by myself. If the sportsman has fair luck, it will be, when the Vichúr tank bed has been beaten, time to halt for tiffin. A fire is lit, the soup is prepared and eaten and an hour's rest in all may be put in. The Tandiri tank is then taken and when this has been beaten out, it is, if there has been a decent number of birds about, quite time to think of turning back. If he has had about enough, and the day is wearing on, the sportsman may retrace his steps, taking, if they are in proper order, the wet cultivation and grassy waste fields above the beds of the tanks which he has already shot over and into which a good many of the birds, which may have been missed, or which got away unshot at on the way out, will have pitched. If, however, he prefers to try quite fresh ground, he can, when facing homewards, turn either right or left-handed, taking, in the former case, the cultivation under the Vichúr tank, the fields intervening between it and the Pittapúr tank and shooting the bed of the latter tank, in which there is a long stretch of grass. Eastward of this, and not marked in the maps, is a small and partly ruined tank, in the bed of which I have bagged very many snipe. Beyond this is the river, and, if this route is taken, the jutka will have to be moved down the road, about a mile or so towards Chingleput and brought along a sandy little lane to the river bank. If the left-hand line is taken, there is, to the north and slightly east of Tandiri, a small and beautifully grassy little tank called Mámbákum Tángal, which, almost always, abounds in snipe and north-east again of this is, what I think is called the Muluméni tank, either the bed of, or the cultivation under, which—the latter for choice—can be worked through and this, brings one out, after a short walk, to the cultivation at the head of the Kávitandalam tank, in the bed of which the start was made in the morning. By this time, at the best season of the year for shooting, it will be very nearly dark: the river is again crossed—a weary trudge after the day's walk—the welcome glimmer of the lantern, which should always form part of the outfit for an expedition covering the whole day out and which the jutka-driver, if he knows his business properly, lights as soon as it grows dusk, is seen as soon as the bank is topped, the jutka is then soon reached, the shooting clothes are bundled off, the dry flannels, which the jehu should have put ready, are slipped on, and then comes the drink and the lounge over a cheroot, before one clambers into the trap and rattles, in more senses than one, back to Chingle-

put; a bit tired, perhaps, but, if the bag has been a good
one, in a contented frame of mind, and quite ready for a
really hot bath, which is the best thing to prevent stiffness,
and then dinner.

When shooting, there are, besides observing the ordinary
rule of not beating up wind, if it can be avoided, two points
to attend to—

(i) Not to allow talking, or noise, amongst the
beaters—a practice to which they are very prone.

(ii) Never to let a cooly run in to pick up a bird that
is dropped; it should be marked by one of the men and
gathered only after the shooter has reloaded and the line
moves on. Many a warm corner is ruined by beaters
rushing in—a very common trick with unbroken hands—to
pick up the first two, or three, fallen birds.

I shall now take the line of railway down from Madras,
as far as I know it and give some of the best places within
easy, or pretty easy, reach of stations. I cannot pretend
to mention every spot, as I have to write a good deal from
memory and to indicate every ground, would be a very
long business, even if I could recollect them all.

It is useless to begin from any station nearer Madras
than Vandalúr. There is but one place which can be got
at from Pallavaram, that is worth anything much, and
that is the ground under the Chembrambákam tank, about
five or six miles from the station and along a good road.
This, however, is pretty well harried by shooting men
from the Mount and the Poonamallee Depôt. Vandalúr,
the next station to Pallavaram, used to be good ground, but
of late years it has been very much shot over, as, when
going out for the day from Madras, one can begin earlier
and leave off later there, than anywhere else.

The best ground in the neighbourhood of Vandalúr
is in the bed of, as well as the fields under, the Maniman-
galam tank, a large reservoir about three and a half or four
miles west of the station, on the road to Striperumbudúr.

To the eastward, on the road to Covelong, there is, or was,
a very good place, about five or six miles out and about
half to three-quarters of a mile south of the road. I have
forgotten the name of it, but think that it is Kárani.
The sportsman should beware of being decoyed into beating the scrub-jungle on the way to the two spots which
I have mentioned, for partridges and hares. There used
to be heaps of them, but they have now been pretty well
trapped and shot out of all this ground, and trying for them
is mere waste of time: a bird, or two, and a stray hare
may, now and then, be picked up, but it may be regarded
as a piece of luck if they are.

There used to be some very good ground under the
Vandalúr tank, and north of it, on either side of the rail;
but this is so much shot over by soldiers from the Mount,
and native shikaries who supply the game purveyors of
Madras, that there is, now-a-days, but little use in trying
it. There is, I believe, some very good shooting ground on
the road to Walajabad, but I have no personal knowledge
of it.

No jutkas, unless one is brought from the Mount, are
to be had at Vandalur and the ordinary country cart,
which, at best, does about three miles an hour, is the only
conveyance procurable there.

Guduváncheri, the next station down the line and at which
there is a good public bungalow, was, for a long while,
the centre of the snipe shooting world of Madras, but it has
been pretty well cut out by the superior attractions of,
and the larger area available at, Chingleput. A marvellous
number of birds has been taken off this place, year after
year, for quite twenty years; the fields around must,
by now, be a young lead mine. The snipe, however, never
seem to get much wiser and still appear, every season, in considerable numbers. The ground usually shot is on both
sides of the line, north and south of the station. There
used to be plenty of grassy, waste land about, but, of late

years, it has, almost entirely, been brought under cultivation. Early in the season, however, there is a good deal of raggi stubble, which is, always, a pretty certain find. There are three or four good tanks to the south-west of the station; but they are some distance off, and can be taken comfortably, only, when one stays for the night at the bungalow. The south-eastern part of the ground, past the station, and on the Chingleput road, is, to my mind, the best. There is beyond it and over a low ridge, a bit which used to be very good. Kondangi, a very fine piece of ground, off which, shooting both alone and with others, I have taken many a good bag, and which lies some seven miles south-east of the bungalow, along a cross country track, used to be worked from Guduváncheri, before Chingleput came to the fore, when it was found that it could be far more readily got at from there. To do Kondangi from Guduváncheri, one must sleep the previous night at the latter place. As at Vandalúr, the only conveyances available at Guduváncheri are country carts, but the ordinary shooting grounds being so close at hand, one hardly requires them.

The station before reaching Chingleput is Singaperumalkovil. This, though a wretched little place, is an excellent centre to shoot from.

Immediately close to the station, and to the eastward of it, there is nothing; but a walk of a mile or two in that direction will bring one to a series of small tanks and to the grass and cultivation at the head of the large Chingleput tank.

This ground may be worked in three ways, *viz*., (i) either by shooting round from the starting point to and along the eastern side of the big tank, and coming out where the line of rail crosses the Chingleput-Sadras road, and then in to Chingleput, or (ii) after working the small tanks, taking the western side of the main tank and coming out on to the trunk road, below the escape weir and then shooting the ground below the bund and so in to Chingleput, or (iii) by shooting the small tanks, working the top of the Chingleput tank, and then beating the ground further south, and returning by that route to Singaperumalkovil station. Each of these lines of country will afford, if the season is a decent one, a full day's sport.

On the western side and close to the railway line, is the large Chettipúnyam tank, the bed of which, with the cultivation under the tank north of it—in the waters of which there are often teal and duck—will, not infrequently, afford a day's shooting, during which one need never lose sight of the station.

Some two or three miles west of the station, beyond a ridge of low hills and beginning at a village called, I believe, Kolatúr, there is some very good ground, which is not much worried.

Yet another line to take, is the bed of the Chettipúnyam tank, and the eastern edge of the cultivation under it: the sportsman can then pass through a gap in the low hills beyond this, cross what is known as the Madavu, which is a wide and permanent water-course, often impassable in the rains, and either shoot the Áhtur ground, to the west of this, and strike the road on the other side of the railway, about a couple of miles, or so, from Chingleput, or work, in a north-westerly direction, to the Villiyampakkam station, on the Conjeeveram line, where the afternoon train may be caught, or a jutka sent out beforehand from Chingleput, may be met, or Chingleput may be reached by going south-east, across country, as soon as one has got over the Madavu. There is, if the last mentioned line is followed, shooting pretty nearly the whole way into Chingleput, and it is often good, but it makes a long day of it and cannot be properly done, unless one delays the return to Madras until next morning.

From Chingleput, ground, at pretty well all points of the compass, may be conveniently got at, if one halts for two nights—running down one evening by the Mail, shooting the next day, and returning by the first train the following morning. The whole of the Singaperumalkovil beats may be thus worked. It is impossible to indicate all the good grounds that there are, as they are so numerous. Taking spots to be reached by rail along the Chingleput-Conjeeveram line, Villiyampakkam, the first station out, affords excellent sport on what is commonly known as the Áhtur beat. This is to the north of the line, and east of the station there is shooting nearly the whole way down to Chingleput, which can easily be reached on foot. Many large bags have been obtained here. Another beat from Villiyampakkam station is the bed of the Pallúr tank, the ground under it, and a long, grassy, tank to the west northwest of Pallúr. On this beat, which is a very good one for snipe, grey quail, often, and duck, teal and partridge, occasionally, are to be picked up. On the roadside, a little beyond the station, there is a lot of scrub-jungle and wild orange trees, out of which I have killed, towards the end of the season, many snipe, and sundry partridges ; but to work this jungle properly, two guns are required.

The bed of the Villiyampakkam tank, not far from the station, is very good holding ground, as are the fields under it.

At Walajabad, the next station towards Conjeeveram, there is also a good bit which is not far from, and on the Chingleput side of, the station and close to the northern side of the line, but the best beat is under the Kattuvákam and Tennéri tanks, on the road from Walajabad to Striperumbudúr and distant some three or four miles from the former place.

This, being somewhat out of the line of the ordinary run of snipe shooters, is not so frequently worried, as is ground closer to Chingleput. There is no halting place at Walajabad, and no jutkas are to be had, unless specially sent out from Chingleput.

There is, I believe, a good ground, across the river, to the south of the station, but I have never shot it, as I could get plenty of sport elsewhere and this bit of country is difficult to get at, as the river has to be crossed, going and returning and the shooting is a good way off. It can be managed by running up by rail to Walajabad and having a jutka sent out, in which to return to Chingleput, but this makes a very long day of the business.

Walajabad is the last place on the line to which it is worth while to go from Chingleput. About Conjeeveram itself, unless one goes south, some four or five miles across the Pálár and another smaller river, into the North Arcot district, where there is a large tank at the side of the Wandiwash road, the shooting is, I do not know why, poor, and there is nothing much to be had until one reaches Pallúr, the last station before arriving at Arkonam, from which anyone wishing to shoot this ground, which is a very good one, but much shot over owing to its proximity to the junction station, should work.

To return now to the railway line southwards from Chingleput. The first station, in this direction, is Kolatur. North and all round this, there is very good ground on which I have, on sundry occasions, bagged florican, both in grass and crop. About a mile north of the station, on the eastern side of the line, and close to it, is a tank called, I think Mosivákam, which is easily identifiable, as it is the only large sized one with a grassy bed in that neighbourhood; in this, when the grass is in order, I have, more than once, spent the whole day shooting, with good results. But, if one does not have like luck, there is ample ground to occupy, for the day, a couple of guns, below the tank, and in the fields under the small tanks around it. One can easily work this beat by going down by the early train from Chingleput, and returning by the last.

There is an excellent and extensive ground, to the east

of the station, which is reached by going through the village of Kolatur, walking about half a mile along a cross country cart road, and then striking eastwards, in which direction there is a chain of small tanks, about which, one may be pretty certain of obtaining good sport.

On the western side of the railway, and north-west of the station, there is, in the Tirumani and Olakur tanks, very good ground. The bed of the tank (name unknown) nearly abreast of the station, and some little distance west of it, sometimes, particularly in November and December, swarms with snipe. Some of the biggest bags, that I know of, have been got on the ground west of Kolatur station, and on it I have killed duck, teal, quail, partridges and occasional florican and hares, in addition to very large numbers of snipe. This beat cannot be fully worked by using the railway, alone. The best way is to take the early train down, shoot the ground, then work up towards Chingleput and have a jutka at the old race course, close to which the shooting ground ends.

Beyond Kolatur, the next station from which to shoot is Padálam, on the southern bank of the Pálár. This is ground which I, myself, never visited much, as I had others which I liked better. I have shot it, occasionally, and have often taken the western edge of it from the Chingleput-Madurántakam road. There are always birds to be had there in the season; but I have never heard of any really good bag being shot about Padálam—certainly, nothing like what I have known taken off the Kolatur beats. There are rice-fields around the station, raggi stubble at the beginning of the season and some swampy grass, but one cannot get from the railway to the really good ground, which is considerably to the westward, and return to catch the train, without much more hurry than is compatible with either proper beating, or good shooting. The best way to work the ground to which I allude, is from Chingleput, using a jutka. Eastward of the station, there is some pretty good country with sundry small tanks, but I don't think very much of it.

Beyond Padálam, is Madurantakam station. There are several grounds about this, which, when I first knew them, were very good, but which seem, of late years, though not much harried by the "out and back" sportsman, to have fallen off considerably.

There are only two beats which one can shoot from the station, if obliged to return the same day. The one is to the east and the other to the west, of the line of rail. The former of these is about a mile and a half, or two miles, from the station and the path to it lies, mostly, along a water channel, in the bed of which one has frequently to walk, getting, of course, wet feet before the day's work begins. There is nothing to shoot on the way. The ground consists of a chain of three shallow tanks, the beds of which are, generally, more than half empty and bear a plentiful crop of grass and weeds, in which I have seen the snipe very thick. It is a very pleasant bit of shooting, even for two guns, and is just enough to fill up the time, nicely, between trains. If one has not trains to trouble one, there is another long, grassy tank, not far north of the last of the chain which I have mentioned, and beyond that, the Kinár tank, with a long expanse of grass; but shooting these means staying for the night at the Karangúli public bungalow, which is two and a half miles north-east of the station, and a very good one.

The other ground starts from close to the station, and a little south-west of it. The best part is around the village and old fort of Karangúli, which is a couple of miles further north, and across the stream rising from the escape weir of the Madurántakam tank: one can beat from the southern end, along the fields abutting the line, cross the stream near the railway bridge and so get on to the Karangúli ground, returning, after shooting that, by the fields along the road, back to Madurántakam.

There are other good places, both east and west, but, to shoot them really satisfactorily, the sportsman must be, in the one case, prepared to camp out, or, at any rate, to have a jutka from Chingleput and stay the night at the Karangúli bungalow, and, in the other, to put in two nights there.

The ground to the eastward is very good indeed, but, practically, unknown. It is about five miles from the Madurántakam station, near the junction of the roads leading to Chéyur and Chúnampett. Here, there is a large tank, which frequently contains, in the cold season, very many waterfowl, and below it there used to be, when I knew it, a long stretch of swampy grass, which was excellent holding ground.

The beats easily accessible from the public bungalow, are, to begin with, the Karangúli ground, already referred to, taken with the beds of the Karangúli and Kinár tanks and the fields below the latter. The others are to the westward and the first of these begins about three-quarters of a mile behind the bungalow. There is here, a small tank, divided only by its bund (there is no land under it), from the waters of the Madurántakam tank, which is a fine one and never entirely dry. I have shot very many teal and some duck, off the small tank by hiding on the bund and sending a man in, on a raft of rushes, or a log of buoyant wood, to flush the birds, which, when making, as they always did, for the large tank, often afforded very good shots, though nothing which was not killed on the spot was, as a rule, gathered, as what carried on fell into deep, weedy water, infested by what are called out here alligators, though they are really crocodiles. The bed of the small tank, to which I have alluded, the fields under another above it and the bed of another small tank still further beyond and on the northern side of the Madurán-takam-Utremerúr road, will always, in an average season, give a very decent amount of shooting.

Westward of the small tank, there is some very good ground, which forms part of the northern foreshore of the Madurántakam tank. I some years ago, frequently killed golden plover on the grass and partridges in the low jungle, bordering on the wet cultivation in the bed of the tank, but that has, probably, now been cleared off. There are sundry small tanks about this spot, which are all good for snipe. One of these is rather remarkable. I have forgotten the name, but the tank is easily recognized by its being full of a tree, like the mangrove, which flourishes in standing water, when not deep, but which is not often met with inland. An ancestor of the ryot who now holds most, if not all, of the lands under it, obtained, what he thought, was the written permission of a Collector who ruled many years ago, to preserve this sheet of water as an asylum for aquatic fowl of all sorts, and, though the document on which the claim is based, confers no such authority, the protection of the birds, has, somehow or the other, been very generally respected, with the result that an enormous quantity of cormorants, herons, cranes, and waterfowl of all sorts, resort to the tank, which is quite a small one, and are wonderfully tame. The perching birds make the trees in it their roosting places, and the ducks and teal, doze out the day on the mud and weeds on its shores. The manurial effect of this congeries of birds on the water of the tank, and, through it, on the crops below, is very marked, and this has probably much to do with the tenacity with which the ryot proprietor adheres to his alleged privileges. The sportsman would do well to leave this tank alone; but it is, at the same time, worth while, if in its immediate neighbourhood, to have a look at it, as it is a curious sight.

There is another good ground further south, at the head proper of the Madurántakam tank, but to work right round this sheet of water, is a long stretch and the mud is deep and tenacious. There is also the channel, which feeds the tank, to be negotiated, and this is, at times, of an uncomfortable depth.

The next point down the line, which may be made a shooting station, is Acharapákam. There is, here, a bungalow, which was formerly a public one, but which can, now, only be occupied with the permission of the Local Fund Engineer, or the Collector of the district. It contains no furniture to speak of, and no conveniences, so anyone halting at it, would have to bring everything with him. There is, however, some very good shooting about the place, and the only really comfortable way of working it is to engage, from the Railway Company, a shooting carriage, which can be detached at the station. To attempt it from Chingleput is out of the question, as the time between the down and up trains is too short. The Acharapákam tank is immediately alongside, and to the eastward, of the station. The bed of this reservoir is good ground and so is the long stretch of waste and cultivation below it. In the low scrub to the eastward of the tank, there used to be a good many partridges and quail, but these have, probably, been long ago trapped. North of the station, and on the western side of the line, is another good beat, near the village of Palliapettai, where, besides snipe, a florican is occasionally to be found, and there used, when I knew it, to be, in the season, a good many grey quail.

About a mile or so westward of the station, is the village of Uttamanellur, in the bed of the tank of which, the ground under it and the country further westward, I have found large numbers of birds. It is reached by going round the northern end of the range of hills to the westward of the station. I have shot along the edge of the Uttamanellur ground, and then, instead of continuing to the westward, kept along the western foot of the hills, alluded to above, beating, the jungle and scrub, in a southerly direction, until I reached the Perambair tank, about two and a half to three miles south-west of the station: this, in the proper season, is about the best place, within reach of the railway, that I know in the Chingleput district for duck and teal. I have seen it pretty well black with them, but the worst of it is that it is a very weedy sheet of water and has a good deal of lotus in it, and this makes it difficult, and sometimes dangerous, to retrieve birds from it. I used a Berthon's shooting boat, which made matters pretty easy. The snipe shooting at the head of the tank, and under it, is fair, but not so good as on other grounds in the neighbourhood. There is good sport to be had at the villages of Irumbali and Perunkáranai, to the eastward of the station, but this involves a rough cross-country walk, of some distance, and, when staying at Acharapákam, I very seldom went in that direction, as there was plenty of shooting closer at hand.

Beyond Acharapákam, I have not shot very much. Olakúr, the last station in the Chingleput district, I never tried, and there are only two places further south to which I have been for sporting purposes. These are Tindivánam and Villupuram, both in the South Arcot district; the latter is the junction of the main line with the Pondicherry and Dharmávaram branches. I do not know the names of the tanks, etc., at either place, and have been only within a day's shooting distance on either side of the railway stations. At Tindivánam, there is a very good, well-furnished and well-kept public bungalow, and there is excellent ground, on both sides of the station, and close at hand. That to the eastward is the better and there is, on the road to it, a Government reserved scrub-jungle (by courtesy a forest), to shoot in which, as in all other Forest Reserves, an annual license, costing Rs. 10, is necessary. In this, there are a good many partridges and hares. The tanks beyond, being out of the ordinary range of the European or native shikari, hold, or used to, duck and teal, sufficiently unacquainted with man to allow of their being approached within shooting distance without very much trouble.

At Villupuram, I shot but once, spending a couple of days there, in the course of which I and a shooting companion, saw a great quantity of birds, but, unfortunately, a cyclone was on and the weather was such that they would not lie, and all that we got, after much cowering under a bush in our waterproofs during squalls, much bad language, much watching of scores of snipe, flying sky high and much expenditure of cartridges, was a comparatively small bag, slain, almost entirely, by using the choke barrels of our guns, only. The ground, of which there is a huge stretch on both sides of the railway, and which is quite handy to the station, is ideal country for snipe, and, in favourable weather, and at the proper time of the year, *viz.*, November and December, there must be no lack of birds on it. We got a teal or two there, and if there had been sunshine and calm, instead of storm and rain, would probably have got more, as there were many about.

At Villupuram, there is very good accommodation at the station, and the sportsman who gives the place a trial, need bring only the bedding which one carries for night travelling on the railway, towels, his clothes and shooting tackle, and, perhaps, if the weather is warm, a box of ice. If turned out of the station rooms, on account of overstaying the time that travellers may occupy them, there is a good public bungalow, close at hand, to which one can go, coming over to the station refreshment room for meals.

South of Villupuram, I have no knowledge of the shooting along the line of rail, but I have heard, from sporting friends, that, about both Trichinopoly and Madura, it is very good, though, at the former place, heavy work, owing to the deep mud which prevails. Tanjore, I believe, is singularly bad anywhere near the railway, not because there are no birds, but because there is such an immense unbroken expanse of wet cultivation, that one may often walk all day without happening on the piece of country in which they lie.

Having dealt with the immediate neighbourhood of railway stations on the southern line, as far as I am acquainted with them, I will now return to Chingleput and say more of it, as a snipe shooting centre, it being, certainly, far and away, the best that there is in the civilized parts of Southern India. I have already mentioned several pieces of country around Chingleput which afford excellent sport, but any account of the shooting along the South Indian line would be incomplete, if I did not add to the list places accessible by road, only, from that point.

To the eastward there are two roads—both very good going for jutkas—which run together for a short distance and then bifurcate, the one to Tiruporúr and the other to Sadras—places on the sea coast. About five miles along the Tiruporúr road is the village of Reddikuppam, and, beginning almost at the roadside, in the grassy bed of a tank, and shooting the ground south of this, one may either go on *via* Ooragadam, until the Sadras road is struck at Keerapákkam (the jutka having been sent round to meet one at this point), or else a circuit may be made, east about, after shooting a couple of miles or so south of Reddikuppam, and the day finished at Konérikuppam, a mile or two beyond Reddikuppam, on the way to Tiruporúr.

It is by this road that the Kondangi ground, to which I have already referred (page 434), can be most conveniently reached. The point nearest to it is Kárambakam, a village on the roadside, just ten miles from Chingleput station and the run out can be made in a little over an hour in a good jutka. The shooting begins about half a mile, or even less, north of the road and the ground is of large extent and very good. There is ample room and sport for a couple of guns here.

South of Kárambakam, there is a good ground, running down to the village of Mullipákkam, where there is a large tank, which, often, holds very considerable numbers of duck and teal; a return may, after shooting the bed of this, be made by turning either left or right handed and working back to the road, coming out, in the one case, about a mile and a half beyond Kárambakam and, in the other, near Konérikuppam. This beat will carry two guns, easily, and partridges and quail are to be found on it.

Along the Chingleput-Sadras road, there used to be an excellent ground at Nemali, a village four miles out : it is, however, a good deal harried, not only by shikaries for the local and Madras market, but by Europeans coming out for a short day. The best way to shoot this place is to begin on the northern side of the road, work the ground under the Nemali tank, then cross the road and go on down south to the Sókandi tank, the bed of which is an excellent bit, and large. If, when this has been finished, there is time for it, the ground below the tank may be taken, and a return be made through the scrub-jungle between this and the railway crossing at the old race course, where the jutka should be in waiting. But few people go to the lower part of the ground, as it can be worked, only, if one stays the night at Chingleput.

About three or four miles beyond Nemali is the village of Keerapákkam, of which I have previously made mention, but only as a terminal point. It is well worth going out there, shooting the ground to the north, which cannot be done properly if one comes across from Reddikuppam, when only the cream of it can be taken. Going up as far as Chinna Irumbédu, one can return to the starting point, or very close to it, *viâ* Periya Irumbédu, Amaradapallam and Ooragadam. This beat is too far for the professional snipe slayer and he never troubles it. A couple of miles or so beyond Keerapákkam, on the right hand side of the road, is a low hill with, on its north-eastern edge, a small jungle-clad gorge, leading into a hollow, which was once cultivated and to the bed of a small ruined tank beyond. Here, in years gone by, I have had, late in the season, with, amongst other companions, the well known "Smooth

Bore," many a day's exciting sport, beating the snipe out of the then low jungle on the hillside. It was like shooting miniature and very fast woodcock, and there was, at times, a bewildering number of birds coming out all round and giving one an equally bewildering variety of shots. There were also many peafowl in it, but, though, now and then, one was to be caught napping, they were not given to getting up until well out of range. A paternal Government has, since then, converted this happy hunting ground into a reserved forest, for the purpose of supplying fuel to future generations, and, though one may, by taking out a license, beat it and other neighbouring reserves, for game, the jungle has now grown up so much and the undergrowth is so thick, that shooting it must be well nigh an impossibility, as beaters cannot get through it without being much mauled by thorns. There are, however, some other spots, of which I shall speak presently, where sport, similar to that which I have mentioned, can still be had.

Of the remaining two grounds to the east of the railway, which occur to me, the one is the entire circuit of the bed of the Chingleput large tank—a long walk—but one which will, often, furnish a good day. The way to work it is to drive out to the escape weir of the tank, close to which one can make a start, sending the jutka to about half a mile or so, beyond the railway crossing, on the Chingleput-Sadras road, to pick one up in the evening. The other ground is one which is of no use, until February, or March and then it is delightful. It lies along the rocky hills, covered with bushes, scrub, euphorbia, and—in the hollows—low jungle, which border part of the old race course and are to the south of it. These hillsides should be beaten by at least half a dozen men, armed with pretty long and stout sticks, who should, generally, be not more than a hundred yards up the hillside, the gun or guns keeping below : if there are two, one should be well in front, and the other about level with the beaters ; all the little ravines, of which there are a good many, should be driven from the top, downwards. The proceedings are varied at times by the appearance of wild pigs, of which there are, owing to the conservancy of Government jungles by the Forest Department, a good many now about. A friend, out with me here, had once the chance of bagging a snipe with one barrel, and a pig, which turned out at the sound of the shot at the bird, with the other, as the latter ran quite close enough to him to be killed with a charge of No. 8. It was spoiled, however, by there being two pigs, which came one on either side of a bush, and, whilst my friend was looking out for No. 1, which was dashing through some thick stuff, No. 2 slipped out, an easy shot, close behind him and was, before he could turn, gone. It was very tantalising to stand as I did on the other side of a narrow ravine, within easy reach if I had had a ball cartridge, but out of the effective range of the shot with which my gun was loaded, and to look on at the "tumash," helpless to take part in it. The best plan to work this beat is to go about half a mile along an old "famine" road leading to Kolatúr, which branches off from the race course and is, close to the hills to be driven. The sportsman should then arrange his line, facing towards Chingleput, and beat along the hill sides, following all the ravines, until the eastern face of the range is reached : beyond this is very seldom productive of much, and the best thing to do, unless one gets a full day, as I have more than once had, on the bit which I have mentioned, is to cross the line at the race course gate, and work the jungle and low hills to the east and north-east of the line, keeping south of the race course until the Chingleput-Sadras road is met, about a couple of miles or so from the station and here the jutka, which can easily get along the race course, should be waiting.

To the westward of the line of rail, there are sundry good grounds, in addition to those which I have already mentioned.

The first of these, in order of distance, is one of use only late in the season and this is reached by going out about a quarter of a mile beyond the escape weir of the Chingleput tank on the road to Madras and then beating the jungle along the base of the hills (the hill slopes, in this case, are of but little value) northwards, for about a mile and a half, or two miles. There used to be a good many hares in this bit, but they have, of late years, since it ceased to be so called "reserved forest," been much trapped, and the appearance of one now-a-days causes pretty well as much excitement amongst the beaters as if a tiger had turned out. There are still a few partridges and, in the season, a sprinkling of grey quail. Its merits as a shooting ground lie, however, in the snipe which are found, at times, pretty thickly along it. These give very good sport, as one can get, where the jungle is fairly high, real driving; the beaters being put in at one end of the cover, and the gun or guns standing at the other. The birds then have plenty of time to get on pace, and, generally, fully avail themselves of the opportunity; coming out, in addition, at all sorts of unexpected places and angles. If, instead of going beyond the escape weir of the tank, one stops short of it, and turns to the left through the village of Kándalur, the western face of the hills, to which I have just alluded, can be beaten, beginning at about quarter of a mile north of the village. There is ground here for about two miles, and the birds are generally much thicker than on the other side, but there being a good deal of prickly-pear and dense, scrubby, thorny, bush, just in the very best part of it, recovering one's game is often an unsatisfactory process. I, once, on this bit, shooting with an ejector gun and without moving from my original post, knocked over, certainly, not less than twenty-six snipe in one short drive. I picked up, owing to the difficult nature of the cover, only thirteen birds, but the like number was gathered, shortly afterwards, by some cow-boys and there were no doubt other birds, which were not recovered. I mention this to show what a quantity of snipe may be found on this ground in, say, the month of February, or the beginning of March and what a large proportion of those shot on it may be lost.

During the early part of the season, there is a very good ground below the Kándalur tank, in the bed of it, and in the waterspread of and under, another tank, about a mile and a half to the northward, the name of which I forget. The Áhtur, Villiyampakkam and other shooting grounds, to the right of the Chingleput-Conjeeveram road and which run pretty well parallel to the railway line, have, already, been sufficiently referred to by me elsewhere (page 436). On the left of the road, however, there is a beat which is some considerable distance out and which calls for special mention. This is the spot on which Captain Baring, A.-D.-C. to the then Governor, Lord Wenlock, bagged, in one day, 92 couple, which, I believe, is the record, in this part of the world, for a single gun. The ground is reached by driving out to Palaya Sivaram, a village nine miles on the Conjeeveram road. The place at which to alight is easily distinguishable by a small hill, at the roadside, on which there is a temple. The Pálár, which is on the other side of the road, has to be crossed. Beyond the river is a walk of quite five miles to the scene of Captain Baring's exploit; there is some very fair ground on the way and a tank out of which one may occasionally get duck and teal, but there is no time to take this and the cream of the beat, too, in the one day, so it is better not to linger *en route*. I, unfortunately, have forgotten the names of the tanks and find that I made no record of these, and I am unable to recall them even with the aid of a map. The course is, however, south by west after crossing the Pálár, and there is a track which commences near an old temple, standing on the river bank, about opposite Palaya Sivaram, runs through a village hard by and then on, until one comes to a small tank on the right hand, the bund of which is covered with palmyra trees. The path must now be left, and the bank of the tank crossed : on the other side of a small rise ; just beyond this, is the beginning of the shooting ground. It consists, mainly, of the beds of and areas under, two tanks, not very far apart, one of which is pretty large and shallow, with a fine stretch of grass at its head. There used to be, and was, when Captain Baring shot his huge bag, a long expanse of grassy, uncultivated land under the tanks, which swarmed with snipe, but of late it has been gradually brought under the plough, and, when I last visited the spot, some three or four years ago, there was, to my disgust, not much of the grass left : it is very possible that, by now, it has entirely disappeared. However, there is plenty of other ground about for snipe, though not of the concentrated kind that there used to be. I have always found jack snipe, sometimes quite a number, in this beat, and grey quail are fairly common in the grass in the bed of the large tank, in January and February.

To do this trip, with anything like comfort, one must make a very early start from Chingleput, and have a horse posted at Palaya Sivaram, to which it is best to drive out in a jutka. It makes a great difference to the sportsman's shooting, if, before beginning business, he rides, instead of walks, some five or six miles in the sun, and it makes a still greater difference in his bodily condition, when he gets back to the jutka, in the evening. I speak this from actual experience, as, upon the first occasion on which I followed in Captain Baring's steps, I did not know what the distance was and walked from the jutka to the ground and back, with the result that, though then as hard as nails, I was pretty well done up, when, at 8-30 P.M., I got back to Chingleput, and would have shot better and had a longer day if I had known what the real distance was and taken a horse. Another good beat on the

Conjeeveram road, but nearer Chingleput, is reached by
driving out about four miles, crossing the Pálár and,
making a start near the village of Sáttanjéri, working on to
that of Kávanipákam, the tank of which is large, with a
lot of good grass—and in places, very deep and tenacious
mud—at the head of it, and then going on to Perunkávani
tank, which is an excellent bit, when the water is low
enough. A return can be made *viá* the Mulaméni tank,
and the top of that at Kávitandalam, to the river and so
across to the jutka, which should have been brought a
couple of miles nearer Chingleput. Yet another beat, along
the same road is reached, by crossing the masonry bridge,
which spans the Madavú not far from Chingleput, on the
Conjeeveram road and taking a lane to the left, a little
further on, which leads to the river on the further side of
which, a commencement may be made in the grassy bed of
a small ruined tank, close at hand. This having been
worked over, either the cultivation under the Pillapúr
tank, which is immediately to the westward, or its bed,
according as the tank is full, or not, can be taken.
Beyond, and still westward, is the Sidhandi tank, the bed
of which is, usually, very good ground. This gone through,
the fields under the Annandúr tank, which adjoins that
of Sidhandi, but in the bed of which there is never any
cover to speak of, can, then, be shot in two beats, one to
the westward and the other to the eastward, and the
sportsman, walking along the bund of the Sidhandi tank,
can return through the cultivation and grass, mixed with
weeds, to be found at the head of the Maiyúr tank, in the
waterspread of which is a grassy and pretty large island,
which, when the water is low enough to allow of one's
getting out to it, is very well worth shooting. To do this,
however, necessitates turning homewards as soon as the
bed of the Sidhandi tank has been beaten, and omitting
the Annandúr tank from the programme. Following the
outer line of the cultivation eastward of the head of the

Maiyúr tank, there is shooting almost up to the river and the day ends but a short distance from the point at which the morning's start was made. The worst of taking this line, is, that one has to cross a supply channel, which is, at all times, pretty well waist deep and, not infrequently, up to one's neck.

The beat just mentioned, may be varied by, instead of going on to Sidhandi after beating the bed of the Pillapúr tank, keeping a little north of west and taking the Sittanakávúr, and the Porupandal tanks, in the low jungle around the escape weir of the former of which, I have often got partridges. The northern edge of the cultivation under the Sálavákam tank, can then be gone through and a return made over the cultivation below the Annandúr and Sidhandi tanks, finishing up in a little, narrow, grassy tank, called Áhtur Tángal, which is good and, frequently, holds a number of birds. This brings one out to the bund of the Maiyúr tank, along which the path to the river lies. The jutka should be brought from the point at which it halted in the morning, through Nattam, a suburb of Chingleput, and stationed abreast of the northern end of the Maiyúr Tope on an old road running along, and down, the river.

South of Chingleput, a very fair, though, perhaps, not full day, may, as the season draws on, be had by shooting round the bed of, and under a queer, circular, tank, which seems never to be either full, or empty, which has grass all round its waterspread and which lies to the left-hand side of the road to Madurántakam, a short distance before it reaches the Pálár river. In the scrubby euphorbia jungle above it, hares and partridges and, now and then, a florican, are to be found. The area under the tank is small, but often holds birds and, late in the season, a fair amount of snipe and a few quail, may be picked up out of the scrub along the slopes of the low hills, to the right of the road, looking south, on which I have, more than once, seen wild pig : in the bed of the tank I have often had very good sport, but the snipe there seem capricious in their comings and goings, and one can never look upon it as a sure find.

Crossing the river, which can always be done in a jutka, unless the stream is in fresh, and turning to the right hand almost immediately afterwards, there is, at a distance of something about a mile, a very good ground, which consists, largely, of the fields and waste lands under the Maiyúr tank : beating these, in a westerly direction, for about a mile and a half, one can then strike southerly, and work out to the Chingleput-Utramerur road, there meeting the jutka, which should have come on from the river bank. There is shooting the whole way down to the spot where the jutka should be—about a mile down the Utramerur road. If the sportsman has time and does not mind taking the chance of negotiating a channel which, occasionally, is unpleasantly deep, he can, instead of going out to the Utramerur road, turn eastwards, about half a mile short of it, and work out to the Chingleput-Madurántakam road, meeting the jutka upon that, a mile and a half or so nearer the river.

There is, some seven miles from Chingleput, on the way to Madurántakam, on the left hand side of the road and quite close to it, an excellent ground, at a village called Palayamuttur, on which I have seen the snipe in swarms. It can be reached, from Padálam, but, as I remarked when writing of that place (page 438), it is ground which can be more easily got at from Chingleput. Starting with this, one can shoot for some distance south, until abreast, or nearly so, of a low hill, on the western side of the road, with a temple on it; when the road can be crossed, and the ground, in a homeward direction, worked until one has had enough of it, or the day closes.

I think that I have now, though I have not by any means exhausted the subject, said enough regarding the snipe grounds of Chingleput and thereabouts.

I thought, when I commenced this paper, that I should be able to say something of the shooting in other districts (North Arcot and Cuddapah), through which the South Indian Railway runs, but I was in these, long before that line came into existence, and on wading through sundry old journals, find that I but seldom noted particular places and that I cannot identify them, when I did. I then led a nomad life, my notes show only the approximate direction in which I went out from the camping ground, or bungalow, at which I halted, and the bags which I then got, when compared with those which I killed afterwards in the Chingleput district, look very insignificant and were what I should, now, call decidedly poor. Added to this, my experiences go back, as regards North Arcot, to thirty-five years ago and, as regards Cuddapah, to twenty-three, and of Nellore I know nothing, except by repute. What I could say, therefore, would not be of much use now-a-days and might prove misleading, especially as one of the first effects of the opening-up of a railway, is the speedy disappearance of all non-migratory game, within easy reach of it, which is not specially protected.

There is, no doubt, good shooting to be had along the Nellore line; snipe are to be found, in satisfactory numbers, about the Trichinopoly and Madura Districts and, possibly, in the portion of the South Arcot District of which I have not knowledge, and in Tanjore, and duck and teal abound, in the season, in parts of the country through which the railway runs from Pilér to Kadiri, in the Cuddapah District. Around Chittoor and Vellore and in the Chandragiri Taluk, of the North Arcot District, too, there used to be, when I knew them, a very fair amount of small game.

The casual sportsman, by which term I mean, the visitor, or the man who does not shoot regularly and who wants something satisfactory when he does, had, however, better not attempt such places as those referred to above, unless he has a friend at, or near, any spot which he wishes to try, who shoots and who can either take him out, or put him, under the guidance of a competent shikari, on to the ground where he will find birds. He will, if he is wise, and desires a certainty of decent, if not always good sport run no risks in exploring the unknown, and confine himself to the country around the main line of the railway, which I have, in the foregoing pages, described, I fear, at somewhat tedious length.

My readers will, perhaps, forgive me this, when I plead, as my excuse, the hope that some of them, at any rate, may, with the aid of what I have written, be able, when their snipe shooting days are over, to look back, as I now do, with never-failing pleasure, mingled, though it be, with a shadow of regret that such things cannot come again, to many a good bag killed along the South Indian line and to many a happy day of freedom from the worries and slavery of official life, spent, often with right good sporting companions and hospitable friends, shooting at Chingleput, and places within reach of it.

J. F. P.

BIG GAME SHOOTING IN SOUTHERN INDIA.

The animals to be found in the jungles of Southern India, which may be classed as " big game," are—the elephant, the bison, the tiger, the panther, the leopard, and the bear. Wolves and hyænas are occasionally come across, but they are not, from a sportman's point of view, worth consideration.

Elephant shooting is truly royal sport, but can. only be enjoyed on very rare occasions, as the killing of elephants is prohibited by special legislation, except in *self-defence*, or when a tusker, because of his mischievous or dangerous nature, has been proclaimed by the Collector of the district. In the latter case a reward is generally offered which goes a good way towards paying the expenses of the " shoot :" the tusks, however, are Government property, but may be purchased from the District Forest Officer at the market rate for ivory. In regard to shooting "in self-defence," I think that if one accidentally finds oneself within fifteen or twenty yards of a wild tusker, unless the opportunity for a speedy and noiseless retreat is extremely good, the safest course, provided one happens to be carrying a heavy rifle, is to kill the elephant then and there. The brain-shot is of course the one to try for ; there are several rules for finding the exact spot to fire at in an elephant's head, from various angles ; the simplest, perhaps, is to imagine a stick driven through the head, in at one ear and out at the other, a bullet breaking that stick at the centre, or even going very near to it, will be instantly fatal and the mighty brute will sink to the ground without a sound. If the brain has been missed and the weapon being used is a 4 bore, the left barrel may be put in behind the shoulder, but dropping him in his tracks is then improbable, and the

dangerous business of tracking up the wounded animal
will have to be undertaken. To those who are ever likely
to go out after elephants, I would strongly recommend the
purchase of that most fascinating and valuable book, the
best book on shooting in this Presidency, so far at least as
big game is concerned, I allude to Sanderson's " Thirteen
Years among the Wild Beasts of India."

Let us now turn to the consideration of how best to do,
and where to go, to secure that magnificent trophy, the
head of a solitary bull bison.

We will suppose we are starting from Tuticorin, and
that we wish to get into one of the best, and (I daresay it
will appeal to the instincts of most English sportsmen if
I add) one of the least known jungles in the Madras Presidency. Granting then that this is the idea, I would say
take tickets for Erode junction, where bullock-carts must
be engaged for the rest of the journey into the wild jungles
of the Bhawani taluq in north-east Coimbatore. The hill
ranges of the Bhawani taluq are almost uninhabited, and
numerous herds of bison are to be found all over them.
Perhaps, however, the best point for a sportsman, who did
not know the ground, to make for would be the little hamlet called Burgoor or, as it is spelt in the maps, " Bargur."
This place is some forty miles from Erode, and would be
three marches from that station ; the road goes by Bhawani
village, and Andiyur, another small village at the foot of
the Burgoor hills. With willing cartmen and good bullocks
Andiyur could be reached in one day from Erode. Next
day's march is the stiffest: it is not such a very long one.
Only some sixteen miles from Andiyur to Tamarakarai
Forest bungalow ; but a severe ghaut of some three thous-
and feet has to be surmounted, the ascent begins seven
miles out from Andiyur and it continues a steep up hill climb
almost the whole way to Tamarakarai. Permission to use
the Forest bungalows on the Bargur hills should be obtained
from the District Forest Officer of Coimbatore (North), to

whom also application must be made for shooting licenses; the fee for the license is Rs. 10. The distance from Tamarakarai bungalow to Tattakarai bungalow is about eight miles, and Bargur lies half-way between the two. Bison are to be got in the jungles, on both sides of the road, throughout the whole of these eight miles, but trackers, or at least men who know where to find the game, must be got hold of; the best men to have are the Sholagars, a few of these wild aboriginals live at Tattakarai, and more are to be found in the jungles to the north-east of that bungalow. In bison shooting, there are two methods which may be adopted for getting within shot of the grand object of pursuit; first and foremost, there is the sure and certain plan of *tracking*, and, if the ground is fairly soft from recent rain, it is, in my opinion, not only the most interesting, but also the most certain way of approaching; the trackers, if good men, should not be hustled, but should be allowed to pick up the tracks, and follow them, at their own pace; by watching them, a sportsman (even if he does not understand their language, which is a dialect of Canarese,) can usually tell at once if they are getting close to the bull; they become very cautious and frequently climb trees to look ahead. A Sholagar who knows his work will, on sighting the animal, stop dead and point to it, stooping down if the beast is very close to enable the shot to be fired over him. If a picked shot can be had within twenty or thirty yards, the neck is the best spot to put the bullet in. As a rule, though, the shot behind the shoulder and *not too high* should be taken. The best gun for the work is undoubtedly the 8 or 10 bore paradox, but an 8 bore rifle burning ten drams of powder is very efficient. A word here on the subject of stalking boots may be of value; the writer has had a very long experience of tracking and stalking in Indian jungles, and can confidently say that there is nothing to beat rubber soles, the solid red rubber ones wear best, but whether two or three pairs of cheap rubber soled tennis shoes will not prove a better investment than one pair of best quality is open to argument. The second method for getting bison can only be adopted in jungles where the hill tops are clear, and open, covered with short grass. In such cases the bison may be sighted and stalked as are the red deer in Scotland. This is most charming sport, and lucky is the man who can enjoy it, for it is the exception, rather than the rule, to come on bison in jungle of this nature.

If, however, after a day or two of tracking such hill tops as I have described, or any large open stretches of short grass have been come across, and with fresh tracks through or near them, a good position should be chosen that will command a clear view, and at the same time be to leeward of the feeding ground. A very early start must be made next morning, for bison never stop in the open for long after the sun has got up.

Tigers and panthers are fairly numerous in these hills, as indeed they generally are in jungles where there are cattle to prey upon, and Bargur is entirely a cattle-grazing village. The best way to get a shot at a tiger is to tie up baits in likely places, and sit up over the " Kill." Great pains should be taken in selecting the position, so that when the tiger comes to feed he may not get the wind ; the direction in which he will probably retire, to lie up for the day, must be carefully studied ; and, the " Machan " or platform, in a suitable tree, should invariably be prepared beforehand, so that the tiger may not be disturbed by the noise of cutting poles, and by (what is probably worse still) the stage whispers of the men employed. I am quite sure that if more attention was paid to these points the shooting of tigers and panthers over " Kills " would be more frequently successful than it is. As the remarks which I have made apply equally where panthers and leopards are concerned, and as the same procedure may be adopted in their case, except that a bleating goat is a better bait for the latter, I will now turn to the consideration of our great friend the black bear.

Black bear shooting is most amusing and exciting sport, and the spice of danger gives a zest to a pursuit which is, in this part of the world at any rate, second only to the tracking of elephants and bison. Bears are very fond of certain fuits, the principal ones in these jungles being the Neral, the Yellchi, and the Attie. I have given the Canarese names of the trees, and all jungle men know perfectly their fruit, when it is ripe, and where to find them. Bears are also very partial to the little black oblong berries of the bastard date bush; in jungles where these grow, if the fruit should happen to be ripe, they will come down from their caves and fastnesses in rocky hills to feed at about sunset, and a shot may often be obtained before it gets too dark. This is also the case when the Yellchi fruit is dropping: if it is at all plentiful, they will come to it quite early in the evening. A couple of years ago I shot three bears, all dropped within a radius of fifty yards. They were feeding on the ruddy brown berries, intent only on the sweet repast, so that I got up close, and had commenced operations with my 12 bore paradox before they dreamt of danger. The right barrel dropped the old she bear, and with the left I mortally wounded one of the two almost full-grown cubs. These two were close together, and, as luck would have it, immediately started fighting. In the midst of a most infernal din I reloaded, and killed them both. This, needless to say, was a red-letter day, but my good fortune did not here come to an end, for the old father bear still remained unaccounted for, and I killed him next evening within 200 yards of the same spot.

From the sportsman's point of view, this is a most excellent habit that bears have, of fighting with each other, when one gets wounded; it generally results in their great undoing, if only the man keeps cool. Therein lies the only difficulty, for the scuffling that ensues, comingled with yells and howls, is quite enough to disturb the equanimity of most men. I am of opinion that they do not intend to fight, and that it is very rough luck on the un-wounded one, who, in the most kind-hearted way possible, has rushed up to see what is the matter with his miserable brother, and to comfort him. The stricken bear instantly goes for his comforter, attacking him ferociously. Proba-bly most of my readers have heard of "a bear with a sore head." So far as my experience goes they are *at all times* inclined to be cross.

And now, let us work out what is best to be done, if one finds oneself in a jungle, where there are tracks of bears, but when, alas! there is apparently no fruit that they are fond of, ripe. In this event, they must be tracked to their caves, and, sometimes, if fresh tracks are come on early in the morning, especially at times when the dew is heavy, they can be followed so speedily that they are caught and encountered before reaching their retreat. Nothing is easier in all the different branches of tracking than the rapid following up of a bear's trail, if he has gone away through grass two feet high, when there has been a heavy dew; the broad dark line of grass with the dew brushed off shows up most distinctly against the silvery glistening shimmer of the herbage on either side. Even if the trail may lead, as it often does over sheet rock, the tell-tale line will usually be clearly visible in the grass on the other side from many yards away.

When the tracks have not been found at a sufficiently early hour, in all probability our black-haired shaggy friend will have made good his point, and with a little skill, and care, may be found lying sound asleep, in a little dry hollow, under an overhanging rock. What a perfect reward for a little toil, and with what eager, though care-fully subdued, delight we make our preparations. At times, to our joy we find that, whereas we have only been following the track of a single animal, now, to our rapture,

there are two, lying snugly, and peacefully slumbering.
As often as not, however, if there are real caves in the
neighbourhood, the sleeping bear cannot be seen from outside. In either case, the supremely important point to be
borne in mind is that the approach *must be noiseless.* If
the final drawing near has been properly done, the effect
of a few taps by the tracker with his little axe at the back of
the cave will be almost magical. Out rushes Bruin by the
front entrance,—the sportsman, it is needless to remark,
has *not* gone behind. By the way, an incident that happened to myself on the Billigarungan hills, some years ago,
leads me to warn the novice at this work not to stand in
the path that will probably be chosen by the fleeing bear.
On that occasion, I *very* nearly came off second best.
The Sholagar had hardly tapped the rock behind, when
out they came, two bears, and down the path they charged,
the very path in which I was standing. A right and left
stopped neither of them, and the next thing I remember
clearly was running round and round a tree with a wounded bear trying to get hold of me. The other, which was
unhurt, had fortunately for me gone straight on. For a few
seconds, the bear had most distinctly the command of the
situation. Had I stumbled and fallen, my chance would
have been a poor one, as it happened, I kept cool, and
kept my feet; the bear was badly wounded, and presently
made off. I reloaded and after a few minutes, greatly
against the wishes of old Jeddiah, the Sholagar (who had
watched the episode from a safe place above with horror-
stricken eyes), we followed the blood tracks, and came up
with him within a few hundred yards, going very slow,
and almost played out, so that I finished him off without
further trouble. I will now, before concluding, give a
few words of advice, which are mainly intended for the
sportsman who knows perhaps very little of Indian big
game shooting, and least of all of the parts I write about.

In the first place, always write to the District Forest

INDEX TO STATIONS.

464

Officer for permission to shoot. A courteous letter to this official will not be thrown away. Secondly, be sure to take enough food for servants and coolies, and metal cooking pots for them, when going into unknown jungles; a fair allowance is 2 lbs. weight of rice for each man, per diem: and for every rupee's worth of rice, 2 annas of curry-stuff (salt, chillies, etc.,) should be purchased. It is advisable also to take a good big bundle of common tobacco, with which to gain the hearts of the trackers. Thirdly, get the topographical map of the parts you are about to explore, and don't forget to carry a compass.

Lastly, one must be prepared to *work hard;* a good collection of trophies is not made by a series of lucky flukes, but by downright hard work, and only after enduring very many disappointments, and recking not of blank days. When all is said and done, if bison and bears could be got without difficulty or trouble, where would the pleasure come in; and, it is well worth all one's pains; at least such is the opinion, formed on experience, of the writer, who was born and brought up in one of the most beautiful parts of Perthshire, and who early acquired a strong liking for shooting and fishing, which has ever since given a charm to his twenty-one years in the bamboo jungles and on the forest-clad hills of Southern India.

BILIGIRI SHOLAGAR.

INDEX TO STATIONS.

59

Lightning Source UK Ltd.
Milton Keynes UK
12 March 2010

151222UK00001B/40/P